THE

Captain Taprell Dorling, whose *nom ae plume* was 'Taffrail', was born in 1883. Joining the Navy in 1897, he was to serve continuously throughout the First World War in small ships in the southern North Sea. During this time he began to write and his first novel, *Pincher Martin O.D.*, became a bestseller. A press officer in the Second World War, his writing career had by then been firmly established. He died in 1968.

"TAFFRAIL."
1917.

ENDLESS STORY

Destroyer Operations in the Great War

'TAFFRAIL'
Captain Taprell Dorling

Introduction by James Goldrick

Seaforth
PUBLISHING

DEDICATED

TO

ADMIRAL SIR REGINALD YORKE TYRWHITT,

BARONET, OF TERSCHELLING,

G.C.B., D.S.O., D.C.L. (OXON.)

WHO LED THE
HARWICH FORCE
THROUGHOUT THE WAR OF
1914–1918
AND EARNED THE
ADMIRATION, AFFECTION, RESPECT,
AND SUPREME CONFIDENCE
OF THOSE WHO HAD THE
HAPPY FORTUNE
TO SERVE UNDER HIS COMMAND.

Copyright © Taprell Dorling 1931
Introduction copyright © James Goldrick 2016

This edition first published in Great Britain in 2016 by
Seaforth Publishing,

Pen & Sword Books Ltd,
47 Church Street,
Barnsley S70 2AS

Despite extensive inquiries it has not been possible to trace the copyright
holder of *Endless Story*. The publishers would be happy to hear
from anyone with further information.

British Library Cataloguing in Publication Data
A catalogue record for this book is available from the British Library

ISBN 978 1 4738 8212 6 (PAPERBACK)
ISBN 978 1 4738 8214 0 (EPUB)
ISBN 978 1 4738 8213 3 (KINDLE)

Printed and bound in Great Britain by CPI Group (UK) Ltd, Croydon, CR0 4YY

NEW INTRODUCTION

ENDLESS Story: Being an Account of the Work of the Destroyers, Flotilla-Leaders, Torpedo-Boats and Patrol Boats in the Great War was written by 'Taffrail', Captain Taprell Dorling DSO, RN, and published in 1931. It remains the most evocative account of the work of the 'little ships' in the Great War, leavened by the author's own expertise and his synthesis of the individual and collective experience of a host of professional colleagues, as well as the official and personal histories that were already in circulation. The narrative is not confined to British ships, but extends to the global operations of the Royal Australian Navy's destroyer flotilla and the units of the United States Navy that deployed to European waters in 1917 and made a vital contribution to the U-Boat war. *Endless Story* gives the reader a window on these aspects of the naval war of 1914–18 that remains unmatched by any other published work.

Henry Taprell Dorling was born in 1883, the son of a British Army Colonel. He changed his name to Taprell Henry Dorling in 1908 and then to H Taprell Dorling in 1910. From the outset of his writing career he would employ the pseudonym 'Taffrail' as a play on his own name. Dorling joined HMS *Britannia* as a cadet in 1897 and went to sea as a midshipman in 1899. He was fortunate enough to be appointed to Captain Percy Scott's large cruiser, the *Terrible*, which was temporarily stationed in South Africa in support of operations ashore. Dorling joined the ship in January 1900 and earned the South Africa medal. *Terrible* then deployed to her proper station in China and was soon embroiled in the Boxer Rebellion. Dorling was part of the naval brigade that operated ashore from late June until early September 1900. He was awarded the China Medal with the 'Relief of Pekin' clasp. The receipt of two campaign medals while still a midshipman may have triggered what became a lifelong interest in medals and decorations.

Dorling's examination record was not distinguished, despite his operational experience, and he completed his sub lieutenant's courses in 1903 with a mixture of second and third class passes, including an initial failure in navigation. He was promoted Lieutenant in December 1904. Dorling had already been appointed to the '30-knot' destroyer *Sylvia* and remained in this ship until his transfer to the armoured cruiser *Kent* for another commission on the China Station in 1906 and 1907. He spent the following year in the battleship *Prince George*, flagship of the

Portsmouth Division of the Home Fleet, before being given his first command, *Lynx*, one of the very first torpedo boat destroyers to be commissioned and by then one of the oldest and slowest in service. Dorling transferred to the larger and faster '30-knot' *Leven* in late 1909 and had a further year in command. Andrew Cunningham, the future C-in-C Mediterranean and First Sea Lord, was a friend and flotilla mate at this time, commanding the destroyers *Vulture* and *Roebuck*.

These small ships were consciously regarded as an apprentice-ship for command and accidents and incidents were accepted as practically inevitable. In *Endless Story*, Dorling commented that 'one soon discovered that the best destroyer officers were more or less born, not made', but this did not mean that the even the best were always able to cope with handling these 'tricky craft'. Dorling himself put *Lynx* aground in June 1909 and received a caution from his Commander-in-Chief. In fact, extended service in small ships without receiving at least one admonition 'to be more careful in future' was the exception rather than the rule. During his time in *Leven*, the ship participated in King George V's Coronation Review, for which Dorling received the Coronation Medal.

Big ship time in the battleship *Agamemnon* in the Home Fleet followed before, in early 1913, Dorling was posted to undertake the newly established War Staff Course. He had displayed little interest in specialising as a gunnery or torpedo officer and was already known for his literary skills. Dorling had capitalised on the increasing popular interest in the Royal Navy and begun to contribute short stories to a wide range of popular periodicals, such as *Chambers' Journal* and *Pearson's Magazine*. A later confidential report was to describe his activities as 'light literature on sea subjects'. He had also already written his first book, *All about Ships*, published by Cassell in 1912. The short stories themselves, many of which were later published in collections such as *Carry On!*, are marked by great descriptive skill and command of narrative. Dorling always told a good story, even if his characterisations were less sophisticated. Along with a contemporary naval writer, Lewis Ricci, a paymaster officer who used the pen name 'Bartimeus', Dorling's work gives a clear view of the daily life of the Royal Navy in the period that is a vital aid to any would-be social historian.

Amongst his 1913 War Staff course mates was Bertram Ramsay, a friendship that was to prove important for Dorling during the Second World War when Ramsay commanded the naval forces for the invasion of Europe. On completing the course, Dorling was appointed to the light cruiser *Patrol*, one of the flotilla leaders assigned to the Admiral of Patrols organisation. He was both the first lieutenant of the ship and responsible for war staff duties. At the outbreak of war in August 1914, Dorling found himself in the Tyne with the *Patrol*, in charge of the Ninth Flotilla, which included a second light cruiser and twenty-three old destroyers. Patrolling the northeast coast was monotonous and unpleasant and Dorling must have been delighted to be appointed captain of the brand new M class destroyer *Murray* in November 1914 and assigned to the Harwich Force under Commodore Reginald Tyrwhitt. He would remain in seagoing command until August 1918.

Endless Story's personal element really begins at this point. Dorling himself noted in his introduction that he had 'not set out to write a destroyer *history*; but merely a destroyer miscellany which I hope will give some idea of their manifold duties in wartime.' Dorling succeeds in every way, cleverly interspersing his own experiences of the southern North Sea and Heligoland Bight with the wider narrative of the destroyer war and a detailed examination of major actions, most notably the day and night destroyer engagements during the battle of Jutland, as well as the Dardanelles, the Dover Patrol and the Zeebrugge Raid. He draws not only on official sources and published material, but the recollections of colleagues and friends who include some of the most distinguished destroyer captains of the conflict. In the next war some, such as Cunningham, would serve in the highest ranks, while others would find new challenges for their practical skills as commodores of ocean convoys.

As shown in *Endless Story*, Dorling's greatest strength as a writer was his ability to convey the realities of the seagoing experience with vivid but never exaggerated description. More than any contemporary, it is he, in both fiction and historical writing, who told the story for an earlier generation that Nicholas Monsarrat was to do so effectively for the battle of the Atlantic in *The Cruel Sea*. The difference between the two authors is that Monsarrat, who also experienced operations in the North Sea, wrote his novel about a war in the deep ocean, while Dorling's subject at this time was largely that of the narrow seas. Dorling himself would have been the first to admit that the extended miseries of the transatlantic passage were a different experience to the routine of a few days at sea interspersed with a night in harbour.

But Dorling's own emphasis on the realities of sea and weather is not mistaken. *Endless Story* is strewn with examples of the appalling conditions with which the little ships had to cope, such as the heavy sea which drove the bridge rails of the destroyer *Tigress* four feet aft and pinned her captain against the compass binnacle, breaking two of his ribs. Dorling himself narrates an experience of a storm in January 1918 in the destroyer *Telemachus*, his second wartime command, in which the ship only just made the shelter of Loch Inchard, after being pooped by a following wave which swept 'practically everything except the after gun ... overboard, even the after binnacle.' The destroyer *Racoon* was not so fortunate and was wrecked with the loss of all hands.

Navigation in poor weather, with often limited visibility and in treacherous tides and currents, was another challenge. Gyroscopic compasses had yet to be fitted to destroyers and they had perforce to rely on their magnetic units. Most were not even fitted with a compass on their bridge at the start of the war but had to rely on the installation in the wheelhouse below. Dorling draws on a fictional account by 'Bartimeus' of the actual wrecking of the destroyers *Narborough* and *Opal* in a snowstorm in January 1918 to reinforce the message about the appalling conditions that saw the two ships lose their way in the Pentland Firth and drive ashore on the Pentland Skerries. There was but one survivor.

Dorling's opening list of the destroyer casualties of 1914–18 tells the story in another way. Sixty-seven flotilla leaders and destroyers were sunk, but only forty-six through enemy action. Thirteen ships were lost in collision and eight were wrecked. The statistics for the Harwich Force in the National Archives confirm just how challenging conditions were. In 1916, there were twenty-two collisions, six groundings and six major berthing incidents, compared with twenty-one collisions, seven groundings and eleven berthing incidents in 1917 and twenty, five and five in 1918. This reflected something that Dorling acknowledged in *Endless Story*. The operational demands were much greater than anything that had been experienced before the war and the environment itself was the greatest enemy. Ironically, it could also sometimes be a friend. The fog which caused so many collisions and near misses – experiences that Dorling claimed were worse for him than being under heavy gunfire – could on occasion cloak ships from a superior enemy. On one minelaying operation, Dorling recalled, 'we had heard strange sirens very close, and had even felt the heavy wash in the otherwise flat calm sea caused by a large ship's passage through the water at high speed.'

Dorling's own extensive experience included an epic tow in November 1915, in which he succeeded in bringing the destroyer *Matchless* safe into harbour after the latter had her stern blown off by a mine. In October 1917, in the *Telemachus*, he rescued the survivors of the Swedish barque *Esmeralda* from their open boat despite appalling weather. For this achievement, he was awarded a gold medal by the Swedish government in 1919. He had already been promoted Commander in 1916 and awarded the DSO in 1917 with the citation that he had 'served continuously throughout the war and distinguished himself on many occasions with the Harwich Force'. Rather to his surprise, his first novel, *Pincher Martin O.D*, published in 1916, had also proved an immediate success with well over 20,000 copies sold in the first six weeks. He followed this with *The Sub* in 1917.

The second half of Dorling's war at sea, in command of the *Telemachus*, represented another important theme of the naval conflict – mine warfare. Assigned to the Twentieth (Minelaying) Destroyer Flotilla at Immingham on the Humber River, Dorling spent much time in covert minelaying operations in and around the Heligoland Bight and off the Belgian coast. These operations, of which Dorling took part in thirty-six, were always at hazard from German minefields, known and unknown and Dorling commented ruefully on seeing the German charts after the war of the number of times that he must have passed unknowing over an enemy field. *Telemachus* was fortunate in this regard, but many other ships were not.

Dorling joined the naval staff in the Plans Division in August 1918. With the end of the war, he was soon seconded to act as secretary to the 'Clasps Committee'. He had already published in 1915 the first edition of what became the standard text on the subject, *Service Medals, Ribbons, Badges and Flags*, which became *Ribbons and Medals* in later editions. The intent was for the British War Medal for 1914–19 to have clasps for individual and fleet actions in the same way as the old Naval and Military General Service Medals had done for the Napoleonic Wars. The Committee produced a detailed list of forty-four clasps and they were listed in Admiralty Weekly Order 2051 of August 1920. However, the cost was considered prohibitive and the clasps were never formally issued. Dorling must have been very disappointed. Later editions of *Ribbons and Medals* included a detailed explanation of the clasps, while Dorling himself retained a miniature of the

British War Medal with the seven clasps that he had earned. Afterwards, he rejoined the Plans Division and his later service there earned high praise from his Director. In 1919 Dorling had found the time to write a precursor to *Endless Story*, which he entitled *H.M.S. "Anonymous"*. Published in 1920, this was an account of many of his personal experiences of the war at sea. It eschews naming individuals or ships, but includes many details that could not be fitted into *Endless Story*.

Dorling returned to sea in the *Telemachus* in 1921, based in a nucleus crew flotilla at Port Edgar. After this commission, he went back to the Plans Division for a short period before being posted to the Tyne Division of the Royal Naval Volunteer Reserve as a staff instructor. By this time it was clear that he would not be promoted captain on the active list. His literary career continued to flourish, however, and when he formally retired with an honorary promotion in 1929 a new novel, *Pirates*, was already in the works. Over the next decade he wrote a number of adventure stories, usually with a maritime background. These included *Cypher K* (1932), *Dover-Ostend* (1934), *Seventy North* (1934) and *Mid-Atlantic* (1936). In 1935 he published *Swept Channels*, a book very much in the style of *Endless Story*, but focused on the dangerous and largely unknown work of the minesweepers of the Great War. *Swept Channels* displays the same combination of sympathy and professional insight as *Endless Story* and was a similar success. Dorling was also approached by Rudyard Kipling's widow to write the poet's biography but, like Carrie Kipling's first choice of biographer Hector Bolitho, he refused the commision, probably because of concerns over her efforts to exert editorial control.

In 1939, Dorling was recalled to active service as a press officer. In December 1942, his links with Admiral Ramsay and Admiral Cunningham were renewed with his appointment as press officer for the Commander of the Naval Expeditionary Force, first in North Africa and the Mediterranean and then for D-Day in France. He found time to publish a novel, *Chenies*, in 1943, as well as books detailing the activities of the navy in the conflict. After the war's end, he spent a further year in the Admiralty working for the Chief of Naval Information before his final release in August 1946. For his war services he received a final decoration, the American Legion of Merit.

Dorling continued his writing career with further novels such as *Toby Shad* (1949), *The Jade Lizard* (1951), *Eurydice* (1953) and *Arctic Convoy* (1956), the latter being a fictional account of an officer's experiences in the gruelling Russian convoys. He also served as a radio broadcaster and as naval correspondent of *The Observer*. One of his most significant achievements was to assist Admiral of the Fleet Viscount Cunningham of Hyndhope with the latter's memoir *A Sailor's Odyssey*, which was published in 1951. It would be an exaggeration to say that Dorling 'ghosted' the book, but he certainly helped make it a very readable record of A B Cunningham's remarkable career. Dorling died in Greenwich on 1 July 1968. He was survived by his widow and their only son.

Endless Story may well be Dorling's finest achievement as a writer, particularly if it is coupled with *Swept Channels*. It is inherently a partial account of the war of the little ships, but nonetheless conveys the realities of 1914–18 at sea in a way that few others have ever matched. It is a book in the best traditions of the naval writers who have done so much to cast a light for the outsider on the hidden world of the seagoing navy.

JAMES GOLDRICK, JUNE 2016

INTRODUCTION

IT has long been my ambition to write a book describing the work of the Destroyers during the war, and with Destroyers I necessarily include other vessels of the same type – Flotilla-leaders, Torpedo-boats, and Patrol-, or P.-boats. It seemed a pity that some scores of half-forgotten actions, adventures, and incidents should be suffered to pass into oblivion, which is my excuse for writing this book. I have not set out to write a destroyer *history*; but merely a destroyer miscellany which I hope will give some idea of their manifold duties in wartime.

I have dealt at some length with Jutland, the engagement off Heligoland soon after the outbreak of war, the Dover Patrol, the destroyers in the Dardanelles and at Gallipoli, as well with the more important phases of destroyer work elsewhere. It was quite impossible, however, to describe every little action, every hair-raising incident, in which they were involved during the four years of war. Those that I have mentioned must be taken as typical of many others.

People to whom I am indebted for information are so numerous and the list of books to which I have referred is so lengthy, that I have included a separate list of acknowledgments and bibliography on the pages immediately following. Several officers who have greatly helped me with personal accounts have preferred to remain anonymous. I hope they also will accept my sincere gratitude.

But this book is not all " scissors and paste." I know my local colour so far as the North Sea and Home Waters are concerned, and as much about destroyers as anything else I am ever likely to in this life. The result, I hope, is a popular account of their work and adventures. In any case, it has been written by one who commanded destroyers for six years in peace and four years in war, and would not have served elsewhere for worlds. Ten years is a considerable slice of a lifetime.

I should add, perhaps, that I have had no access to any official documents or records other than those available to the general public. Moreover, Volume V. of *Naval Operations*, the final volume of the official Naval History of the War, compiled from official sources, did not appear until the manuscript of this book was in the hands of the printers.

TAFFRAIL.

CONTENTS

LIST OF ILLUSTRATIONS

BIBLIOGRAPHY

The Grand Fleet. Admiral of the Fleet Earl Jellicoe.

The Crisis of the Naval War. Admiral of the Fleet Earl Jellicoe.

The World Crisis, Vols. I. and II. Mr. Winston Churchill.

Naval Operations, Vols. I., II., III. Sir Julian Corbett.

Naval Operations, Vol. IV. Sir Henry Newbolt.

A Naval Lieutenant, 1914–1918. Commander Stephen King-Hall.

Encyclopædia Britannica, 14th Edition.

The Battle of Jutland Official Despatches. H.M.S.O.

Narrative of the Battle of Jutland. H.M.S.O.

The Fighting at Jutland. Lieutenant-Commanders H. W. Fawcett and G. W. W. Hooper.

The Truth about Jutland. Rear-Admiral J. E. T. Harper.

The Jutland Scandal. Admiral Sir Reginald Bacon.

Falklands, Jutland, and the Bight. Captain Barry Bingham, V.C.

The Dover Patrol, 2 vols. Admiral Sir Reginald Bacon.

Keeping the Seas. Rear-Admiral E. R. G. R. Evans.

The German Submarine War. R. H. Gibson and Maurice Prendergast.

Submarine and Anti-Submarine. Sir Henry Newbolt.

Our Navy at War. Josephus Daniels.

Harwich Naval Forces. E. F. Knight.

Official History of Australia in the War, Vols. I. and II. C. W. Bean.

Official History of Australia in the War, Vol. IX., " The Royal Australian Navy." A. W. Jose.

Gallipoli. John Masefield.

Gallipoli Diary. General Sir Ian Hamilton.

The Navy in the Dardanelles Campaign. Admiral of the Fleet Lord Wester Wemyss.

Pincher Martin, O.D. Taffrail.

The Sub. Taffrail.

A Little Ship. Taffrail.

H.M.S. " Anonymous." Taffrail.

ACKNOWLEDGMENTS

I AM indebted to the following persons and firms for permission to make use of, and to quote extracts from, the books mentioned :

The Controller of His Majesty's Stationery Office.
> (i.) Vols. I. to IV., *Naval Operations*, the Official Naval History, by Sir Julian Corbett and Sir Henry Newbolt.
> (ii.) *The Battle of Jutland – Official Despatches.*

A. W. Jose, Esq., and the Publishers.
> Vol. IX., *The Official History of Australia in the War :* " The Royal Australian Navy."

General Sir Ian Hamilton.
> *A Gallipoli Diary.*

Mr. John Masefield.
> *Gallipoli.*

Lieutenant-Commander H. W. Fawcett, R.N., and Messrs. Hutchinsons.
> *The Fighting at Jutland.*

Captain Barry Bingham, V.C., and Messrs. John Murray.
> *Falklands, Jutland, and the Bight.*

Messrs. W. & R. Chambers Ltd.
> For permission to reprint the account of Zeebrugge, which originally appeared in my book, *A Little Ship*, published in 1918.

Messrs. Herbert Jenkins.
> *H.M.S. " Anonymous."*

Messrs. George Doran & Co., New York.
> *Our Navy at War*, by Mr. Josephus Daniels.

Mr. Shane Leslie.
> *The Epic of Jutland.*

Paymaster-Commander L. da C. Ricci, R.N. (" Bartimeus ").
> *The Navy Eternal.*

To the following I would also tender my grateful thanks for valuable assistance :

The Director of Naval Construction.
The Librarian and Staff of the Admiralty Library.
Captain W. W. Hunt, D.S.O., R.N.
Captain A. F. W. Howard, R.N.
Captain Arthur Marsden, R.N.
Commander G. H. Barnish, D.S.O., R.D., R.N.R.
Major Cecil Paddon, late Otago Mounted Rifles, New Zealand Expeditionary Force,
and
some dozens of other officers whose request for anonymity I must observe.

CHAPTER I

A DESTROYERS' WAR

I

IN these days of peace and naval retrenchment, and " yard-sticks " for the limitation and apportionment of navies, it is a little difficult to realise that during the 4 years, 3 months, and 7 days that the war lasted, we lost no fewer than 67 flotilla-leaders and destroyers – 17 in action against surface ships, 8 sunk by submarines ; 20 by mines ; 13 in collision ; 8 wrecked ; and 1 through a cause unknown, though usually supposed to have been a floating mine. This meant on an average the loss of a destroyer every 23½ days. The total number of casualties, according to present-day reckoning, would make up seven whole flotillas. Over and above this, we lost 11 torpedo-boats and 2 patrol-boats.

How many more of these little vessels, battle-scarred or other-wise damaged, limped or were towed back into harbour, some barely afloat, is almost beyond computation. Moreover, for every casualty, or partial casualty, there must have been twenty and one narrow shaves of disaster.

There cannot be an officer or a man who served in T.B.D.s during the war who could not spin his crop of hair-raising stories. What is more, they would probably be true.

Those were the days when destroyers were ubiquitous. They were maids-of-all-work, flaunting their blackened, weather-worn ensigns all over the North Sea and English Channel, into the Heligoland Bight, from the Dardanelles and the Suez Canal to Gibraltar, and thence halfway across the Atlantic almost to the Arctic Circle. Whenever the great battleships or battle-cruisers put to sea, destroyers went with them, whatever the weather. Destroyers convoyed transports and food-carriers from 30° west in the North Atlantic to the Channel and Irish Sea. They es-corted transports across the Channel to Havre, Dieppe, Boulogne, Calais, and Dunkerque, traffic up and down the east coast, food-ships to and fro between Orfordness and Holland, neutral ship-ping across the top of the North Sea between the Shetlands and Scandinavia. They hunted submarines, scooped up enemy outpost boats in the Heligoland Bight and the Kattegat, patrolled the British coast, accompanied aircraft-carriers for raids on Zeppelin sheds, and minelayers on their nocturnal excursions. They laid mines and swept for mines, landed troops in their boats on the beaches of Pacific Islands and the Gallipoli Peninsula, and, both in Gallipoli and on the Flanders coast, bombarded the enemy troops and shore positions.

In February 1915, one destroyer, the *Beagle*, employed on cross-Channel escort duty from Portsmouth, had her fires alight for no less than twenty-six days out of the twenty-eight. Her case was not altogether exceptional.

" Destroyers," wrote Sir Julian Corbett, " were run off their legs, and no praise can be too high for the men who endured the strain, or for those who built the no-less-sorely-tried hulls and engines." [1]

Someone once remarked that the work of the Royal Navy during the war consisted of " periods of intense monotony alleviated by moments of intense excitement." So far as the destroyers were concerned, this is hardly true. Their jobs were so multifarious that there was no time for boredom or monotony. If we lacked the ghastly excitements of trench warfare, we had the fierce gales of the North Sea, the Atlantic, and English Channel, when there was no coming into harbour for " stress of weather." The green seas came over everywhere, while the ship lurched and tumbled, pitched and rolled, wallowed and buried herself without ceasing. The water found its way through our oilskins, and down into our sea-boots, within a quarter of an hour of leaving harbour. One remained wet, or partially so, for four or five days on end, and snatched what meals one could on the reeling bridge or in the chart house beneath it.

Though I was not personally afflicted, some of us were seasick. Shall I ever forget a wretched, white-lipped signalman, with the beads of cold perspiration on his forehead, who habitually retched over a bucket in the tail of the bridge in anything approaching a lop ? And nobody without a hardened stomach could bear the sights and sounds and smells on a destroyer's mess-decks in a real gale of wind.

Then the blinding fogs which were a curse to us ; the suppressed anxiety of making the land at 20 knots in thick weather with the lights of lighthouses and lightships extinguished lest they should point the way to submarines ; the station-keeping at night in

[1] *Naval Operations*, Vol. II, p. 403.

close formation without lights; the return into harbour to
replenish the oil-fuel after several days at sea, followed by a
warm sponge-down in front of the blazing stove in one's cabin in
a bath like an exaggerated saucer. That, with the arrival of the
mail from the depot ship, a square meal with the ship at rest, and
a night's uninterrupted sleep in a bunk, was bliss to the wartime
destroyer captain. Then off to sea again, whatever the weather,
with the prospect of three or four days' respite for boiler-cleaning
once every month, and a short refit in a dockyard twice a year.
And so it went on. One grew weary of counting the thousands
of miles thrashed out by our whirring propellers.

I remember the dark night when my own ship, the *Murray*, met
her sub-divisional mate broadside to broadside with an appalling
crash during an alteration of course in the middle of the North
Sea. I don't think much blame was attributable to anyone, but
with our side looking like the flank of an underfed greyhound,
and some of our boiler-room fans displaced, we managed to
steam home without being towed.

Can I ever forget the British submarine we nearly rammed in
the *Telemachus*, but just managed to avoid, while entering the
Humber on a dark night in a sluicing tide? We missed her by
perhaps thirty feet, literally scraping across her bows. Then
there was the filthy night with a strong easterly gale when a
convoy of merchantmen without lights was crossing the entrance
to the Firth of Forth at the same time as the cruisers and destroyers were putting to sea. Steaming 22 knots and literally blinded
by spray, we sighted one of the escorting destroyers at a distance
of something less than 100 feet steaming at right angles across our
bows. There was just time to yelp with the siren as the helm
went hard a starboard to swing our bows clear. Then, the next
instant, the helm went hard a port to swing our tail clear. Again
we must have missed her, and she us, by a matter of thirty feet.
It was a nerve-racking moment, worse by far than being under
heavy gunfire. I felt physically sick, and trembled all over.
If we had hit that destroyer at the speed we were travelling, we
should have carved our way clean through her, to leave her ship's
company struggling in a sea in which no boat could live. When
we breathed again, how we cursed those who steamed unlighted
convoys across the entrance to our base when destroyers, cruisers,
battle-cruisers, and battleships were hurrying out to sea!

Once, while steaming from Dover to Dunkerque during daylight, our next ahead, the *Redgauntlet*, came into contact with

one of the mine-nets used for catching submarines. The consequent explosion blew a considerable hole in her bows. Closing to offer assistance, we were informed she could still steam, so followed her back to Dover. The captain of that vessel was Commander (now Captain) Malcolm Goldsmith, an officer with a keen sense of the ridiculous.

" What is your damage ? " the admiral signalled by semaphore on our arrival.

" My damage is comparable to a collision of the second magnitude," Goldsmith replied.

" What is a collision of the second magnitude ? " the admiral demanded. (I could almost see his frowns at this unaccustomed levity.)

" When portions of the bow are still adhering to the hull," answered Goldsmith, utterly unabashed.

But many are the tales of Malcolm Goldsmith bandied about the Service. After the war, he was captain of a flotilla-leader employed in the Black Sea and Sea of Azov helping the White Russians during the Bolshevist invasion of the Crimea. To the east of the Perekop Peninsula, which joins the Crimea to the mainland, is a more or less inland sea known as the Sivash. But on the British charts and maps it has an alternative name.

Goldsmith, having done his turn of duty in this apparently rather depressing neighbourhood, was being relieved by a cruiser whose captain was new to the work. And the moment that cruiser's upperworks hove in sight over the skyline, Goldsmith's searchlight was busily flashing a signal.

" Welcome," it spelled out letter by letter. " Welcome to the Putrid Sea ! "

There was the other occasion, also in the Crimea, or in South Russia, where a cruiser bombarded a Bolshevist railway station and was rather pleased with the result. Her captain signalled to Goldsmith, " I bombarded railway station this morning, firing ten rounds of six-inch, and obtained nine direct hits." Goldsmith waited until the next day before he made the answer. Then, on returning into harbour he replied, " Your bombastic 1623 of yesterday. I note that the 9.25 train this morning left according to schedule."

More recently, in 1926, having been appointed Captain of the Dockyard and King's Harbour Master at Malta, Captain Goldsmith sailed single-handed from England to Gibraltar in his yacht, a 20-ton cutter called the *Rame*. Afterwards, with some companions, he voyaged on to Malta. It was an adventurous, arduous journey which won him the Royal Cruising Club Challenge Cup for 1926, the premier award of the only Yacht Club in this country which encourages deep-sea cruising among its members instead of racing.

This passage, however, adventurous though it was, was not quite so hair-raising as that home in 1928, when, again in the *Rame* and with two companions, Goldsmith was blown 180 miles out into the Atlantic off the Spanish coast by a succession of heavy gales, and in a truly mountainous sea for so small a vessel. The *Rame* finally reached the Spanish port of Ferrol with her crew more dead than alive, and for this feat her owner was again awarded the R. C. C. Challenge Cup for 1928. I have told the story of those two voyages in *Chambers's Journal*. The yarn was well worth the telling, if only to show that the spirit of adventure is not quite dead in naval post-captains of forty-six and over!

There is another and well-known destroyer officer whom I cannot forbear to mention, and this is George Piercy Leith.[1] Some time before the war he was in command of a destroyer which happened to be in dry-dock at, I believe, Devonport. On a Saturday or Sunday, when the dockyard was closed for the week-end, orders came for his flotilla to proceed to sea. His ship was ready, but in ordinary circumstances would not be floated out of dock until the Monday morning, by which time it would be too late. Exasperated at the delay, he proceeded to flood the dock himself, floated his ship, raised steam, and went to sea. History relates that he received an Admiralty letter of appreciation commending his zeal and ingenuity for getting to sea, and, by the same post, another communication from their lordships conveying a mild reproof for leaving the caisson which sealed the entrance of the dry-dock floating about the harbour, together with an intimation that the next officer who did it would be tried by court martial!

"Georgie" Leith was the hero of another story during the war, when, taking his destroyer through the Downs in a fog as thick as a blanket, he came into contact with a merchant-ship at anchor. All collisions and groundings have to be reported on a special form, one of the questions being, "Where was the ship collided with first sighted?" or words to that effect.

In the blank space for the answer Leith wrote, "Overhead"!

[1] Now Captain, C.B.E.

It was literally true. The first sight he had seen of the other ship in the prevailing weather conditions was her overhanging-counter high over his own vessel's forecastle.

2

Most of the officers who commanded the larger destroyers in the war had served their early apprenticeship in command of torpedo-boats, or the old 27 and 30 knotters built between 1894 and 1901, numbers of which were still in the patrol flotillas on the east coast and at Dover in August 1914, and served until the end of hostilities. During peace, these flotillas were stationed at Portsmouth, Devonport, and Harwich or Chatham. They did their gunnery and torpedo practices at sea, and occasional cruises round about the British Isles. But except on mobilisation, or during the annual summer manœuvres, they carried skeleton or " nucleus " crews only.

It was the general, though not the invariable, rule that no lieutenants under four years' seniority should be considered for destroyer commands. Moreover, in 1908 the Admiralty inaugurated preliminary examinations in navigation and torpedo, adding gunnery and signals within a year or two. The navigation test, which was severely practical, was a good thing, for most destroyer captains were *ipso facto* their own navigators. For the life of me, however, I could never see the use of the examinations in torpedo, gunnery, and signals, except, perhaps, to eliminate the hopelessly incompetent. We all went through an intensive course of study in the set subject before we presented ourselves for examination. In other words, we crammed fiercely, and the knowledge thus acquired and soon forgotten did not make us any better destroyer officers.

Experience in command taught, and taught quickly. But one soon discovered that the best destroyer officers were more or less born, not made. Destroyer sense is like " road sense " when driving a motor-car, which some people never seem to acquire.

Being long and narrow, of light draught and easily influenced by every wind that blows, destroyers are tricky craft to handle. They are very sensitive, while no two can be manœuvred exactly alike. Each one has her own peculiar idiosyncrasies, which have to be studied and humoured. No amount of theoretical knowledge will ever teach one to turn one's ship in her own length in a narrow, congested harbour in a tideway, or to take her alongside another ship or a jetty in a gale of wind and a strong tide without damage.   Some people can do it neatly straight away. Others, after months of practice, are never really successful.

The worst destroyer officer I ever came across was a commander who had achieved five first-class certificates and early promotion when passing for lieutenant.   He had afterwards become a very shining light in a branch of the Service that I will not mention, and, on attaining the coveted " brass hat " of a commander at an early age, applied for, and obtained, the command of a destroyer.   He had never handled a ship in his life, and his name, like that of his ship, soon became a byword in the flotilla.   He was for ever asking for divers to clear his propellers of wires that had become wrapped round them, and invariably when he came into harbour we used to watch with interest out of the wardroom scuttles while he made three or four abortive attempts to pick up his buoys at bow and stern, while bawling from his bridge through a megaphone.   At sea, when we were sometimes condemned to following him, he was a public nuisance – steering a serpentine course, increasing or decreasing speed without a signal, shaving past oncoming or overtaken ships, and generally behaving in an utterly unseamanlike and incomprehensible way.   He was quite oblivious to the maxim, " Remember the Next Astern," which I notice occupies a prominent position on the bridges of the *Nelson* and *Rodney*, our newest battleships.

Frequently he lost himself at sea, and, as often, ran blindly into danger.   We soon learnt to distrust him and his navigation, and, like Agag, walked delicately.   However, he did not last long. Three bumps and a fairly bad smash in something like six months led to his transference to the comparative safety of a big ship. That particular officer lacked the destroyer sense, and no amount of experience would ever have instilled it.   On the bridge of a destroyer he was a danger to himself and a terror to his friends. In his own scientific, specialist job he was a very big noise indeed. Wild horses will not make me divulge his name.

After two years or eighteen months in a nucleus crew destroyer, a young commanding officer before the war was either moved on to a destroyer in one of the " running," fully commissioned flotillas attached to the sea-going fleet, or in the Mediterranean or China, or, if there were no immediate vacancies, to do a year or two of purgatory in a battleship or cruiser.   It was rather a come-down to find oneself one of the many lieutenants in a large wardroom after tasting the mingled joys and responsibilities of independent command.   After being " the captain," it upset one's dignity to have to muster the seamen's kits, and to find oneself keeping watch on the quarter-deck in a frock-coat and sword-belt with a telescope under one's arm.   But, however irksome, it was doubtless good for one's soul, and one always had the satisfaction of knowing, if one had been favourably reported upon, that in two years or eighteen months one would be back in command of a newer and better destroyer.

There were some officers, however, who had served in destroyers for six or seven years or so continuously before the war, and remained in them practically throughout the whole period of hostilities.   Among others, the present Rear-Admiral Dashwood F. Moir, D.S.O., Commodore Andrew B. Cunningham, D.S.O., and Captains Arthur M. Lecky, D.S.O., Aubrey T. Tillard, D.S.O., and Claude F. Allsup, D.S.O., are cases in point.   Commodore Cunningham must hold the record for length of service in one ship, for he commanded the destroyer *Scorpion* from January, 1911 to January, 1918 – a period of seven years !

In those early days there was a feeling of pride and joy at being in command of one's own small ship at the age of twenty-five or thereabouts, to know that one was the " Lieutenant and Commander,"[1] and that one had certain privileges denied to ordinary lieutenants in big ships.   It was not merely because we drew an increase of pay over and above the bare 10s. a day for lieutenants of under eight years' seniority.   The increase amounted, if I remember rightly, to an additional 6s. 3d. – an automatic 1s. for being in command, 3s. 9d. command money, and 1s. 6d. " hard lying money " for the wear and tear of clothing and the " discomfort " of destroyer life.   And in 1909–10 an additional 6s. 3d. a day, or £114 1s. 3d. a year, over and above our bare lieutenant's pay of £182 10s. a year, was comparative affluence to those without private means.   Living was cheap in those days.

Another privilege was the drawing of a cask of pickled tongues on appointment to the command of a destroyer, and another cask thereafter whenever one commissioned another.   (I once succeeded in drawing three such casks, or twenty-four tongues, in one year.)   This perquisite, I have been given to understand, dated from the early part of the nineteenth century, when William IV, himself a naval officer, inspected one of the naval Victualling Yards.   The tongues, liver, kidneys, and so forth of the beasts killed to supply fresh meat to the fleet used, I believe,

---

[1] This was before the introduction, in 1914, of the specific rank of " lieutenant-commander " for lieutenants of over eight years' seniority.

to become the property of the butchers and officials. But on the King asking the superintendent what became of them, the latter replied that the tongues were issued to the captains of His Majesty's ships. And so they continued to be until the Navy took to the consumption of imported meat instead of the home-killed variety. I always felt grateful to King William.

I think, perhaps, that the gunnery, torpedo, and other special-ists in big ships used rather to look askance at their destroyer brethren in the days before the war. The specialists – those who went in for " instrumentalisms of all kinds," as Mr. Winston Churchill once expressed it – regarded themselves, and perhaps rightly, as the brains of the Service. Certainly service in big ships under the immediate eyes of admirals brought its own reward in the shape of promotion far more readily than to those officers who had held independent commands. Destroyers were rather a backwater so far as advancement was concerned.

Moreover, destroyer life was considered to be rather free and easy compared with the strenuous life of a battleship, a refuge for those who were not ambitious and aspired to a good time while the going was easy. Destroyer officers were " salt horse " – that is, non-specialists. They were pirates, said some people, who never did a really hard day's work in their lives, and got ashore at 1.30 in the afternoons to play golf while their hard-worked opposite numbers in big ships were frowned upon if they dared to land before 3.30. Most destroyer officers, their detractors averred, went in for " destroying " because they were married men, or engaged to be married, and needed the extra pay. Mar-ried men, said the bachelors, were the bane of the Service.

How often did I hear all these statements made during dinner round the wardroom table of a battleship before the war ? Was I myself not warned against going in for destroyers because they were considered " bad service " ?

Did that warning have any effect ? No.

Do I regret having been a destroyer officer ? Again, no.

One never hears those derogatory remarks about destroyers nowadays, for it was during the war that they came into their own. How often was I told by some big ship officer, " Lord, I envy you your job ! "

Quite frankly, I did not envy him his.

CHAPTER II

THE BATTLE OF THE BIGHT

I

THE *Lance*, Commander Wion de M. Egerton,[1] of the 3rd Flotilla from Harwich, was the first British destroyer, if not the first British ship, to open fire in the war. Well I remember the thrill of excitement that passed through us when we read of it in the newspapers. It was almost unbelievable that scenes such as those we had read of as happening off Port Arthur ten years before during the Russo-Japanese War were now taking place under our very noses in the North Sea. For the first time in their history, British destroyers had been in action.

The day after the outbreak of war, on August 5th, 1914, the 3rd Flotilla, under the command of Captain Cecil H. Fox in the light-cruiser *Amphion*, was making the first of its many sweeps of the southern portion of the North Sea. Other destroyers from Harwich, with Commodore Reginald Tyrwhitt, in the *Amethyst*, were also at sea.

During the morning, Captain Fox was told by a British trawler that a suspicious steamer had been seen " throwing things overboard twenty miles north-east of the outer Gabbard " lightship, or, roughly, thirty miles off Southwold. The destroyers were spread out to search the neighbourhood, and the *Lance* and *Landrail* sent on at full speed to the position indicated.

At 10.30 they sighted a small grey steamer, which promptly made off at full speed to the eastward. She was, indeed, the *Königin Luise*, a small, fast mail-steamer belonging to the North German Lloyd which had been taken over by the German Government before the outbreak of war and converted into a minelayer. Leaving Borkum roads on the night of August 4th, she had spent the early morning of the 5th laying her minefield to the west of longitude 3° east. The mines had been planted regardless of the rulings of International Law or the time-honoured customs of sea warfare, which permitted them to be laid only in an enemy's territorial waters. The *Königin Luise's* field, in international waters, was just as likely to destroy neutral ships as British.

---

[1] Now Rear-Admiral, D.S.O.

Hotly chased by the *Lance* and *Landrail*, the marauder was brought to action at about 11 o'clock, and the destroyers very soon had the satisfaction of seeing some of their shells drive home. The *Lark* and *Linnet* joined in the chase, followed by the rest of the flotilla, and the *Königin Luise*, hit again and again, was soon reduced to a crawl. By shortly after noon she was sinking, and her men had started to jump overboard to save their lives. Her engines, however, had not been stopped, and she continued to move slowly ahead until she finally turned over on her side and settled down.

Approaching the scene, the British vessels lowered their boats. Out of the German ship's complement of about 100 men some 43, several of them severely wounded, were rescued. The story that some of the men saved had been shot in the back by their own officers is believed to be utterly untrue.

Thus, within thirteen hours of the outbreak of hostilities, was the first enemy ship sunk in the war.

Feelings of satisfaction, however, were shortlived, for at about 6.35 next morning, while on her return journey to Harwich, the *Amphion* struck a mine, which exploded under her forebridge. Practically all the men in the forepart of the ship were killed instantaneously, as well as 18 of the 20 German prisoners that the *Amphion* had rescued from the sea.

Captain Fox and the other officers on the light-cruiser's bridge were stunned and badly burnt. The explosion had caused a fire, and very soon, blazing between decks forward, the *Amphion* began to settle by the bows. For a few minutes she continued to move in a circle until the engines could be stopped.

There was no confusion or panic. The men fell in on deck. It was soon realised that the vessel was doomed, and orders were given for the ship to be abandoned. The boats were lowered, and the destroyers sent theirs to assist in the work of rescue. Within twenty minutes of the first explosion all the survivors were safely on board the destroyers.

Hardly had this work been done when the fire in the *Amphion's* bows either reached the fore-magazine, or else she struck another mine. Whatever the cause, there came a heavy explosion which wrecked what remained of the bows of the ship, and shot skywards in a spout of flame and smoke. Débris went whirling into the air, to come raining into the sea all round the rescuing destroyers. There were several casualties, one 4-inch shell falling on board the *Lark*, to kill two of the *Amphion's* men just rescued, and another of the German prisoners.

The *Amphion* slowly disappeared, bows first, and of the ship's company, 1 officer and 150 men perished. They were the first naval casualties of the war. Their sudden loss in an enemy minefield within thirty-two hours of the opening of hostilities came as rather a shock, and certainly caused the Navy to realise something of the ruthlessness of modern warfare.

2

The first real action of the war in which destroyers took part was the battle of the Heligoland Bight, on August 28th, 1914. It was a confused, hardly fought engagement, or series of engagements, which started at daylight in misty weather and a glassy sea within a few miles of Heligoland, and lasted until about 1.30 p.m., when the British squadrons and flotillas finally withdrew in safety. Contrary to popular belief, the guns of Heligoland did not actually come into action against British surface vessels ; but it was probably the only time its red cliffs were sighted by any British ships other than submarines.

The general idea was quite simple. From the earliest days of the war our submarines had maintained a watch off the German ports. They had noticed that enemy destroyers patrolled each night off the Bight, and on their return at daylight each morning were met by light-cruisers about twenty miles north-west of Heligoland. Commodore Roger Keyes,[1] commanding the submarine flotilla, suggested that a well-organised sweep, coming down from the north and starting from well inshore just before dawn, would have excellent results.

He was to station a line of three submarines close to Heligoland with orders not to come to the surface before a certain time. Three more submarines were to be placed forty miles to the westward, to draw the enemy destroyers out to sea, while a couple more were to watch the mouth of the Ems River.

Commodore Tyrwhitt, with the newly commissioned light-cruiser *Arethusa*, the 3rd Flotilla of 16 L. class destroyers, together with the light-cruiser *Fearless*, Captain W. F. Blunt, and 15 more destroyers of the 1st Flotilla, was to approach Heligoland from the northward, reaching a point about twelve miles west of the island at 8 a.m. The two light-cruisers, with

[1] Now Admiral of the Fleet Sir Roger Keyes, Bart., G.C.B., K.C.V.O., C.M.G., D.S.O., L.L.D., D.C.L.

their flotillas, were then to sweep out to sea, covering a wide front.

The two battle-cruisers *Invincible* and *New Zealand* were detailed to act in support farther to seaward, while another force of older cruisers was stationed off Terschelling, about 100 miles from Heligoland.

At the last moment, however, the plan was somewhat altered. A brigade of Royal Marines was due to land at Ostend on the 26th, and some counter-move on the part of the German High Seas Fleet in the Jade River was not improbable.   It was therefore arranged that Commodore Tyrwhitt's inshore flotillas should be further supported by Sir David Beatty, with the *Lion*, *Queen*

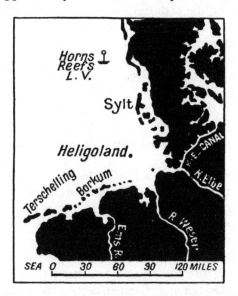

Mary, and *Princess Royal*, and by Commodore W. E. Goodenough's second light-cruiser squadron *Southampton*, *Falmouth*, *Birmingham*, *Nottingham*, *Lowestoft*, and *Liverpool*.

Neither Commodore Tyrwhitt nor Commodore Keyes, who was on the scene in the destroyer *Lurcher*, with the *Firedrake*, in charge of the submarines, was told of this reinforcement.   Commodore Tyrwhitt, however, discovered it for himself at 3.30 a.m. on the morning of the operation, when the 2nd Light-Cruiser Squadron was sighted by his destroyers and nearly attacked as hostile.   Only a prompt interchange of recognition signals saved a regrettable incident.

Commodore Keyes remained unaware of the presence of the six additional light-cruisers until much later in the day.   His lack of knowledge greatly complicated the situation when he eventually sighted the vessels in the mist, and, quite naturally, reported them as hostile.

Wireless was not used with the same discrimination in the early days of the war as it was later on, and shortly before midnight on August 27th signals intercepted from seaward warned the Germans that a considerable force was approaching the Bight. Their normal dispositions were therefore altered, the offshore destroyer patrols being ordered to retire before the British destroyers in the hope of enticing the latter well into the Bight, where light-cruisers would be ready to cut them off.

At 5 o'clock on the 28th the *Arethusa* was steering south-south-east for her 8 o'clock position to the westward of Heligoland. With the commodore were the 16 L. class destroyers steaming in four columns. Two miles astern of the *Arethusa* steamed the *Fearless*, with her 15 destroyers similarly disposed. The morning was grey and overcast, with hardly a ripple on the water. To the westward – that is, to seaward – the horizon was reasonably clear. To the east, however, it was hazy, and the visibility during the morning never exceeded four miles. Sometimes it was considerably less.

Shortly before 7 o'clock a hostile destroyer was sighted on the *Arethusa's* port bow at a distance of about three and a half miles. Without altering course himself, the commodore detached his nearest column of destroyers, *Laurel*, *Liberty*, *Lysander*, and *Laertes*, led by Commander Frank Forrester Rose,[1] to deal with her. The enemy made off at full speed to the south-east into the Bight, with the *Laurel* and her consorts in pursuit. Very soon Rose sighted ten more German destroyers, which he promptly engaged, and chased at full speed towards Heligoland. The range was so great, however, that little or no damage was done on either side.

At about 7.30, having lost sight of his detached division in the mist, but hearing the sound of their gunfire to the eastward, Commodore Tyrwhitt swung round to port to support them. Before long he was able to see the enemy flotilla with which his destroyers were engaged, and at 7.40 altered course to the eastward and increased to full speed, with the *Fearless* and 1st Flotilla following some distance astern.

Just before 8 o'clock he sighted a German light-cruiser to the eastward. She was the *Stettin*, and the *Arethusa* altered course

[1] Now Rear-Admiral, D.S.O.

to bring her to action. A moment or two later another light-cruiser, the *Frauenlob*, was seen coming up from the south-east from the direction of Heligoland, and about four miles astern of the *Stettin*. The *Arethusa* and destroyers were soon in action.

On sighting the *Fearless* and her destroyers, the *Stettin*, which apparently had not yet raised steam for full speed, disappeared into the mist. The *Arethusa* thereupon turned to the southward to engage the *Frauenlob*, which had turned round and was making off in that direction.

At 8.10 the range was no more than 6,000 yards and still dropping, and very soon the *Frauenlob's* excellent gunnery had its effect. The *Arethusa*, which had commissioned on about

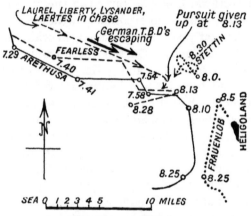

PHASE I. 7.29 – 8.25.

German destroyers sighted and chased to S.E. by *Laurel's* division. *Arethusa* sights *Stettin* and *Frauenlob*, and is engaged by both. *Frauenlob* then engaged by *Arethusa*. Action broken off at 8.25.

August 11th and had done no real target practice, suffered severely.[1] Within ten minutes, according to one account, she was hit thirty-five times, and lost 11 killed and 16 wounded, one of the killed being Lieutenant Westmacott, the signal officer, who was on the bridge with the commodore.

By 8.25 the range had dropped to about 3,500 yards, and the

[1] The Commodore's broad pendant had been transferred from the *Amethyst* on August 26th on the arrival of the *Arethusa* at Harwich. The latter, though she had been in commission about fifteen days, was hardly in a condition to fight a general action. Her speed on trials had reached only 25 knots instead of the estimated 30, while her 4-inch semi-automatic guns almost invariably jammed as soon as they were fired. Target practice was carried out after leaving Harwich on August 27th. The guns, however, continued to jam, and the practice was soon discontinued lest they should not be ready the next morning.

Arethusa had only one 6-inch gun left in action. It was at this moment, however, that the enemy was hit forward under the bridge by a 6-inch shell, which caused 37 casualties and made her sheer off to the eastward. Unable to take any further part in the action, she returned to Wilhelmshaven. The destroyers, meanwhile, had not been idle. Some of them were attending to a tramp steamer flying Norwegian colours which was crossing the *Arethusa's* bows as though she might be laying mines, while others had severely pounded a German torpedo-boat, which escaped, blazing, to the eastward.

At about 8.30 the *Arethusa* turned to the westward for the sweep out to sea, the *Fearless* and her destroyers, now about eight miles to the northward, having turned in this direction about a quarter of an hour earlier, in accordance with the instructions.

So ended the first phase of the action, in which the *Arethusa* had been badly damaged. On the other hand, the *Frauenlob* had been put out of action, and a German destroyer and two torpedo-boats had been hit and badly battered by our flotillas.

The destroyer V.1 had been badly hit in the after boiler-room by a shell which killed 1 man and wounded 2 others. The boilers being damaged, the compartment became untenable, and her speed was reduced to 20 knots. Zigzagging to save herself from further punishment, she was hit again on the starboard side, and had her steering-gear damaged. But for the timely arrival of the *Stettin* she would probably have been sunk. D.8 and T.33 were German torpedo-boats, and the first-named was hit five times. One shell, striking the after-side of the bridge, killed the commanding officer and wounded about 15 men, besides cutting the steam-pipes and enveloping the ship in an impenetrable cloud. D.8, a small twenty-five-year-old vessel, armed with only three 4-pounder guns, was exposed to heavy fire for forty minutes, and made a most gallant fight. After the captain was killed, the crippled ship was fought by the first lieutenant until she could fight no more. She eventually crawled out of action and had to be towed home, with a loss out of her small crew of 13 killed and 11 wounded.

T.33, a minesweeping torpedo-boat, commanded by a warrant officer, was also badly hit and had to be towed in. Her escape was a miracle, for at one period, according to the German account, the *Arethusa* approached her within 900 yards and then altered course away, probably under the impression that she was done for. Her casualties were slight – 2 killed and 6 wounded.

Both these small torpedo-boats fought gallantly, even firing their puny 4-pounder guns at the *Arethusa*.

The mist was getting thicker. Soon after she turned to the westward at about 8.15, the *Fearless* sighted a destroyer ahead. Captain Blunt ordered one of his divisions to chase ; but about the same time intercepted a wireless signal from Commodore Keyes in the *Lurcher* which seemed to indicate that he was coming in from seaward. Thinking the stranger might be the *Lurcher*, Blunt accordingly cancelled the pursuit. Soon afterwards, the destroyer altered course and disappeared in the mist.

She was actually the enemy destroyer V.187, the German commodore's vessel, and at 8.25 the 5th Division of the 1st Flotilla – *Goshawk, Lizard, Lapwing, Phœnix* – again sighted her steaming to the southward. They at once turned to pursue at full speed, opening a heavy fire at a range of 6,000 yards.

The shell could be seen splashing into the water all round her, as, for some minutes, the chase continued. Then, to the amazement of those in the British destroyers, the German suddenly put her helm over and doubled back to the northward, straight into arms of the *Ferret, Forester, Druid*, and *Defender*, which had also been detached.

What had happened was that V.187 had sighted the *Nottingham* and *Lowestoft* to the southward. Coming under heavy fire from their 6-inch guns, the German commodore, hemmed in on all sides, decided to turn upon his pursuers. The result was a foregone conclusion. Engaged by all eight of the British destroyers, V.187 was reduced to little more than a wreck, circling helplessly in a cloud of smoke, steam, and leaping shell fountains. " One gun after another was put out of action, and the commander wounded by a splinter," wrote one of the German officers who survived. " Hit after hit found her. The ship was completely covered in smoke and steam ; a great part of the crew was dead ; V.187 could only move at slow speed."

The British destroyers flashed past their crippled opponent, firing into her at a range of no more than 600 yards. Every shot told, and very soon, on fire and badly down by the bows, V.187 was apparently sinking. Though her ensign was still flying, she had ceased firing. To save useless slaughter, the British destroyers also ceased fire, and sent away their boats to save life. The survivors of V.187, however, possibly imagining that what remained of their ship was about to be boarded and captured, reopened fire, and the *Goshawk*, commander the Hon. Herbert

Meade,[1] lying stopped at a distance of 200 yards, was hit in the wardroom. Another short burst of fire silenced V.187 for ever, and at 9.10, after explosive scuttling charges had been fired by her crew, she sank with her colours flying.

The British boats closed the spot to rescue the swimmers in the water; but hardly had the work started than the grey mist to the eastward was rent by bright stabs of flame, and projectiles started to splash into the sea and to whir overhead like coveys of partridges. The grey hull and four funnels of a light-cruiser appeared through the murk. It was the *Stettin*, which had steamed to the south-westward after her first engagement.

Her fire was very accurate. Five of the destroyers had boats in the water picking up their drowning and wounded enemies. Four of them managed to get them alongside, and hurriedly removed their crews, together with the German commodore and 26 men, who were made prisoners. But as the *Stettin's* salvos still continued to pitch all round them, they could not delay further. The boats were left adrift, and the destroyers steamed off to save themselves.

Now there occurred one of the most curious incidents of the battle. The *Defender* had drifted some distance away from her whaler and dinghy, and came under such heavy fire that her lieutenant-commander considered it advisable to save his ship and to leave his boats behind with the men still in them.

But the British submarine E.4 – Lieutenant-Commander Ernest W. Leir[2] – was in the vicinity. She had made a bold attempt to torpedo the *Stettin*, and, though her shot had gone wide, forced that ship to turn away and disappear in the mist.

Watching through his periscope, Leir had seen the end of V.187 and the rescuing destroyers scattered. Returning to the spot, he then saw the boats left behind, and at 9.30, when the cruiser had disappeared and everything seemed quiet, came to the surface and approached them.

They were full of badly wounded Germans, whose hurts had been roughly bandaged by our seamen with torn-up clothing stripped from their own bodies. There were also 2 unwounded German officers and 8 men, besides, of course, the men from the *Defender*. These latter, together with 1 unwounded German officer and 2 men " as a sample," Leir took on board E.4. He had no room for further passengers, no means of dealing with

---

[1] Now Vice-Admiral the Hon. Sir Herbert Meade, K.C.V.O., C.B., D.S.O.
[2] Now Captain, D.S.O.

numbers of badly wounded, so, leaving 7 unwounded behind to row the boats and look after the injured, he provided them with water and biscuits, saw that they had a compass, gave them the course for Heligoland, only fourteen miles away, and allowed them to make the best of their way home. Her work done, E.4 then submerged as dramatically as she had appeared.

It was a calm summer day, with every promise of fair weather. It has been said, with what truth one cannot say, that those boats never reached Heligoland. If this was the case, it was no fault of ours. Even the enemy testified to the humanity of our destroyers. " The British," wrote a German officer, " without

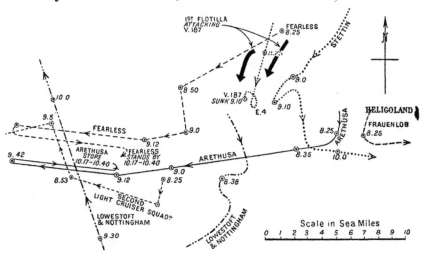

PHASE 2. 8.25 – 10.40

Arethusa proceeding to the westward with 3rd Flotilla. *Fearless* proceeding to westward. Two divisions of 1st Flotilla attack V.187 and sink her at 9.10. *Stettin* comes down from N.E. and opens fire on rescuing boats. Submarine E.4 attacks her, and then rescues *Defender's* boats. *Lurcher*, not shown in plan, sights *Lowestoft* and *Nottingham*, and then four other ships of 2nd Light-Cruiser Squadron, reports she is in touch with enemy, which accounts for *Arethusa's* turn to eastward at 9.42. *Fearless* conforms. *Arethusa* stops to repair damages from 10.17 to 10.40, while *Fearless* and 1st Flotilla stand by.

stopping to consider their own danger, sent out lifeboats to save our men."

At 8.30, Commodore Goodenough, with four of his light-cruisers, had reached his appointed position about twenty miles south-west of Heligoland, and altered course to the westward. About twenty minutes beforehand, intercepting the *Arethusa's* signals that she was in action, he had detached the *Nottingham* and *Lowestoft* to assist her. A little later these two light-cruisers were sighted by Commodore Keyes in the *Lurcher*. Unaware that any British four-funnelled cruisers were taking part in the operation, and seeing them dimly in the mist, the commodore proceeded to shadow them, reporting to the *Invincible* by wireless that he was in touch with the enemy. This message was intercepted by Commodore Goodenough in the *Southampton*, who decided to go to the *Lurcher's* assistance.

At 8.53, after turning to the north, the *Southampton* had the *Lurcher* in sight, though the result was only to increase the complexity of the situation. Commodore Keyes, knowing nothing of the presence of Goodenough's squadron, now thought he was in touch with four Germans. Steaming off to the northward towards the battle-cruiser supports farther out at sea, he wirelessed to the *Invincible* that he was being chased, and was trying to lead the enemy towards her.

Commodore Goodenough followed the *Lurcher* to the northward for about twelve minutes. Then, realising something was amiss, he turned again to the westerly course for the sweep out to sea. This led to another *contretemps*. At 9.30, those on the *Southampton's* bridge suddenly sighted a periscope 500 yards on the starboard bow. The cruiser, travelling at high speed, swerved to ram, and the submarine just managed to avoid destruction by making a " crash dive."

This submarine was actually the British E.6 – Lieutenant-Commander C. P. Talbot.[1] Diving deeply, those in her heard the roar of the *Southampton's* propellers as she passed overhead. But for Talbot's clever handling and wonderful presence of mind, the loss of the E.6 would have provided a regrettable incident.

Soon afterwards, sighting the *Lurcher* again, the mystery of Commodore Keyes's " enemy " cruisers was cleared up as between himself and Commodore Goodenough. But Keyes's submarines did not know of the presence of the 2nd Light-Cruiser Squadron, nor could they be informed. As his ship might be attacked on sight, Commodore Goodenough thought it advisable to continue to the westward.

To Commodore Tyrwhitt, however, still steaming to the west with the 3rd Flotilla, with the *Fearless* and some of her destroyers about two and a half miles to the north, the situation was nebulous in the extreme. At about 9.45 the *Firedrake*, the other destroyer attached to the submarines, passed him the *Lurcher's* signal that she was being pursued. Though his *Arethusa* was badly damaged and her speed was gradually failing, Tyrwhitt swung round to the

[1] Now Captain, D.S.O.

eastward with his destroyers to assist Commodore Keyes. His movement was conformed to by the *Fearless* and the 1st Flotilla.

After being vouchsafed a fleeting glimpse of a hostile light-cruiser, which rapidly disappeared in the mist, Commodore Tyrwhitt, after steaming some eight miles to the eastward without any sight of the *Lurcher*, realised he was again getting very close to Heligoland. Enemy light-cruisers might appear in force at any moment, so he turned again to the west with the *Fearless* and both flotillas of destroyers.

Severely damaged in the engine-room, the *Arethusa* could now steam no more than 10 knots. Her feed tank had been holed, her torpedo-tubes demolished, and all her guns but one put out of action. At about 10.17, there being no enemy ships in sight, Commodore Tyrwhitt directed the 3rd Flotilla to steam on to the westward at 10 knots. He himself closed the *Fearless* and the 1st Flotilla, and ordered them to stop and to cover him while he affected temporary repairs to his crippled ship. By about 10.40 both the light-cruisers and the 1st Flotilla were under way again, steaming slowly to the west, with the destroyers spread out ahead. The *Arethusa* was reduced to a crawl ; but all her guns except two 4–inch were again ready for action. She was not to be left in peace for long.

The Commander-in-Chief of the High Seas Fleet, lying in the Jade River some twenty-two miles to the south-south-west, could not bring his heavy ships to sea on account of the state of the tide. He was, however, doing his utmost to concentrate all his available light-cruisers to attack the British flotillas on their way out to sea. The *Mainz* had left the Ems River at 9 o'clock, and was hoping to join the *Strassburg*, which sailed from the Jade at 9.30. The *Cöln*, *Ariadne*, *Stralsund*, and *Kolberg* left the Jade at intervals after the *Strassburg*. The *Stettin*, too, was on her way west from Heligoland.

Seven enemy light-cruisers were then endeavouring to cut off the retiring British. The damaged *Arethusa*, as already mentioned, was reduced to 10 knots, and, though most of her armament had been repaired, she was in no fit state to fight another action. The 3rd Flotilla, having been ordered to steam on, were some miles to the west of Commodore Tyrwhitt when he steamed slowly on at 10.40. In close company with the *Arethusa* was the *Fearless* and her 1st Flotilla.

At 10.30, Commodore Goodenough's 2nd Light-Cruiser Squadron was about thirty miles to the west of the *Arethusa's* position.

and Sir David Beatty, with the battle-cruisers some ten miles more to the west-south-west. The nearest reinforcements were thus over an hour's steaming from the *Arethusa*.

It was lucky that the thickening mist made it impossible for the enemy to work in unison. Had those light-cruisers been able to concentrate, had they realised that no British reinforcements were within easy supporting distance, nothing but a miracle could have saved the *Arethusa* from destruction.

As it was, her position from about 11 o'clock onwards was precarious in the extreme. She was only saved by her own hard fighting, the splendid, self-sacrificing gallantry of the *Fearless* and the destroyers of the 1st and 3rd Flotillas, and the rapidity and dash with which Commodore Goodenough and Sir David Beatty brought their light-cruisers and battle-cruisers to the scene of action when once her dangerous situation was realised.

3

It is not easy to follow the course of the main action, which lasted intermittently from 11 a.m. to 1.30 p.m. The weather, let it be remembered, was thick, the visibility rarely exceeding 6,000 yards, or three miles, and, except in the more important incidents, no two narratives quite agree as to precisely which enemy ships were sighted at any particular time. The fighting was very confused, and in the published plans of the battle, which was fought over an area of about twenty by fifteen miles, the tracks of the vessels engaged cross and re-cross in every direction.

Very soon after resuming their course to the westward, the *Arethusa* and *Fearless* and the 1st Flotilla were in action with an enemy light-cruiser, probably the *Strassburg*, which appeared from the south-east. After a few ineffectual salvos at long range, she disappeared in the mist. At 11.5, another German, the *Cöln*, was sighted in the same direction, and passed to the north after firing a few shots. The *Arethusa* had turned south to engage, while Captain Blunt in the *Fearless*, with the 1st Flotilla, steamed between the commodore and the Germans to draw their fire from the crippled *Arethusa*.

Both British ships, with the destroyers, turned to the west at 11.12, only to sight the *Strassburg* again to the north in a few minutes. Once more her grey sides sparkled with flame as she opened a heavy and accurate fire on the *Arethusa*. The latter, with the *Fearless* and destroyers, at once replied.

The situation was becoming desperate. The sound of the battle would inevitably attract more Germans to the scene. Already the *Fearless* had flashed off an urgent call for help, and already, before receiving it, Sir David Beatty had ordered Commodore Goodenough to detach two of his light-cruisers to the *Arethusa's* assistance. Steaming hard, they were coming in from seaward towards the sounds of gunfire. It remained a question whether they would arrive in time to save her.

Hard pressed, Commodore Tyrwhitt asked Captain Blunt to

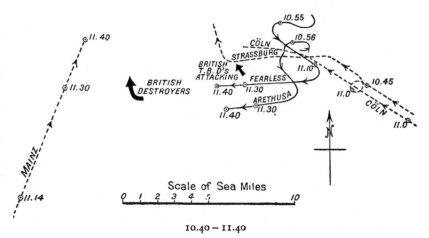

Scale of Sea Miles

10.40 — 11.40

Strassburg and *Cöln* appear from S.E. *Arethusa* and *Fearless* engage, *Fearless* coming under *Arethusa's* stern to protect her. *Strassburg* and *Cöln* then go to northward, and former reappears, to be driven off by destroyers. *Mainz* is sighted by destroyers six miles ahead of *Arethusa* at about 11.30, and is chased off to northward.

send in his destroyers to drive off the persistent *Strassburg* to the northward. " We received a very severe and most accurate fire from this cruiser," the commodore wrote. " Salvo after salvo was falling between twenty and thirty yards short, but not a single shell struck."

According to some accounts, this German ship was not the *Strassburg*; but, whoever she was, the result was the same. Steaming off at full speed to the north-west, the destroyers soon found the enemy and attacked under heavy fire. Several torpedoes were fired, but, though none of them hit, the *Strassburg* was forced to turn away to avoid them. For the time being, the *Arethusa* was left in peace.

To Sir David Beatty, about forty miles out to sea, the situation was fraught with anxious uncertainty. Several urgent calls for reinforcements had told him that the *Arethusa*, *Fearless*, and destroyers were still in action, and apparently with superior forces. Fighting had been going on for nearly four hours, and since 8 a.m., when the sweep to the westward from Heligoland was timed to begin, Commodore Tyrwhitt had advanced barely fifteen miles.

Something clearly was wrong. The flotillas were still within easy reach of the enemy bases, the Jade River being barely twenty miles to the south-south-east, and the Ems about thirty to the south-west. In the Jade lay the High Seas Fleet, and when the tide served the German Commander-in-Chief would send some of his heavy ships to sea. There was palpable danger of the light-cruisers inshore being overwhelmed unless they were supported, and supported thoroughly. The risk of enemy mines and submarines was considerable. The mist to the eastward was thickening ; but Sir David, with characteristic boldness, determined to take his whole force into the Bight to clear up the situation and to extricate the *Arethusa*, *Fearless*, and the flotillas. At 11.30, Commodore Goodenough, with his four remaining light-cruisers, was ordered to the eastward with all possible despatch, and at the same time the *Lion*, *Queen Mary*, *Princess Royal*, *Invincible*, and *New Zealand* swung round towards the scene of action and started to work up to full speed.

At about 11.30 some of the destroyers about six miles to the westward of the *Arethusa* sighted an enemy light-cruiser ahead steaming to the north-eastward at high speed. This was the *Mainz*, which had left the Ems at 10 a.m. The *Ariel*, followed by the *Lucifer* and *Llewellyn*, and then by eight more destroyers in line ahead, turned to the north to get into position for attacking with torpedoes. The enemy, opening fire, pursued them to the north for about twenty minutes, when, at 11.50, she suddenly swung round again to the south. The destroyers turned after her.

What had happened was that the *Mainz* had suddenly sighted Commodore Goodenough's light-cruisers coming down at full speed from the north-west. The visibility seems to have improved, for the *Southampton* and her consorts opened fire at a range of 10,000 yards. The *Mainz*, " very wisely," as wrote one of the *Southampton's* officers, " fled like a stag." Chased for some time at full speed, she was under the fire of about fifteen 6-inch guns, to which she made a feeble reply with her after 4.1's.

After being hit at least twice, the shell-bursts showing yellow against the red flashes of her guns, she disappeared in the mist.

A few minutes after noon, still running hard to the southward, the *Mainz* was sighted on the starboard bow of the *Arethusa*. Chased by Commodore Goodenough, she had no alternative but to cross the *Arethusa's* bows. The *Fearless*, about two miles to the north of the commodore, turned to engage her on a northerly course, while the *Arethusa* swerved slightly to starboard to bring her guns to bear.

Once more the latter was in fierce action at a range of little more than 5,000 yards, and, not aware that his enemy was already flying from the 2nd Light-Cruiser Squadron, Commodore Tyrwhitt ordered the five divisions of destroyers in company with him to attack with torpedoes.

Many torpedoes were fired, but the brunt of the *Mainz's* resistance fell upon the 4th Division of the 3rd Flotilla, the *Laurel*, *Liberty*, *Lysander*, and *Laertes*, which, according to one account, approached within 1,000 yards. The enemy's fire was remarkably accurate, and just after the *Laurel* had fired two torpedoes, and was turning to get away, she was very badly hit. A shell bursting in the engine-room killed 4 men and did much damage. Another struck near the foremost gun and killed 3 more. Another, hitting aft, detonated the lyddite shell in the ready racks on the upper deck, which put the after gun out of action, practically demolished the after funnel, and hid the ship in a cloud of dense smoke. Commander Frank F. Rose, her commanding officer, was seriously wounded in the left leg by the third projectile which struck. Shifting his weight on to the other leg, he continued in command. Then he was hit again, this time on the right leg. He was knocked down ; but continued to give orders until he lost consciousness. The ship still being under heavy fire, Lieutenant C. R. Peploe[1] continued to fight the ship, one of the petty officers tying a lifebelt round the wounded commander as he lay insensible. Thanks to the efforts of the engineer officer, Engineer-Lieutenant-Commander H. T. Meeson, the *Laurel*, in spite of her damaged engines, boilers, and funnel, was eventually able to limp away. For his gallantry on this occasion Rose was awarded the D.S.O., and Peploe the D.S.C.

The *Liberty*, the destroyer astern of the *Laurel*, was partly hidden by the latter's smoke as she steamed in to attack. But as she also turned away, after firing her torpedoes, she was hit

[1] Now Commander, D.S.C.

on the bridge by a shell which brought down her mast, shattered the searchlight, and killed Lieutenant-Commander Nigel Barttelot and a signalman. Her first lieutenant, Lieutenant H. E. Horan, [1] took over the command, and continued to fire on the *Mainz* until she disappeared in the mist to the southward.

The third destroyer of this group, the *Lysander*, Commander H. F. H. Wakefield, was luckier. Unhit by the salvo intended for her, she fired torpedoes at the *Mainz* and then turned away to attack another German cruiser which had just appeared to the northward – probably the *Strassburg*.

The last destroyer in the line, the *Laertes*, Lieutenant-Commander Malcolm L. Goldsmith, [2] was hit by four shells of one salvo. Her casualties were 2 killed and 6 wounded, her boilers were severely damaged, and she was brought to a complete standstill through the consequent lack of water. Thanks again to her engineer, Engineer-Lieutenant-Commander Alexander Hill, she was eventually able to proceed unaided. The *Laurel*, not so lucky, had to be towed home.

These torpedo attacks – indeed, all the attacks made by the *Fearless* and the destroyers during the day – were made at close range in misty weather, and utterly regardless of consequences. They were pushed home with the greatest gallantry, the destroyers never hesitating to engage light-cruisers with gunfire. Many torpedoes were fired during the series of engagements. An officer, describing the scene at one period, speaks of the sea as being " furrowed " by their whitened tracks. Soon after the battle the Admiralty was forced to issue an order reminding all concerned that the stock of these expensive weapons was not inexhaustible, and that too lavish an expenditure might endanger the future supply.

All the same, one of the destroyer's torpedoes hit the *Mainz* amidships in a terrific upheaval of smoke and spray. " The ship reared," wrote one of her surviving officers, " bent perceptibly from end to end, and continued to pitch for some time. Every bit of glass between decks was smashed, and the electric light faded and went out. We had to find our way about with electric torches. The ship was slowly sinking by the bow."

The *Mainz* had fought brilliantly, and continued to fight until the end. Before being torpedoed, she had been set on fire forward and aft, had had her port engine disabled, most of her guns

---

[1] Now Captain, D.S.C.   [2] Now Captain, D.S.O.

put out of action, and her rudder jammed with 10° of port helm. Horribly battered, but apparently still steaming at slow speed, she turned to the west straight into the arms of Commodore Goodenough and his four light-cruisers.

" We closed down on her," wrote one of the *Southampton's* officers[1] " hitting with every salvo. She was a mass of yellow flame and smoke as the lyddite detonated along her length. Her two after funnels melted away and collapsed. Red glows, indicating internal fires, showed through gaping wounds in her sides." One of her guns still fired spasmodically ; but in ten

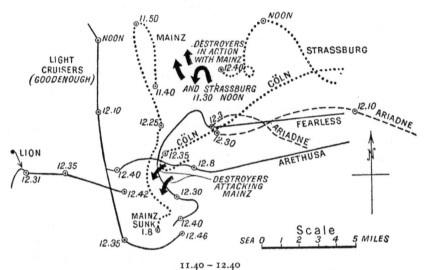

11.40 – 12.40

Mainz steaming northward after destroyers, until, at 11.50, she sights Goodenough's light-cruisers and turns south. *Mainz* is engaged by *Fearless* and destroyers and attacked with torpedoes. She is re-engaged by Goodenough's light-cruisers, and finally sinks at 1.8. *Arethusa* and *Fearless* in intermittent action. At about 12.30 Tyrwhitt sights Goodenough's light-cruisers to the N.W., and soon afterwards the *Lion* and other battle-cruisers. (To avoid too many tracks, *Stettin* and *Stralsund* are not shown.)

minutes she lay a blazing, smoking wreck, sinking by the bows. Her men could be seen jumping into the water. Then " the mainmast slowly leant forward, and, like a great tree, quite gradually lay down along her deck."

" The *Mainz* was incredibly brave," wrote another British officer in a published letter. " The last I saw of her was as a complete wreck, with a smoking hell in the centre. On the poop and forecastle respectively a gun was nevertheless sending forth death and destruction."

[1] Commander Stephen King-Hall, in *A Naval Lieutenant, 1914–18*. (Methuen & Co.)

As to what it was like on board the *Mainz* we know from the account of a German petty officer : " The wireless telegraphy room was a heap of ruins, and burning fiercely. Two of the funnels had been brought down, the searchlight shot to pieces, and an increasing number of shells hit the deck, tearing great holes in it. Guns' crews, voice-pipe men, and ammunition supply-parties were literally blown to pieces. The upper deck was a chaos of ruin, flame, scorching heat, and corpses, and everything was streaked with the green and yellow residue of the explosives, that emitted suffocating gases. The hail of shell increased, and death and destruction were wrought not only by 200 or 300 shell falling on an area of only 460 by 46 feet ; but also by splinters torn from the ship's side and decks. Our guns were knocked out one after the other, till finally only one remained. This gun continued to fire until the last shell was expended ; but it only fired slowly, the captain of the gun and all its crew being dead or wounded. The enemy then ceased fire."

The *Mainz* struck her colours at 12.50, and Commodore Goodenough, leaving her to steam on towards the sound of heavy gunfire to the westward, detached the *Liverpool* to rescue the survivors. She lowered three boats and picked up many of the swimmers. Commodore Keyes now appeared with the *Lurcher* and *Firedrake*, and, as it could be seen that the *Mainz's* smoking decks were littered with wounded, he actually took the *Lurcher* alongside. He was able to save practically all the survivors before, at 1.8, the stricken cruiser suddenly turned over on her side and went to the bottom. Her end was hastened by scuttling charges fired by her crew. As she disappeared, the *Lurcher* barely avoided being damaged by her propellors as the stern came out of water. Of the *Mainz's* crew of 380 officers and men, 348 were rescued, 60 of them being seriously wounded.

From noon until 12.30 the *Arethusa* and *Fearless* had endured another severe gruelling. The *Cöln* and *Ariadne* were fast coming up from astern, followed by the *Stralsund* and *Stettin*, while about five miles away to the north-east the devoted destroyers were engaging the *Strassburg*. For a time the *Fearless* was heavily engaged with two ships, and then ran on to draw the fire of the *Mainz*.

It was at this time that Commodore Tyrwhitt saw four light-cruisers coming down at high speed out of the mist to the north-west. They were steaming in line abreast, and for a moment of breathless suspense those in the *Arethusa* thought that they were

German, and that this was the end of everything. Then they were seen to be firing heavily on the crippled *Mainz*. They were friends – Commodore Goodenough's 2nd Light-Cruiser Squadron.

Recalling her scattered destroyers, the *Arethusa* resumed the course to the westward. As the destroyers began to re-form, salvos of shell began to fall among them from two ships dimly to be seen to the northward, the *Cöln* and the *Stettin*. Once more the situation was fraught with grave danger. Then, quite suddenly, the shape of a very large ship loomed out of the murk to the westward. She was steaming at full speed, the smoke rolling from her funnels and the white bow wave piled up round her sharp stem. One by one four more huge hulls came into view astern of her. After another moment or two of hideous anxiety, the newcomers were made out to be Sir David Beatty's *Lion*, with the four other battle-cruisers.

At that moment the hearts of those on board the crippled *Arethusa* must have been filled with supreme thankfulness. Many times during the last four hours the situation had seemed desperate, if not hopeless. But now the pendulum of chance had definitely swung over. Salvation was in sight. Instead of the enemy being the pursuers, they would now be the pursued. No light-cruiser that was ever built could stand up to the 13.5 and 12-inch guns of the British battle-cruisers.

For the *Arethusa*, the *Fearless*, and the destroyers the battle was over. For the *Lion* and her consorts it was just about to begin – the first time they had fired their guns in anger.

Steering about midway between the *Arethusa* and the stricken *Mainz*, the *Lion* sighted the *Cöln* on her port bow steaming hard to the north-east. A few salvos from the flagship and the *Princess Royal* disabled her engines. Before her destruction could be completed, however, the *Ariadne* appeared in the mist, travelling fast to the south-east across the *Lion's* bow. She was at once engaged. Escape was utterly impossible. Hit again and again, she staggered on ; but within a few minutes, with one boiler-room out of action, a coal bunker blazing, and the ship on fire almost from end to end, the *Ariadne* had developed a heavy list and was obviously sinking. She floated until the afternoon, when, her survivors having been rescued by the *Danzig*, she rolled over and went to the bottom. She had lost 3 officers and 61 men killed, and 65 wounded.

Leaving her to her fate, Sir David steamed on, and at 1.10, when about thirty-two miles from the Jade River, made the general signal, " Retire." Before proceeding to the westward, however, he made a wide circle to the north to find the crippled *Cöln*. At 1.25 she was again sighted, steaming slowly to the south-east. Her flag was still flying. There was nothing for it but to complete her destruction, and at a range of about 3,500 yards the *Lion's* 13.5's thundered.

The second salvo hit, and only one more was needed. The *Cöln* listed heavily over to port, and at 1.35 disappeared to the bottom. Destroyers were sent to the spot to rescue any survivors, though for some unexplained reason none were picked up. According to the account of the one solitary survivor, however, a stoker called Neumann, who was rescued from the water on August 30th, 250 of the *Cöln's* men assembled on the quarter-deck on the order being given to " abandon ship " just before she sank. When she took her final plunge, large numbers of men took to the water and clung on to pieces of wreckage, only to drop off one by one through cold and exhaustion as the weary hours passed and no help came. Neumann was finally left alone, to be saved, practically at his last gasp, forty-eight hours after his ship had been sunk. The *Cöln's* losses consisted of the German admiral, 21 officers, 17 warrant officers, and 467 officers and men, a total of 506.

Thus, in little less than an hour, Sir David Beatty's decision to take his battle-cruisers into the Bight to Commodore Tyrwhitt's assistance turned a very awkward situation into a victory.

The British squadrons and flotillas withdrew in safety, only two ships, the *Arethusa* and the *Laurel*, having to be towed home. Our losses in all amounted to about 35 killed and 40 wounded, the *Arethusa's* casualties being 11 killed and 16 wounded. Only the *Arethusa* and two destroyers were really seriously damaged.

Considering the very heavy fire which many of our vessels had suffered, the small casualty list was a matter for congratulation. Contradictory as it may sound, it was largely accounted for by the excellence of the German shooting and the nicety with which their guns were calibrated. Their shell mostly fell together in bunches, and if one missed its target the others probably did likewise. As proof of this, we may cite Commodore Tyrwhitt's remark to the effect that at the period of engagement salvo after salvo fell between twenty and thirty yards short and not a single shell struck, and the extreme accuracy of the *Mainz's* fire on the *Laurel, Liberty, Lysander*, and *Laertes* when they attacked her with torpedoes.

The Germans, on the other hand, lost 3 light-cruisers and 1 destroyer. Their casualties in personnel amounted to 712 officers and men killed, 149 wounded, and 381 prisoners of war, a total of 1,242.

The moral effect, however, was even greater than the material. " August 28th," wrote Admiral Von Tirpitz, " was a day fateful, both in after-effects and in incidental results, for the work of our Navy. . . . The Emperor did not want losses of this sort. . . . Orders were issued by the Emperor . . . to restrict the initiative of the Commander-in-Chief of the North Sea Fleet ; the loss of ships was to be avoided ; fleet sallies and any greater undertakings must be approved by His Majesty in advance. . . . "

So the unwillingness of the German High Command to venture the High Seas Fleet at sea throughout the war was perhaps brought about by the early British success off Heligoland.

Upon the Royal Navy, on the other hand, the effect was stimulating. Light forces had pushed their way into the Bight until they actually sighted the red cliffs of Heligoland. Young destroyer officers had not hesitated to tackle light-cruisers, and certainly acquired a feeling of superiority over the German destroyers and a profound faith in their own leaders.

Admittedly, there was a good deal of luck on our side. Seeing that the *Arethusa* had been in commission such a short time, and had not really tested her guns, it seems rather to have been tempting Providence to send her in on a raid where hard fighting was to be expected. It is as well to remember, however, that she was a brand new ship, superior in speed and gun-power – indeed, in every way – to the little *Amethyst* from which Commodore Tyrwhitt had just turned over. Most of us, if given our choice, would have chosen the *Arethusa*, in spite of the fact that her crew was newly joined and rather unfamiliar with the armament.[1]

Had not Sir David Beatty taken his battle-cruisers into the Bight at the critical moment, however, the *Arethusa* could hardly have survived. Moreover, the bad staff work which left Commodores Tyrwhitt and Keyes in ignorance of a most important alteration in the operation orders showed that we still had a lot to learn. This omission, as has already been explained, all but brought about disaster when the *Arethusa*, *Fearless*, and their flotillas turned again to the westward in response to the *Lurcher's* signal that she was being chased by " enemy " cruisers.

[1] See footnote, page 27.

The Germans fought gallantly, and after Heligoland no British officer under-rated their bravery or efficiency. They, however, " knew nothing of our defective staff work and of the risks we had run," as Mr. Winston Churchill has written. " All they saw was that the British did not hesitate to hazard their greatest vessels as well as their light craft in the most daring offensive action, and had escaped apparently unscathed. They felt as we should have felt had German destroyers broken into the Solent and their battle-cruisers penetrated as far as the Nab."[1]

[1] *The World Crisis, 1911–1914*, p. 309.

CHAPTER III

DESTROYERS IN THE DARDANELLES

I

BEYOND saying that the final object of the Dardanelles campaign was the desire to pass an Allied Fleet into the Sea of Marmora and thence to Constantinople, it is unnecessary here to enter into the precise circumstances which caused the British and French Governments to attempt the forcing of the Dardanelles and the capture of the Gallipoli Peninsula in 1915. Moreover, the tragic story of the campaign in all its lurid detail has been told many times over by worthier pens than mine.

I would refer those who wish for a general and picturesque narrative of the fighting ashore which is not overburdened with technical detail to Mr. John Masefield's *Gallipoli*, first published in 1916. Volume II. of Mr. Winston Churchill's *The World Crisis*, dealing with the year 1915, and published in 1923, describes in detail the events which led up to the decision to attempt the forcing of the Dardanelles by the Royal Navy, the subsequent landing of troops on the Gallipoli Peninsula, and the course of the fighting afloat and ashore. The military aspects of the campaign are fully dealt with in the two volumes of General Sir Ian Hamilton's *A Gallipoli Diary* (1920), while among many other books on the subject may be mentioned Mr. Ellis Ashmead-Bartlett's *The Uncensored Dardanelles* (1927), Admiral Lord Wester Wemyss's *The Navy in the Dardanelles Campaign* (1924), and, of course, *The Final Report of the Dardanelles Commission* (1919).

The circumstances in which the troops, with the aid of the Royal Navy, landed on the bullet-swept, shell-ridden beaches of the Gallipoli Peninsula, and the almost incredible gallantry with which they advanced and maintained their foothold ashore in the face of vastly superior forces, are rather apt to overshadow the major object of the campaign. The capture and occupation of the Peninsula, had it come to pass, would have been incidental, a step in the passage of the fleet through the minefields and past the guns of the inner Dardanelles defences to the Sea of Marmora and Constantinople.

Constantinople, with all the advantages its possession would give, was the ultimate prize. What were these advantages?

If the Dardanelles had been forced and the Gallipoli Peninsula occupied, it would have severed the link by which Turkey maintained her foothold in Europe. The Allied command in the Black Sea would have eased the situation for the Russian armies in the Caucasus, which were heavily beset by the Turks ; would have enabled vast quantities of wheat from the granaries of South Russia to be exported to Allied countries ; would have provided an avenue for the import into Russia of the munitions and weapons which she sorely needed ; and have given the Allies access to the mouths of the Danube. Not the least advantage of a great feat of arms by the Allies in the Near East would have been its effect on the various Balkan nations.

Greece, unable to make up her mind, would probably have thrown in her lot with the Allies. Bulgaria, which afterwards joined the Central Powers, might have done the same. So would Roumania. The effect upon Italy, too, which had not yet joined in the war, and still belonged to the Triple Alliance, would be stupendous.

The mere appearance of Allied men-of-war before Constantinople would probably have finished the war so far as Turkey was concerned. As said one well-informed German officer, [1] " I have no doubt whatever that Turkey would have made peace. There would have been revolution. The appearance of ships before Constantinople would have been sufficient. Constantinople *is* Turkey. There were no troops to speak of in Constantinople."

Constantinople was the prize, the whole aim and object of the attempted forcing of the Dardanelles by the fleet and the subsequent bloody campaign in the Gallipoli Peninsula.

The project failed in circumstances that we already know. But let us consider the campaign, not as a disaster, but as a stupendous human effort involving seemingly insurmountable risks and difficulties. It came, " more than once," as Mr. Masefield writes, [2] " very near to triumph, achieved the impossible many times, and failed, in the end, as many great deeds of arms have failed, from something which had nothing to do with arms, nor with the men who bore them."

---

[1] Lieutenant-Commander Balzer, who was A.D.C. to the representative of the Minister of Marine at Berlin, a clever and capable German officer, who had studied Turkish politics closely, and had definite and reasonable opinions. His statement is quoted by Mr. Churchill in *The World Crisis, 1915,* p. 264.

[2] *Gallipoli,* pp. 3–4.

Moreover, the campaign was a naval one, which depended entirely upon the power of the Navy. By the Navy the troops were carried to and landed on the Peninsula, maintained there, and finally carried away. During the nine months that the partial occupation lasted, over 300,000 men and vast quantities of weapons and stores were taken to Gallipoli by the Navy from places 3,000, 4,000, and even 6,000 miles away. During the fighting, some 150,000 sick and wounded were evacuated by the Navy to ports from 500 to 3,000 miles distant. Every day the Navy supplied the Army with the food, the drink, and the munitions without which it could neither exist nor fight. Day after day the men-of-war, battleships, cruisers, and destroyers moved up and down the rugged Gallipoli coast, searching the hills with gunfire, bombarding the Turkish positions and trenches. The campaign, moreover, was not merely a wonderful illustration of sea power, but an almost perfect example of successful co-operation between the two great fighting Services.

After describing various landing operations, Sir Ian Hamilton referred to the Royal Navy as " The sheet-anchor on which hung the whole of these elaborate schemes." Elsewhere he has written, " The Navy was our father and our mother."

2

At 9.50 on the morning of February 19th, 1915, a fleet of seven British and four French battleships, together with one British battle-cruiser, began the bombardment of the outer forts of the Dardanelles at Cape Helles and Kum Kale. At 2 o'clock in the afternoon, when the forts had been hit repeatedly and made no reply, the bombarding ships closed in to within 6,000 yards and continued a deliberate fire. At 4.45, when certain vessels advanced within 5,000 yards, some of the more modern enemy guns came into action until, in the failing light, the fleet withdrew at 5.30. The result of this inconclusive operation was to show that the ships must anchor before accurate shooting could be hoped for, that direct fire was better than indirect fire, and that direct hits must be registered on the enemy guns to put them out of action. It was not sufficient merely to hit the forts.

For five days no further bombardments were possible because of a gale ; but on the morning of the 25th the operation was recommenced with deliberate fire at 12,000 yards. All the four long-range guns defending the mouth of the Straits were knocked out, and in the afternoon the ships closed in to within short range and battered the forts to pieces.

Minesweeping trawlers, accompanied by destroyers, swept the approaches and entrance to the Straits on the nights of the 25th and 26th, and on the latter date three battleships moved inside and completed the destruction of the outer forts. On the 26th and following days demolition parties of from 50 to 100 seamen and marines were landed by destroyers to complete the actual destruction of the guns at Sedd-el-Bahr, near Cape Helles, and at two forts near Kum Kale, on the Asiatic shore. These were not seriously opposed by the enemy, and returned to their ships with a loss of 9 killed and wounded, having destroyed with guncotton, or found in a disabled condition, 48 guns of various calibres.

By March 2nd the outer defences were destroyed, and the fleet was able to sweep and to enter the Straits for a distance of about six miles. The inner and intermediate defences were now exposed to naval attack. These consisted of the forts and batteries situated along the European and Asiatic shores, together with ten lines of mines in the narrower portion of the Straits between Kephez and Chanak. The minefields were protected by mobile batteries of field-guns, while numbers of heavy howitzers were hidden in the clefts and gullies on both the Asiatic and European shores. These latter, in temporary emplacements and invisible to the ships, soon proved themselves a serious annoyance.

The most serious obstacle of all, however, was the extensive minefield which started about eight miles from the entrance to the Straits, and covered a distance of about four miles. The battleships could not approach until it had been swept, and this was the work of the minesweeping trawlers protected by destroyers.

But " protection " seems hardly the word for it. The destroyers were in as dangerous a situation as the trawlers themselves. The work was carried out at night, in a strong current, often in bad weather, under the rays of occasional searchlights and the heavy fire of guns of all calibres, many of them shooting at range of a mile or less. Since the enemy weapons were mobile and easily hidden, they could rarely be silenced.

In a letter to me, an officer in one of the destroyers writes of this period : " At the beginning, when we were patrolling, and a gun was fired at the ship, one instinctively moved quickly and thought the ship was going to be hit. But in a very short time we got used to being shot at, and came to realise that the percentage of hits to shots fired at you was very small. . . . We were employed attending on ships firing inside the entrance to the Straits during the day, and at night went up with the trawlers to protect them or try to, while they endeavoured to sweep. It was interesting watching the big ships in action. The Turks, who couldn't resist the larger bulk of a battleship as a target, seldom fired at us, and from a distance of a few cables we would watch shell bursting and literally rattling on the battleship's armoured sides.

" The night business, however, was distinctly nasty, and all calibres of Turkish guns let us have it. Occasionally there would be an enormous splodge quite different to the rest, with an unusual sound unlike that of an ordinary shell striking the water. Some people maintained they were firing their ancient muzzle-loaders, with the huge stone shot, samples of which we afterwards found at Sedd-el-Bahr. As the days went on the Turkish *morale* improved, and their shooting became more accurate and better in every way."

That close-range gunfire at night was trying enough to the regular naval personnel, but doubly trying to the erstwhile civilian crews of the trawlers, who, accustomed to mines, had never encountered artillery fire. The sweeping progressed very slowly, and eventually the trawlers were manned by regular naval personnel. Even so, it soon became evident that the clearing of the minefield could not be accomplished until the mobile guns defending it were silenced. Desperate attempts were made nightly ; but with little or no success.

A condition of stalemate had been reached. Until that minefield had been swept, the bombarding ships could not approach sufficiently close to fire with any effect at the numerous forts and gun emplacements. Moreover, on each occasion when the battleships tried to bombard, they were constantly hit by the gradually increasing number of concealed howitzers. By March 3rd, Rear-Admiral de Robeck, the second-in-command to Vice-Admiral Carden, is said to have reported that the Straits could not be forced unless one shore or the other were occupied, and that no further progress could be made without the co-operation of the Army.[1]

That the time for the successful employment of landing-parties

[1] *Encyclopædia Britannica*, 14th edition, Vol. xxiii., " World War," p. 783.

for destroying guns ashore was past was emphasised on March 4th, when a demolition party consisting of a considerable number of marines, landed at Kum Kale, on the Asiatic shore, was repulsed with severe loss. Forced to take what cover could be found on the beach, the survivors were rescued by the destroyers *Wolverine*, Commander O. J. Prentis, and *Scorpion*, Lieutenant-Commander A. B. Cunningham, which ran in after dark. The *Scorpion's* armed whaler, with eight men under the command of Mr. T. W. W. Thorrowgood, Gunner (T.) pulled twice into the shore under very heavy rifle fire and brought off 2 officers and 5 men, 2 of whom were wounded, a gallant piece of work which won Thorrowgood the Distinguished Service Cross, and his eight seamen Distinguished Service Medals.

Again and again the minefield off Kephez was attacked after nightfall by the sweepers, escorted by destroyers, who engaged the enemy batteries; but again with little success. On March 6th the expedient was tried of sending in the light-cruiser *Amethyst* to cover the destroyers and sweepers; but she was heavily engaged by the shore guns, and forced to retire with severe damage and many casualties. On March 9th, 10th, and 13th attempts were made to sweep with the picket-boats of the fleet covered by destroyers; but once more with little results, in spite of the greatest gallantry and devotion to duty on the part of all concerned.

Vice-Admiral Carden speaks of the destroyers' work during this period as "invaluable," and refers to their "boldness in action and untiring devotion to duty." They certainly deserved the recommendation. They were tireless.

"On the day after the outer forts were reduced," the destroyer officer continues, "we reconnoitred the southern side of the Straits, going dead slow and stopping to fire at field-guns and any other targets which offered. They didn't open fire until 4 o'clock in the afternoon. There is no doubt the reduction of the outer forts shook them. They had temporarily lost their courage, but soon got it back. Another incident I remember in those early days was on March 1st, when the whaler had been sent ashore with the sub-lieutenant in charge to destroy a fishing-craft in Morto Bay, just east of Sedd-el-Bahr. They were pouring paraffin into her to light her, when down the valley leading to the beach came a large body of Turks – about a battalion. With the flash of our first gun at a few hundred yards they turned and bolted like rabbits, and we got several shell into them as they ran. The moral effect of our guns at the beginning was tremendous, but they soon learnt that they didn't always hit. To summarise the early operations : targets were easy at first, and the Turkish firing was wild and inaccurate. Some destroyers had great fun firing at a camel train near Kum Kale. But the enemy shooting improved daily. The trawlers trying to sweep were always under a very heavy fire, and efficient sweeping was impossible."

3

For some days the First Lord of the Admiralty had been urging Vice-Admiral Carden to new efforts. " The results to be gained," telegraphed Mr. Churchill on March 11th, " are . . . great enough to justify loss of ships and men if success cannot be obtained without. . . . We shall support you in well-conceived action for forcing a decision, even if regrettable losses are entailed." [1]

A great naval attack on the forts in the Narrows was planned for March 18th ; but on the 16th Admiral Carden's health broke down, and he was forced to relinquish the command to Vice-Admiral de Robeck.

On the brilliant, sunlit morning of March 18th, the whole Allied fleet advanced to the attack. It consisted of the *Queen Elizabeth, Agamemnon, Lord Nelson*, and *Inflexible*, which were to fire at the forts in the Narrows at a range of 14,000 yards, and the *Triumph* and *Prince George*, which were simultaneously to engage the intermediate defences. The four French battleships *Suffren, Bouvet, Charlemagne*, and *Gaulois*, were later to fire at the forts in the Narrows at 8,000 yards, when they had been battered at longer range, while the *Cornwallis* and *Canopus* were to cover the minesweepers during the night, by which time it was hoped the forts commanding the minefields would be reduced. The *Vengeance, Irresistible, Albion, Ocean, Swiftsure*, and *Majestic* were detailed as reliefs.

Firing started at about 11.30, when the ships immediately became the targets for the mobile howitzers and the field-guns of the intermediate defences. They were hit several times, though their armour protected them from much damage. A few minutes after noon the four French battleships steamed ahead and through the line of British vessels to engage at closer range. All the forts and enemy guns were now in hot action, to which no fewer

[1] *The World Crisis, 1915*, pp. 217-18.

than twelve great ships were replying with every gun that would bear.

The scene at this period was magnificent and awe-inspiring. The sea was intensely blue and calm, and the sun shone overhead in a sky of almost cloudless azure. The large grey hulls of the bombarding battleships wreathed themselves in orange flashes and billowing clouds of tawny cordite smoke as they wheeled and circled amid forests of dazzling white spray fountains flung up by the enemy shell. The forts spouted great clouds of dust and smoke, mingled every now and then with the flame of their guns and the redder flash of exploding shell. The thundering roar of the terrific cannonade rumbled across the water, echoed

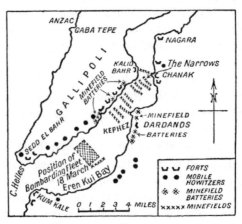

DEFENCES OF DARDANELLES

and re-echoed from the frowning hills on either side of the Straits, the brownish-green shores of which sparkled with the flashes of mobile howitzers and field-guns. For rather more than an hour this intensive bombardment continued, until, by 1.30, the fire of the forts had appreciably weakened.

The destroyers *Colne*, Commander Claude Seymour, and *Chelmer*, Lieutenant-Commander Hugh T. England, had been fitted with light sweeps and ordered to sweep in ahead of the *Queen Elizabeth*.

" The first incident I remember concerning the naval efforts to force the Straits occurred on the evening of March 17th," writes an officer of the *Chelmer*, " when we returned to coal at Tenedos and received a signal from the *Ribble* telling us to look up a passage in the Bible – verse 15, chapter xi., of the second book of Samuel. We did so, to read, ' And he wrote in the letter, saying, set ye Uriah in the forefront of the battle, and retire ye from him, that he may be smitten and die.' The *Ribble* had read her orders for the next day, and we had not received ours ; but on opening them we found that the *Chelmer* and *Colne* were to sweep ahead of the fleet entering the Straits next morning, and understood the jest. . . . As things turned out we were all right, the *Agamemnon* being detailed for counter-battery work and keeping the fire down, so that we did our sweeping unscathed. The first part of the day went well, and in a short time we saw explosions in the forts at the Narrows. We had a good view, as we remained inside the Straits until ordered to clear out by the Commander-in-Chief."

By 1.45, by which time the fire of the forts had almost ceased, the minesweepers were ordered to advance under the cover of the four destroyers *Basilisk*, *Grasshopper*, *Racoon*, and *Mosquito*, to start clearing the Kephez minefield.

So far everything had gone well. Though various ships had been badly knocked about, the *Gaulois* having been forced to discontinue the action with much damage forward, and the *Bouvet* having been heavily hit, the injury was no more than had been expected and the casualties in personnel were comparatively light.

The French squadron had been ordered to retire, and now it was that a new factor came into play. In the early dawn and low visibility of March 8th, a small Turkish steamer had crept down the Straits unseen to lay a line of twenty mines in Eren Keui Bay, just in the area in which the bombarding ships had manœuvred on March 6th and 7th. And just before 2 o'clock, as the French battleship *Bouvet* was following the *Suffren* out of the Straits, onlookers were appalled to see a great gout of flame and smoke and spray rise up at her side. Her magazine had exploded. In two minutes she rolled over and disappeared in a cloud of smoke and steam.

As she was still under heavy fire, it was thought at the time that she had been destroyed by a shell. It was not until later that it was realised she had struck one of the mines laid in Eren Keui Bay.

The River class destroyer *Wear*, Captain Christopher P. Metcalfe, which had been in attendance on the *Queen Elizabeth* throughout the operation, and frequently under heavy fire, at once dashed at full speed to the *Bouvet's* assistance. By the time she reached the spot the battleship had sunk, but, lowering her whaler under a storm of dropping shell, she succeeded in rescuing 66 men.

The action was continued by the British vessels until about 3 p.m., by which time the forts were practically silent. The minesweepers, covered by their destroyers, were steaming towards the Kephez minefield, advancing slowly because of the 3-knot current which sweeps constantly down the Dardanelles from the Sea of Marmora.

The battle-cruiser *Inflexible*, which had been hit during the action, had had her bridge wrecked and set ablaze. Without being aware of it, however, she had been manœuvring in or near the hidden minefield all day, and at 4.11 struck and exploded a mine. She heeled over, and was in considerable danger ; but managed to steam out of the Straits at slow speed, reached Tenedos in safety, and was anchored in shallow water. After her injuries had been patched up, she had to be sent to Malta, and thence to Gibraltar, for repairs.

At 4.14 p.m. the battleship *Irresistible* also struck a mine, and at once took up a heavy list and was unable to move. The old vessel was slowly sinking, and obviously could not last long. Seeing her stopped and heeling over, the enemy reopened their fire, but within a few minutes Captain Metcalfe was alongside with the *Wear*. At 4.50 he was back alongside the *Queen Elizabeth* with his decks crowded with 28 officers and 582 men of the *Irresistible's* crew, the remainder having elected to remain on board their ship, in case the unexpected happened and she remained afloat.

Admiral de Robeck was now in a position of horrible uncertainty. It was not thought possible that moored mines had been laid in the water in which the fleet had been manœuvring throughout the day. Indeed, it was not known until after the war. The *Bouvet*, which had been under heavy fire, might have been destroyed by a shell ; but both the *Inflexible* and *Irresistible* had been mined.

What mines were they ? Were they floating mines set adrift by the enemy higher up the Straits, to be carried down by the current upon the bombarding squadron ? Were they perhaps torpedoes, fired from some station concealed ashore ? Whatever this new agency of destruction might be, the fleet was obviously in highly dangerous waters, and, beset by this fresh anxiety, Vice-Admiral de Robeck determined to break off the action.

Nobody can question this decision. Two ships had been put completely out of action in almost as many minutes. The remainder of the fleet might be destroyed piecemeal.

The two battleships ordered to cover the minesweeping during the night could not remain in the Straits, and, as some of the forts were still firing, the minesweepers could not do their work. The entire operation must be broken off, and at about 5 p.m. the admiral ordered a general retirement. There was no alternative.

Let us revert again to the tale of the little 550-ton destroyer *Chelmer*, which, at some time before 2 p.m., had been ordered out of the Straits.

" The *Gaulois* arrived outside the Straits steaming slowly with her forecastle awash, or nearly so, so we deemed it advisable to offer to take off some of her crew in case she sank. We went alongside and took off about 400, and very soon afterwards, with these Frenchmen on board, we intercepted a wireless message to say that the *Inflexible* had been mined and was in danger of sinking. We put the men from the *Gaulois* on board the *Dartmouth*, outside the Straits, and then proceeded inside and met the *Inflexible* coming out. *Irresistible* had also been mined."

While the retirement was in progress, the *Ocean*, standing by the stricken *Irresistible*, struck another mine, and was seriously damaged. The time was 6.5 p.m., but, in spite of the very heavy fire which was being poured upon her from both sides of the Straits, destroyers went to her assistance. The names of these destroyers were the *Colne*, Commander Claude Seymour ; *Chelmer*, Lieutenant-Commander Hugh T. England ; *Wear*, Captain Christopher P. Metcalfe ; *Jed*, Lieutenant George F. A. Mulock ; *Kennet*, Lieutenant Charles E. S. Farrant ; *Racoon*, Lieutenant-Commander A. G. Muller ; and *Mosquito*, Lieutenant-Commander James L. C. Clark.

The enemy gunfire at this period has been described as " terrific," and it is surprising that none of the rescuing destroyers was sunk, and that they sustained comparatively few casualties. The *Racoon* was damaged by the concussion of a large shell bursting under water, and was deluged with shrapnel bullets, and here are the experiences of the *Chelmer*.

" Just after we got inside the Straits the *Ocean* struck a mine, so we stood by her. She had a good many of the *Irresistible's* crew on board, a large number of the remainder having been taken off by the *Wear*. While we were standing by the *Ocean* she took a list of about 15°, and looked as if she might capsize at any moment, so we went alongside her port side and took off about 500 of her crew. Other destroyers went alongside the other side. It was rather a nasty situation, as she was under fire from a battery of fairly big guns – howitzers, I think – and was turning slowly round and round in the current. Salvos of five or six heavy shell, about 8- or 10-inch, were arriving frequently. Eventually one of these salvos, having just missed us, burst under water and lifted the little *Chelmer* bodily into the air. I remember the azimuth ring of the compass going into the air over my head, and dropping on the deck of the bridge. The damage done to the ship was eighteen feet of the bottom blown in, and the centre boiler-room flooded.

" People said that men on the upper deck, though they were holding on to the berthing-rails, were blown off their feet by the explosion.– One entertaining thing happened. Just before the explosion, a yeoman of signals belonging to the *Irresistible* or *Ocean* had been sent aft to ask the senior officer on board if he would care to use the captain's cabin. We were anxious to get the officers down below, to leave more room on the upper deck. Apparently the yeoman reached this officer at the same time as the explosion ; but the message was faithfully delivered. He sent back the reply, " Thank the Captain for his kindness ; but I will stay on deck and see it out to the end." This officer had already abandoned the *Irresistible* to come to the *Ocean*, only to be mined again.

" With our decks crowded, we finally left the *Ocean* and struggled slowly down the Dardanelles to the *Lord Nelson*, going alongside her and transhipping all the shipwrecked personnel. After borrowing the *Lord Nelson's* collision mats and securing them under our injured bottom as far as we could, we then crawled off to our depot-ship, the *Blenheim*, at Tenedos.– The end of a hectic day.– I have only mentioned major incidents ; but there was hardly a moment we were not doing or seeing something. After temporary repairs by the *Blenheim*, we went on to Malta and had new plates put in the bottom ; but managed to get back to the Dardanelles in time for the landing."

That same night destroyers were sent into the Straits to look for the *Irresistible* and *Ocean*, which were still afloat when last seen. Not a trace of them could be found. Both battleships had gone to the bottom.

In his despatch of March 26th, Vice-Admiral de Robeck particularly mentioned the names of the *Wear, Colne, Chelmer,*

Jed, and *Kennet*, and their commanding officers.   The saving of
valuable lives, he wrote, " was a brilliant and gallant performance
on their part."

And so the attack of March 18th failed.   The forts in the
Narrows, though severely battered, had not been put out of
action, while the minefield, the key to the whole system of
defence, was still intact.   The Allies had lost 3 battleships,
while at least 3 others were badly damaged.

It is not for us to say whether, as Mr. Churchill suggests in
The World Crisis, 1915, it would ever have been possible for the
destroyers fitted as minesweepers, together with the other minesweepers that generally arrived upon the scene, ever to have
swept a passage for the fleet through that formidable mine barrier
between Kephez and Chanak.   The fact remains that the idea
of forcing the Straits with the fleet was abandoned, and that
henceforward the energies of the Navy were concentrated upon
landing and maintaining the Army upon the rugged Peninsula
of Gallipoli.

CHAPTER IV

DESTROYERS AT GALLIPOLI

I

BY the third week in April 1915 the Expeditionary Force had been concentrated in their transports in the harbour at Mudros. Some days were spent in rehearsing the landings, drawing up the final orders, and completing the arrangements. This delay has sometimes been criticised by the uninitiated ; but the weather was unusually fickle for the time of year, and it was quite impossible to attempt the landings on the small open beaches of the Peninsula itself without the prospect of two or three days of fine weather.

The enemy had had ample warning of what was coming, and had had time to concentrate troops to repel the landing. It is true that the landings might be made at various widely separated points, and that some of them might be feints to distract attention. The Peninsula, moreover, had no railways to move troops rapidly from place to place, while what roads it possessed were bad. But everybody was aware that our men would not get ashore except under heavy fire from the high ground by which all the beaches were commanded. The situation was ideal for defence. Indeed, many German and Turkish officers believed that a serious landing was altogether impossible. To expect our men to land from long strings of towed boats and lighters under heavy fire with a bad surf breaking on the beaches was to court disaster at the outset.

Moreover, food, guns, ammunition, sandbags entrenching-tools, clothing, medical stores, horses, mules, fodder, and even water had also to be put ashore. All this heterogeneous mass of material, quite apart from the men themselves, had to be allocated to boats and lighters in such a way as to ensure the least possible confusion at the landing-places.

It was on the afternoon of St. George's Day, April 23rd, 1915, that a huge fleet of transports, escorted by the men-of-war, slowly left the harbour of Mudros for Tenedos amid a great tumult of voices as the seamen cheered the soldiers, and the soldiers the seamen. The island of Tenedos lies about fifteen miles south-south-west of the entrance to the Dardanelles, and it was here, on the 24th, that the first parties to land left their transports and embarked in the battleships and minesweepers that were to put them ashore. The Australian and New Zealand Army Corps, which was to be landed to the north of Gaba Tepe, sailed thither direct from Mudros.

A demonstration by men-of-war and transports containing the Royal Naval Division was to be made at the Bulair Lines, in the Gulf of Xeros, in the hope of preventing any enemy troops in that area from leaving it. Sir Ian Hamilton's main attacks, however, were to be launched at the southern end of the Peninsula, the 29th Division, afterwards reinforced by the R.N. Division, being simultaneously put ashore at five different spots near Cape

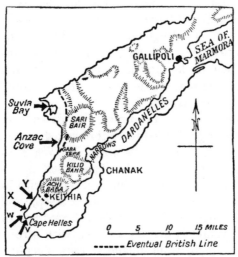

GALLIPOLI PENINSULA AND DARDANELLES
SKETCH MAP SHOWING LANDING PLACES

Helles – Beaches S, V, W, X, and Y. The Australians and New Zealanders were intended to land near Gaba Tepe, on the narrow neck of the Peninsula opposite Maidos.

There was to be intensive artillery fire from the men-of-war to cover the landings in the Helles area. The landing at Gaba Tepe, however, was to take place without artillery preparation shortly before dawn, and it was hoped that while the Turks were heavily involved with the simultaneous attacks at Helles, the Anzacs would make good headway and be able to occupy the high ridges of hills commanding the Narrows.

The story of " The Battle of the Beaches," as it has been called, has often been told. Thrilling accounts of what occurred, and the desperate gallantry displayed, have been written by, among others, Mr. Winston Churchill and Mr. John Masefield. Here, where I am principally concerned with the doings of the destroyers, the landing at what afterwards became known as " Anzac Cove " is by far the most relevant.

In this area the arrangements provided for the troops from the battleships *Queen*, *Prince of Wales*, and *London* to be landed first, every ship sending in four tows each of three large pulling boats towed by a steamboat. The seven destroyers *Beagle*, Commander H. R. Godfrey, which also carried Captain C. P. R. Coode, the Captain (D) of the Flotilla ; *Bulldog*, Lieutenant-Commander W. B. Mackenzie ; *Scourge*, Lieutenant-Commander H. de B. Tupper ; *Foxhound*, Commander W. G. Howard ; *Colne*, Commander Claude Seymour ; *Chelmer*, Lieutenant-Commander H. T. England ; *Usk*, Lieutenant-Commander W. G. C. Maxwell ; and *Ribble*, Lieutenant-Commander R. W. Wilkinson, their decks crowded with soldiers, and towing the transports' lifeboats, were then to approach close to the shore and disembark their troops.

The landing had been timed for before dawn, successive waves of 1,500 men being intended to be thrown ashore at a rugged and difficult spot about half a mile north of Gaba Tepe, unlikely to be elaborately defended. Gaba Tepe itself is a steep cliff or promontory about ninety feet high, covered with low scrub, and the ground above the landing-beaches is steep, sandy cliff, much broken by a tangle of deep gullies and ravines running inland. Most of the ground is densely covered with scrub between two and three feet high, while inland it rises steeply in a series of broken hills and spurs to the ridge known as Sari Bair, nearly 1,000 feet high. There are occasional clumps of stunted pine, with dense undergrowths of scrub struggling for existence in a loose, sandy marl which speedily becomes dust in dry weather, and very sticky in wet – altogether a bleak, inhospitable, and very difficult country for fighting.

It was an intensely calm, still night, with a sea like satin. Without a glimmer of light, the ships arrived off the coast at about 3.30 a.m., while the moon was still above the horizon. For a little time they waited until it set. One can imagine the scene – the almost uncanny silence, disturbed only by the rippling of the water, and the dim moonlight shining feebly on the glassy sea, and the troops crowded on the decks of the destroyers.

" You fellows can smoke and talk quietly," said Wilkinson, the captain of the *Ribble*, leaning over his bridge rails. " But

I expect all lights to be put out and absolute silence to be kept when I give the order." The galley, meanwhile, was working overtime. The *Ribble's* seamen, hospitable as ever, were serving out basins of cocoa, biscuits, and corned beef sandwiches to their guests. For many of those men it was their last meal.

Then the moon set. In the pitch darkness the ships again crept slowly shorewards. " Lights out, men, and stop talking," came the voice of the *Ribble's* captain to the troops on deck. " We're going in now."

" I can never forget my feelings that night as we steamed slowly across from Mudros with those wonderful Australians on board," writes another destroyer officer. " They were the cream of the men of Australia. We had practised and organised the arrangements for landing them to the best of our ability. There was nothing more to be thought of in that respect, but there was ample time to think as we crept slowly across to the Peninsula. ... We were embarked upon the greatest adventure of our lives, and on such an occasion men become very close and intimate with each other. I well remember a very fine Australian officer asking me if he could speak to me privately. We went to my cabin, and he spoke to me of his wife and his children, showing me snapshots of them. He asked me, ' Was I right to volunteer and come ? ' – I trust my answer helped to reassure him. Such thoughts must have been passing through the minds of many men that night during the tense hours of waiting for action, and in the morning they proved their courage up to the hilt."

The seven destroyers, in line abreast, with the boats in tow astern of them, moved on to where the dark loom of the land was becoming plainer and plainer every minute. About 500 yards from the shore, with their leadsmen sounding from their forecastles, they stopped and started to haul the boats alongside the wooden stagings built along their sides.

The string of boats, with the troops from the battleships, passed ahead in tow of their steamboats, whose engines seemed to be unusually noisy in the intense stillness. In the darkness, however, the tows stood a little farther to the north than they should have done, due to an unsuspected northerly current near the shore. They actually reached the coast in a small bay steeply overhung by cliffs called Ari Burnu, but for ever afterwards " Anzac Cove." This accident led them to a spot where the enemy were not expecting them.

Forty yards or so from the shore the steamboats slipped their boats, which then pulled in towards the shore with muffled oars. The time was about 4.30 a.m., and the dawn was breaking. Suddenly a bright yellow light flickered out ashore and then disappeared. The figure of a man showed for a moment silhouetted against the sky on a plateau above the beach for which the boats were making. There came the sharp crack of a rifle shot, and the whizz of the bullet as it passed overhead. Then three or four more reports, followed by a straggling, independent fire, which gradually increased to the crackling uproar of more and more rifles as a number of Turks came rushing along the beach from the direction of Gaba Tepe, firing as they came.

Men in the boats were soon being hit ; but, pushing on, the cutters grounded in about three or four feet of water and the troops scrambled out and waded ashore. The heavier launches and pinnaces took the ground farther out, their men sometimes leaping out in water well above their waists. A few went in out of their depths, and were carried under and drowned by the weight of their packs and equipment.

The men already landed were climbing up the steep hillside, clutching at the insecure roots of the shrubs, driving in their bayonets to pull themselves up. There came the faint knocking sound of a machine-gun – first a few single shots. Then a continuous rattle, like water boiling in a kettle – the sound of the fighting by the men already ashore.

The light, meanwhile, was gradually increasing as the destroyers hauled their boats alongside their wooden stagings for the troops to disembark. Already the bullets were whistling overhead, first singly, then in droves. The high forecastles of the little ships gave some protection to the troops on deck ; but they had to wait until their boats came back from the beach before all their soldiers could be landed.

The delay seemed ages long. Men were being hit on the destroyers' decks by the gradually increasing rifle fire from the shore. The machine-guns had the range accurately, and the shots were hitting the steel bows of the destroyers with a sound like hail on an iron roof. The water through which the boats pulled to the shore was ripped with bullets, man after man in the boats being killed or wounded. In this storm of fire young midshipmen of sixteen and seventeen years of age calmly stood up in the stern-sheets of their boats directing operations. Those boys set an example remembered by all who saw them. They were wonderful.

The coxswain of one destroyer received a bullet which passed through both cheeks, removed two teeth on either side, and then killed a signalman alongside him. Bleeding, and spitting out the remains of his teeth, with, one expects, the inevitable nautical ejaculations, the petty officer remained at his post of duty.

Four men on the upper deck of the *Ribble* had been hit as she waited, and one had fallen into the water. Then a steamboat and a cutter came alongside to land the rest of her troops. " Good-bye and good luck ! " called a naval sub-lieutenant, leaning over the ship's side and waving his hand as they left. Almost as he spoke he fell, shot through the head.

As the troops already ashore pressed on into the tangled and confused ravines and gullies leading down from the mountain of Sari Bair, the Turkish artillery opened fire. More and more enemy reinforcements were arriving. The ships lying off the coast were firing inland to assist the advance. Four thousand men had landed by full daylight, and by 7.30 their number had roughly been doubled. And still they came.

I will not attempt to describe the fighting ashore ; but here is an account of the landing as taken part in by the destroyer *Chelmer*.

" We took part in this first landing, and afterwards remained at Anzac supporting the flanks the whole time the place was occupied. We had practised landing the troops at Mudros, and the arrangement was to get them into the boats – ships' lifeboats – some distance from the beach, towing them alongside on separate boat-ropes. We hoped they would not have to pull at all, but have way enough to reach the shore when the ship stopped close in. The plan worked out perfectly, except that we got too close and got the bows ashore. However, they came off again when we went astern. Five boats got away splendidly ; but the sixth got hung up by the boat-rope getting foul. As the ship was being drifted broadside on to the beach, the captain had to go astern with his port propeller. The wash rather upset things, and the boat was delayed in getting away. The skipper hailed her from the bridge – ' Damned sorry, you fellows ! But you'll be clear in a minute ! '

" A chorus of voices came back – That's all right ! Never you mind. We'll make up for lost time when we get ashore ! " They were absolutely undefeatable. I met one of the Australians from that boat in London after the Armistice – I believe the only survivor. He remembered the *Chelmer* with great affection.

He told me his house in Australia was to be named *Chelmer*, his dog was to be *Chelmer*, and his expected offspring *Chelmer* too !

" It was anxious work landing those damned good fellows in the early days, as, once one got near the beach and started disembarking them into boats and lighters, we were under fire from guns in the Olive Groves south of Gaba Tepe, as well as from machine-guns and rifles at closer quarters. Some were hit on board before they even left the ship.

"A young midshipman properly put the wind up us one day. We had finished disembarking troops, but during his last trip the snotty had got the tow-rope foul of the screw of his steamboat. We were under heavy fire at the time, but he proceeded all the same to dive under water to try and clear his propeller, taking no notice of our rather heated ejaculations that we proposed moving out of the danger zone before he started his bathing operations. All the midshipmen were wonderful. Bullets left them completely unmoved. This was told us over and over again by the Australians."

By 2 o'clock in the afternoon, 12,000 Australian infantry and two batteries of Indian mounted artillery were ashore at Anzac, occupying a semicircular position of considerable extent, but literally hanging on by their eyelids and fighting desperately for every foot of ground. The second Australian Division, which included a New Zealand brigade, landed later, so that, within twenty-four hours of the first men stepping on the beach, 20,000 men were ashore.

The Turkish heavy howitzers were shelling the beach, and their hidden field-guns the transports. The latter were forced to move farther out to sea, which gave the tows a greater distance to travel to the shore under round after round of shrapnel and high explosive. Shell constantly burst on the strip of beach, about 500 yards long by 40 broad, and every box of stores or ammunition landed had at least one projectile and fifty bullets fired at it before it was finally dropped on the sand.

" The boatmen and the beach working-parties were the unsung heroes of that landing,"[1] Mr. Masefield wrote. We can agree. The boats' crews came in under heavy fire with troops or stores, waited until they were disembarked under a concentrated " hate " of every description, and then shoved off, went slowly back to the transports, and came in with more. Boats were sunk or smashed, and men killed in the water ; but the work went on

[1] *Gallipoli*, p. 48.

for hour after hour. All day long the beach-parties were wading out to the boats to carry ashore the masses of munitions and stores required for some thousands of soldiers. For these gallant fellows, boats' crews and beach-parties alike, there was no possible chance of taking cover. Regardless of risk, they had to see it through if the troops were to have the slightest chance of consolidating their precarious foothold. The boats' crews and beach-parties, let it be said, belonged to the Royal Navy. I sometimes wonder whether it was a seaman or an Australian who gave the name of " Hell Spit " to that deadly little excrescence south of Anzac Cove.

Ashore, the battle still continued furiously, with the Turkish reinforcements constantly arriving. In the actual fighting-lines more than half the men engaged on both sides were killed or wounded. The position was critical, so critical that at midnight on the 25th-26th, about nineteen and a half hours after landing, General Birdwood and some of the Australian brigadiers counselled re-embarkation. But, as writes Mr. Churchill, " The Commander-in-Chief showed himself a truer judge of the spirit of the Australian troops than even their most trusted leaders. Steady counsel being also given by Admiral Thursby, Sir Ian Hamilton wrote a definite order to ' Dig in and stick it out.' From that moment, through all the months that followed, the power did not exist in the Turkish Empire to shake from its soil the grip of the Antipodes."[1]

" On the night after the landing," an account from a destroyer continues, " we were all suffering from strain, and it was a question whether or not we could hold on ashore. Various orders and counter-orders were given about getting off the wounded, and in the dark it was difficult to identify boats. Our leading signalman was hailing them as they came off from the beach, and from one we could get no answer, though she was quite close. The captain told him to hail the boat and to tell her she would be fired upon if she didn't answer. This the leading signalman proceeded to do in a stentorian voice, and the answer came back at once – ' Rear-Admiral – *Queen* ! ' Dear Admiral Thursby. he didn't mind an atom. – For the first few days we were continuously landing troops, ammunition, and stores from the transports which were anchored clear of rifle fire from the shore. As an example of the hardness of an Australian, I remember while alongside one of the big transports – the *Minnewaska*, I think

[1] *The World Crisis, 1915,* p. 324.

– a large Australian, complete with pack, full equipment, rifle, and ammunition, fell on our steel deck from the top deck of the transport, about forty feet. I was close to the spot at the time, and immediately said to a seaman, ' Get the doctor.' The Australian overheard my remark, rose slowly to his feet, and, looking at me as if he meant every word, said, ' Don't be a bloody fool ! ' He was apparently quite undamaged, and bruises were of no consequence."

Rear-Admiral Thursby,[1] whose flag was flying in the *Queen*, was in charge of the naval side of the disembarkation at Anzac. " The destroyers under Captain C. P. R. Coode,"[2] he wrote in his official despatch, " landed the second part of the covering force with great gallantry and expedition, and it is in my opinion entirely due to the rapidity with which so large a force was thrown on the beach that we were able to establish ourselves there."

On the day of the landing, and the three subsequent days, destroyers swept for mines inside the Straits to allow the big ships to come up on the right flank of the Army to bombard the Turkish positions with their heavy guns. These destroyers were the *Wolverine*, Commander O. J. Prentis ; *Scorpion*, Lieutenant-Commander A. B. Cunningham ; *Mosquito*, Lieutenant-Commander A. M. Lecky ; *Renard*, Lieutenant-Commander L. G. B. A. Campbell ; *Grampus*, Lieutenant-Commander R. Bacchus ; *Pincher*, Lieutenant-Commander H. W. Wyld ; *Rattlesnake*, Lieutenant-Commander P. G. Wodehouse ; *Racoon*, Lieutenant-Commander A. G. Muller ; and *Grasshopper*, Lieutenant-Commander R. T. Amedroz.

I am told by an officer in one of these ships that the first day's sweeping was " not too bad," as the Turks were rather taken by surprise and " only turned loose their howitzers ! "

But on the other days the galling fire of a battery of very accurate 4.1-inch guns on the Asiatic coast occasioned many casualties. On the third day, runs the account of an officer who was present, " we started passing the sweeps well inside the Straits, and much higher up than had been customary before. No sooner had the destroyers taken up their formation for passing their sweep-wires from one ship to the other,– we were working in pairs, of course – than the Asiatic 4.1's opened fire. The *Wolverine* had just secured her end of the wire and the *Scorpion* was opening out from her. At this moment, when the two ships were seventy yards apart or less, they were straddled by a salvo. Two projectiles fell over the *Scorpion*, two between the two ships, and the fifth on the *Wolverine's* bridge. It burst on the pedestal of the starboard engine-room telegraph, and instantly killed Commander O. J. Prentis the senior officer of the sweeping destroyers, an R.N.R. midshipman, and the coxswain. The yeoman of signals, who was also on the bridge, was seen to come down the ladder, and then and there to make a semaphore signal to say that the captain was killed and the bridge out of action. It showed wonderful presence of mind, as I believe he was wounded. He was a curious sight, with practically every rag of clothing blown off him."

On one or the other of the days spent in sweeping, the *Racoon* was also hit by a shell in one of her boilers, while the *Mosquito* sustained heavy casualties and had her first lieutenant, Patrick E. Maxwell-Lefroy, killed.

" It was not very pleasant," runs one account, " paddling along at 12 knots against a 2 or 3 knot current, tied by the tail to another destroyer and being fairly constantly straddled by the salvos from those high-velocity guns."

One can quite well believe it. The sides of a destroyer do not afford protection against anything much larger than a rifle bullet.

2

It is impossible here to describe the wonderful gallantry of the troops at Helles and Anzac, the successive attacks and counter-attacks by the enemy, and the means by which, with the assistance of the Royal Navy and the Mercantile Marine, the Army maintained itself ashore in these two areas in circumstances of unparalleled difficulty and danger. " No army in history has made a more heroic attack ; no army in history has been set such a task," writes Mr. Masefield, in referring to the landing. " . . . Our men achieved a feat without parallel in war, and no other troops in the world (not even Japanese or Ghazis in the hope of heaven) would have made good those beaches on the 25th of April."[1]

This was true of the landings. But it was equally true of the wonderful way in which the soldiers fought to maintain themselves on those slices of arid, waterless, hostile territory, under constant shell and rifle fire, in pestilence and famine, in burning

---

[1] *Gallipoli*, p. 25.

heat and bitter cold, and in all the horror and filth and agony of constant slaughter.

Read the last paragraph of Mr. Masefield's book published in 1916. This is what he writes, and it is quoted with his permission.

" ' Still,' our enemies say, ' you did not win the Peninsula.' We did not ; and some day, when truth will walk clean-eyed, it will be known why we did not. Until then, let our enemies say this : ' They did not win, but they came across 3,000 miles of sea, a little army without reserves and short of munitions, a band of brothers, not half of them half-trained, and nearly all of them new to war. They came to what we said was an impregnable fort, on which our veterans of war and massacre had laboured for two months, and by sheer naked manhood they beat us and drove us out of it. Then, rallying, but without reserves, they beat us again and drove us farther. Then, rallying once more, but still without reserves, they beat us again, this time to our knees. Then, had they had reserves, they would have conquered, but by God's pity they had none. Then, after a lapse of time, when we were men again, they had reserves, and they hit us a staggering blow, which needed but a push to end us, but God again had pity. After that our God was indeed pitiful, for England made no further thrust, and they went away.' "

Owing to the lack of artillery ashore, the ships of the fleet, all classes of ships, supplied the covering fire for the troops ashore, work which, after the arrival of the German submarines in the Ægean in May 1915, proved doubly dangerous and difficult. It was the Royal Navy's task, too, to land the reinforcements, ammunition, stores, food, and, in many cases, the water without which the troops could neither fight nor exist in country barren of any supplies ; to evacuate the wounded and sick ; in short, with the sterling help of the Mercantile Marine, to transport every man, every horse and mule, every gun, every cartridge, every pound of stores, across the sea and up the beaches as far as high-water mark. Then, and not before, the naval responsibility in the work of disembarkation ended. In course of time the landing-beaches, with their sunken ships forming breakwaters and piers, became regular little enclosed harbours, and busy ones at that, though generally under enemy shell fire.

It is impossible to follow the operations in detail ; but let us take the doings of a typical destroyer.

Gaba Tepe is a steep promontory about ninety feet high, with a rounded summit and steep, precipitous sides, with the cliff-foot washed by deep water. It commanded Anzac Cove, and at dawn on May 4th, says one account, " we tried to capture it by landing troops from destroyers together with other parties going out from Anzac. But it was honeycombed with machine-guns ; in fact, a veritable fortress."

Stopping a short distance from the shore, and following the same procedure as at Anzac, the destroyers sent in the boats laden with soldiers. They were soon discovered, and the water became whipped into flying spray from the droves of bullets from many machine-guns and hidden riflemen. One who was present describes them as hitting the bows and sides of the destroyers with a sound like a hundred pneumatic riveters busily at work.

" The troops we landed only got as far as the sandy beach, and any fellow who got any distance from the sea was instantly shot up. We had to evacuate the survivors under heavy barrage fire from all the destroyers present. – Afterwards, we were watching the beach under Gaba Tepe and saw one of the Australian casualties moving. (It had been reported that only the dead had been left behind.) Admiral Thursby gave us permission to send in a boat with a Red Cross flag to bring him off. There were lots of volunteers to man the dinghy, and two men were sent in with the Red Cross flag flying, with orders to *waste no time* in bringing off the wounded Australian. The two A.B.'s, I think they were, did precisely the opposite. Having got the wounded man into the boat, they then strolled calmly about the beach collecting rifles from the dead. I think they brought off half a dozen. The point of the story is that the Turks absolutely played the game. They respected the Red Cross and never fired a shot. Later on, when we had taken the wounded man to a hospital ship – he was hit in the head, but I heard afterwards that he recovered – we steamed in close under Gaba Tepe and threw the rifles one by one into the sea, to show Johnny Turk that we didn't intend not to play the game. I hope they saw, and realised what we were doing.

" In the early days we were always doing odd jobs in addition to landing troops, and were never idle for a moment. I remember we landed Lionel Lambart, who was a commander on the Commander-in-Chief's staff, at Nibrunesi Point, at the southern end of Suvla Bay, to search for observation-posts for spotting the fire of enemy ships in the Narrows firing over the Peninsula at transports off Anzac. He strolled about ashore for half an hour and nobody interfered with him. After coming off again, he said he would like to do the same thing in a bay farther north ; but this time the Turks gave us a hot reception with machine-guns, and we had to clear out quickly. Fortunately the landing-party hadn't left the ship."

On May 25th the old battleship *Triumph* was torpedoed and sunk by a German submarine off Anzac. She was steaming slowly in circles with her torpedo-nets out ; but the torpedo went through them like tissue-paper, to find its mark beyond. The *Chelmer* was screening her at the time, but never saw a sign of a periscope. Rushing up alongside the *Triumph's* stern-walk, the *Chelmer*, by a " very fine display of seamanship," to quote the *Official History*, took off many of the men from the battleship before she capsized and sank. In all, the destroyer and her boats rescued 500 officers and men.

" She behaved very well," says an officer of that destroyer. " She took about twenty minutes before she capsized, and gave us time to get most of her crew on board. She had a list of about 15°, and we went alongside her port side with her torpedo-net-booms underneath us. Just before she turned over she gave a resounding creak, which warned us to clear out. So we cut the painter and cleared out – full speed astern both, and just in time."

I can imagine no more horrible feeling than being in a 550-ton destroyer alongside a sinking battleship of 12,000 odd tons, with the prospect of being rolled upon !

Everywhere the destroyers were busy. We read of the *Scorpion*, *Wolverine*, and *Renard* shelling the enemy trenches in the Helles sector where they came down to the sea ; the *Racoon*, *Beagle*, *Basilisk*, and *Bulldog* screening the light-cruiser *Talbot* while she silenced enemy batteries with her 6-inch guns ; the searchlights of the *Scorpion* discovering two battalions of Turks creeping along the cliffs in mass formation in an endeavour to turn the sea flank at Anzac, and her guns opening fire with such effect that the enemy fled, leaving 300 dead and wounded behind. Before the enemy attacked on that night they had shot out both the *Scorpion's* searchlights, probably deliberately, and had inflicted casualties on the crews. The lights were only repaired again just in time to answer the call for gunfire from the shore.

The light-cruiser *Minerva* and the destroyer *Jed* landed a raiding-party at the head of the Gulf of Xeros ; while the strain on the destroyers and other small craft was increased by the necessity of having to make systematic searches of all the islands and coasts in the Ægean Sea, where innumerable coves and indentations and harbours might offer excellent facilities as bases for German submarines.

On May 28th, for instance, the cruiser *Bacchante*, with the destroyer *Kennet*, visited Budrun, in the Gulf of Kos, well south of Smyrna, which was suspected of supplying U-boats. A French cruiser, sending in her boats under a flag of truce some days before, had had them fired upon. She thereupon bombarded the town. On hearing of this, Admiral de Robeck ordered the *Bacchante* and *Kennet* to proceed thither and destroy the shipping. This they did, destroying also the castle and barracks.

Here is the tale of one of his trips in a destroyer which, by permission of General Sir Ian Hamilton, I am allowed to quote from his *Gallipoli Diary*. With other highly placed officers, he was embarking at V beach, near Sedd-el-Bahr. " When we got to the pier, which ends in the *River Clyde*, we found another destroyer, the *Wolverine*, under Lieutenant-Commander Keyes, the brother of the Commodore. She was to take us across, and (of all places in the world to select for a berth !) she had run herself alongside the *River Clyde*, which was, at that moment, busy playing target to the heavy guns of Asia. I imagined that taking aboard a boss like the Commander-in-Chief as well as that much bigger boss (in naval estimates) his own big brother, the Commodore,[1] our Lieutenant-Commander would nip away presto. Not a bit of it ! No sooner had he got us aboard than he came out boldly and very, very slowly, stern first, from the lee of the *River Clyde*, and began a duel against Asia with his 4-inch lyddite from the *Wolverine's* after gun. The fight seems funny to me now, but, at the time, serio-comic would have better described my impressions. Shells ashore are part of the common lot ; they came all in the day's work : on the water ; in a cockle-shell – well, you can't go to ground, anyway ! "

I am glad that Sir Ian Hamilton had also experienced that naked, helpless feeling which so many of us have felt when under heavy fire in a destroyer. Perhaps we were not quite such cowards for feeling frightened as we sometimes thought we were.

Elsewhere, Sir Ian mentions " the redoubtable *Wolverine*, under that desperado Lieutenant-Commander Keyes," of whom

---

[1] Sir Ian refers, of course, to the present Admiral of the Fleet Sir Roger Keyes, who at that time was serving as Chief of Staff to Vice-Admiral de Robeck.

a brother officer remarks, " Adrian Keyes was one of those officers who never knew when it was time to beat a retreat while one still had a whole skin."

In so kindly giving me permission to quote from his book, Sir Ian adds, " During the campaign I sampled nearly every destroyer with the Fleet, and I never wish to meet with a more adventurous, gallant lot of officers, petty officers, and men. No matter how risky the deals Government make in disarmament, my confidence returns to me when I reflect that many of those destroyer lads of Dardanelles days may now be in command of battleships."

That, from a very distinguished and gallant soldier, is a fine tribute to the destroyer service.

3

From the end of May, when the arrival of enemy submarines made it extremely dangerous for the battleships and large cruisers to do the work, two destroyers worked twenty-four hours on and twenty-four hours off on the left flank of the Army at Helles performing the duty of a battery of artillery, and using, for the most part, indirect fire. The right flank, within the Dardanelles, was held by French troops, and was usually protected by French destroyers, though occasionally British T.B.D.s took a turn. Destroyers also guarded the northern flank after the Suvla Bay landing in August, and every night the Anzac right flank had its destroyer.

The two destroyers on the left flank at Helles were the *Wolverine* and *Scorpion*. Except for a few weeks' rest towards the end of September 1915, they did this duty until the evacuation.

The left flank supporting fire was well organised. Firing, as already pointed out, was nearly always indirect, and a permanent spotting officer, Lieutenant Gordon H. Seath,[1] of the Royal Marines, lived ashore with a few naval signal ratings. Many firings were also spotted by aeroplanes. Until the cruisers fitted with anti-torpedo "bulges " or "blisters" arrived, the destroyers were alone unless an attack by the left flank troops was contemplated. On such occasions a cruiser or other ship, strongly escorted by destroyers, came out to lend weight to the fire.

The destroyers served the same purpose as a battery of artillery, answering calls for fire from the shore and doing counter-battery

[1] Now Major, D.S.O.

work. Having plenty of ammunition, they probably fired
rather more than their fair share.

" It was strange at first," writes one of the officers, " to have
to deal with indirect fire, and many previously unthought-of
problems arose and had to be solved on the instant. I remember
on one occasion not being able to get at a target because of the
flatness of the trajectory of the 4-inch gun. So we cut the 4-inch
charges in half with a knife and used the gun as a howitzer. We
were heavily indebted to Lieutenant-Commander John B. Waterlow, the first and gunnery lieutenant-commander of our depot-
ship, the *Blenheim*, for all the assistance he gave us. On the
above-mentioned occasion a range-table for 4-inch half-charges
arrived on board next day."

The firing procedure was fairly simple. There were three
moored buoys, and most targets, generally enemy batteries,
was registered from each buoy. When fire was called for, the
destroyer steamed to the most convenient buoy and fired slowly
until the signal " O. K." was received from the observation officer
ashore. Then she put in about ten rounds rapid fire.

It often happened that the destroyer was shelled out of her
position before completing the shoot, in which event she went to
another buoy and repeated the process. " After a few weeks,"
says one account, " one could usually predict where the next
enemy salvo was going to fall, especially as the Turks used only
field artillery to keep the destroyers quiet. It usually took them
six to eight salvos to get anywhere near.

" At night the soldiers showed a light on the left extreme of
their front line trench, and this was used as an aiming mark."

" I think it was in June that the number of destroyers at Anzac
were reduced to two," another account mentions. " These were
the *Chelmer* and *Colne*, and they were always there, except when
coaling at Mudros. After the *Triumph* and *Majestic* were torpedoed and sunk, and until the blistered cruisers[1] and monitors[2]
arrived, the destroyers did all the flanking and naval supporting
fire at Anzac. Any special firing in the way of naval artillery
support was done by a cruiser sent from Mudros, who carried out
her shoot and then returned.

" The flanking destroyer was much appreciated by the troops
at Anzac, especially after dark, and on the right flank we kept

---

[1] The old cruisers *Theseus*, *Endymion*, *Grafton*, and *Edgar*, which had been
fitted with anti-torpedo " blisters " or " bulges."
[2] Four large war-built monitors mounting 14-inch guns, and four smaller
monitors with 9.2 or 6-inch guns, were all on the scene by the end of July.

our searchlight burning all night. We did a certain amount of indirect firing ; but the most effective firing was direct, and sometimes we could enfilade the Turkish trenches with excellent results. I remember that our largest gun, the 12-pounder 12-cwt., was worn out and had to be replaced at the exact number of rounds corresponding to its muzzle velocity in feet per second – I think 1,375. The bores of the three 12-pounder 8-cwt. guns became smoother and smoother as time went on and behaved rather like howitzers, which was all to the good. We never replaced them, and they fired a countless number of rounds.

" We made pictures of the Turkish trenches and positions viewed from the sea, and on the left flank laid down three small buoys from which the different positions were accurately registered. We used to go in to one of these buoys just before dark and fire a few deliberate rounds at the Turks. This invariably produced a reply, whereupon, having seen that they had more or less registered on the buoy we were then at, we cleared out. The point was that during the rest of the night we always fired from one of the other buoys, a mile or so away, while Johnny Turk wasted his ammunition and his energy by pelting our original position. It was a simple ruse, but successful, and it was extraordinary how used we got to it. Often one heard shell after shell whizzing over one's head, and nobody turned a hair.

" In the daytime one had to be more nippy. One or two Turkish guns were not very disturbing, for we could always move about and dodge the shell. But a four-gun battery was the devil, especially when they were firing shrapnel. Six guns were worse. Then we had to move pretty quick.

" On the right flank, buoys were no good. They had too many machine-guns at Gaba Tepe, and were for ever altering their zones of fire. Here our plan was to go in shortly after dusk, and try and register the positions on which their machine-guns were trained, and afterwards to avoid these positions when doing our own firing. We could only fix the positions by angle and bearing, and once I remember we fixed one spot too well and received the best part of a machine-gun belt through our funnels. Here, on the right flank, it was usually a case of going in very close, putting the searchlight on the Turkish trenches, getting the firing done as quickly as possible, and then clearing out. On the left flank, however, we could fire more or less deliberately from the buoys and take our time. But the unexpected often happened, and sometimes the Turks left us severely alone.

Perhaps on these occasions we were wasting ammunition on an empty trench and the Turks were smiling. One could never tell.

" One yarn showing the audacity of the Australians is worth recounting. A friend of ours in the Light Horse, Macloughlin by name, came off one morning and asked us to bombard a trench with some speckled sandbags opposite his position on the extreme right of our flank next the sea, from which he had been much annoyed by the Turks. He pointed out the position, and we agreed to bombard that night, arranging that he should be in his trench with a signal lantern in case we couldn't find the speckled sandbags with our searchlight, or wanted any help. After dark we went in close, and had no trouble at all in finding the speckled sandbags when we switched on the searchlight. In fact, they showed up better than in the daytime. We put in about forty rounds of 12-pounder shell, which disturbed the trench considerably. Then, as the Turks hadn't opened fire an us, we signalled in to our friend, ' Is that enough ? ' He replied immediately, ' Wait a bit. I will go over and see.' ! – After a few minutes, which seemed like half an hour, back came the further reply from Macloughlin – ' Quite enough. . . . You have blown the place to hell ! ' That was the spirit of the Australians. They were indomitable, and they and the New Zealanders at Anzac were the finest fellows I have ever seen in action. By the end of July a large percentage were pretty sick. Dysentery was rife among them ; but nothing could cool their ardour. They knew the August push was coming on, and they weren't going to miss it. We usually had one or two of them on board recuperating for a few days, and whenever we went to Mudros to coal we used to load up as many cases of tinned milk and other stuff as we had room for. These we served out to them. Their gratitude was delightful."

I have before me a letter from Major Cecil Paddon, late of the Otago Mounted Rifle Regiment, a New Zealand Corps then being used as infantry.

"It was entirely due to the *Chelmer*, *Colne*, and *Rattlesnake*," he says, " that Nos. 2 and 3 posts were held, and that any of the O.M.R. are alive to tell the tale to-day. – By day it was purgatory, heat, flies, and one pint of water a man for twenty-four hours, not to mention the everlasting sniping from all sides. At night it was the nearest imitation of hell that I want to meet, only mitigated by the fact that ' Mamma ' – *Chelmer* – and ' Nursie ' – *Colne* – always rolled up when Abdul got nasty. Two nights late in May – the 28th and 30th, I think – earned them their names. Things were getting sticky on the neck of land between Nos. 2 and 3 posts, and our people were having a nasty time, when some destroyer steamed in on the left flank – it looked as if her skipper were holding her against the beach – lit up the dog-fight, and got busy with her guns, very busy. Abdul went home in a hurry, and the *Chelmer* earned her nickname. Later on, the

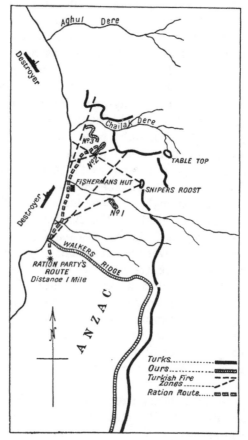

ROUGH SKETCH OF POSITION DURING PERIOD
APRIL 25TH TO AUGUST 7TH AT ANZAC

fact that she was handy stopped the enemy raiding. They also let our ration-parties alone when bringing supplies out along the beach from Anzac at night. They had it properly taped (see sketch), and we got a bad doing for a while until the destroyers took hold. If I have one record because I – a soldier – commanded a 4-inch gun in action in one of H.M. ships, the officers and men of the *Chelmer* have another by sending their soft bread rations and tomatoes ashore to our people. The *Chelmer*, *Colne*, *Racoon*, and *Rattlesnake* will never be forgotten by the survivors of the O.M.R.

"Water was as gold at Anzac," Major Paddon continues; "one pint a man a day, and water from Alexandria at that. This was brought out in petrol tins at night to Nos. 2 and 3 posts for about a mile along the beach, two-thirds of which was covered by the enemy machine-guns. In spite of the greatest care, something occasionally gave the ration-party away – a tin clanked, or someone stumbled. Then the fun began. Everyone fell flat and hugged their precious water-tins. ' Plunk ! ' – and a tin was punctured, and the wretched carrier tried to plug the holes with anything handy, usually his fingers, and called on every Deity he could think of to know where in hell ' Mamma ' or ' Nursie ' had got to. Then something would loom up in the darkness to seaward, and we would hear someone giving orders. On went the searchlight. Crash went the destroyer's 12-pounders, and the ration-party got up, shook themselves, and strolled home quite happy, unattended by any more hate. The Navy had taken hold.

"The left flank of No. 3 post was overlooked by a Turkish machine-gun and sniping position," says Major Paddon. "This made life hazardous to any poor wretch who wanted to sit in the sun in the daytime and chase the ' big game ' (lice) in his shirt or shorts, not to mention the fact that it put a stop to our night bathing, and thereby increased our livestock. The Turks were only 300 yards away, and something had to be done. Having arranged for various dummy targets to be exposed to draw their fire, I joined the *Racoon* off Anzac, and we lobbed a few shell from her foremost 4-inch into the Turk trenches. Shortly afterwards, No. 3 post signalled that the sniping had started. The after gun of the *Racoon* spotted the position, and put in three beauties. The first was a little to the right, and flushed a brace of Turks. The second was a shade low ; but after the dust blew away the whole of their position was exposed to the view of the delighted men in No. 3 post. (As one man put it, ' It wasn't hardly decent. Just like lifting the whole front from a house.') The *Racoon's* third round hoisted machine-gun and crew to glory, and thereafter peace descended on that flank and our ' big game ' got well and truly strafed. All the same, the men in No. 3 post had a grouse. The third shell, they said, spoilt what looked like a real chance to get some of their own back after the second had exposed the Turk position. Not one man out of many got in a single round."

On the night of June 9th a scouting patrol went out from Anzac to examine the country towards Suvla Bay. " For some reason," runs Major Paddon's account of the incident, " they delayed their return until dawn, and were pinned down to the sandhills at the mouth of the Aghul Dere, about 1,300 yards to the north of our position in No. 3 post. One of our officers, Captain Twisleton, and a small party, by clever use of the sand-hills, got out to them, but they also were held up. – We got through to H.Q. at Anzac, and in a very short time *Colne, Chelmer,* and *Rattlesnake* came up at full speed. Then the fun began. They opened fire, and pinned the Turks down whenever they showed themselves, which allowed our isolated party near the Aghul Dere to begin retiring on No. 3. In the meantime, the Turks on another hillock overlooking the scene lined their trenches and had sitters at our people as they bolted from sandhill to sandhill. This encouraged still more Turks. Things got hotter and hotter. We managed to keep down some of the fire ; but what really finished it was the *Colne, Chelmer,* and *Rattlesnake* solemnly coming in in line ahead well within rifle range, and shepherding the patrol and its relief home at the patrol's own walking-pace. It looked outrageous, and the Turk evidently thought so too, and fairly plastered the three destroyers as they came slowly along. But the 4-inch and 12-pounders were too much for Abdul. He gave in, and holed up under cover again. I got a cheery signal – from the *Rattlesnake,* I think – ' Do it again, please. Haven't had so much fun for a long time ! ' "

4

The landing at Suvla Bay on August 6th-7th, in conjunction with a holding attack in the Helles area and a heavy attack from Anzac on the dominating ridge of Sari Bair, had as its main object the capture of Koja Chemen Tepe (Hill 971), the highest peak of the Sari Bair range. If this eminence were occupied, it might be possible, working from there, also to occupy the narrow neck of the Peninsula between Gaba Tepe and Maidos. This would cut off the bulk of the Turkish Army in Gallipoli from communication by land with Constantinople ; would provide gun positions commanding the Narrows, thus cutting the Turkish sea communications with Asia and Constantinople; and would secure Suvla Bay as a winter base for all the troops in the Anzac neighbourhood. It is unnecessary to go into much detail; but full naval co-operation was arranged for at Helles and Anzac, while

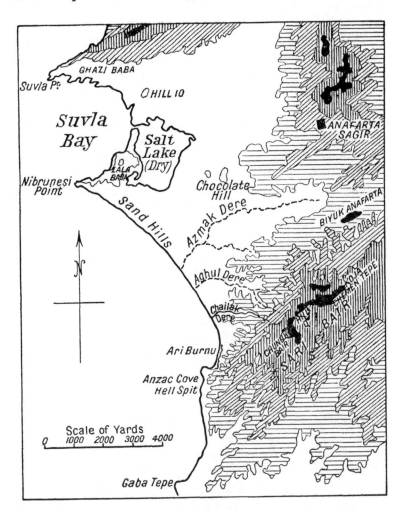

at Anzac the troops had been largely and secretly reinforced in readiness for the attack.

At Suvla Bay, where the general conduct of the landing was in the hands of Rear-Admiral A. H. Christian, the ships concerned were the *Talbot*, *Grafton*, *Theseus*, and *Endymion*, together with a host of destroyers, sloops, trawlers, and "beetles." These latter were motor-lighters specially designed for carrying 500 infantry and had been sent out from England. They were intended for landing troops on a hostile coast, and were of very shallow draught, bullet-proof, and fitted with landing brows in their bows. Under their own power they could travel about 5 knots.

The main landing in the Suvla Bay area was to be carried out at Nibrunesi Beach, south of the Bay. For this, 3,000 soldiers had to be crowded into the *Endymion* and *Theseus*, the sloop *Aster*, and six trawlers, the sloop and trawlers each towing horse-boats, with guns and horses. Seven destroyers – the *Grasshopper, Basilisk, Arno, Foxhound, Scourge, Racoon,* and *Mosquito* – each had 500 troops on board, and towed a " beetle " with another 500. They were to steam close in to the shore, slip their " beetles," and send them in, after which the latter would return to land the other men from the destroyers. Three thousand five hundred men would then be landed in the first wave so to speak, and the same number from the destroyers shortly afterwards. The remaining 3,000 from the cruisers would then be put ashore.

Another landing, inside Suvla Bay, was to be made of 3,000 men from the destroyers *Beagle, Bulldog,* and *Grampus,* and their towed " beetles."

Suvla Bay and its environs was thought to be weakly held by the enemy ; but, whatever happened, the landing must come as a surprise. The beach inside Suvla Bay was unsurveyed and the chart unreliable, so that delays and difficulties might be expected. A flat calm night with no moon was essential to success.

The embarkation took place without any hitch at Kephalo, on the eastern side of Imbros and about twelve miles from Suvla. Organisation and weather were both perfect. With every light extinguished, the large collection of vessels moved through the blackest of black nights towards their objective.

A destroyer, showing a dim light to seaward, had been anchored off Nibrunesi Beach as a leading mark. The seven destroyers carrying troops steamed in, in line abreast, with their " beetles " towing astern. Behind them came the *Endymion* and *Theseus*, then the trawlers and the *Aster* towing their horse-boats.

The sea was like glass and the night intensely still. But the surprise was complete. Beyond a few scattered rifle shots fired by the enemy outposts along the shore, there was no resistance. The " beetles " were slipped by the destroyers at about 10 p.m.,

and landed their 3,500 men without a single casualty. They
returned at once to the destroyers and landed the next 3,500,
so that by midnight 7,000 men were ashore. By 1.30 a.m. the
Endymion and *Theseus* also had been cleared, so that by 1.30 a.m.
on the 7th two brigades were ashore with their guns and horses.
The Nibrunesi landing had been comparatively easy, and the
arrangements had worked perfectly.

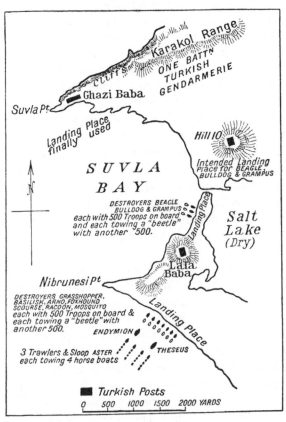

But at A Beach, that inside Suvla Bay, things were rather more
difficult. The landing had been intended to take place opposite
Hill 10 ; but with nothing whatever to guide them in the pitch
darkness, the destroyers, with their " beetles," steered too much
to the south, and anchored about 600 yards off the coast
some 900 yards from the intended landing-place. The mistake
was not realised until daylight ; but the " beetles " were cast off
and made straight for the shore.

Trouble started almost at once. One after the other the motor

lighters grounded 100 yards out in three feet of water. The
Turkish outposts ashore opened fire ; but our men leapt out and
waded ashore. The water deepened again towards the beach ; but
with the help of ropes stretched between the lighters and the
shore the 1,500 troops were landed without much loss.

Heavy fire had meanwhile been opened by the small Turkish
forces on Ghazi Baba, Hill 10, and Lala Baba, while two small
guns somewhere inland were firing shrapnel.

The lighters, meanwhile, were so hard and fast aground that
they could not return to the destroyers to land the next 1,500
men. Picket boats were sent off to fetch reserve tows of pulling
boats. By 11.30 p.m. the *Grampus* had got her " beetle " afloat
and alongside again, her 500 men being ashore by 12.30 a.m.
The *Bulldog* succeeded in landing her contingent by 2.30 ; but
it was not until nearly 5 that the *Beagle's* troops were landed
in pulling boats towed by steamboats.

The landing of the reinforcements, which started to arrive at
dawn, took place on Nibrunesi Beach and in two small coves
under Ghazi Baba, which subsequently became the main landing-
places. At daylight the Turks started shelling the bay and all
the beaches they could reach, and at 8.30, or thereabouts, the
destroyer *Scourge* was hit in the engine-room by a shell and had
to retire.

We need not write of the Battle of Suvla Bay, so vividly
described by Mr. Winston Churchill in chapter xxi. of *The World
Crisis, 1915*. Due to a variety of causes, it ended in failure.

Desperate fighting, meanwhile, had been going on at Helles
and Anzac. It lasted from August 6th to the 10th. The Australian, New Zealand, British, and Indian troops at Anzac, under an intense covering fire from the ships, strove
valiantly among the ravines and gullies to attain the ridge of
Sari Bair, with its three dominating peaks Koja Chemen Tepe,
Hill Q, and Chunuk Bair. The Turks, however, rushed reinforcements to the scene, and, in spite of the gallantry of our
troops, they could nowhere effect a permanent lodgment on the
all-important ridge commanding the Narrows. The Suvla
offensive had failed to link up with the attacks on Sari Bair. All
the advantage gained from the heavy and continuous fighting of
these five blazing days in August, during which many of the men
landed at Suvla suffered the torments of raging thirst, was a
footing at Suvla and the use of a comparatively well-sheltered
landing-place on the outer coast of the Gallipoli Peninsula. The

position at Anzac had been extended and improved.   Nevertheless, all the high ground within easy artillery range of the landing-
places, and which overlooked the whole of the occupied territory,
still remained in the hands of the enemy.

5

Here is a short description of the fighting at Anzac as seen
from one of the destroyers : " One of the most successful ruses we
carried out was the shelling of No. 3 post and Table Top on the
left flank at the same time each night for some weeks before
August 6th, so that both these positions were taken by the New
Zealanders with hardly any loss when they advanced out of
Anzac on that night.   No. 3 post was near the beach, and had
changed hands pretty frequently during May, June, and July.
Our wheeze was to get the Turks used to the shelling, so that they
would evacuate the positions when it became due, and that the
New Zealanders, when they attacked, would find them empty.
So far as I remember, we used to switch on the searchlight and
start in on No. 3 post at 9 p.m. with slow, deliberate fire until 9.25,
then a rapid burst until 9.30.   At 9.30 we shifted to Table Top,
which was above No. 3 post, and literally a table top, with a cliff
face towards the New Zealanders.   We fired deliberate rounds
from 9.30 to 9.55, and then five minutes rapid until 10 p.m.

" The *Chelmer* and *Colne* did this every night for about six
weeks before August 6th, and on that night the same routine was
carried out.   The result was excellent.   Both positions were evacuated.   The trenches were empty, and Turkish officers were found
in their dug-outs on the side of the positions in their pyjamas! "

" For a while," writes Major Paddon, " the efforts of the
destroyers produced tangible results – wails from some unfortunate who had been hit, and loud curses, calls on Allah, supplemented by heavy rifle fire.   After a time nothing used to occur
at all, and we often chuckled over the destroyers' nightly hates,
and wondered what they meant.

" The night of August 6th at 9.30 p.m. saw us going over the
top to clear the right flank of the Suvla Bay landing.   As usual,
the destroyer had fired her nightly ' hate,' and at 9.30 her searchlight lifted.   That was our zero time.   Over we went, and no
sign from the enemy.   The men on our right passed through their
wire, went over fourteen land mines, and gathered in the front-
line trench without a shot fired.   It was empty!

" Then the joke struck us. Abdul is a fatalist, but has common sense, of a sort. ' Why sit here and be shelled night after night ? ' he asked himself. ' Why not go back a little, and shelter in peace ? ' – They did, and that was how the destroyer's brain-wave saved us from being badly mauled. – A little later that same night we ran into a sticky nest of trenches. On went the *Chelmer's* lights, right in the Turks' eyes. We went on too where we hadn't expected to, except at a price. That was just another little wheeze – but they all counted."

To continue the story from the point of view of a destroyer ; " When our troops were driven off the crest of Koja Chemen Tepe – the most conspicuous peak in the Sari Bair ridge – on August 10th, as a result of the Suvla Bay crowd not having been able to make their way up the Anafarta valley, all the ships present opened a furious fire. We expended practically the whole of our remaining outfit of ammunition at the masses of Turks coming over the crest. It was bitterly disappointing to see our troops driven back down the hill, but one must give the Turks full marks for bravery. They came over in sort of double companies in echelon in close order, standing out conspicuously on the skyline. We and the other ships pumped shell into them as fast as we could load and fire ; but their advance never wavered."

Sir Ian Hamilton, in his subsequent despatch, particularly referred to the services of the Navy during the Anzac operations in August. When describing the first attack on Chunuk Bair, he writes, " Nor may I omit to add that the true destroyer spirit with which H.M.S. *Colne* (Commander Seymour) and H.M.S. *Chelmer* (Commander England) backed us up will live in the grateful memories of the Army."

The lines of trenches at Helles, Anzac, and Suvla now formed the homes of thousands of our troops until the final evacuations in December and January 1916. There, writes Mr. Masefield, " They lived and did their cooking and washing, made their jokes and sang their songs. There they sweated under their burdens, and slept, and fell in to die. There they marched up the burning hill, where the sand devils thrown up by the shells were blackening heaven ; there they lay in their dirty rags awaiting death ; and there by the thousands up and down they lie buried, in little lonely graves where they fell, or in the pits of the great engagements."[1]

Out at sea, waiting to take off their freights of wounded, lay

[1] *Gallipoli*, p. 161.

the hospital ships, their white hulls, with broad green bands broken by their red Geneva crosses, showing conspicuously against the background of sea and sky. Then the grey-painted transports and storeships, and, passing between them and the beaches, an everlasting procession of small craft carrying troops and provisions and munitions to the shore. Nearer to the coast were the black shapes of the destroyers and other vessels protecting the flanks, and, right inshore, the sunken hulls of vessels scuttled to form breakwaters for the landing-places. Some of the beaches were littered with wrecks, battered by enemy shell fire, or driven ashore in bad weather. There, too, were the shattered remains of the naval and other boats used in the first landings.

Most of the beaches used for disembarkation had their piers and landing-places, always under shell fire ; but always scenes of great business. On the foreshore beyond high-water mark, in dug-outs in the hillsides, or in the more sheltered gullies and ravines, were the temporary hospitals, the ammunition and provision dumps, the horse and mule lines, the stores of fodder, the spare guns, the wheeled transport. The men, thousands of them, lived in dug-outs. There were offices with typewriters and telephones, armourers' forges, smitheries, a constant stream of men coming and going along the dusty, makeshift roads between the beaches and the front-line trenches.

Late in November came the Great Blizzard, which will live in the memories of all those who experienced it, and probably had some effect in bringing about the final evacuation.

The morning of November 26th was cold and wet, with a biting north-easterly wind. By the afternoon it was blowing half a gale, with heavy sleet. The wind freshened to a gale, with thunder and rain – rain which fell in torrents, and converted every ravine into a tumbling river, and every trench into a canal. The water poured down the hillsides with such rapidity that men had to leave their trenches hurriedly, leaving most of their belongings behind them. Some were drowned at their posts. In the midst of the inevitable confusion, the enemy opened up a heavy rifle and shrapnel fire.

For three awful days the blizzard continued, with sleet and snow, the mud freezing in the trenches, and a great sea breaking on the coast and hurtling the spray far inland. Men were frozen to death. Hundreds, who had stuck it out up till now, were forced to go sick through frost-bite.

When the weather cleared, the beaches were freshly littered with the wreckage of boats and lighters and piers. But worse than the material damage was the loss of men. One division lost two-thirds of its numbers. At Helles, Anzac, and Suvla more than 200 were drowned, or perished through exposure ; 10,000 were rendered unfit for further service ; and at least three times this number were temporarily incapacitated.

But in spite of the wind and the sea the destroyers do not seem to have sought shelter. " We were on the right flank at Anzac during the blizzard," writes a destroyer officer. " We let go our anchor and veered all our cable, hoping that we should not drag ashore under the noses of the Turks at Gaba Tepe. We kept the searchlight burning on a bearing of their trenches. It was a bad night, but had its compensations. A large number of quail which were blown off the shore flew into the rays of the light and hit the ship. We picked up quite a number of birds on deck next morning, and, like the Israelites, enjoyed our free gift of game very much. It blew so hard during the night that one couldn't hear oneself speak on the bridge. Our R.N.R. officer managed to indicate that something was wrong with him, and eventually we understood that he was trying to tell us he had been hit by a bullet over the heart ! We went down to the chart house to have a look, and, sure enough, there was a hole through his oil-skin in the right place. On opening his coat, a bullet fell out. It was a spent one, and had gone through his oilskin and monkey-jacket, just making a blue mark on his chest over his heart !

" Another narrow escape occurred to an officer in a destroyer. He was standing on deck by the circular hatch above the ward-room lobby, when a small howitzer shell came down, grazed him all down the left side, burning his coat, flattening out the buttons, and incidentally breaking his watch. But beyond bruises he was undamaged. The shell passed on through the hatch and burst below, causing several casualties."

When once the evacuation had been decided upon, the withdrawal of the vast accumulation of stores about the beaches at Suvla and Anzac, and of the bulk of the troops, was a gradual process spread over ten nights. The organisation was masterly, no less than 44,000 men, about 3,000 animals, 130 guns, and vast quantities of stores and munitions being evacuated from these two areas in eight nights without arousing the suspicions of the enemy. There remained ashore about 40,000 men with 65 guns and sufficient stores and ammunition for four days.

It is unnecessary to describe the actual details of the final evacuation of Anzac and Suvla on the nights of December 18th-19th, and 19th-20th. Vessels of every class took part, and at 4.15 a.m. on the 20th the last soldier had left and the beach-parties were ready to embark. An hour and a quarter later the last man had left Suvla.

The minute organisation, the ingenious ruses by which the enemy were hoodwinked into believing that nothing unusual was happening, are set forth in detail in the official naval and military histories. But on ten nights 83,048 soldiers, 186 guns, 1,697 horse-drawn vehicles, 21 motor-vehicles, and 4,695 horses and mules were withdrawn with no greater casualties than half a dozen men wounded. When it is realized that the official esti-mate of losses during the evacuation was from thirty to forty per

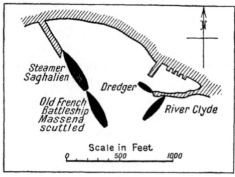

ROUGH SKETCH OF HELLES OR V BEACH AT
TIME OF EVACUATION

cent. of the troops to be embarked, the bloodless withdrawal in the face of a superior and watchful enemy who had been temporarily hypnotised by the excellence of the naval and military staff work was little short of miraculous.

The Australians and New Zealanders cursed loud and deep at having to leave the ground they had so dearly bought. " We all hated leaving Anzac," writes an officer of the *Chelmer*. " There were plenty who said the Australians wouldn't go."

At Helles, the plan for evacuation was much the same as that at Anzac and Suvla, though, as the enemy might be expecting an evacuation and bad weather had set in, its preparation and execution were considerably more difficult. Some 37,500 men, 142 guns, about 4,200 animals, over 1,900 vehicles, and huge quantities of munitions and stores had to be embarked.

The preliminary stage started on December 29th, but so great was the accumulation of stores that it was found necessary to load up the lighters in the daytime. Secrecy was of vital importance. The enemy had aeroplanes, and whenever they appeared the work had to cease. The opportunity was taken, however, of reversing the process of disembarkation – troops on their way to the landing-places turning back, and a show being made of disembarking stores and animals, so that the aircraft could only take back news that the position was being strengthened, not abandoned.

The bad weather and the enemy shell fire gave constant trouble, though covering squadrons working in the Ægean and against the Asiatic guns did much to keep down the gunfire. V and W Beaches and Gully Beach, the first two of which had small enclosed harbours formed by sunken ships, were the embarkation places, and both were exposed to southerly winds. The preliminary embarkations, though greatly interrupted by bad weather, proceeded more or less smoothly. It soon came to be realised, however, that two fine nights in succession for the last stage of the evacuation was more than could be hoped for.

Fifteen thousand men were originally to be left for the last flight, and they might hold on for twenty-four hours. If, however, they were to be weatherbound ashore, possibly for several days, some 17,000 men and 50 guns were the least that would be required for the front of eight miles.

If only the Navy could re-embark them in one night, instead of in two, all might be well. It was Commodore (now Admiral of the Fleet Sir Roger) Keyes who suggested the use of destroyers as additional troop-carriers.

The final act was definitely arranged, weather permitting, for the night of January 8th-9th, 1916. On the morning of the 7th, 19,000 men and 49 guns were still ashore. If the Turks made a really resolute attack, anything might happen, and, if they realised that an evacuation was in process, attack they assuredly would. They were obviously uneasy, for the beaches were persistently shelled and their airmen were very busy. Moreover, at 11.30 a.m. on the 7th there began a furious artillery attack on both our flanks which could only be the prelude to an onslaught. Far worse than anything that had ever before been experienced, the bombardment continued for three hours. Then the enemy trenches could be seen bristling with bayonets, and at 4 p.m. Turkish officers could be seen trying to force their men to leave their trenches.

It was an anxious moment ; but only in one portion of the line did the attack develop, and there it was easily repulsed. Meanwhile, the guns of a battleship, 3 bulged cruisers, 4 large and 1 small monitor and a destroyer, the *Wolverine*, had been pouring in a withering fire on the enemy troops crowded into their reserve and communication trenches. The latter, having expended all her ammunition, had to summon a consort to her assistance. And by 5 o'clock the threatened attack of a vastly superior force had been definitely frustrated, with a loss to our side of 164 killed.

On the night of the 7th more men and animals and guns were embarked, until, on the morning of the 8th, only 17,000 men and 40 guns remained ashore. At 8 p.m. the final embarkation began

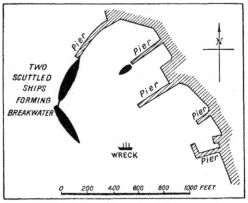

ROUGH SKETCH OF W BEACH AT TIME OF
EVACUATION

rapidly and smoothly, the motor-lighters, troop-carriers, and destroyers going alongside the piers and hulks at V, W, and Gully Beaches in succession to take the troops out to the ships that were to receive them.

At W Beach the destroyer *Lawford* was already alongside one of the hulks. It had started to breeze up, and at 10.15, when the destroyer *Lydiard* relieved a troop-carrier alongside, she managed to get there only with the greatest difficulty. Wind and sea increased rapidly. The floating bridge from the shore to the inshore hulk became impassable, and the last of the *Lydiard's* troops had to be ferried out to her in motor-lighters, a slow and laborious business in the rising sea. She finally got away without damage.

At V Beach, where 1,600 troops remained, a very heavy sea was soon running. Notwithstanding, the destroyers *Grasshopper*, Lieutenant-Commander R. T. Amedroz, and *Bulldog*, Lieutenant-Commander W. B. Mackenzie, were taken alongside the hulks in pitch darkness by their commanding officers. It was a fine display of seamanship which evoked the admiration of all who saw it. Laden with troops, they got clear at 3.20 a.m.

At W Beach, where the destroyers *Staunch* and *Fury* were brought in alongside the outer hulk with great danger and difficulty after the *Lawford* and *Lydiard* had left, the bridges between the hulks and the shore, as already mentioned, could not be used. The troops had to be ferried out to them in motor-lighters, which, with their puny engines, were almost unmanageable in the heavy sea.

Gully Beach was on the left of the British line. Situated on the west coast of the Peninsula at the end of Zighin Dere, a ravine running down to the sea, and between X and Y Beaches, it had no protecting breakwaters, and was open to the weather from any direction from south, through west, to north. Here were Major-General F. S. Maude with a small headquarters staff and the last 680 men to leave.

At midnight the cruiser *Talbot*, with two motor-lighters and two steamboats, arrived to embark them. By this time, however, there was a heavy surf running, and one of the " beetles " was driven ashore and wrecked. The other, with the greatest difficulty, was taken alongside the little pier, where she managed to embark 525 men and to get away in safety. In pitch darkness, the remaining 160 had to make their way two miles to W Beach, cutting their way through the wire, the man-traps, and other obstacles which had been prepared to delay the enemy. General Maude himself, his medical officer, and a dozen men attached to his headquarters, stayed behind with the naval beach-party with the idea of embarking in the *Talbot's* steamboats. This was found to be impossible, so the general and his little party had to follow the remainder to W Beach. It was a race against time. They had two miles to go in circumstances of great difficulty, and it was nearly 3 a.m. Thanks, however, to the delay and difficulty with the embarkation at W Beach, they arrived with time to spare.

From here, shortly before 5 a.m., the destroyers *Fury* and *Staunch*, laden with men, at last got clear, leaving a few lighters waiting inshore for stragglers. A heavy sea was breaking over the hulks as the unwieldy " beetles " clawed their way seaward in the light of the blazing store and ammunition dumps. One of the latter exploded prematurely; but by 5.30 the last man was off the Peninsula. Not until then did the Turks realise that the evacuation was complete.

Where, as already mentioned, the estimate of loss during the withdrawal was expected to be thirty or forty per cent. of the men re-embarked, it had successfully been accomplished with the loss of one seaman accidentally killed by the premature explosion !

So marvellous an evacuation from the restricted embarkation places of a difficult coast, under the eyes of a brave and greatly superior enemy, was a wonderful tribute to the staff-work of the Army and Navy. But it was also a wonderful testimony to the seamanship and resource of the officers and men of the destroyers, troop-carriers, lighters, and a horde of boats and trawlers, upon whom had fallen the brunt of the work inshore. Many of these craft were commanded by officers of the Royal Naval Reserve, and all of the boats by midshipmen not out of their teens. But every one of them had helped to make history. The impossible had been achieved. Throughout the long period of our island story the evacuation of the Gallipoli Peninsula has no parallel.

And so, in the rising wind and sea, with the shrilling of the gale in the rigging and the thresh of the waves alongside, those British soldiers and seamen left Gallipoli, and the Dardanelles campaign became a thing of the past.

Many had been left behind ; but those who remained treasured their memory – treasured also the memory of an unforgettable nine months during which the men of the Navy and Army, men from every walk of life and from every part of the British Empire, had fought and laboured together as blood brothers.

6

No account of the work of the destroyers of the 5th Flotilla in the Dardanelles or Gallipoli can be complete without some reference to their Captain (D), Captain C. P. R. Coode – now Rear-Admiral C. P. R. Coode, C.B., D.S.O. – in the *Blenheim*.

" You can have no idea how he influenced everyone under his orders," one of his destroyer commanders writes to me. " It is quite impossible for one who was not there to understand what an all-pervading influence his outstanding personality and forceful character had upon all who served under him. To junior officers especially he presented rather a sinister and terrifying appearance ; but though at times apparently harsh and unsparing in his judgments, he was very human and, above all, absolutely just. He inspired everyone to do their utmost, and a word of commendation from Captain Coode was highly valued and eagerly sought after. Outspoken condemnation was the certain portion of those who blundered or failed to live up to the high standard expected of them by Captain (D). Under his stimulating direction, backed up by the untiring efforts of his officers, the *Blenheim* was a mother ship indeed to the destroyers attached to her."

" As you know," writes one of the Mediterranean destroyer officers of this period, " there was usually nothing but growling about the depot-ships on the part of the destroyers, and as far as I could see during my subsequent service with the Grand Fleet the destroyers had good reason to be dissatisfied. The *Blenheim* was a wonderful depot-ship, the only one I have ever heard of that attached destroyers bestowed unstinted praise upon. . . . J. B. Waterlow, the 1st and G, and afterwards commander of the *Blenheim*, was a wonderful chap. No trouble was too much for him to ease the ways for us. He even sent a picket-boat round all the destroyers nightly when we were in harbour to collect the officers to dine in the *Blenheim*, and returned them to their ships after dinner."

In time of war, depot-ships meant much to destroyers, and in my own personal experience I realise what a tremendous debt of gratitude we, the Harwich Destroyer Flotillas, owed to the *Dido*, our mother ship alongside Parkeston Quay throughout the war. Captain W. M. Moir, now Rear-Admiral W. M. Moir, C.B.E., together with all his officers and men, did everything in their power to help us. This was not always the case with other parent ships.

The *Dido*, however, like the *Blenheim*, was rather an exception. Here are some extracts from an article I wrote about her at the time.

" You have only to ask the destroyers what they think of their parent, and there is not one of them who would not tell you that they could not get on without her. Of course they cannot ! Destroyers, like delicate children, are prone to catch mumps, whooping-cough, and measles. They cannot thrive without careful nursing, particularly in wartime.

" So if the depot-ship receives a plaintive wail by signal to say that one of her children has been punctured through the bows by a projectile, or that another, in a slight altercation at sea with one of her sisters, has developed a small dent in herself to the accompaniment of leaky rivets and seams, she merely says, ' Come alongside ! '

" The destroyer does so. An army of workmen step on board with their tools, and with much hammering and drilling, the outward application of a steel plate, some oakum, and some white lead, her hurts are plastered and she is rendered seaworthy once more.

" Sometimes the defects may be even more serious, as, for instance, when one of her charges, having been badly cut into in a thick fog, or having unwisely sat down upon a mine, limps back into harbour with several compartments full of water and severe internal injuries as well. But mother is quite equal to the emergency. She sends her shipwrights, carpenters, and other experts on board the afflicted one, and, with a large wooden patch, more oakum, and buckets of red and white lead, the destroyer is made sufficiently seaworthy to proceed to the nearest dockyard.

" Again, there may be engine-room defects—such things as over-heated thrust-blocks, stripped turbines, and leaky valves. There are boiler troubles, and the periodical cleaning of the boiler tubes. There can be defects in the guns, torpedo-tubes, searchlights, or electrical fittings ; defects anywhere and everywhere, even in the galley stove funnel or the wardroom pantry. Mother has a large family, and its ailments are very varied and diverse. But she competes with them all and, save in cases of very severe damage, rarely confesses the job to be beyond her powers and has to send her troublesome children to a dockyard.

" But this is not all she does. If Able Seaman Murphy carves the top off his finger or complains of ' 'orrible pains in the stummick,' he is sent to mother to be nursed back to health by her doctors. If Stoker Jones imagines he has not received the pay to which he is entitled, if he wishes to remit a monthly sum to his wife, or desires to become the possessor of a pair of boots, a toothbrush, and a pair of new trousers, mother will oblige him. Moreover, the fond parent distributes the mails, and supplies the beef, vegetables, bread, rum, haricot beans, tinned salmon, raisins, sugar, tea, flour, coffee, cocoa, and a hundred and one other comestibles necessary for the nourishment of those on board her *protégées*. She will also supply many other unconsidered trifles in the way of ammunition, torpedoes, rope, canvas, paint, emery paper, bath-brick, oil, bolts, nuts, pens, red ink, black ink, hectograph ink, foolscap, pencils, paper fasteners, postage stamps . . . I will leave it at that.

" Heaven alone knows what else she can disgorge if need be. She seems to resemble a glorified Army and Navy Stores, with engineering, ship fitting, ship chandlery, outfitting, haber- dashery, carpentry, chemists, dry provisions, butchers, bakers, stationery, postal, and fancy goods departments. . . . In addition to all this, the officers of the flotilla are honorary members of mother's wardroom, where, in spite of the fact that she some- times has great difficulty in collecting the sums due at the end of the month, she allows them to obtain meals, drinks, and tobacco. Lastly, she gets up periodical cinematograph or variety shows, to which all are invited, free, gratis, and for nothing. . . . What more could her children want ? Mother is an old cruiser ; but she is a very good parent to her destroyers. Years ago she was the pride of the Mediterranean Fleet, with white decks, twinkling brass- work, and the black hull, red water-line, white upper-works, and cream-coloured masts and funnels of the old-time Navy. Now- adays she is painted a dingy grey, and her decks are no longer spotless—she has other things to think about than mere cleanli- ness. But she is a good mother. Her greatness has not departed."

Photo, Russell, London

SIR REGINALD TYRWHITT.
1917.

H.M.S. MIRANDA.
10TH FLOTILLA. AT SEA OFF EAST COAST, 1915.

All destroyers were painted black until after Jutland, when grey was decided upon as a better colour. As the White Ensign and the German naval ensign looked much the same at a distance, while British and German destroyers were not dissimilar in appearance, the former were provided with the special recognition mark shown in the photograph. This was changed at intervals to a diamond, or a triangle point up. This cumbrous arrangement of wooden laths was afterwards abolished, and for recognition purposes destroyers at sea flew the Red Ensign or Union Flag at the yard-arm.

A WARTIME GROUP. *H.M.S. MURRAY*, 1915.

From left to right: Engineer-Lieutenant-Commander James Ashton (p. 140); Surgeon Probationer R.N.V.R. A. G. Lennon-Brown (p. 231); Midshipman R.N.R. Bernard Coles; Sub-Lieutenant R. D. Oliver (p. 119); Lieutenant-Commander Taprell Dorling.

THE AFTER GUN OF *H.M.S. MATCHLESS.*
See page 123.

H.M.S. MATCHLESS IN THE FLOATING DOCK AT HARWICH AFTER
BEING BLOWN UP BY AN ENEMY MINE.

The stern of the ship has completely vanished, with the rudder and propellers.
The doorway leading to what was the wardroom can be seen in the upper part of the
photograph, and the small black rectangle on the left is the serving-hatch from
the pantry.

WARTIME PETTY OFFICERS. *H.M.S. MURRAY*, 1915.
From left to right:—Chief Stoker Martin; Petty Officer Nason; Chief Petty Officer
William Ewles (p. 147); Chief Engine-Room Artificer Cockerell.

THE DOG " BOOSTER.'
The unnatural position of the near hind leg was due to the injury sustained in the fight mentioned on page 315.

H.M.S. TELEMACHUS. 20TH FLOTILLA.

August 2nd, 1918. This photograph was taken the afternoon previous to the loss of the *Vehement* and *Ariel* in an enemy minefield.   In the photograph the ship is carrying 40 mines which are invisible behind the painted canvas screen over the after part of the ship. See page 380.

CHAPTER V

DESTROYERS IN THE ÆGEAN

AFTER the final evacuation of the Gallipoli Peninsula in January 1916, most of the troops were sent to Egypt and Salonika. Enemy submarines were very active in the Mediterranean, and a blockade not only of the Dardanelles, but also of the western and southern coasts of Turkey-in-Asia and the coast of Syria, together with a constant watch upon the Greek islands in the Ægean Sea, had still to be maintained if the many natural harbours and anchorages were not to be used as bases by U-boats working on the crowded transport route between Egypt and Salonika.

A considerable portion of this work was undertaken by destroyers, though I can obtain practically no details of the tedious and soul-destroying task carried on by the patrols off the Dardanelles, Smyrna, the south coast of Turkey-in-Asia, and Syria. The work, though arduous and important, was monotonous and largely devoid of picturesque incident, according to those who took part in it.

I am more fortunate, however, in regard to the 150 miles of the transport route between Rhodes on the south and the island of Nicaria on the north, where it passed the Dodacanese and the two groups of islands shown on the maps as the Sporades and Cyclades.

In about March 1916, a force under the command of Captain Frank Larken, [1] in the light-cruiser *Doris*, was sent to work in this area, with its headquarters at Maltizana, in the island of Stampalia – or Astropalia, as it is marked on most maps. Part of this force consisted of the destroyers *Scorpion*, *Wolverine*, *Rattlesnake*, and *Pincher*.

The harbours on the mainland which might be used by enemy submarines were mined, though in most cases a narrow channel was left open for the use of our small craft – destroyers, trawlers, etc. The duty of the destroyers was to patrol among the numerous islands by day, and to occupy the transport route at night.

After about a month of this routine the *Doris* was relieved by

[1] Now Vice-Admiral, C.B., C.M.G.

the *Edgar* – Captain Douglas L. Dent[1] – and a new policy was inaugurated. A minor base was established at Port Laki, in Leros
Island, and a force of 2 destroyers – *Scorpion* and *Wolverine* – 3
trawlers, and 11 drifters was sent to work from there. Though
still under the orders of Captain Dent, the operations of this detached group were directed by the commanding officer of the
Scorpion, Commander A. B. Cunningham, D.S.O.

Very briefly, his orders were to patrol the scattered islands and
the mainland, from Samos on the north to Rhodes on the south, a
distance of about 120 miles, to search for hostile submarines. The
mainland harbours were also to be investigated, and any boats or
native craft found which might be used for communicating with
the outside world were to be destroyed. Villages firing on the
searching vessels were to be shelled and destroyed, though this, as
a rule, was rather beyond the capability of destroyers, with their
comparatively small outfits of ammunition.

An intelligence system was in force under Professor J. L.
Myres, then, as now, Wykeham Professor of Ancient History and
Fellow and Librarian of New College, Oxford. He had been given
the rank of Lieutenant-Commander, R.N.V.R., and had an excellent lot of workers among the Greek fishermen. His Greek
sympathies, however, made him by no means popular with the
Italian governors of the Dodacanese Islands.

As time went on, Lieutenant-Commander Myres, who was very
keen on carrying the war into the enemy's own territory, raised a
force of Greek and Cretan irregulars – most people called them
brigands – which was used for raiding the mainland covered by
destroyers.

" We used to land some 300 brigands," says one account, " who,
having shot up the small Turkish posts containing about thirty
men and generally about twenty miles apart, raided the Turkish
cattle. There were large numbers of cattle on the open fertile
plains which were said to be Government property, and used for
feeding the Turkish Army. We used to land the brigands late at
night, the idea being that they surrounded the Turkish post and
shot it up at dawn. They were always about ten to one, and I
give the Turks full marks, for, so far as I know, they seldom surrendered. After the Turkish post had been dealt with, the cattle
were raided, and some 200 or 300 head generally carried off in the
trawlers and native craft."

There followed a bright and busy few months for the destroyers,

[1] Now Vice-Admiral, C.B., C.M.G.

upon whom devolved the entire work of examining the enemy coast and harbours, and covering the operations of the brigand landing-parties.

" Most of the Turkish coast villages," says an account from an officer in the *Scorpion*, " were found to be protected by entrenchments, which were generally manned on our approach, though by no means all of them showed fight. In the case of harbours with bottle-neck entrances, the usual enemy plan was to allow the destroyer to enter without opposition, and to open a heavy rifle fire upon her as she came out through the narrows. Some of the narrow harbours were strenuously defended, both on our entry and withdrawal. Fearsome rifles were used by the Turks, and the old .55 inch Graas were very popular. Their large bullets made a splash in the water like a 1-inch aiming rifle bullet.

" It was soon discovered that the protective mattresses round our bridges offered no resistance to close-range rifle fire. We were therefore supplied with ½-inch loopholed steel plates by our depot-ship, the *Blenheim*, which were fitted round the bridge whenever we made a raid. They made it comparatively safe ; but the mounting of them was a laborious business which took some hours. Moreover, when once they were in place, navigation had to be done entirely by eye, as the magnetism of the steel affected the compass and made it quite useless. Later on, two 56-foot picket-boats were supplied to the force to enable the small harbours to be entered at night.

" One of the first places to be examined, and one which gave good results, was a place where submarines had been reported as using a river-mouth as a base. This was proved to be quite impossible, but at a village near by a number of lighters and native craft were found and destroyed. The surrounding hills were heavily entrenched ; but on that occasion we met with no opposition.

" Among many exciting incidents, two remain particularly in my memory. It had been decided to search a narrow inlet inside the Gulf of Mendalia – Mandelyah on the Admiralty charts – at the head of which was a village called Kujak. We decided to do so at night by sending in the picket-boat, covered, if necessary, by our gunfire. She closed the entrance at about 11 p.m., and on entering was fired on from both sides, to which she effectually replied with her .303-inch maxim. Unfortunately, before she arrived within half a mile of the village she bumped heavily over an obstruction, and was found to be in very shallow water which was not shown on the chart. The obstruction proved to be a large drain-pipe running transversely across the harbour. At first sight there seemed to be little hope of re-passing it stern first, and owing to the shallow water it was quite impossible to turn.

" Fortunately the rifle fire had abated to some extent, so by dumping coal and lightening the stern, the picket-boat was gradually worked backwards over the pipe, her exit from the harbour being hastened by heavy rifle fire from both sides of the entrance. Nothing at all was gained by this enterprise, as no native craft were found, and it nearly resulted in the loss of the picket-boat. The destroyer, with her bridge protected by steel plates, tried to enter next morning. She was received with a hot fire in the entrance at ranges of well under 100 yards. The village escaped bombardment, as it was round a bend, and the heavy rifle fire did not allow our guns to be manned.

" On the Budrum Peninsula is a small harbour called Port Gumishlu, and we had received information that this place was being used constantly by native craft communicating with the islands. We therefore decided to send the picket-boat in at night to destroy any craft found. On her approach she was discovered by her flaming funnel, to be received with very heavy rifle fire in the narrow entrance. The coxswain was shot through the back, and his convulsive movement of the wheel nearly put the boat ashore. Only one half-sunken native boat was discovered and destroyed with explosive, while the picket-boat's retreat was harried by heavy rifle fire.

" The next morning the *Scorpion* closed the harbour, intending to bombard the village at close range as a reprisal. On arriving within 600 yards, however, we were hotly received and had 3 men of the 4-inch gun's crew wounded. Considering that the reason for this obstinate defence required investigation, we decided to enter the harbour in daylight with the bridge defences rigged, the upper deck clear of men, and to meet rifle fire with rifle fire by manning the bridge loopholes and mess-deck scuttles.

" Navigational dangers made progress rather slow, but, closing in, we had a great small-arms battle in the entrance. Very heavy fire came from a small rocky promontory on the starboard side of the entrance. It was replied to vigorously by our seamen, who could see their opponents lying behind rocks and bushes, at times at ranges of fifty yards and less. Bullets banged incessantly on the steel plating round the bridge ; but it effectively prevented our having any casualties. Nothing was found in the harbour to justify this resistance ; but agents afterwards reported that at the time of our visit a company of Turkish troops were in the village collecting taxes in kind. The camels for removing the grain were later discovered behind a hill and shelled, many of them being destroyed. The village was also heavily bombarded.

" These are merely two from many similar incidents. I have no knowledge of the effect of these operations on the safety of the Egypt-Salonika transport route, but, speaking from memory, I do not recollect a single steamer being attacked by an enemy submarine in that area during the four or five months that we were there."

That some of H.M. destroyers had the supreme excitement during the war of engaging Turkish soldiery at a range of fifty yards, with not a man on deck and the seamen sniping out of the mess-deck scuttles, will be news to many people.

Here is another story of the same period from the destroyer *Harpy* – Commander H. T. England. " We had done a successful raid at the top end of the Gulf of Mendalia, and, while the commandeered cattle were being embarked, Professor Myres asked us to go across the bay to a little land-locked harbour, where there were supposed to be some boats drawn up on the beach which were used for fishing, and which he said ought to be destroyed in order to maintain a strict blockade. – We steamed over and had a look at the place, and it didn't look pleasant. There were some nicely made trenches covering the whole harbour and entrance, and some earthworks had been erected where apparently they were going to mount guns. When Myres was told we didn't think it worth while going into the harbour, where there wasn't room to turn and we could only come out stern first, he remarked that the *Scorpion* and *Wolverine* had often done it, and that when the Turks saw our forecastle 4-inch gun they would cut and run.

" Eventually, against our captain's better judgment, we decided to go in close and have a look at the trenches first. If we could see no loopholes or steel plates, and no sign of their being occupied, we would go on inside the harbour. – We steamed in and had a close look. Saw no sign of life at all – old man Turk behaving like Brer Rabbit – so in we went, having previously got everyone down below except our foremost 4-inch gun's crew.

" The Turks behaved with great circumspection. They waited until the *Harpy* was right up against the town and couldn't come any closer, and the captain had just remarked to Professor Myres that there weren't any bally boats on the beach at all, when crack, crack, crack, rifle fire from all sides at a range of about 100 yards ! The 4-inch gun fired at once ; but one couldn't see a soul, and we were temporarily in a shower of bullets. We only had one casualty ; but this, unfortunately, was Commander England, who was seriously wounded. Professor Lieutenant-Commander Myres was very apologetic, as the captain had been persuaded to go in against his better judgment. The Professor's last remark to Commander England was, ' You must come to New College after the war. We haven't got an exceptionally good cook ; but our port is excellent ! ' "

As a result of this incident, Rear-Admiral Thursby stopped the cattle-raiding expeditions. They were not worth it if valuable personnel was to be lost.

Apart from his personal courage, Professor Myres was undoubtedly the man for leading cattle-raids in Asia Minor. Most of his brigands were recruited from the Greek islands, and, besides a profound knowledge of Greece and Greek history, he had travelled extensively in Greece, Asia Minor, and Crete, had conducted excavations in Cyprus, and so knew the neighbourhood and its people like the palm of his own hand.

The war certainly produced some strange situations. One of the strangest, however, must surely have been that of the Wykeham Professor of Ancient History at New College, Oxford, an M.A., Hon. D.Sc., Fellow of the British Academy, and F.S.A., on the bridge of a destroyer in action, and leading a band of bloodthirsty freebooters on cattle-forays in Asia Minor.

CHAPTER VI

MISHAPS IN THE BIGHT

I

O N a morning in April 1915 the Harwich Force had arrived within measurable distance of the island of Borkum, immortalised several years before the war by the late Erskine Childers's delightful adventure story, *The Riddle of the Sands.* At the time of which I write, Erskine Childers himself, if I mistake not, was serving as a lieutenant R.N.V.R. in the seaplane-carrier *Engadine,* a commandeered cross-Channel passenger steamer. I think he had already earned the Distinguished Service Cross for his services as an observer in one or other of the air-raids on the German coast.

We were steaming on an easterly course in three columns, the light-cruisers and a couple of seaplane-carriers in the centre, and lines of destroyers close on either flank. We had attempted this particular operation, an air-raid on some German aerodrome in or near Borkum, several times before, but always without success. Invariably we had started off from Harwich with everything in our favour – a flat, calm sea, gentle breeze, and clear visibility. As certainly, the fates had arrayed themselves against us after covering our 250 miles and arriving near the enemy coast – a boisterous south-westerly gale and a heavy sea, or a fog as thick as a blanket, in neither of which conditions our seaplanes could do their business.

We detested the gales, and the horrible, short, steep seas which wetted us through and through and made our destroyers uncomfortably skittish. We disliked the snow and the sleet, and the ice with which our decks were sometimes covered and the muzzles of our guns choked. But above all we hated the fogs – cold, clammy fogs which dripped from our eyebrows and cap peaks and sometimes came down at a few minutes' notice to reduce the range of visibility to a few yards.

It was only natural that fog should be our chief bugbear. We invariably steamed at high speed, 20 knots or more, with anything up to 30 ships in close formation. At one moment it might be beautifully clear and sunny. The next, we would run into a wall of impalpable vapour, to find ourselves utterly blind, with sirens yelping and wailing in all directions.

But on this particular morning the dawn broke bright and clear, and 5 o'clock found us speeding along with the horizon ahead suffused with the wonderful prismatic colouring of a gorgeous sunrise. Then the blood-red sun, flattened like an orange, sailed up into space over a bank of low-lying, purplish cloud, and the day began.

Drinking our morning cocoa and smoking our pipes on the bridge, we congratulated each other on the weather. At 6 o'clock the operation was timed to start. We had another hour to wait, another twenty miles to travel.

At 5.50 the *Arethusa*, which flew the broad pendant of Commodore Reginald Tyrwhitt, hoisted the blue and white striped *Preparative* flag. Hauled down at 5.55, it would give the seaplane-carriers the signal to sheer out of the line, to stop engines, and to hoist their seaplanes out on to the water.

We travelled on over the glassy sea, the sun, now well over the horizon, bathing us in its brilliance, a lovely, breathless morning. All the same, I had not liked the look of the sunrise. The " morning red " presaged bad weather, possibly a blow from the southwest. But all we wanted was two hours of fine weather – just 120 minutes.

As I looked to the eastward I noticed that the horizon was gradually becoming blurred and indistinct. Patches of mist seemed to be moving slowly across the surface of the calm sea, wreathing eddies and tentacles stretching out towards us.

" That's torn it ! " observed the first lieutenant glumly, glancing in the same direction.

It had. I noticed the tall mastheads of the light-cruisers slowly becoming hidden. Then a white flag with five small black crosses appeared over the *Arethusa's* bridge rails, to climb aloft, to disappear.

" Negative, sir ! " the signalman called.

I could have cursed. For the fourth or fifth time the operation was postponed. It seemed as if we should never bring it off.

The outlines of the more distant ships lost their sharpness, then disappeared. Nearer vessels became swallowed up in the murk. With an inexplicable suddenness, like the dropping of a curtain, we steamed into a wall of thick fog. We were alone, rushing through it at 20 knots with a visibility of perhaps fifty yards. All we could do was to steer by compass and to keep a watchful eye upon the trail of whitened water in the wake of the next ahead.

The *Arethusa's* siren howled frenziedly from somewhere on the port bow in the longs and shorts of the Morse code.

" Signal for 10 knots, sir," said the signalman, his ear cocked.

The yelping was taken up by ship after ship, repeated all down the lines. Then the long blast of the *Executive*, which meant that the purport of the signal was to be obeyed.

I gave an order over my shoulder. The engine-room revolution telegraph clanged noisily as a man twisted the handle until the pointer stood at 180. The speed decreased – 10 knots.

For a moment or two there was silence, disturbed only by the usual noises of the ship and the rippling sound of the water alongside. Then another burst of yelping from the *Arethusa's* siren repeated by other ships.

"Alter course leaders together the rest in succession 8 points to starboard, sir," the signalman interpreted.

The fog had thickened appreciably. Looking over the bows, we could barely see the flattened, swirling wake of the next ahead. At 10 knots a destroyer leaves little trace of her passage through the water. Even as I watched I saw the dim shape of her stern looming up out of the mist a few yards from our bows. We were closing fast. I reduced speed, sheered slightly out of the line. We continued to overtake her, until her funnels, and then her bridge, appeared out of the murk as we ranged alongside. Hailing through a megaphone, I was told her speed was 7 knots, while following her next ahead, her captain told me, was like trying to follow the curves of a wriggling serpent.

" They're all bunched up anyhow ahead," he concluded. " I've got three of 'em in sight now ! "

I tried to edge our ship, the *Murray*, back into her proper station ; but, glancing aft, saw the sharp bow of our next astern dangerously close to our port quarter. I hailed her through a megaphone, told her of the situation ahead – that the others were steaming dead slow.

Her captain had rather a bad temper that morning, and asked, in no uncertain language, what the hell I thought I was playing at. I retaliated. There was no time for explanation. Station-keeping during an alteration of course in a thick fog is always irritating. There were eight destroyers in our line. They were closing in on each other like the folds of a concertina, sheering out of the line to port and starboard to avoid collision – a regular " pot-mess," as a bluejacket would call it.

The *Arethusa's* siren gave a prolonged shriek as a signal for the course to be altered 8 points, or 90 degrees, to starboard. It was an evolution simple enough in clear weather, but not so simple in fog. We were steaming in three columns, and while the *Arethusa*, heading the centre column of light-cruisers and seaplane-carriers, swung straight round to the new course and maintained an even speed, we, the starboard wing column, had, so to speak, to mark time and drop back to maintain our relative positions. The port wing column, on the other hand, had to increase speed and alter course gradually.

For a few minutes everything went well, and we managed to drop back into station and to follow on in the wake of the next ahead. Then, quite suddenly, two frantic yelps from a siren somewhere close on the starboard bow warned us that some other ship was altering course to port – the wrong direction.

A moment later we heard three shrill blasts from our invisible next ahead. For some reason unknown to us, she was going astern.

I stopped our engines, put the telegraphs to slow astern, hooting thrice on the siren to warn the ship behind us. Almost at the same moment there came an appalling, smashing thud from somewhere right ahead as two ships collided. Then the sound of men shouting.

My impressions of what happened during the next few minutes are rather blurred, for at that moment everything seemed utter confusion, with ships steaming in every direction. A great bulk slid out of the mist perhaps forty yards under our bows. She was a light-cruiser, heading in the opposite direction to ourselves. We manœuvred to avoid her, just succeeded in slithering past without hitting.

Someone on her bridge shouted through a megaphone. " Destroyer ! " he hailed. " Stand by. We're badly damaged ! "

She was the *Undaunted*, and we could see her plight for ourselves. There was a huge V-shaped gash in her port side aft, through which the water must be pouring into her hull. We could hear the twittering of boatswain's pipes, see the shadowy figures of men hurrying to place a collision mat over the hole.

We travelled on, intending to circle round when clear and to go to her assistance. Before we could turn, however, another vessel appeared out of the fog to starboard. This time it was the *Landrail*, the destroyer which had crashed into the *Undaunted*.

She was a horrible sight – her forecastle half its original length, and some twenty feet of her bow crumpled, twisted, and forced bodily aft. Through the torn, jagged holes in her plating we could look right into her fore mess-deck, could even see the mess-stools and tables. The forepart of her forecastle deck had collapsed downwards until the original stem-head was nearly touching the water. It formed a vertical wall, as it were, over the top of which protruded the muzzle of her 4-inch gun as though it were mounted on the edge of a cliff. Men on her forecastle were running forward with the collision mat. Another destroyer was standing by her.

It was now, when we were still moving ahead, that the lookout on our forecastle howled frenziedly, pointed over the bows, and then started to run aft. I didn't wonder.

On our starboard bow, moving rapidly at right-angles across our track, was the heavy white bow-wave of another light-cruiser. It cannot have been more than fifty yards distant.

It was an agonising, sickening moment. We were moving at 12 knots, and it seemed a certainty that we should hit her. With my heart in my mouth I gave orders for full speed astern.

Æons of time seemed to pass before the turbines responded. We saw the cruiser's hull, then her mast, then her three funnels. Her grey side seemed to be travelling past our bows for ever – within thirty yards, thirty feet, then a couple of fathoms. We braced ourselves, waiting for the crash that seemed inevitable. We escaped hitting her by a miracle, missing the rounded stern by a matter of six feet before we finally gathered sternway. Feeling physically sick, and trembling all over, I breathed again. The whole incident lasted less than thirty seconds. It seemed more like ten minutes.

We were in a nasty predicament, well into the Heligoland Bight, within ten or a dozen miles of Borkum. The *Undaunted* was seriously damaged, though she might be able to hobble home under her steam. The *Landrail*, however, was in a sorrier plight. Her bows were utterly collapsed, and, even if she did not sink, she would have to be towed home stern first. With two lame ducks and the possibility of bad weather, much might happen before we saw England again. Moreover, it was before the time when we had learnt to be cautious about the use of wireless in enemy waters. Some ship had been using it. The chances were a hundred to one that the signals would be intercepted by the enemy, that they would realise that something untoward had happened within a few miles of one of their roosting-places. If the fog held, all might be well. If not, we might expect our retreat to be harried by a cruiser squadron or two and flotillas of destroyers.

Indeed, within ten minutes our leading telegraphist was reporting unusual activity on the part of the German shore wireless stations. What is more, their signals were being answered by ships fairly close at hand.

The *Undaunted*, having patched up the enormous rent in her side as best she could, presently limped off to the westward, escorted by one other destroyer besides ourselves. She could only steam at slow speed, but, as luck would have it, fog or thick mist held throughout the day as we gradually left the German coast farther and farther astern. And that afternoon, as we steamed homeward, we heard the *Undaunted's* bugles sounding the " Last Post," and the crackle of the three volleys as the remains of some poor fellow were committed to the deep. We did not know until afterwards that one man had been killed instantaneously by the collision and two others injured.

The mist cleared and bad weather came on as we neared the English coast, though, under the lee of the land, it mattered little to us. We saw the *Undaunted* into the Thames estuary on her way to Chatham dockyard, when we parted company and returned to our base.

The *Landrail's* adventures are a story in themselves. At first she managed to struggle to the westward at slow speed, using her own engines. Then the collision bulkhead started to strain and to leak, while the cable-locker became flooded. The ship was badly down by the bows. Before long, bulkheads were showing signs of collapse, and the foremost oil-fuel tank was leaking into the sea.

Stopping her engines to diminish the strain, weights were moved aft to bring the bows higher out of the water. The bulkheads forward were shored up with spars, planks, mess-stools, and tables, the same being done with the top of the large oil-tank in the bottom of the ship, which showed signs of bulging upwards. Shell from the foremost shell-room and some shackles of cable were transported aft. By the time this work had been done it was 8 o'clock in the morning, and the fog was as thick as ever. A gentle breeze from the westward rippled the water into minute corrugations. As yet it had no malice, but was increasing gradually in force. Before long it would blow the fog away. To judge from the barometer reading and the gory-looking sunrise, a gale from the south-west might be expected. The enemy wireless signals showed no signs of abatement. Some devilment was in preparation to the eastward.

For a time the *Landrail*, having completed temporary repairs, managed to steam on to the west, working up to 10 knots. The fog was still as thick as ever, and no other ships were now in sight. She reported her damage and estimated position to the *Arethusa* by wireless ; there was no alternative.

" Am returning to search for you," Commodore Tyrwhitt replied. " Use siren."

It was soon after 10 o'clock that the *Arethusa's* siren was heard trumpeting in the murk, and ten minutes later the *Landrail*, still steaming at 10 knots, was following the silvery disc of her larger sister's searchlight.

So far, so good. The cripple was no longer alone at the mercy of any prowling enemy that might suddenly appear. She went on her way rejoicing.

Soon after noon the fog rolled away as suddenly as it had come, to leave a clear horizon to the westward. But it was not a fair weather horizon. The glass had gone down and the look of the sky was threatening, with the sun hidden behind a hard, grey pall dappled all over with lumps of dark cloud driving down from the west on the wings of the new wind. Wind and sea rose fast, so that by 2 o'clock the *Landrail* was pitching to the motion of the crisp little waves, and occasional whiffs of spray came rattling against her canvas bridge-screens. Before long it would be blowing hard from the south-west.

Word came on to the bridge that the bulkheads showed signs of bulging and that some of the shores were working loose with the motion. Speed was reduced to 8 knots, the Commodore being informed.

" I anticipate bad weather," he said in reply. " Do not risk your ship unnecessarily. Are you sufficiently seaworthy to steam at slow speed against a heavy sea ? "

The answer was in the negative.

" Prepare to be taken in tow by the stern," came back at once. " Turn stern to sea and stop engines. Hawser will be sent."

The sea was still rising, but a destroyer, the *Mentor*, took the *Landrail* in tow, and, with the latter's propellers jogging slowly astern, tugged her slowly to the westward, with the waves breaking in cataracts over the stern. Then the *Landrail* took a sudden sheer and became unmanageable, and the 3½-inch wire parted like pack-thread. Another destroyer then made an attempt, with a like result, and then the cruiser *Aurora*. The same thing happened once more, until the *Arethusa* herself came to the rescue.

Finally, when the 4½-inch steel wire had been passed across

between the ships, the procession staggered slowly on to the westward at a speed of little more than 6 knots.

When darkness fell it came on to blow great guns from the south-west, with a heavy, toppling sea. The speed dropped to 5 knots, to 3, and finally to nothing worth mentioning. Even so, the huge frothing combers, crashing against the *Landrail's* blunt stern and erupting on board ten and twelve feet deep, removed every movable fitting from her after part, and made the stern un-inhabitable. The store-rooms containing the food were right aft, so, after making a succession of perilous journeys to salve suffi-cient food for the journey, the stern portion of the ship was aban-doned and the officers camped forward for the rest of the trip.

Wet through, exhausted, and weary-eyed, they watched through the terrible night. But the stoutest watertight hatches, let alone the light ones in a destroyer, would never have stood the trip-hammer blows of the seas. Try as they would, they could not prevent water from finding its way below, and every gallon in the after compartments decreased the buoyancy of the ship and made things worse.

The night passed dismally. At daybreak next morning it was blowing a full gale, with a heavier sea than ever. The *Landrail*, jerking to the pull of the towing-hawser, was crashing and thud-ding as though she would break in halves. Destroyers, steaming ahead, dribbled oil in the water, but though by so doing they prevented the seas from breaking, nothing could subdue the steep rollers that threatened to engulf the crippled ship.

At 10 o'clock in the morning, to make things worse, the towing-wire again snapped like a harp-string. For two mortal hours the *Landrail* rolled dizzily in the trough of the sea, while her ex-hausted men, sliding about her reeling deck, hanging on for their lives, man-handled on board the end of a destroyer's chain-cable. Both ends being made fast, the weary progress was resumed at about noon, until, at 12.30, the cable itself parted and the *Land-rail* again fell off broadside on to the sea, rolling fifty degrees either way.

Then it was they thought they would have to abandon ship, for, though the pumps were kept going, all the after compartments were flooded. The foremost bulkheads, too, were starting to bulge like cardboard, so that parties of men had constantly to be kept at work replacing and wedging up the timber shores. For a time it seemed as though the ship were doomed.

The Commodore, however, was the last person on earth to

think of abandoning one of his crippled children while there remained the least prospect of saving her. Steaming the *Arethusa* quite close, he lowered a boat and passed the *Landrail* the end of another hawser. It was followed by the end of his stout chaincable, the end of which, after three hours' back-breaking work, was finally dragged bodily on board the *Landrail* and secured, every soul in the ship lending a hand. Then the *Arethusa* went slowly ahead, and this time the cable held.

It was seventy-one hours after the collision, seventy-one hours of agony and suspense, that daylight came and those on board the *Landrail* saw the faint blue streak of the English coast peeping up over the far horizon ahead. Exhausted, unshaven, wet through, and hungry, they gazed greedily at the thin line of land with expressions of gratitude on their lips.

The wind lulled and the sea died away as they drew under its lee.

And so the *Landrail* came home.

2

I am reminded of another *contretemps* in the Heligoland Bight, which happened on the night of August 17–18, 1915.

The minelayer *Princess Margaret*, escorted by two divisions of the 10th Destroyer Flotilla from Harwich, had been detailed to lay a minefield off the Amrun Bank, some twenty-five miles north of Heligoland. Commodore Tyrwhitt's light-cruisers from Harwich, escorted by more destroyers, were farther out at sea as a support.

Having passed through several trawlers fishing, one of which, being German, was sunk, the inshore force made the Horns Reef Lightship after dark, and turned south towards the minelaying position. The senior officer of the escorting destroyers was Commander E. T. Inman, in the *Mentor*, and when darkness came the divisions had been disposed on each quarter of the *Princess Margaret*.

It was a very dark night, calm but heavily overcast. Shortly before reaching the area to be mined, the force sighted a division of hostile destroyers, which at once fired torpedoes and then made off at full speed in the darkness. They had fired at the *Princess Margaret*, which, with her huge hull and three funnels, was a conspicuous and tempting target. The torpedoes luckily missed her ;

but one unfortunately hit the *Mentor*, the resulting explosion completely blowing away her bows under water.

The *Princess Margaret* turned back, and in the resulting confusion the escort lost touch. Presently there came a wireless signal from the Admiralty countermanding the operation, as directional wireless had located strong enemy forces at sea in the neighbourhood of the intended minefield.

The *Mentor*, meanwhile, seemed to be completely disabled, and found herself quite alone within a few miles of the enemy coast, and in water which generally teemed with German patrol vessels. The lower portion of her bows had been completely blown away, until the deck of the forecastle, from about the foremost gun, hung vertically down towards the water with the stem-head submerged. Considerable other damage had been done by the explosion, including the wrecking of all the signalling lamps on the bridge, and the smashing of the oil lamps. Surprising to relate, however, the ship was not making much water.

Realising the danger of capture, Inman destroyed his confidential books. Then, with his guns and torpedoes ready for instant action, he set the rest of his men to work to shore up bulkheads, place collision mats, and do all in their power to make the ship tolerably seaworthy for the 360-mile passage home. Luckily the weather was fine, and showed every prospect of remaining so.

While this work was still in progress, Inman sighted some ships in the darkness and wished to ask them to stand by him. To his great annoyance, the smashing of all the lights and lamps made any communication impossible, and the vessels steamed on and vanished in the darkness. It was not until some days later that he blessed the failure of his lights. Those ships were German cruisers. They passed him within a few hundred yards. Had he shown a solitary gleam he would have been sunk outright.

Her temporary repairs finished, the *Mentor* made tracks for home, gradually working up to 10 knots. At this speed, in the words of her captain, " she pushed the whole ocean in front of her." The fine weather held, and she duly arrived at Harwich, where we watched her coming up harbour, an extraordinary sight. The fact that she was safely brought home after such extensive damage reflected the greatest credit, not only on those who had brought her in, but on the firm who built her – Messrs. Hawthorn Leslie & Co., at their well-known shipyard on the Tyne.

Commander Inman met his death in distressing circumstances while in command of the destroyer *Simoom* during one of the night actions between the Harwich Force and German destroyers near the Schouwen Bank Lightship, off the Dutch coast about midway between the Hook of Holland and Zeebrugge. It happened on the night of January 22–23, 1917, and a letter from Captain A. F. W. Howard, who was present in another destroyer, the *Mansfield*, shows the hideous anxiety and uncertainty of these close-range night mêlées between opposing torpedo craft.

" We had been detached at Dover for about a week," he writes to me. " You know what that meant. We had been at sea the whole time, and never on the same course for more than half an hour at a time, which meant no sleep. Returning to harbour dog-tired and hoping for a rest, we were greeted with a signal to return to Harwich with all despatch. We legged it for all we were worth, and on arrival found the Harwich Force putting to sea. We received orders to complete with oil and join up with another division of T.B.D.s off the Schouwen Bank."

What had happened was that Commodore Tyrwhitt had had orders from the Admiralty to intercept some enemy destroyers known to be proceeding from the Ems to Zeebrugge to relieve or reinforce the flotilla already there.

It was a calm, cold, very dark night, with a peculiar mistiness in the atmosphere. " We succeeded in finding the division after dark," Captain Howard continues, " and tailed on to a long line of destroyers without being blown to pieces. Rather an anxious business, and on my way there my first lieutenant and I checked our recognition signals and orders again and again in case of mistakes. As you know, a mistake on these occasions of joining up after dark meant playing a harp for the rest of one's days. Shortly after we joined up, gun flashes were sighted ahead, and we increased to full speed with the others."

Eight enemy destroyers had been sighted passing close under the sterns of Commodore Tyrwhitt's light-cruisers farther ahead. A general mêlée followed at a range of 1,000 yards and less, the cruisers firing hard with their 6-inch guns, and the enemy destroyers retaliating with torpedoes. The scene was an extraordinary one. As the enemy fled at full speed, their funnel-tops were crowned with a vivid red glow, until a scarlet canopy seemed to hang over each vessel.

It is hopeless to attempt to describe the course of the action, but, as Captain Howard writes, " we were still proceeding in the direction of the gunfire when the whole sky was lit up by a heavy explosion. It seemed as if a giant had taken a running kick at a huge bonfire. Sparks flew up several hundred feet and came down in a beautiful golden rain."

The *Simoom*, indeed, had been torpedoed forward, and the explosion had fired her fore magazine.

" We were going anything from full speed to stop, sometimes even going astern, so I had all my work cut out to keep more or less in station and to avoid collision. I had no time to look about and to take in the situation. My first lieutenant, who was in the gun-control position above the bridge, reported two submarines on our starboard beam. I told him to open fire if he could ; but he lost sight of them almost at once and never picked them up again. In any case, two of our guns were stuck up and choked with ice, though they had been worked frequently during the night. (It was bitterly cold ; but in spite of it I had the greatest difficulty in keeping awake.) I heard afterwards that those two ' submarines ' were really enemy destroyers which must have passed down our line on an opposite course and just out of sight of most of us. Somebody then put a searchlight on the *Simoom*, or what was left of her. She had all gone up to the foremost funnel, and we never expected her to be afloat at daylight. However, she was, and the remains were sunk by gunfire, as you know.

" I was very depressed when I saw the forlorn *Simoom* in the morning and knew that poor Inman had gone. . . . My ship, the *Mansfield*, was his sub-divisional mate, and it is curious that I was not with Inman on the occasions that the *Mentor* and *Simoom* came to grief. For some reason I had both times been on some special job or other. Inman liked to have me astern of him, as he thought I was lucky, and although by my seniority I should have had a sub-division of my own, I was by his special request kept with him."

It was during this particular night action that the opposing destroyers, steaming at full speed, fought each other within pistol range. The German leader, horribly battered and barely afloat, eventually reached the Dutch port of Imuiden, while another, also damaged, was chased into Zeebrugge.

It is easy to talk of " decisive results " at night. In the confusion of a mêlée in pitch darkness, however, with all ships steaming at high speeds, the blinding effects of gunfire, the uncertainty as to what is happening, and the extreme difficulty of distinguishing between friends and enemies, the result is largely a matter of luck. And so it was on this occasion.

To close this chapter more cheerfully, Captain Howard reminds me of one or two stories of the war. Early in 1915 he had just taken over the *Mansfield* at Messrs. Hawthorn Leslie's works in the Tyne. It was 7.45 in the evening, and the officers had just started dinner in the wardroom when the heavy thump of an explosion close at hand brought them quickly on deck, as it did the men.

It was the first Zeppelin raid on the Tyne, and the monster could be seen overhead. The *Mansfield* at once went to action stations, but could do nothing, as there were no anti-aircraft guns of much use in those days. However, a hoary-headed reservist sentry, wearing the Egyptian ribbons of 1882 and only half his uniform, opened fire with his Martini carbine. A shout of laughter went up from the seamen. Then came the inevitable " voice " " Why don't you fix your ruddy bayonet, mate, and charge the blighter ! "

Another yarn. A destroyer had been in station in sight of a battleship all through the night, and was suddenly challenged at dawn. The destroyer's commanding officer, thinking it quite an unnecessary demand considering the hours his ship had been in sight, did not respond in the usual manner. Instead, thinking of Tom Clare's *On the Telephone*, he flashed back with his search-light : " You very funny dis morning, don't you ? " and steamed ahead into his day station before he could be found out. One cannot always vouch for the truth of stories of this sort, though plenty of destroyer officers were capable of such a retort.

I asked Captain Howard for his most vivid recollection of the war. " So many things happened in those years," he replied, " that only a few impressions have stuck. Unless recalled by some conversation or incident, the remainder won't come out. But," he went on to say, " I can still picture one morning off the west coast of Ireland when the whole sea was strewn with dead mules, and then picking up the survivors of a vessel which had been sunk by shell fire from a submarine. Curiously enough, what impressed me most was a huge buck nigger, his shirt saturated with blood from a horrible wound in his back, and the broadest grin on his face I have ever seen on a human being.

" Talking of gory shirts," he adds, " reminds me of a Dutch ship sunk off the Galloper. She just went up on a couple of mines, and the crew, some of them wounded, took to the boats. I managed to pick them up on my way back to Harwich. They were most grateful to us, and I still have a telegram and letter sent to me by them and their owners on their return to Holland.

Another letter came from one of the seamen, begging us to send him his gory shirt, which had been changed when a wound was dressed on board. A shirt *was* sent, soaked in blood ; but I strongly suspect the blood was squeezed out of our ration beef. However, I have no doubt it is a much-treasured relic of the war in the house of some Dutch seafaring family."

CHAPTER VII

SATURDAY NIGHT AT SEA

I

IN my brief leisure during part of the war I once wrote a book called *Pincher Martin, O.D.* It appeared serially in *Chambers's Journal*, starting early in 1916, and was published as a book in November. Completing it at all was difficult, for writing on board a destroyer at sea in time of war was impossible, for more reasons than one. I could only put pen to paper while we were in harbour. Often I received telegrams from Edinburgh, such as, " Please send next instalment Pincher long overdue." I did my best. It was very difficult. Sometimes I thought I had undertaken more than I could accomplish.

Each chapter was submitted to the Censors at the Admiralty Press Bureau before publication, and, so far as I remember, there were no excisions. In the autumn, before *Pincher's* publication as a complete book, the whole manuscript – 120,000 words – was again sent to the Admiralty. This was to make doubly certain that I should not be hanged, drawn, and quartered for disobeying an article in the King's Regulations and Admiralty Instructions, which says, in so many words, that no officer or man upon the active list can publish, or cause to be published, indirectly or otherwise, any book, or any article in a newspaper, periodical, or journal, unless Admiralty approval has first been obtained.

In due course the Censor returned the proofs to the publisher requiring the deletion of certain passages in a chapter describing the Battle of Jutland, which had been written entirely from hearsay, newspaper accounts, and my own local knowledge of the North Sea. One of the deletions was fifteen lines descriptive of the British Fleet steaming eastward during the night of May 30th, 1916, in which, perhaps, I had hinted that Sir John Jellicoe had previous knowledge that something unusual was in the wind. Further blue pencillings described the *Lion*, Sir David Beatty's flagship, being hit by enemy shell, and the loss of the *Indefatigable*, *Queen Mary*, *Defence*, and *Warrior*. One of the excisions in regard to the latter ship consisted of the twelve words – " and then came the piteous and gruesome task of identifying the dead." The Censor was perfectly within his rights, but my publishers, meanwhile, acting on the assumption that everything was in order as each individual chapter had been officially stamped " Passed by Censor," had printed a first large edition of 20,000 copies.

What should they do? Must the whole of the first edition be scrapped?

No. They determined to have a run for their money. Armed with the chapters, their representative came hot-foot to London. He penetrated into the Admiralty, saw the Chief Censor, and suggested that as the original chapters had been duly passed before publication and were merely being reprinted in book form, the cost of scrapping the first edition because of *subsequent censorship* should fall upon the Navy Estimates instead of the publishers.

I should like to have seen the Chief Censor's face, provided I had been present strictly incognito. Mr. George Morris, Messrs. Chambers's representative, was a far braver man than myself.

Nevertheless, the Chief Censor met him half way. The first edition might be passed as it stood. The second edition must be altered.

So all was peace.

To my great surprise, 22,004 copies of *Pincher* were sold between November 15th, 1916, and December 31st, and a good many have been sold since. The book had a good " press," and I had many letters concerning it. One of the most amusing was written in red ink in very strange handwriting on the back of a newspaper wrapper. Sent to the publishers from St. Anne's-on-Sea, Lancashire, where I believe there is an asylum, it was forwarded on to me. It was short and to the point, blasphemous as well: " What the devil is Pincher Martin? Tell us about Jesus. We are fed up of your stories." It was strictly anonymous.

And among other communications I received an anonymous poem called " Saturday Night at Sea," sent by someone who described himself or herself – I suspect the latter – as " A Spirit in Prison." Here it is.

SATURDAY NIGHT AT SEA

I

It is Saturday night, my darling,
Yes, Saturday night at sea,
And somewhere across the ocean
They are toasting you and me.

Brave sailormen, my darling,
  Are thinking of you and me.
Can't you see them round the table
  This Saturday night at sea ?

2

But they're not all there, my darling,
  Though Saturday night it be,
For someone must still be watching
  With eyes strained out to sea.
The foe may be near, my darling,
  Menacing you and me,
So they " carry on " from Sunday morn
  To Saturday night at sea.

3

High on the bridge, my darling,
  A figure I can see,
And eyes that are ever straining
  To windward and to lee.
The wind is cold, my darling,
  The night as black can be,
But they never cease their vigil
  On any night – at sea.

4

And down below, my darling,
  Far down, beneath the sea,
Where the engines pound and clatter
  And the flames are roaring free,
They're " carrying on" my darling.
  Their work for you and me,
And they never cease their labours.
  Ev'n on Saturday night – at sea.

5

But round the table, darling,
  Empty places I can see
Of sailormen who gave their all –
  Yes, all, for you and me.
They met their death, my darling,
  To keep us safe and free,
And they'll ne'er drink " Sweethearts and wives " again
  On Saturday night at sea.

6

So they " carry on," my darling,
  Out in the grim North Sea.
Or they grope along the Channel
  In their little T.B.D.

Or perhaps in the Downs, my darling,
Or where'er their duty be,
They wait in the dark and wind and cold
All Saturday night – at sea.

7

Then let us give thanks, my darling,
To the God of the Wind and Sea
For these brave and glorious sailormen
Who are guarding you and me.
Tho' some have gone west, my darling,
To the land where the soul is free,
Yet those who remain are carrying on
Their noble work – at sea.

" A Spirit in Prison."

I fear I read it out in the wardroom, amid hoots of ribald merriment. As it contained the words " my darling " no less than fourteen times, we came to the conclusion it must be intended as a cradle-song.

The engineer-lieutenant-commander strongly objected to the aspersion cast upon his department by the line "where the engines pound and clatter." The *Murray* had turbines, he pointed out. If they dared to pound and clatter, there would be trouble for him and everybody else !

Neither could we see ourselves " round the table " on Saturday night at sea in wartime, drinking the time-honoured toast " Sweethearts and wives," with the waggish member of the mess murmuring under his breath, " May they never meet ! "

No. We had other things to do.

The most exciting Saturday night I ever passed was spent in an enemy minefield off Southwold.

2

It was a dark winter evening in November 1915 when five destroyers of the Harwich Force were groping their way back to their base after two days and two nights at sea. I cannot remember the names of three of the ships, but the *Matchless*, Commander George L. D. Gibbs, was at the rear of the line, and we, in the *Murray*, came next.

All the time we had been at sea we had had the usual North

Sea weather – a thick haze accompanied by occasional rain. On the return journey, however, half a gale of wind had sprung up from the south-west, with a nasty, toppling sea. It was nearly 6 o'clock. We were fairly close to the English coast, trying to make Orfordness Lighthouse, the light in which had been asked between certain times. But, though we should have been feeling the shelter of the land, it was still blowing as hard as ever, with a heavy, perpendicular lop which caused us to pitch and to wallow.

The sky was overcast, and the night as black as a cave. For the last forty-eight hours we had had no sight of the sun, or stars, or land. We had been steering erratic courses, and our position was more or less a matter of guesswork. Even the soundings did little to help us.

We were steaming, as usual, without lights. The sub-lieutenant, the usual men, and myself were on the bridge watching the next ahead, when, at 5.51 precisely, there came a crashing report from somewhere close astern. It was not like the sharp sound of a gun, but more sustained and muffled – a sort of reverberating thud which shook the ship.

Looking anxiously aft, we suddenly saw the *Matchless's* signal-lamp flickering in and out.

" Have – struck – a – mine," our signalman read out.

We answered that we were coming to help her.

I sent Oliver,[1] the sub-lieutenant, flying aft to warn Buchanan,[2] the first lieutenant, to be prepared for towing and to have the boats turned out ready for saving life if the *Matchless* sank. While he was away, I turned the ship short on her heel with the propellers, and stopped about fifty yards abreast of the damaged ship, which had fallen off into the trough of the sea. Our men, or those who were below, had flocked on deck at the sound of the explosion, and were soon making preparations.

" Are you all right ? " I howled through a megaphone, as, rolling heavily, we slid slowly past the *Matchless*.

" I don't know about all right," Gibbs's voice came back. " I think she'll float, but my stern's been blown off, with the rudder and screws. We can't move ! "

" Right ! " I shouted. " We'll take you in tow ! Will you stand by with your wire ? "

" Right ! "

It was going to be easier said than done. When we put the

[1] Now Commander Robert Don Oliver, D.S.C.
[2] Now Captain Edgar W. Buchanan, D.S.C.

searchlight on the *Matchless*, it could be seen she was in a bad way. She was not rolling very heavily, for some portion of her damaged stern was still connected with the hull. But she lay over to starboard towards the wind and sea until her mast was at an angle of 30° to the vertical. She was badly down by the stern, and broken water was washing half way across her deck. The spectacle was alarming.

We had drawn slightly ahead, rolling so heavily that at one moment the rails on the upper deck were under water, and the next high in the air. The men had the greatest difficulty in keeping their footing.

I manœuvred the *Murray* until our stern was level with the *Matchless's* bows, and about twenty feet off. I could not go nearer, for if our stern, with the vulnerable rudder and propellers, came into contact with the other ship, there might be two vessels disabled instead of one. That would be a hopeless state of affairs, particularly as the three others destroyers who had been with us when the incident happened had completely disappeared.

We wanted to get heaving lines between the two ships, for once the gap was bridged a wire hawser could be hauled across, and after that the *Matchless's* 3½-inch steel wire hawser for towing. But time and time again the wind blew the lines back in the men's faces. They could not heave them across, and were in constant danger of being shot off into the sea by the violent movement.

There was nothing for it but to lower a boat. It was no night for a destroyer's whaler, for it still blew half a gale, with a heavy sea. But it had to be risked. Oliver, the sub-lieutenant, and six men took their places in the whaler at her davits, which was slowly lowered towards the water. From the bridge I watched as she descended, and my heart was in my mouth.

The ship was still rolling heavily. The farther the boat was lowered, the longer became the arc through which she swung. At one moment she was suspended at an impossible angle over the water. The next, she swung in towards us, to hit the ship's side with a crash which threatened to smash her to matchwood and to throw every mother's son of her crew into the sea.

I felt rather nervous. We didn't want seven men in the water on a night like this. It was with a feeling of heartfelt relief that I heard someone shout, " 'Vast lowering ! " and then Oliver's : " Out pins ! – Let go ! "

She fell with a splash on the back of a heavy breaking sea, to be flung bodily aft and all but deposited on deck as the ship lurched towards her. We rolled the other way, and the whaler sank some-where out of my sight under the bottom of the ship, to reappear a few seconds later with her crew tugging at their oars. To this day I do not really know how they got clear.

Going under our stern, the boat passed a line across to the *Matchless*, the coir hawser followed, and then the end of her wire. This was hauled on board and shackled to the two shackles of chain-cable we kept aft, ready for such emergencies.

The two ships were connected. Everything was ready for going ahead, and the whaler was hoisted after another tussle. The time was 7.15 – an hour and twenty-four minutes since the explosion occurred. So far, things had been fairly easy. What we now had to do was to tow the *Matchless* head to wind and sea and drag her into safety.

We were both lying broadside on to the wind, with our heads pointing about south-east. Unaware of our exact position, we judged that the best course to steer to get the *Matchless* back to Harwich was south-west. In other words, we had to pull her through at right angles before we could start to go ahead.

There was a danger of carrying away the wire if we went too fast, so I started by going slow ahead with both engines and the helm over to port. Nothing much happened, except that the wire jerked out of the sea humming like a harp-string and seemed in imminent danger of parting as the ships pitched. A destroyer is not an ideal vessel from which to tow another. She is light and long, and pivots when turning at a point somewhere beneath her after funnel. With the tow-rope made fast right in the stern, much of the manœuvring power is lost. And on this occasion the *Matchless*, with her stern blown off and much of the tangled wreckage trailing in the water astern of her and acting as a huge rudder, did her damnedest to pull us round the wrong way – that was, to the east, instead of through south to south-west. We prayed for patience and that the towing-wire would hold ; but it felt like towing a derelict motor-car with a bicycle and a piece of string.

We had to work the engines very carefully, and tautened out the tow with the helm to port, then gradually increasing the revolutions of the turbines until they should have been giving us 8 knots.

We travelled round through 20°, and there we seemed to stick.

" Isn't she moving ? " I asked the coxswain, after about ten minutes.

" All over the shop, sir," said Ewles, gazing at the compass card
in his usual imperturbable way. " Up to sou'east one minute,
and back to south eighty the next."

We wanted to steer south-west. There seemed little chance of
getting there.

Time after time the ship's head came round with a rush to
starboard, only to fall back again. For an hour we tugged without
effect, while all the time the *Matchless* made signals. – " Please
tow me head to wind and sea as soon as possible. Sea may smash
in the after bulkheads."

" Am doing my very utmost," was all we could reply.

At 8.30 a thin driving rain came to add to our discomfiture.
We had had the *Matchless* in tow for an hour and a quarter, and
had not budged an inch so far as direction went. We were
beginning to feel desperate. I sent for Buchanan, the first lieutenant, who was watching the wire aft.

" We shall have to go a bit faster," I told him.

" If we do, we'll carry away the wire," he objected. " It's
within an ace of parting as it is, and what then, sir ? "

What then, indeed ?

But something had to be done, something rather drastic. We
wanted to turn to starboard, so I put the starboard engine-room
telegraph to slow astern, and the port to half ahead, gradually
increasing the revolutions of the latter until they should be giving
us the equivalent of 16 knots. This exerted a greater thrust. At
last the *Matchless* began to move.

Sometimes the ship came round ten or fifteen degrees with a
rush, only to fall back twelve a moment or two later. Sometimes
the lubber's line on the compass bowl went back beyond the
original starting-point, but generally we managed to gain a degree
or two.

The *Matchless* was in tow at 7.15. It took three hours, with a
constant fear in our hearts that the wire would part, to coax her
round to south-west.

We steamed slowly off towards the land, making good about 3¼
knots, while steaming the revolutions for 8. The damaged ship
yawed terribly in our wake, but by midnight we were under the
lee of the land and in safety. At dawn next morning Orfordness
Lighthouse and the Suffolk coast were in sight on the starboard
bow.

A light-cruiser from Harwich came out to meet us.

" Can't you go a little faster ? " she asked.

" Am steaming 8 knots," we replied.   " Wire may carry away if we increase."

" Try 10 knots," she semaphored.

I worked up the revolutions gradually, ten at a time.   At 9½ knots the towing-wire parted like a piece of pack-thread.

But it did not matter.   We were in calm water, under the lee of the land.   The cruiser took the *Matchless* in tow.

I went on board her when they put her into the floating-dock at Harwich, and a nasty sight she was.   All the wreckage trailing astern had been wrenched off when the cruiser took her in tow. The stern had disappeared as far forward as the foremost bulkhead of the wardroom, so that the wardroom, the magazines and shell-room beneath it, and the store-rooms farther aft, together with the rudder and both propellers, had vanished into the sea.

The after 4-inch gun was salved in a peculiar way.   When the mine exploded under the stern, the after part of the ship flicked upwards like a spring and shot the gun into the air.   Here, after turning a complete somersault, it landed on deck about twenty feet farther forward, with its muzzle through the roof of the sub-lieutenant's cabin.   The sub was asleep in his bunk at the time !

But not an officer or a man in the *Matchless* was killed.   Nobody was even hurt, and when she had been patched up for the journey she was taken to Chatham and provided with a new tail.

It was not until we were safely back in harbour that I discovered that we had been on top of a German minefield, a prohibited area which had been outlined in red on the charts almost since the beginning of the war.   We were glad I had not realised it at the time.   From first to last we must have been in it for something like five hours.

I may be superstitious ; but I attributed our escape to a Chinese joss that we carried on the stern-piece right in the eyes of the ship. I never really knew of what it was the presiding genius – whether, indeed, it represented a man or a woman.   It was a carved wooden image about seven inches high sitting in an armchair, with a yellow face, slanting Chinese eyes, and rather a weatherbeaten complexion, due to wind and spray.   He wore a sort of golden dressing-gown, picked out in scarlet and blue, and received a fresh coat of gold-leaf and enamel every time the ship refitted.

It was a junk joss, originally picked up in Hong-Kong harbour after the great typhoon of 1906, when many junks were capsized and lost, with great loss of life.   The joss – for he had no real name – was with me in every destroyer in which I had served since 1908.

At the end of July 1918, when I was in the *Telemachus*, of the 20th Flotilla of minelaying destroyers, and the joss was in his usual position on the stern-head, a malcontent broke it in pieces one night and flung the remains overboard. The remainder of the ship's company, who regarded the little image as their mascot, was furious. And so was I.

It was strange that on the very next occasion we went to sea, on August 2nd, the 20th Flotilla lost the *Vehement* and *Ariel* on an enemy minefield in the Heligoland Bight.

Was it pure coincidence ?

I wonder.

But sailors are so superstitious, as someone said as they saw me throwing salt over my left shoulder not ten days ago.

CHAPTER VIII

"THE BEEF TRIP"

I

PART of our routine work in the Harwich Force was the protection of the Dutch Convoy which, from 1916 until the end of the war, passed regularly to and fro between the Shipwash Light-vessel, off Orfordness, and the Maas Lightship, off the river of that name leading up to the Dutch port of Rotterdam. It is a run well known to Continental travellers, a distance of about 120 miles.

In 1917, for instance, 520 eastbound and 511 westbound merchant-vessels were convoyed between England and Holland with the loss of 6 ships–4 by submarine attack, 1 by destroyer attack, and 1 by mine. In carrying out the duty the Harwich Force, in the same year, lost 4 destroyers by mines and 1 by collision. Three more destroyers were damaged by mine or torpedo, and 1 light-cruiser and 5 destroyers by collision. "The frequent collisions," says Lord Jellicoe in his book *The Crisis of the Naval War*, "were due to the conditions under which the traffic was carried out at night without lights, and to the prevalence of fogs."

Speaking from personal experience, it is remarkable that our losses were not even greater.

To quote Lord Jellicoe again: "The extraordinarily small losses in the convoys were a very great tribute to the handling of the protecting force and to the organisation in Holland for arranging sailings, when it is borne in mind that it was almost impossible to prevent leakage of information to German agents once the time of sailing was given out, and that the convoys were open to attack from destroyers and submarines operating either from Zeebrugge or from the Ems or other German ports."

From Zeebrugge, the Maas Lightship, which marked the eastern end of our route, was about fifty miles, or about two hours' steaming. From the Ems it was about 180 miles.

The Dutch Convoy was inaugurated not so much because we wanted the butter, cheese, eggs, and so forth that Holland could give us, but because, I imagine, we wished to stop her surplus miscellaneous provender from finding its way to Germany, and so helping to invalidate our blockade.

The convoys went to and fro about once a week, sometimes more frequently. We always referred to our work in connection with them as "The Beef Trip." This was not because the merchantmen we escorted carried beef, or, so far as I am aware, any other kind of meat, but because in some remote way it reminded us of our days as midshipmen. Then, in charge of the "blood boat," generally a sailing pinnace or a cutter, we left our ships at early dawn to bring off from the shore the quarters of raw and bleeding beef which would presently be cut up by the marine butchers and served out to the ship's company.

It was before the time of refrigerators. In the old Channel Fleet we lived on a hand-to-mouth principle, drawing two or three days' allowance of fresh bread and meat at a time. The seamen had lusty appetites, and the men of a battleship would consume over a ton of beef in three days, though, after a couple of days at sea, we were usually eating salt beef and pork out of casks, together with ships' biscuit instead of bread.

All that is changed now, for modern men-of-war have large refrigerating plants, and embark two or three months provisions at a time. Moreover, the meat nowadays is of the chilled, imported variety, not home-killed.

But being in charge of the "blood boat" was never a pleasant job. Indeed, it was delegated to the most junior midshipmen as being beneath the dignity of the more senior ones. Who would like sailing or pulling off to the ship with a grisly pile of flesh sliding and wobbling about in the stern-sheets of the boat? Who would like being routed out of his hammock at six in the morning to be sent ashore before breakfast to see ten or a dozen bullocks slaughtered on the beach? That is what sometimes happened in the more outlandish places in China.

And the escorting of the Dutch "Beef Trip" during the war was also an unpleasant job when the weather was really bad or foggy. Frankly, we detested it.

It would have been easier if the ships of the convoy had all steamed the same speed. But they did not. There were ships of all ages, speeds, and sizes, some of which could steam 10, 12, or even 14 knots, and others no more than 7. They all put their best feet foremost, so that the head of the convoy lengthened out from the tail at the rate of seven miles an hour. When the leader arrived at the Maas the convoy was spread over fifty miles of sea, with sometimes no more than four destroyers to guard it.

What would have happened if the enemy had concentrated a

dozen destroyers at the eastern end of our route, to run down the line sinking as they went, I dread to imagine. But he never did. He gave us credit for a considerably greater strength at sea than we actually had, though somehow I cannot imagine a convoy of German merchantships, some of them steaming 7 knots, passing regularly to and fro within fifty miles of a British destroyer base.

In course of time, when we learnt more, the slower ships in the " Beef Trip " were eliminated altogether, and the convoy proceeded in regular formation, with destroyers spread out on either side zigzagging at high speed as a protection against sub-marines. Out of sight, too, but within easy reach, were a couple of light-cruisers acting as supports in case of a hostile destroyer raid.

The route was frequently altered ; but later still the Germans took to laying mines off the Dutch coast. Then the convoy, on nearing the dangerous areas, used to form into single line, while minesweepers and destroyers with their paravanes streamed went ahead to cut from their moorings any mines that might be in the way.

Mines were always our bugbear, for the submarines from Zeebrugge were very busy. Indeed, the whole area between Orfordness and the North Foreland soon became an ocean grave-yard. Our chart became dotted with the little red-ink symbols denoting sunken ships. At the end of 1916 it showed no less than forty-three.

The signals we so frequently received – " The port of Harwich is closed, due to mines " – rarely seemed to make much difference. We went to sea just the same.

One is compelled to give the enemy full marks for his sub-marine minelaying. The U.C. boats from Zeebrugge used to plant their detestable " eggs " in the very approaches to Harwich with uncanny prescience. It was on one of these that Sir Regi-nald Tyrwhitt's light-cruiser, the *Arethusa*, came to grief on February 11th, 1916. The explosion killed 11 men in one of the boiler-rooms and disabled her engines. A south-easterly gale was blowing at the time, with a nasty sea, and, though destroyers tried to take her in tow, the hawsers parted. The little cruiser eventually drifted ashore on the South Cutler shoal off Felixstowe, where she broke her back and settled down, a total loss.

2

At 10.45 p.m. we were moving seaward in line ahead through the opening in the boom which stretched between Harwich and the Suffolk shore opposite. Steaming on past the Beach End buoy, we headed up the fairway towards the Cork lightship. There were four of us destroyers in company, and, passing the lightship, we headed to the northward for Orfordness.

" Twenty knots," came a signal from the leader. " Show no lights at all."

Shortly before midnight, when the regular five-second flash of Orfordness Lighthouse was abeam, we altered course to the eastward for the North Hinder Lightship, the half-way milestone on our journey to the Dutch coast.

We were becoming a little weary of month after month of this same old route across the North Sea, or the southern portion thereof. We hated the short, snappy sea kicked up almost at a moment's notice by the sharp south-westerly gales, and the dense fogs of early spring and summer. We were tired of the perpetual vista of grey sky and grey water dappled with white horses, and burdened with the squat shapes of our bustling convoys passing to and fro along the line of the Shipwash, North Hinder, and Maas Lightships.

The submarines were always with us, ready to fire a torpedo into the brown of a convoy if they were given a chance. There was always the possibility, too, of tumbling across an enemy destroyer flotilla from Flanders. Our respective tracks must have crossed and recrossed each other many times, though we rarely sighted them.

The sea, in spite of the chill easterly breeze, was not so bad as it might have been. We trundled along with no further discomfort than the usual sheets of spray flying over forecastle, bridge, and upper deck. But spray was all in the day's work ; oilskins, sou'wester, leather sea-boots, and a variety of woollen undergarments and mufflers were the regular seagoing kit during winter.

We passed our old friend the North Hinder, and had the Maas in sight ahead by the time the first sign of dawn was encroaching on the dark sky to the eastward. We steamed on, until, beyond the lightship, we saw the red and white lights of the Dutch pilot steamer off the Hook of Holland. A nearer approach was inadvisable, for there lay Dutch territorial waters – *Verboten*.

Putting our helms over, we steamed to and fro, waiting for the homecoming convoy to appear.

The darkness of night gave way to the curious half-light which sometimes obtains between dawn and sunrise. The colour in the sky to the east gradually deepened, until sky and sea alike were dyed a vivid, transient pink. Elsewhere, the sea was a deep purple-blue, ruffled by the breeze until it looked soft to the south, like velvet rubbed the wrong way.

There was mist over the low-lying coast, but presently we saw a thin smear of funnel smoke staining the clear sky above it. Then the shape of a merchant-ship loomed up out of the haze – another, another, until we counted ten in a long straggling procession. They were our precious convoy, laden with butter, cheeses, eggs, and the miscellaneous produce of the Netherlands.

We checked their names and number from our sailing-orders, to find them all correct and present. Then one destroyer took station ahead and started to zigzag, two more went to port and starboard respectively, and the fourth astern.

I am writing of 1916, before the time when the ships of the Dutch Convoy kept close company and steamed in formation. Here we had ten ships, the fastest going 15 knots, the slowest, $7\frac{1}{2}$, and the remainder 11, 10, and 9. At the end of an hour, by which time it was full daylight, the 15-knotter was leading the others by a good two miles. Already the convoy was stretched out over seven miles of sea, while in three hours the leader would be over twenty miles ahead of the rear ship. We, for our sins, were responsible for the tail of the procession, the ship pounding along at 9 knots, and the other at $7\frac{1}{2}$. To protect ten merchant-men, all going different speeds, against submarine attack with only four destroyers was ever a matter of some difficulty. By the time the leader reached the English coast the laggards would be sixty-five odd miles astern. In short, four destroyers had to guard double this distance. What it meant was that we could not guarantee their safety. We could only hope that our presence would deter any submarine from making an attack, which, strangely enough, it generally seemed to do. I think I am right in saying that not more than a dozen merchantmen were lost on this route during the war.

We did our best to spur on the slower ships by making encouraging signals ; but it was little use harrying vessels that were already doing their utmost. From our very hearts we pitied the men condemned to go to sea in such crocks. They had surprising pluck, and we admired them, every one !

By 11 a.m. the leading ships of the east-going convoy, escorted by their destroyers, were passing us on an opposite course, and at 1 p.m., when we again sighted the North Hinder, only five of our convoy were still in sight, the 10-knot brigade practically hull-down, and the solitary 9-knotter six miles ahead.

That Dutch lightship, the North Hinder, a favourite lurking-ground for U-boats, seemed free of them on this occasion, and at about six in the evening, by which time the sun had set and darkness was coming down, we made the first of the buoys mark-ing the swept channel up and down the English coast. Our lumbering old tramp altered course to the southward with an ironical waggle of her rusty stern and disappeared into the night. We were glad to be quit of her. She was an anxious charge.

We still had to wait until the eastward-bound convoy reached its destination in safety, but after a brief delay the usual wireless signal came speeding over a hundred miles of space.

" Convoy arrived intact," said the senior officer of the escort in code. " Am returning."

It was the signal for us also to return to our base. We went on to 22 knots, and a couple of hours later, with our funnels caked white with salt, were peacefully secured alongside the oilers in Harwich harbour replenishing our fuel preparatory to securing to our buoys.

Another " Beef Trip " was finished. Yet another consignment of Dutch cheeses, margarine, butter, eggs, and lard had found their way to the United Kingdom.

3

Our jaunts to and fro across the Narrow Seas were not always so uneventful.

I remember once steaming through several acres of bobbing red Dutch cheeses after some ship or another had been torpedoed and sunk, while our sailors clustered along the ship's side and gazed wistfully at them as we passed. Had we been able to stop, we could have supplied ourselves for weeks. But Fritz was somewhere in the neighbourhood. I did not fancy our ship as a cockshy for a possible torpedo. I can only hope those cheeses duly floated home to England.

On another occasion we were near the *Copenhagen*, of the Great Eastern Railway Company, when she was torpedoed in full daylight and bad weather midway between the English coast and the North Hinder. The destroyer escort was unable to keep up in the heavy sea, and the *Copenhagen*, trusting to her 18 knots, pushed on alone.

A submarine's torpedo hit and exploded in her boiler-room. The ship did not sink, and was eventually got back into harbour and repaired ; but the incident brought us one or two exciting moments.

With more destroyers, we were at sea to the eastward on other business when her S.O.S. came, and raced back at full speed to help her. She was heeling over to a dangerous angle, with the passengers and crew tossing about in their boats in the heavy sea. The submarine was still in the neighbourhood, for as we circled round, while the other destroyers carried on their work of rescue, we suddenly saw a torpedo coming towards us. It was travelling on the surface, more or less, its blunt copper head and striker clearly visible in the trough of the seas.

I did not wait, but ordered the helm to be put hard over to port, and dashed at the starboard engine-room telegraphs and put it to " Full astern." The ship swung round on her heel, and the torpedo passed ahead and travelled on towards the horizon.

During another " Beef Trip " one of the merchant-vessels was set on fire, and a destroyer, running alongside at night in a heavy sea, rescued the crew before the vessel sank. And there were collisions fairly frequently. One pitch dark night a T.B.D. came into contact at high speed with one of a convoy steaming in the opposite direction. What happened to the merchantman I do not know ; but the destroyer limped back into Harwich with one side of her bows completely torn out and the huge gash stuffed with hammocks to keep out the water.

On Saturday, August 12th, 1916, the destroyers *Lance*, *Laverock*, *Lassoo*, and some others left Harwich to escort a few merchant-men to Holland. The latter had not formed up in close order at their rendezvous, the consequence being that at dawn on the 13th they were considerably scattered. The *Lassoo* – Lieutenant-Commander Vernon S. Butler – was cruising across the front of the convoy at 25 knots as a protection against submarines, and was in the act of turning, when, at 5.30 a.m., an explosion occurred abreast of the after torpedo-tubes. The commanding officer, who was in the chart house underneath the bridge examining the chart, found himself shot backwards on to the settee. Recovering himself, he reached the bridge in a few seconds, to find the coxswain just regaining the wheel, and the officer of the watch still on his back with most of the breath knocked out of him by a heavy wooden range-dial which had struck him in the stomach.

A column of water about eighty feet high shot into the air in the spot where the explosion had taken place. The shock was so violent that an able seaman on the opposite side of the ship was lifted off his feet, and was so surprised and jarred that he did not see the column of water at all.

The *Lassoo* had struck a mine. Her back was broken, and by the time she had come to a standstill the two halves of the ship were separated and it was necessary to take a boat from one portion to the other, the stern portion of the ship being under water.

A stoker attending the dynamos in the compartment adjacent to the explosion was killed instantaneously, as were three officers sleeping in the cabin flat aft. The fourth officer down there had a miraculous escape, managing to get his head out through the great gash in the deck overhead, and being hauled through it to safety by two men who happened to be on deck at the time. Beyond being badly bruised and " full of oil fuel," he was unhurt.

Summoned by wireless, the other destroyers were soon on the scene. As it was thought that the *Lassoo* had been hit by a torpedo from a submarine they all got out their explosive sweeps. The *Laverock's* presently exploded, and it was hoped that the U-boat had been bagged. But no wreckage came to the surface. The sweep must have detonated against some obstruction on the bottom, so the *Lance* stood by the *Lassoo* and sent the other two destroyers on ahead to protect the convoy.

The boats were lowered from both the *Lance* and *Lassoo* and the ship's company of the latter were ferried across with as many of their belongings as they could collect. The *Lassoo* seemed to be doomed ; but there was still a slight chance that she might be towed into safety, as the weather was calm. The captain and about a dozen men remained behind to make the necessary preparations.

" I was amused to see our Maltese wardroom steward," the *Lassoo's* commanding officer writes. "With every single article he possessed intact, he got down into the whaler, his face one broad grin, and saying, ' No more dese 'blotty destroyers for me! ' – a dictum he stuck to, as I couldn't get him to come with me again to another one."

The *Lassoo* was gradually sinking deeper in the water amidships as one bulkhead after another collapsed under the pressure of water. The captain, Lieutenant-Commander, now Captain

Vernon Butler, went down into the foremost boiler-room with an engine-room artificer in the pitch darkness to see if it was possible to shore up the after bulkhead. But it was too close to the back of the boiler for anything to be done. "This was a most unpleasant business, and we were jolly glad to get on deck again, especially as we found that the bulkhead we had been looking at was by then the next one due to go!"

Preparations had just been completed for taking the remains of the ship in tow when the after bulkhead of this boiler-room collapsed. The sudden inrush of water finished the ship. She suddenly fell over on her beam ends to starboard, and the signalman, who was on the roof of the bridge signalling to the *Lance*, shot with a splash into the sea. He was wearing two life-belts, and, protesting to all and sundry that he could not swim, did a record ten yards to the whaler, whose occupants, greatly amused, cheered him on.

The men still on board were released from further duty, and dived overboard from the forecastle, being picked up by the boats. But the engine-room artificer, who had been down with the captain in the boiler-room, had unfortunately got oil on his boots. In trying to climb over the high side of the ship he slipped backwards, became entangled in the berthing rails, and went down with her.

"I finally found myself walking out along the foremost funnel, which was then horizontal," Captain Butler's account runs. "The forepart of the ship then started to sink, taking me with it by suction. However, after coming up and swimming aft as hard as I could to clear the rigging, the ship broke in two, and the two parts sank one after the other. I was just in a nice position to go down with the stern portion, when a large coir fender shot up right in front of me. I was able to support myself on this until picked up by a boat, which took me to the *Lance*. In her we went back to Harwich.

"The weather was fine, the sea calm, and the water warm. No other mines were found in the area, and I understand that the one which bagged us was a stray specimen released by a German minelaying submarine on her way back home. In spite of her terrible damage, the ship took thirty-five minutes to sink, which speaks volumes for the firm that built her – John Brown's, Clydebank. I had taken her over there as a brand-new ship in October 1915."

It was on the night of December 23rd, 1917, however, that the

Harwich Force suffered one of its severest blows. I had left Harwich by this time, and know only of what occurred through hearsay and what has already been written.

The Germans had laid an extensive minefield off the Dutch coast, and four destroyers, accompanying a convoy, the *Surprise*, *Torrent*, *Tornado*, and *Radiant*, ran into it.

One of these vessels struck a mine, and a second went to help her, only to be blown up herself. A similar fate met the third ship while she was trying to rescue the crews of the other two. The *Surprise*, *Torrent*, and *Tornado* had gone. Only the *Radiant* was left. Her captain, Commander Geoffrey F. S. Nash, knew what had happened; but, undeterred by the horrible danger, steamed his ship to the spot where the survivors were struggling in the icy water, lowered his boats and was the means of saving many lives. Several of the *Radiant's* officers and men jumped overboard to save drowning men.

Barely a quarter of the crews of the three ships survived. But not one of them would have been saved if it had not been for the coolness and gallantry of the *Radiant's* captain. How his ship ever got clear without coming to grief is a mystery. When the chart of the German minefields was delivered up after the Armistice, it was discovered that over 400 " eggs " had been deposited in this particular locality.

So from time to time, during more than four years of war, many good men served their last commissions in that stretch of water which lies between England and the Netherlands – the old " Narrow Seas " of Lord Howard of Effingham. They were our friends and our flotilla-mates, men whom we regarded almost as brothers.

Their sepulchre is the grey, wind-lashed water; their tombstones, a myriad foaming whitecaps. Their epitaphs are written across the sky in the trails of smoke from passing shipping.

CHAPTER IX

RUNNING THE GAUNTLET

I

I AM never likely to forget Easter Monday, April 24th, 1916. The depredations of enemy submarines in the English Channel and the southern portion of the North Sea were becoming a menace. The barrages of mines and mine-nets between Dover and the French coast had done little to prevent U-boats from proceeding down-Channel and doing their worst. Many of the marauders, minelayers among them, hailed from Zeebrugge, the Germans having a large submarine base about ten miles up the canal at Bruges.

It had been decided to enclose the whole of the Flanders coast, from Dunkerque to the Scheldt, in a sort of ring fence about forty miles long. It was to be composed of double lines of mines backed up by mine-nets, the lines being laid parallel to the shore at a distance of between twelve and fifteen miles. At either end they would curve inwards towards the land.

The many thousands of mines would take some weeks to lay, the minelayers from Sheerness having to make several trips and being able only to deposit them at night. The placing of the nets would be undertaken by a whole fleet of little fishing-drifters, each vessel being able to lay 1,000 yards of net in one operation.

When this Belgian coast barrage was finally complete, it was intended that it should be patrolled by monitors and destroyers throughout the summer.

Dover, with the great amount of escort and patrol work that had ever to be done, was always short of destroyers. So, about two days before the Belgian coast operation was timed to start, a division of four M class destroyers from the Harwich Force were sent to assist. These four ships were the *Medea*, Commander George L. D. Gibbs; *Melpomene*, Lieutenant-Commander Hubert De Burgh; *Milne*, Lieutenant-Commander Hugh R. Troup; and *Murray*, Lieutenant-Commander Taprell Dorling.

On the afternoon of April 23rd, the minelayers *Princess Margaret*, *Orvieto*, *Biarritz* and *Paris* sailed from Sheerness under the escort of eight other destroyers from Harwich. The minelayers were all converted merchant-vessels, the first two being passenger liners. The little *Biarritz* and *Paris* will be familiar to many cross-Channel passengers.

They arrived off the Belgian coast soon after 4 a.m. on April 24th, and started to lay their mines, completing the job at 7.30 and then returning to Sheerness to embark more.

We, the party from Dunkerque – my own ship being the *Murray*, detached thither from Harwich – sailed before dawn.

We formed quite a respectable armada. In the van went six paddle minesweepers, ex-pleasure steamers which, in peace, took seasick trippers at so much a time between London, Southend, Margate, Clacton, Brighton, Worthing, and a dozen other watering-places. Being of very shallow draught, they were useful craft, and, with their sweeps out, were clearing a way for the rest of us to pass. We were, so to speak, treading on virgin ground.

Behind the sweepers came the four M class destroyers, steaming for us, at the dismal speed of 9 knots. Astern of us again, fading into the distance on the horizon, came the long lines of ordinary little fishing-drifters who were to lay the mine-nets. They were manned for the most part by their ordinary fishing crews and commanded by their own skippers, each division being led by an R.N.R. lieutenant, and the whole bunch by an " admiral " in the shape of a retired captain, R.N. They had homely names – *Girl Ethel, Clover Bank, Au Fait, Boy Charlie, Try Again,* and the like. Indeed, drifters' names sometimes led to mild amusement.

One of H.M. ships was once sent off on detached service from Dover, with a drifter to work with her. Bad weather coming on, the captain of the man-of-war decided to anchor for the night and to keep the drifters with him. So he made a signal by wireless to the admiral – a signal, unfortunately, that could be intercepted by every ship in the neighbourhood, and was rather loosely worded : " Threatening to blow," was flashed off into the ether. " Have arranged for *Girl Annie* to lie close to me during the night " ! The officer concerned was afterwards rather perplexed at the tender and facetious enquiries for his lady friend. [1]

To return, however, to the morning of April 24th, 1916.

The columns of drifters, which seemed to be there in scores, were flanked by more destroyers of the Dover Patrol, which acted the part of watch-dogs and shepherds. Astern of the whole procession came two strange-looking blister-sided monitors, the

---

[1] The story is told in Admiral Sir Reginald Bacon's *The Dover Patrol*. I am not responsible. – " Taffrail."

Prince Eugene and *General Wolfe.* Of very light draught, built especially for work on the Belgian coast, and provided with twin screws and engines really meant for steam tramps, they seemed to waddle rather than steam. Their full speed, if I remember rightly, was about 5½ knots. Keeping station on them in destroyers, as we sometimes had to, was rather difficult at 4¼. All the same, their 12-inch guns, filched from the old battleships of the *Majestic* class, gave us a tolerable feeling of security. The enemy guns on the Belgian coast, we had been told, could drop a 12-inch or 11-inch projectile on a bit of sea the size of a tennis lawn at the prodigious range of 38,000 yards, or nineteen sea miles. The day, from what we saw of it, was going to be exceptionally clear and fine. We were venturing considerably closer than nineteen miles. It was good to think we had something big to run for if anyone was really unkind.

It was flat calm, the sea shining like burnished silver in the reflected glory of the approaching sunrise. The water was furred here and there by gentle zephyrs passing along its surface, while long streaks of troubled water showed where the strong tide played and rippled along the edge of the hidden sandbanks.

We were off Nieuport, steaming slowly north-east between the East Dyck and Outer Ratel shoals. The low line of coast to starboard, perhaps eight miles away, showed black against a broad band of dull mauve stretching across the horizon. Above this the sky was shot with the prismatic colouring of the dawn.

The white beam of a searchlight at La Panne, to the west of Nieuport, swung questingly across the water. Nieuport itself, or what remained of it, was clearly marked by the occasional glitter of a star-shell. On our starboard bow, where lay Ostend, the rosy sky sparkled and flashed with a myriad pin-points of light, like dancing fireflies. It was a pretty sight, but we knew well enough what those flashes meant. They were anti-aircraft shell and other abominations fired at our aircraft returning from their night bombing expeditions on Zeebrugge and Ostend. The clear upper sky was spotted with smoke-bursts. They showed purple, brown, and blue. Nieuport was where the opposing lines came down to the sea. The guns had been silent as we left our anchorage. Now, with the rapid approach of daylight, they seemed to be waking up. Their thunder came rolling seaward in an ever-increasing volume.

The light grew as we advanced. The low mist over the land was dissipated as the sun rose. Soon we saw the buildings and spires of Ostend silhouetted against the sky, then Blankenberghe, then

Zeebrugge. Five observation balloons rose and hung motionless over the hostile coast. It was uncanny to feel that beneath every one of those inflated sausages was an astute German gentleman with a pair of high-powered glasses watching our every movement, to know that he was in telephonic communication with the batteries below. We were twelve or thirteen miles away from where they floated ; though even at that range the sea must be spread out before them like a map. We were within easy range of the heavier guns ; but they did not open fire. Perhaps we were not worthy of their attention.

The first covey of drifters reached the mark-buoy which showed them where to lay their nets, swung out of the line, and began operations.

Pair after pair followed, while we steamed slowly up and down, to and fro, guarding our smaller sisters against submarine or a possible destroyer attack from Zeebrugge.

The smell of frying kippers rose to the bridge from the galley below, and presently my steward arrived on the bridge to tell me that my breakfast was ready in the chart house. I was hungry. The coffee smelt good. But before I had finished my third piece of toast there came the thump of an explosion from outside. I abandoned the meal ; scrambled on to the bridge.

It was merely a few enemy seaplanes worrying the drifters. They were a full 10,000 feet up. Our 2-pounder pom-poms opened fire, with their ugly snouts cocked up to the sky. I doubt very much if their tiny shell burst anywhere near their target, for the seaplanes circled overhead quite unconcerned, dropped their bombs in among the drifters, and retired shorewards. There were no casualties, though time and time again I could have betted that some ship had been hit.

Throughout the little bombardment the drifter crews worked on without appearing to mind it. The skippers merely stuck their red faces out of their wheel-house windows, glanced overhead, and blasphemed a little. I do not know what they blasphemed ; but, looking through glasses, I could see their expressions, and watched their lips moving. Something pungent was being said.

By the middle of the morning the drifters, working in pairs, were spread over twenty miles of sea and within twelve miles of the enemy coast. There were some submarines in the vicinity, that we knew. Indeed, we sighted the conning-tower of one well inside the line of explosive mine-nets, and spent some time in hunting him, though without effect. On the whole, however, the forenoon was rather dull than otherwise. Perhaps we had expected too much. All the same, we were within easy range of the German guns, and not one of them opened fire until, at about 12.40 p.m., the Tirpitz battery near Ostend suddenly straddled the *General Wolfe* with four 11-inch salvos at a range of 32,000 yards.

The monitor, at her full speed of about 5½ knots, tried to scuttle out of range. The salvos followed her, and it was a wonderful sight to see the tall plumes of spray, four at a time, darting out of the water all round her. She was not hit.

I believe there was a certain amount of liveliness in other parts of the line. At about noon a submarine fouled the nets of the *Arndilly Castle* and was afterwards harried with depth-charges, though I believe she made her escape. At 2 p.m., too, there was a heavy explosion in a British minefield just outside Dutch territorial waters, which we fervently hoped meant the destruction of another.

Perhaps the most exciting incident, however, was when the skipper of the little *Gleaner of the Sea* sighted a periscope quite close to his bow. The submarine had fouled the drifter's wire cable and was clearly visible. Rushing forward with a lance bomb – a small bomb at the end of a short wooden staff like a large broomstick – Skipper Hurren hurled it on to the foredeck of the visitor, where it exploded. The U-boat slid bows first down the wire, which parted. Oil and air bubbles came to the surface, more bombs were dropped, and the position marked with a buoy. Later in the afternoon, as oil was still coming to the surface, a destroyer passed over the spot and fired her explosive sweep. That effectually finished the business. It was a certain " kill." She was U.B. 13 – obviously an unlucky number.

2

Our day had started at about 2.30 a.m. We were to be out all night, the whole of which I must spend on the bridge. So at about 2 p.m., as there was nothing particular going on, I retired to the chart house for a nap, leaving the officer of the watch in charge.

At about a quarter to three I was suddenly awakened by a messenger pulling at my shoulder, the ringing of the alarm gongs, and the rattle of the engine-room telegraphs as the ship increased speed.

" It's enemy destroyers, sir ! " said the man, his voice very excited.

It was.   Arriving on the bridge with a rush, I could see, about 9,000 yards away towards the shore, the slim shapes of three grey vessels steaming in our direction.   They were travelling at full speed, throwing up the water on either side of their sharp stems in white, plume-like bow-waves.   They were evidently about to attack our drifters at work on their nets about a mile shore-ward of where we were patrolling.

The *Medea, Murray*, and *Melpomene* were in company in the order named, the *Milne* having been detached to hunt for a sub-marine.   Our men were at action stations and the guns ready. We were working up to full speed with the stokehold fans roaring, and followed the *Medea* as she swung round and made for the nearest gap in the line of mine-nets.   The waves at our sterns mounted higher and higher as we gradually increased to 30 knots. It was wonderful to feel the old ship really moving at last.   Ash-ton,[1] the engineer-lieutenant-commander, was driving her all he knew.

The enemy, seeing our approach, altered course until they were steering about west-south-west, parallel with the coast. The range dropped rapidly to 8,000 yards – to 7,500.   Then I suddenly saw the orange flashes rippling down their sides.   It was curious to realise that we were being fired at, that even now a covey of hostile shell were driving through the air towards us. I felt not exactly nervous : but intensely excited, anxious to close the range.

Their first salvos fell a good 600 yards short.   Their second splashed into the sea all round us, projectiles seeming to whir and to whine in all directions.   We were not hit, but the shooting was too close to be pleasant.

Steaming at full speed through the gap in the nets and past a drifter reeling drunkenly in our wash, we turned on to a slightly converging course to the enemy at a range of about 6,500 yards. It seemed absurdly long, the targets very small, impossible for our guns to hit.

The *Medea's* three 4-inch flamed out as she straightened out on her course.   We steamed through the brown haze of her cordite smoke with the sweetish smell of it in our nostrils.

---

[1] Now Engineer-Captain James Ashton, D.S.O. Known as " Jaggers " to his real intimates.

" Shall we commence, sir ? " asked the sub, the gun control officer.

Intent on conning the ship, I nodded over my shoulder. There was a crash, a sheet of flame, and the hot stench of burning cordite as our guns opened fire – and went on firing.

My recollections of what happened during the next thirty-five minutes or so are rather hazy. I was far too busy conning the ship and watching the next ahead to take much notice of details. But in between the reports of our own and our neighbours' guns one heard the WHEE – W – WHEE – W of passing shell, and a peculiar purring sound as they fell short and ricochetted. The sea seemed to be vomiting spray fountains, almost as if some giant was flinging handful after handful of huge pebbles into a pond. It seemed surprising that we were not hit.

Occasionally, glancing momentarily towards the enemy, soon at a range of about 5,000 yards, I noticed shell splashes all round them – comforting, very comforting. We were using every ounce of steam we had to close in to decisive range. The Germans, however, were steaming as fast, or faster, zigzagging to avoid being hit, gradually edging away towards the land.

There was one amusing incident. We had an officer's steward in the wardroom, one of the long-haired fraternity whom, and probably quite unjustly, we suspected of having joined the Navy to avoid the trenches in Flanders. (Whether or not a destroyer in the North Sea was preferable to the trenches I don't pretend to know.) Anyhow, the steward's station in action in the *Murray* was on the after part of the bridge, where he was required to manipulate some sort of a fire-control instrument.

When the enemy fire was at its hottest, I noticed he kept his head well down. Then, in a partial lull in the action, he suddenly bobbed his head over the bridge screens with the remark, " Have we sunk 'em yet ? "

We hadn't. As he spoke, a salvo plopped close alongside, and down went his head again.

That man was like the ostrich hiding his head in the sand. I don't think he realised that only one-eighth of an inch of painted canvas was between him and the enemy.

We saw in the after part of the second ship in the enemy line a dull reddish glow, a cloud of black smoke, and a rush of white steam. One of our shell had hit and burst. Her speed dropped. Her friends closed in and started to circle round her.

We had been in action for nearly forty minutes, and by this

time were well inside the line of our drifters. Indeed, when we afterwards worked it out on the chart, we discovered we had reached a position within about 10,000 yards of the shore. I recollect that the sun was behind us, so that every detail of the low, sandy coast was visible to the naked eye. Looking through glasses, one could even count the windows in the buildings on the sea-front at Blankenberghe.

We had done what we set out to do, which was to prevent the enemy from interfering with our drifters. There was no sense in going closer. Our helms went over. We started to steam out to sea as fast as we could leg it. Then the fun began.

The eight miles of sand-dunes from Knocke through Zeebrugge to Blankenberghe contained, as we afterwards discovered, fourteen batteries mounting fifty-four guns – four 12-inch, eight 11-inch, eight 8-inch, twelve 6-inch, four 5-inch, and eighteen 4-inch. I will not pretend that every weapon of this varied and formidable collection of artillery opened fire upon us on that unforgettable afternoon. I will confine myself to saying that the moment we turned our sterns towards the land, at least five miles of the coast started to wink in and out with red gun-flashes. Within a few seconds we were receiving the full attention of a fair proportion of those fifty-four pieces of ordnance varying in size from 12-inch downwards. We could tell that from the size of the splashes – waterspouts.

People say that one cannot hear a shell until it has passed ; but it was certainly not true on this occasion. They roared at us like trains tearing through a station, whistled, whined, hummed. They splashed and burst on striking the water, the splinters driving in all directions. Geysers of all sizes and shapes leapt out of the sea all round us, their white plumes reaching higher than our masthead. I saw a great upheaval of water rear itself out of the sea within three feet of our stern – waited for a crash as it came in through the side to wreck the steering gear. But no – nothing happened ; the ship still steamed on.

A fountain leapt out of the water under our bows and cast its shadow across the bridge and forecastle. We actually steamed through the tumbling spray of it, suddenly to find ourselves wet and blinded and coughing with the bitter smell of high explosive – rather like the smell of an expended squib. The blue sea was pock-marked with large, circular areas where shell had pitched, with here and there patches of scummy-looking discoloration where others had burst. They looked exactly as if someone had been emptying large buckets of ashes. It was supremely, wildly exciting, but I cannot pretend that I liked it. Nobody liked it. If one of those great things hit us and exploded, we might crumple in two, burst open.

A thudding clang and a quiver warned us that we had been hit somewhere fairly close to the bridge. Personally, I waited for what seemed minutes for a gout of flame and a shower of splinters. They never came. Looking forward, I saw a ragged hole in the steel deck of the forecastle. The shell had driven its way through two decks and passed out through the ship's side about eight feet above the waterline without exploding.

If that fuze had been up to its work, the whole of our forecastle guns' crew must have been killed or wounded. As it was, we merely had a large, irregular-shaped hole above the waterline which, for the time being, was plugged with a hammock. Within a foot of me as I write is a jagged lump of steel mounted on a mahogany plinth, with a little brass plate bearing an inscription. It is a small piece of the riding bitt of the *Murray* removed by that 6-inch shell.

The whistling, howling, and screeching continued, and the spray fountains persisted.

" God damn those sons of bitches ! " I heard the coxswain mutter.

I thought that perhaps a splinter had found lodgment in Chief Petty Officer William Ewles's well-favoured anatomy. But it was nothing so serious. The top of our bridge was uncovered. The wind of a passing projectile had merely removed his cap. He looked at me with a wry smile, his face, streaked with perspiration, rather redder than usual.

" 'Strewth, sir ! " he said. " This is no place for a married man ! "

It wasn't.

Soon after the shore guns had opened we had started to dodge this way and that. At the same time, I had signalled to the engine-room to " Make smoke." In point of fact, in my agitation I had pressed the gong once too often or too little, which meant " Negative make smoke." Ashton, however, had his head up the engine-room hatch, and realised what was wanted. Before long the transparent haze at our funnel-tops started to darken. A few seconds later a cloud of inky blackness, so thick and so black that it seemed as if one could have walked upon it, was pouring out of the funnels and rolling away astern.

I think it saved us. Still dodging, we withdrew under the smoke screen. We had been in action with the enemy destroyers from 3 to 3.40. It was now 3.50.

The line of drifters working at their mine-nets were soon about three miles ahead of us. We steamed on towards them to find a gap in the nets through which we could pass in safety. The enemy fire had ceased, and our fourth destroyer, the *Milne*, which had been detached to search for a submarine and had not taken part in the action, was steaming towards us to rejoin.

Then it was that we noticed the *Melpomene*, which had been in action with us, gradually dropping astern. We put it down to a temporary loss of steam which could soon be rectified. It was not until she made a signal asking for help that we realised that she had been badly hit.

We were told afterwards that at about 3.40 she had been hit in the engine-room by a ricochetting 4.1-inch shell, one of the last fired by the enemy destroyers before we broke out of action. This projectile, entering the ship sideways, had happily not burst. If it had, the ship would probably have been lost. As it was, it made a hole in the ship's side below the waterline, through which the water poured in a torrent. The engine-room filled up and the men were finally forced to abandon it, but for twenty minutes the ship had still managed to steam with her turbines awash, and then entirely under water.

Her speed dropped fast. At last she came to a standstill. The sea was flat calm, and the *Milne*, seeing the *Melpomene's* predicament, at once went alongside the port side of her damaged sister with the idea of towing her into safety.

All the destroyers of the Harwich Force carried two shackles – twenty-five fathoms – of chain-cable aft ready for shackling on to the end of a towing-wire to assist a damaged consort. On this occasion, however, through no fault of her captain's, the *Milne* had bad luck. A loop of the cable was dropped by accident over her port propeller while it was being shackled on to the *Melpomene's* wire. The revolving screw caught up the loop and tangled it round the propeller shaft and " A " bracket until it was tied in a tight knot and the propeller came to a standstill. One of her screws was thus out of action until she went into dry-dock.

The *Medea*, Commander G. L. D. Gibbs, signalling to us to go ahead to find a way out through the mine-nets, thereupon went alongside the starboard side of the *Melpomene* to tow her clear, the three ships thus forming a sandwich with the *Melpomene* in the middle.

For twenty-five minutes or so they steamed thus, while the *Murray* went ahead of them to find the gap. But the enemy destroyers had seen what had happened, for at 4.30, looking astern, we sighted their white bow-waves again as they steamed towards us at full speed.

From that moment all sense of time seemed to vanish. I recollect signalling to the *Medea* to tell her the Germans were approaching, and the *Medea* replying, " Please show us the gap in the nets." I went ahead, hailed a drifter, found out where the gap was, and told the others.

The next thing was a series of gun-flashes from the enemy, then about 8,000 yards astern – and several pillars of silvery spray in the water all round the three destroyers tied in a bunch. They must have presented a tempting target.

More salvos fell, rather closer this time. Before long someone would be hit.

There was only one thing to do, and that quickly. The *Murray* must make a smoke-screen under the sterns of the other three. I did not feel very happy about it. It would be a matter of ourselves alone against three Germans until the only other undamaged ship, the *Medea,* came into action with us.

Our telegraphs rattled over to full speed, the helm went over and, signalling to the engine-room for smoke, we dashed past the three ships still lashed together. Our heavy wash caused them considerable inconvenience and carried away some of their wires ; but even as we passed more clusters of shell fell about them.

Straightening out under their sterns, and pouring a dense cloud of black smoke from our funnels, we opened fire on the approaching enemy at a range of about 6,000 yards. We saw the splashes of our falling shell somewhere near them, whereupon they again turned to a course more or less parallel to the coast and transferred their attention to us. It was distinctly unpleasant until the *Medea* cast off from the *Melpomene* and came into action ahead of us. Two against three was not quite such long odds.

To give the *Melpomene* and *Milne* a chance of getting well clear, it was necessary that we should drive the Germans well in towards the coast. This we proceeded to do, while a monitor farther out to sea, the *Prince Eugene*, cocked her 12-inch guns in the air and let them have a dose of shrapnel, until they were out of range.

Our second little battle lasted from about 4.40 to 4.55, at ranges of between 5,000 to 8,000 yards. I think the enemy were hit once or twice, though they never succeeded in hitting us. Firing very fast, they seemed to be missing by fathoms.

It was when we turned to come out again, shortly before 5 o'clock, that the shore batteries again let loose. We adopted our old tactics, zigzagging and making thick smoke, and, though plenty of large projectiles sailed down into the sea all round us, to raise their terrifying waterspouts, we were never actually hit.

The *Medea* was not so lucky. I saw a flash of reddish-golden flame and a puff of black smoke as a shell struck fair and square on her quarter-deck. Then another struck close alongside the funnels. I waited with my heart in my mouth, thinking that she must inevitably be damaged – that we should have to do a sort of " death or glory " exploit under a withering fire and tow her out of action.

To my heartfelt relief, she did not wobble in her course. She steamed on at full speed, and in another five or six minutes it was all over and we were safe.

The *Medea* had been hit three times. A shell, bursting in the wardroom where men were handing up ammunition to the after gun, killed two poor fellows and wounded several more. It had also caused damage to her stern, while rendering the wardroom uninhabitable. I went on board her when we arrived in harbour. It was a nasty sight, blood splashed over the deck and the white enamelled bulkhead, the ship's side perforated in places like a colander. How the detonation of that shell did not explode the magazine and wreck the ship I do not pretend to know.

As for ourselves, we were merely hit once by that single 6-inch shell during the first phase of the action. That we were not struck more often was due to sheer good luck, to Ashton's smoke screens, and to the fact that we zigzagged like a snipe. Fully five miles of coast had concentrated its guns upon us.

Out of the 360 rounds of ammunition that we carried for our three 4-inch guns, we fired no less than 230 during the fifty-five minutes odd we were in action with the German destroyers.

All four of us had been in the wars. The *Melpomene* had to be placed in dry-dock at Dunkerque to be patched up before going to an English dockyard ; the *Medea* went straight to Chatham to have her damage made good ; the *Milne* was put into the floating-dock at Dover to have several fathoms of chain-cable unwound from her port propeller ; while we, the *Murray*, had to endure a makeshift patch over the hole in our bows until they fitted a proper one the next time we did a refit in Chatham dockyard. I remember the temporary plaster leaked infernally every time we pitched into a head sea.

I lunched the day after our little fight with the captain of the monitor *Prince Eugene* at Dunkerque, who seemed anxious to hear of our experiences under heavy fire.

" Humph ! " he said. " I don't know how the devil you managed to escape. At times you'd disappear in splashes, and we all held our breath until you bobbed up again."

I could well believe it. Even Sir Reginald Bacon seemed rather surprised, though, I must confess, rather annoyed at two of us being *hors de combat* so soon after our arrival at Dover. Afterwards, he wrote in his book,[1] " Why the shore batteries ceased firing goodness only knows. They should have made a good bag of destroyers if they had gone on. The whole episode was a piece of fine, cool destroyer work, aid being given to one another under fire at the right moment, and a firm front shown at the same time to the enemy. This was our first experience of the German destroyers, and we learned, what afterwards we were to experience on the coast, that the greater elevation of their guns enabled them always to out-range our boats. Also, we found out that they mounted more 4-inch guns than did our boats."

Some time later Commander George L. D. Gibbs of the *Medea* received his D.S.O. for " the dash and gallantry with which he led his division " on this occasion, as did also Engineer-Lieutenant-Commander William H. Clarke of the *Melpomene* for the remarkable feat of steaming his ship out of action with the engine-room flooded. There is no doubt that she was saved from destruction by his efforts, and those of the petty-officers and men of the engine-room department.

I was ordered to submit names for honours, and our chief engine-room artificer and Chief Petty Officer Ewles, the coxswain, were both awarded Distinguished Service Medals for their good work, while one officer and two men were " mentioned in despatches."

Attached to a beam overhead on the fore mess-deck at the spot where our 6-inch shell penetrated we ever afterwards had a mahogany strip bearing an inscription in brass letters : " Lest we forget our Easter Monday, 1916." It served to remind the men that there was a war on – not that they needed any reminding –

and certainly gave the older hands something to talk about when youngsters joined the ship.

I do not wish to infer that our little engagement was anything at all remarkable, for we certainly did not achieve much beyond protecting the drifters. All the same, we were rather heavily fired upon, and of all our " windy corners " in the war, that of April 24th, 1916, was perhaps the " windiest."

It was a thrilling experience, and if anybody asks me if I had rather a cold feeling in my inside, the answer is in the – affirmative. How can I honestly deny it ?

CHAPTER X

DESTROYERS AT JUTLAND: AFTERNOON MAY 31st.

I

IN a book which deals primarily with the work of destroyers, it is unnecessary to describe in any great detail the events which led up to the Battle of Jutland – of how, during the late evening of May 30th, 1916, on the receipt of news from the Admiralty that there were signs of unusual activity among the ships of the German High Seas Fleet in the Jade River, off Wilhelmshaven, the three detachments of the Grand Fleet sailed from Scapa Flow, the Cromarty Firth, and the Firth of Forth. We must imagine that huge collection of vessels, the mightiest fleet the world has ever known, steaming eastward through the calm night for their rendezvous off the Skager Rack, in the eastern portion of the North Sea.

There were 16 battleships and 3 battle-cruisers from Scapa Flow; 8 battleships from Cromarty; 6 battle-cruisers and 4 battleships from Rosyth: in all, 37 great capital ships. With the several detachments went 8 cruisers; 26 light-cruisers; 6 flotilla-leaders, one, the *Abdiel* being fitted as a minelayer; 73 destroyers; and one seaplane-carrier, the converted cross-Channel passenger steamer *Engadine* – a grand total of 151 vessels of war under the command of Admiral Sir John Jellicoe, with his flag in the *Iron Duke*.

The Admiralty arrangements for intercepting and decoding enemy wireless signals were as near perfection as could be expected.

NOTE.—In writing the four chapters descriptive of the work of the destroyers at Jutland, I have derived information from many sources; but in particular from *The Battle of Jutland: Official Despatches*, published by His Majesty's Stationery Office; volume iii. of *Naval Operations*, by the late Sir Julian Corbett, published by Messrs. Longmans, Green & Co.; and *The Fighting at Jutland* (5th impression), edited by H. W. Fawcett, R.N. and the late G. W. W. Hooper, R.N., Messrs. Hutchinson & Co. For permission to make use of the first two volumes mentioned I am greatly indebted to the Controller, H. M. Stationery Office, as I am to Lieutenant-Commander H. W. Fawcett and the publishers for their readiness to allow me to use *The Fighting at Jutland*. Where quotations have been made from these sources, I have acknowledged them as follows for the sake of brevity:

The Battle of Jutland: Official Despatches as B. J. O. D.
Naval Operations, vol. iii., as N. O. iii.
The Fighting at Jutland as F. J.

It was realised that some important operation was in prospect in the German harbours. Yet precisely what this operation was nobody could guess. It might mean another battle-cruiser raid on the east coast of England, or perhaps some expedition towards the Flanders coast or Straits of Dover. On the other hand, as 16 enemy submarines were thought to be in the North

BATTLE AREA

Detachments of Grand Fleet leave Scapa, Moray Firth, and Rosyth at about 10 p.m., May 30th. High Seas Fleet leaves Jade River (Wilhelmshaven) at 2.30 a.m., May 31st.

Sea, the unusual activity might point to a sortie on the part of the High Seas Fleet. Yet the same sort of thing had happened before, and nobody in Whitehall expected a fleet action within twenty-four hours. The British movements were more precautionary than hopeful.

Moreover, of the many thousands of officers and men in the three detachments of the Grand Fleet which sailed after dark on May 30th, not one had any inkling of what the morrow was to bring. As wrote the late Sir Julian Corbett, there was " nothing to encourage them to believe that what had set them in motion was anything more than one of the many alarms which had so often ended in disappointment."[1]

The meeting, when it came, was unexpected. It was not until 4.33 p.m. on May 31st, after the British and German battle-cruisers and destroyers had already been in action for three-quarters of an hour, that it became definitely known to Sir John Jellicoe and Sir David Beatty that the battleships of the High Seas Fleet were actually at sea and steaming north towards the scene of battle. This surprising piece of news emanated from Commodore W. E. Goodenough, in the light-cruiser *Southampton*,

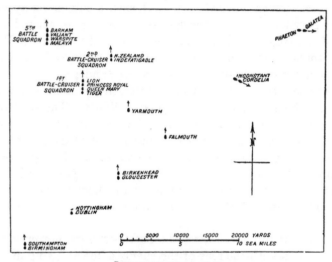

SITUATION AT 2.20 P.M.
Galatea nineteen miles from *Lion*, having just sighted steamer and two enemy T.B.D.s about eleven miles to eastward.

who had pushed on to see the long line of pale-grey enemy hulls stretching far away to the southern horizon.

The *Galatea*, the light-cruiser on the eastern wing of Sir David Beatty's look-out line, nineteen miles away from the *Lion*, first sighted and reported enemy destroyers and light-cruisers to the eastward between 2.20 and 2.30 p.m. At that time Sir David's force had already turned to join Sir John Jellicoe sixty-five miles away to the north. Commodore E. S. Alexander-Sinclair,[2] in the *Galatea*, however, noticing a merchantman stopped and blowing off steam about twelve miles to the east, stood over to examine

[1] *N. O.* iii., p. 325
[2] Now Admiral Sir Edwyn Alexander-Sinclair, G.C.B., M.V.O.

her before turning, presently to see two German destroyers, and then enemy light-cruisers, with whom she and the *Phaeton* were soon in action. Steaming fast to the north-east, the *Galatea* sighted heavy smoke still farther to the eastward – the smoke of the five German battle-cruisers commanded by Vice-Admiral Hipper.

Immediately on receiving the *Galatea's* first signals, the British battle-cruiser force swung round to the southward and then to the east to cut off the enemy from the Heligoland Bight. At 3.33, the *Lützow* and her four consorts were in sight from the *Lion's* bridge. The first shots were fired fifteen minutes later, and furious engagement ensued, with both sides steaming on approximately parallel courses to the southward until 4.40, when, having sighted the High Seas Fleet coming up from the south, Sir David swung round to lead the enemy towards his commander-in-chief.

But many things happened between 3.48 and 4.40.

When the action started, it was a calm, sunny afternoon, with a gentle south-easterly breeze and good visibility. The six British battle-cruisers were more or less in line ahead with the enemy abaft the port beam at a range of about 16,000 yards, or eight sea miles – no very great distance for naval guns. The 5th Battle Squadron – *Barham, Valiant, Malaya, Warspite* – under the command of Rear-Admiral Hugh Evan-Thomas, was roughly eight miles astern of the *Lion* when the run to the south started.

Steaming at full speed after the battle-cruisers, however, they were in action with the rear of the enemy's line at 3.56 p.m., at a range of 19,000 yards. Their shooting was very accurate, though the German line was so obscured by haze and smoke that there was little more to aim at but the flashes of the hostile guns.

Looking to the eastward, indeed – that is, towards the enemy – the light was deceptive and difficult. Both from the *Lion* and the *Barham*, the enemy hulls were difficult to make out against a bank of heavy grey mist upon the horizon. Looking from the German squadron towards the British, on the other hand, the shapes of the *Lion* and her consorts stood out like cardboard silhouettes against the light of the westering sun and a clear, bright horizon. These conditions had their inevitable effects on the shooting of both sides.

As regards the disposition and allocation of destroyers, the light-cruiser *Fearless*, Captain (D)'s ship, and nine destroyers[1]

---

[1] *Acheron, Ariel, Attack, Hydra, Badger, Goshawk, Defender, Lizard, Lapwing.*

of the 1st Flotilla were attached to the 5th Battle Squadron. Originally screening the 2nd Battle-Cruiser Squadron – *New Zealand* and *Indefatigable* – which formed the rear of the battle-cruiser line during the engagement, were six destroyers of the 9th and 10th[1] Flotillas from Harwich. When the enemy was sighted, these six were ordered to take station five miles ahead. The four L class, though steaming their fastest – about 28 knots – were only able to creep up on the battle-cruisers, who were travelling at 25 knots. " I had therefore to remain on the engaged side of the Battle-Cruiser Squadron or drop astern," Commander M. L. Goldsmith, their senior officer in the *Lydiard*, wrote in his report. " I chose to remain where I was rather than lose all chance of making a torpedo attack."

The two M class, the *Moorsom* and *Morris*, being newer and speedier craft, managed to get ahead and to join up with the attacking flotilla. Commander Goldsmith, however, to his intense disappointment, did not achieve his ambition. Steaming up the engaged side of the battle-cruisers, he was eventually ordered by the *Lion* to keep clear, and took station astern.

The light-cruiser *Champion* the Captain (D)'s ship, with eight destroyers[2] of the 13th Flotilla, two of the 10th Flotilla,[3] together with the *Moorsom* and *Morris*, which soon joined them, steamed at their utmost speed to take station ahead of the *Lion*.

For a few breathless minutes they were suffered to remain passive spectators of the terrific duel that was taking place a short distance away, and an unforgettable scene it was.

The enemy were practically out of sight in the haze on the port quarter at a distance of about eight miles, and little could be seen of them except their trailing smoke and the wicked red flashes of their guns flickering in and out over the horizon.

But immediately astern, within a mile or less of some of the rear destroyers, came the long line of British battle-cruisers, headed by the *Lion*. Their huge grey hulls were being driven through the calm sea at 25 knots, the white bow-waves piled up at their stems, their wakes heaped up astern, and the smoke pouring densely from their funnels. They were firing fast, the billowing clouds of golden-brown cordite smoke alternating rapidly with sheets of orange flame as their great weapons gave tongue. Pillars and

---

[1] *Lydiard, Liberty, Landrail, Laurel* (9th Flotilla) ; *Moorsom, Morris* (10th Flotilla), Harwich Force.

[2] *Nestor, Nomad, Narbrough, Obdurate, Petard, Pelican, Nerissa, Nicator*, of the 13th Flotilla.

[3] *Turbulent* and *Termagant*, of the 10th Flotilla, Harwich Force.

waterspouts of dazzling white spray from falling enemy shell spouted out of the water all round them – leaped higher than their mastheads, sometimes blotted them completely out from view. The deep rumble of heavy gunfire boomed out across the calm water in a continuous roar, a resonant clamour which caused the air to vibrate and seemed literally to rend the sky. It was deafening, shattering to the senses.

Those great grey ships looked invincible, invulnerable – yet they were not.

In the turmoil of smoke and shell-splashes it was impossible

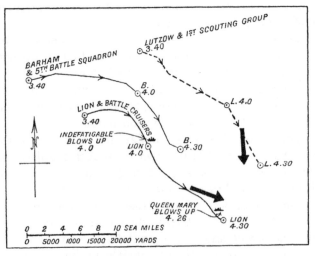

SITUATION BETWEEN 3.40 AND 4.30 P.M.
Black arrow-heads show general direction of British and
German flotillas moving out to attack.

really to see how they were faring. But the *Lion* was being struck repeatedly, and shortly before 4 o'clock she was hit in the centre 13.5-inch gun turret by a shell which killed practically every man inside it, ignited the cordite charges, and sent a shaft of flame and smoke higher than her funnels. She continued to blaze, and but for the gallantry of her badly wounded Major of Marines, who gave the order to close the magazine doors, the ship would have blown up.

Other vessels were also being struck. Almost immediately after the *Lion* incident, the *Indefatigable*, at the rear of the line, was hit by two enemy salvos in rapid succession. The shell were seen to burst in little puffs of red flame and smoke. There came a brief pause, and then the unfortunate ship blew upwards in a sheet of fire and clouds of dense, dark smoke, through which masses of heavy débris could be seen whirling skywards. When the pall of smoke had drifted aside, all traces of the *Indefatigable* had completely disappeared.

The destroyers' turn was soon to come.

At 3.55 the *Lion* wirelessed to the *Champion*, ahead of her : " Opportunity appears favourable for attacking," following it a minute later, with the flag signal : " Proceed at your utmost speed."

At 4.9 came another wireless signal : " Attack the enemy with torpedoes." A few minutes later the *Champion* was repeating it by flags to her flotilla.

They did not tarry. It was the opportunity for which they had been waiting for twenty-two months, the purpose for which they existed and had been trained for years.

At 4.15 the port division, led by Commander the Hon. Barry Bingham[1] in the *Nestor*, swerved out of the line at full speed to attack. Other divisions followed, until, steaming at speeds of nearly 34 knots, as fast as they could be driven, a dozen destroyers were tearing for the area of " no man's sea " between the opposing squadrons.

It was a chance vouchsafed to few destroyer officers, and then only once in a lifetime. They had started on the most exciting race in the world, a race towards the enemy, a race which had as its prizes honour and glory – possibly death.

2

It is a little difficult to follow the fighting that followed. Hipper's battle-cruisers were on the port quarter of the British flotilla at a distance of about $8\frac{1}{2}$ miles. Almost as soon as our destroyers moved out to attack, fifteen enemy destroyers, accompanied by a light-cruiser, the *Regensburg*, emerged from the head of the German battle-cruisers to deliver an attack upon our battle-cruisers. From the German commander-in-chief's despatch we now know that this was launched to relieve the pressure on the *Lützow*, *Derfflinger*, *Seydlitz*, *Moltke*, and *Von der Tann*, which were suffering severely from the accurate fire of the 5th Battle Squadron.

---

[1] Now Captain the Hon. Barry Bingham, V.C., O.B.E.

The British destroyers steered at full speed for a position on the enemy's bow whence to fire their torpedoes, their course gradually converging on that of the German flotilla. At 4.40 the *Nestor*, Commander Bingham, followed by the *Nicator*,[1] Lieutenant Jack Mocatta,[2] and the *Nomad*, Lieutenant-Commander Paul Whitfield,[3] swung round to north to fire their torpedoes, and also to beat off the enemy's destroyer attack. These three ships were followed at intervals by the *Petard*, Lieutenant-Commander E. C. O. Thomson,[4] and the *Turbulent*, Lieutenant-Commander Dudley Stuart. Also engaged during the period that followed were the *Obdurate*, Lieutenant-Commander C. H. Hulton-Sams[5]; *Nerissa*, Lieutenant-Commander M. G. B. Legge[6]; *Termagant*, Lieutenant-Commander C. P. Blake[7]; *Moorsom*, Commander J. C. Hodgson[8]; and *Morris*, Lieutenant-Commander E. S. Graham.[9] Not all these vessels had the chance of firing torpedoes at the enemy's heavy ships, though most of them took part in the action with the hostile destroyers.

Immediately the *Nestor*, *Nicator*, and *Nomad* turned in to attack the enemy's battle-cruisers, the German flotilla turned to an appropriately parallel course. Almost at once the destroyer fight started at a range of about 9,000 yards. Both sides fired rapidly as the distance decreased, and to onlookers the opposing flotillas were only seen as lean black shapes pouring smoke from their funnels as, with their guns blazing, they tore at full speed through a welter of shell-splashes.

At about 4.45 the *Nomad* was hit in the engine-room, the explosion killing or wounding many men and destroying steam-pipes. Steam poured into the engine-room. The main and auxiliary engines came to a standstill, and the ship stopped automatically. But in spite of her casualties and injuries she still continued to fire until her guns would no longer bear. Two torpedoes, running deep, passed under the ship as she lay helpless. Paul Whitfield, her commanding officer, gave orders to prepare the ship for being towed ; but, realising very soon that she was sinking slowly by the stern, set about the destruction of his confidential books, charts, and papers, lest they should fall into the hands of the enemy. It

---

[1] The *Nomad* should really have been astern of the *Nestor* ; but the former had been unable to keep up at the start. *Nicator* had gone ahead.

[2] Now Commander Jack Mocatta, D.S.O.

[3] Now Captain Paul Whitfield, D.S.O., O.B.E.

[4] Now Captain, and D.S.O.   [5] Now Captain.   [6] Now Captain, and D.S.O.

[7] Now Commander, and D.S.O.   [8] Now Captain, and D.S.O.

[9] Now Commander.

was while he was going aft to dispose of the documents in his cabin that he saw the van of the High Seas Fleet looming up over the horizon on the starboard quarter – battleships, enemy battleships !

His ship was gradually heeling over ; but enemy battleships were the legitimate targets for a destroyer's torpedoes. His first thought was whether or not those distant shapes would arrive on a possible bearing to enable him to fire before the list would prevent the torpedoes from leaving their tubes. They were actually fired, though with what result we do not know. This, his primary duty, done, Whitfield went down to his cabin to dispose of his confidential books. There, for the time being, we must leave him.

Meanwhile, a close-range destroyer action between the opposing battle-cruiser lines was still raging to the northward. Closing in at full speed, the *Nestor* and *Nicator*, followed at an interval by the *Petard* and *Turbulent*, and supported by the other destroyers already mentioned, engaged the enemy flotilla at a distance which eventually dropped to about 600 yards – almost point-blank range. The Germans were outgunned, and in a very few minutes their attack was beaten off. Leaving two sinking ships behind them, and with several more hit and damaged, they made at full speed for the comparative safety at the head and tail of their battle-cruisers, closely pursued by our craft. The enemy had actually fired twelve torpedoes at the British battle-cruisers, though, thanks to our destroyers' onslaught they had been unable to approach within a range that gave much chance of hitting.

Two of their ships, V. 27 and V. 29, were left behind sinking on the scene of the action. The former had been hit by a shallow-running torpedo fired from the *Petard*. It took the German amidships, to explode in an upheaval of smoke and spray. A few minutes later, as the *Petard* dashed by at full speed, she gave her stopped and stricken enemy salvo after salvo of 4-inch shell to complete the work of destruction.

Events were happening fast. Reaching a favourable position, the *Nestor* and *Nicator* each fired two torpedoes at the enemy's battle-cruiser line at a range of about 5,000 yards, while continuing to engage the German destroyers. The torpedoes missed, for, seeing the tell-tale splashes as they left their tubes, the German admiral turned his ships away. The *Petard*, firing three torpedoes later at a range of about 7,000 yards, was luckier, for one of hers hit the *Seydlitz*, tore a hole thirteen feet by thirty-nine under her armoured belt, and put one heavy gun completely out of action. Like all German ships, however, the *Seydlitz* was stoutly built, and was still able to steam on.

Swinging round to the eastward, followed by the solitary *Nicator*, the *Nestor* found herself rapidly approaching the head of the enemy battle-cruiser line, all four ships of which were soon pouring in a withering fire from their secondary armaments. The sea vomited splashes and spray fountains ; but, pressing home his attack, Bingham fired his third torpedo at a range of about 3,500 yards. Throughout this period both the *Nestor* and *Nicator* were

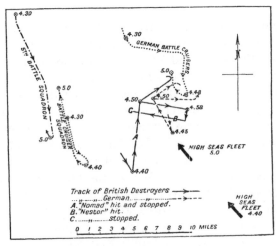

Situation Between 4.30 and 5.0 p.m.
Showing approximate track of *Nestor* and other destroyers during attack.

escaping destruction by feet and inches, for the shell were falling all round them. According to one of the *Nicator's* officers, that ship avoided being hit by altering course towards each salvo as it fell, thereby confusing the enemy's spotting corrections. " Throughout the whole action," says the same officer, " the captain [Mocatta] was leaning coolly against the front of the bridge smoking his pipe, and giving his orders to the helmsman." [1]

His work done, Bingham, still followed by the faithful *Nicator*, swung round through 180° and made off at full speed to the westward to rejoin the British battle-cruisers, which, at 4.40,

[1] *F. J.*, p. 53.

having sighted the approaching High Seas Fleet, had altered course to the northward.

Here there occurs a slight discrepancy between the official reports of the *Nestor* and *Nicator*. Mocatta states that during the run back both ships were subjected to a very heavy fire at a range of about 3,000 yards from the leading battleships of the High Seas Fleet. Bingham says nothing of the battle-fleet, but mentions a light cruiser, the *Regensburg*, which emerged from the head of the German battle-cruiser line and opened a tornado of fire.

The result, whoever inflicted it, was the same, for just before 5 o'clock the *Nestor* received direct hits which put two of her boilers completely out of action and shrouded the ship in a dense cloud of steam. She managed to stagger on for four miles at a gradually diminishing speed, until, at 5.30, she came to a complete standstill within a couple of miles of the sinking *Nomad*, her subdivisional mate.

The *Nicator*, which narrowly escaped colliding with the *Nestor* when she was hit, was ordered to go on and rejoin the *Champion*, which had been flying the destroyer's recall for some time. In spite of the deluge of fire through which she had passed, she had been hit by nothing worse than a few splinters.

On her way back from the final attack, the *Petard* came across the *Nestor* struggling to the westward. Easing down, Thomson closed to within hailing distance, and offered his damaged flotilla-mate a tow. " This," writes Bingham in his official report, " I was obliged to refuse, for I could not see my way to involving a second destroyer in a danger which probably only applied to one, for at the time we were still under fire and able to steam slowly. In the light of subsequent events, I am convinced that my decision was justified."[1]

The *Moorsom*, Commander J. C. Hodgson, had taken part in the destroyer action, but was unable to fire her torpedoes at the German battle-cruisers because of their alteration of course to the northward. Searching for a likely target, Hodgson saw the van of the High Seas Fleet, and, steaming in that direction, made two attacks on the leading enemy battleships. Coming under heavy fire, his ship was hit twice, and, though no immediate damage was done to her fighting efficiency, the after oil-tanks were badly holed. The fire-main was running at the time to keep the decks wet as a precaution against fire, and water poured through shell-holes into the oil fuel tanks, which happened to be in use at the

[1] *B. J. O. D.*, p. 347.

time. There was nobody in the compartment when this happened, and the water speedily found its way through the pipes into the sprayers of the furnaces. The ship's speed dropped rapidly. She was still under heavy fire, and might have stopped altogether, with disastrous results, had not the engineer officer – Engineer-Lieutenant-Commander Sidney G. Wheeler – switched over to another tank in the nick of time. As it was, the *Moorsom* had a narrow escape of destruction. As she had expended all her torpedoes and was short of oil fuel, she was ordered to return to her base soon after nightfall.

By 5.30 p.m. the *Nestor* and *Nomad* lay stopped and helpless within two miles of each other almost in the track of the advancing High Seas Fleet, the *Nomad* being slightly to the southward. The British and German battle-cruisers, still in hot action, had disappeared to the north, from which direction the sound of heavy gunfire still rumbled across the calm water. A heavy bank of mist and funnel-smoke lay stretched across the northern and north-eastern horizon. Not a friendly ship was in sight – no ships at all except the silver-grey battleships of the enemy fleet approaching remorselessly from the south.

We may imagine with what feelings those on board the two injured destroyers awaited their inevitable end.

Whitfield, I believe, was still in his cabin disposing of his confidential books when his crippled and sinking *Nomad* became the target for the secondary armaments of four German battleships at very short range. The ship was soon being badly hit by their rapid salvos, and her foremost magazine blew up. Whitfield himself was seriously wounded, but, seeing that the ship could not float much longer, ordered her to be abandoned. Her crew took to the water in what boats remained serviceable – Carley floats, lifebelts, and planks of timber. The enemy firing continued.

" I went round the ship and, ascertaining that her life was a matter of minutes, left her," Whitfield wrote in his report. " Firing was continued at her up to a range of 500 yards, and a salvo was fired at her after she sank, about a minute and a half after my leaving her."[1]

The ship went to the bottom with her ensign still flying. One officer and 7 men had been killed, and various others wounded. Four officers and 68 men were rescued by a German destroyer, and became prisoners of war.

Those on board the *Nestor* had watched the destruction of their

[1] *B.J.O.D.*, p. 351.

sister ship. Literally smothered with salvos, nothing could be seen of her except leaping columns of spray and the smoke of exploding shell. Their own turn was coming next. The problem was to keep the men occupied until the end, to prevent them from thinking, if that were possible.

While Bingham and his sub-lieutenant threw overboard their confidential books and charts, the first lieutenant, M. J. Bethell, and his men were providing water and biscuit for the boats, and lowering the motor-boat and whaler to the water's edge. The Carley floats were hoisted out and secured alongside, and the wounded lowered into the motor-boat.

The enemy battleships were approaching; but as yet had not opened fire. Time still remained on their hands, and to keep the ship's company occupied Bethell suggested that the cables should be ranged on the forecastle, ostensibly for use in the unlikely event of a tow being forthcoming; but really to keep the men busy until the last.

The High Seas Fleet came on, and then, from a distance of about five miles, the grey sides of the leading battleships flashed into scarlet flame. A cloud of dun-coloured cordite smoke drifted astern of them, and in a few more seconds, with a demoniacal shrieking and whining, projectiles started to drop into the sea all round the doomed *Nestor*. Waterspouts and fountains of spray leapt to the heavens; but in the midst of the turmoil she managed to fire her last torpedo.

Very soon, heavily hit, she began to settle by the stern and to heel over to starboard. The " centre of a whirlwind of shrieking shell," men were falling on deck. She was sinking fast. Bingham gave the order, " Abandon ship."

The boats and floats were soon filled in perfect order and discipline. Just before leaving the ship the commander turned to Bethell, his first lieutenant.

" Now where shall *we* go ? " Bingham asked.

" To heaven, I trust, sir ! " Bethell replied.

" His answer," Captain Bingham writes, " was only characteristic of that gallant spirit. . . . At that moment he turned aside to attend to a mortally wounded signalman, and was seen no more amidst a cloud of fumes from a bursting shell." [1]

The captain climbed into the whaler, where he found eight others waiting. For some time they remained alongside, hailing

[1] *Falklands, Jutland, and the Bight,* by Commander the Hon. Barry Bingham, V.C., O.B.E., p. 146. (Messrs. John Murray.)

the ship for any further survivors. Finally they pushed off, only to have the damaged boat sink under them before they had pulled more than a few strokes. Bingham managed to swim to the motor-boat, where he was pulled on board. The others were also able to save themselves.

The ship now lay with the water lapping over the upper deck, and her forecastle high in the air. She was still being subjected to a heavy fire. But the end came soon. In three minutes or less, with her ensign still flying, she reared her bows perpendicularly in the air, and slid stern first to the bottom. A mass of oil and floating débris alone remained to mark her final resting-place fathoms beneath.

The survivors cheered their ship as she disappeared, and then sang a verse of the National Anthem. Then some stout-hearted able seaman suggested " Tipperary," in which they all joined lustily.

The *Nestor's* survivors, in Captain Bingham's own words, were " sixty odd miles from the nearest shore, in an overladen, leaking, and broken-down motor-boat, with nothing in sight except the enemy's fleet vanishing in the distance. . . . The weather was still calm and fine, but the slightly freshening breeze increased my anxieties as to the length of time the motor-boat would remain afloat."

After about twenty minutes' suspense, however, a division of enemy destroyers was detached from the High Seas Fleet. Closing rapidly, they picked up the *Nestor's* and *Nomad's* survivors, those from the first-named finding themselves prisoners of war on board S.16. Of the *Nestor's* company, 2 officers and 4 men had been killed. Five officers and 75 men were made prisoners, several being wounded.

Sir David Beatty, in referring to the destroyer attacks of the afternoon, wrote in his official despatch : " The attack was carried out in the most gallant manner and with great determination. . . . These destroyer attacks were indicative of the spirit pervading His Majesty's Navy, and were worthy of its highest traditions. I propose to bring to your notice a recommendation of Commander Bingham for the Victoria Cross, and other officers for some recognition of their conspicuous gallantry."[1]

Of the commanding officers of destroyers in the 13th Flotilla, and the attached vessels of the 10th Flotilla, Bingham was awarded the supreme honour of the Victoria Cross. Whitfield of

[1] *B. J. O. D.*, p. 133.

the *Nomad*, Thomson of the *Petard*, Legge of the *Nerissa*, Mocatta of the *Nicator*, Hodgson of the *Moorsom*, Blake of the *Termagant*, Tovey of the *Onslow*, and Alison of the *Moresby* all received D.S.O.s for services at Jutland.

3

The *Onslow*, Lieutenant-Commander J. C. Tovey,[1] and *Moresby*, Lieutenant-Commander R. V. Alison,[1] both of the 13th Flotilla, have not hitherto been mentioned.

At 2.50 p.m. these two destroyers had been detached to screen the seaplane-carrier *Engadine*, which stopped and hoisted out her seaplane at 3 o'clock, after the enemy had been reported in sight by the *Galatea*. The machine returned and was hoisted in at 3.45, and five minutes later the *Onslow* and *Moresby* sighted Hipper's battle-cruisers being engaged by the British ships.

At 4.12, bursting with natural impatience to rejoin his flotilla and to get into action, Tovey signalled to the *Engadine*: " Can you dispense with my services? If so, I will join 5th Battle Squadron." The reply was, " Yes, certainly," and at 4.55 the *Onslow* and *Moresby* were steering south-south-east at 30 knots for the scene of action.

Sir David Beatty had turned northward at 4.40, and, sighting his squadron and Hipper's steering about north-north-east, the *Onslow* and *Moresby* stationed themselves three miles on the engaged bow of the *Lion*. Tovey soon discovered that he was opening out from the *Lion* and rapidly closing in on the enemy. He could see no light-cruisers or destroyers ahead of the German line, " so," as he says in his report, " deemed it a favourable opportunity to deliver an attack with torpedoes, and with this idea proceeded to close the enemy more."[2]

But, before getting into effective torpedo range, four light-cruisers appeared ahead of the hostile battle-cruisers. They at once opened a heavy and very accurate fire on both destroyers, which, smothered in falling salvos, were forced to turn away and to separate.

For the time being Tovey's gallant attempt was foiled, though he and the *Onslow* had more than their share of excitement within the next hour or two, all of which will be related in due course.

---

[1] Now Captains, and D.S.O.s.
[2] *B. J. O. D.*, p. 236.

Alison, in the *Moresby*, separating from the *Onslow* to avoid giving too good a target, steered to pass astern of the British battle-cruisers. At about 5 o'clock he saw an enemy battle-squadron to the southward, the van of the High Seas Fleet. This was a target very much to his choice. Swinging round, he proceeded at full speed to attack.

At 5.10 he fired a long-range torpedo at the third ship in the enemy line, coming under heavy fire as he did so at a range of about 8,000 yards. " The enemy shooting was very good," he observes in his report. " Had they fired double salvos, they would have hit. By observing attentively and using large helm, the ship was not straddled more than six times, and only one piece of H.E. was picked up. . . . The enemy bad station," he adds, " did not justify further expenditure " (of torpedoes) " in view of the night work expected to follow."[1]

It was a pity that so gallant an attempt ended in failure, for the *Moresby's* torpedo missed. But this ship, like the *Onslow*, had not yet played her full share in the Battle of Jutland.

The German destroyers, as already described, had fired twelve torpedoes without result. In the earlier stages of the action, before 5.30, British destroyers had fired twenty-two, or possibly twenty-six, the exact number being uncertain, because the *Turbulent*, which attacked with the *Nerissa*, was sunk in action during the night. Their targets had been the enemy battle-cruisers and battleships, and some of the attacks, as already described, were pushed home with the greatest gallantry and determination to within little more than a mile. Yet of the torpedoes fired, only two went home, and both were fired by the *Petard*. One, discharged during the destroyer mêlée, struck the German destroyer V.27, and the other, fired at about 4.50, the *Seydlitz*.

" Yet," as writes Sir Julian Corbett in the Official History, " small as was the result, the whole affair must ever stand as an exemplary piece of flotilla work in battle."[2]

We can agree. The enemy destroyer attack was completely foiled and broken up. Moreover, the dash and determination with which the British flotilla had pushed home its onslaught forced Hipper's battle-cruisers to turn away to avoid its torpedoes. This undoubtedly saved the British battle-cruisers from further severe punishment during the highly critical period after 4.40, when, having sighted the High Seas Fleet to the southward,

---

[1] *B. J. O. D.*, p. 238.
[2] *N. O.* iii., p. 342.

Sir David Beatty made his 16-point turn to the north. So far as actual losses went, the opposing flotillas had each lost two boats. Nevertheless, these early attacks inculcated in the minds of the Germans a healthy fear for the British destroyers, and something akin to a lack of faith in their own.

CHAPTER XI

DESTROYERS AT JUTLAND : LATE AFTERNOON AND EVENING, MAY 31ST.

I

SIGHTING the High Seas Fleet to the south, the British battle-cruisers, at about 4.40, swung northward 16 points – 180° – in succession to join the Grand Fleet by the shortest possible course.

They had suffered severely. The *Indefatigable*, as already mentioned, had been lost earlier in the action, but at 4.24 the *Queen Mary*, the third ship in the line, suffered the same fate. Fired upon by the *Derfflinger* and *Seydlitz* at ranges of between 16,000 and 14,500 yards, she was struck by a salvo abreast of one of her turrets. Onlookers in other ships saw the dull red flash, the flying splinters, and a cloud of oily smoke as the shell burst. Before another breath could be drawn, there came a shattering concussion, and a blaze like the outpouring of a volcano. The 28,500-ton ship seemed to collapse inwards, the masts and funnels falling together, the side of the ship being blown outwards, and the armoured roofs of the turrets being hurled 100 feet high ; then a dense cloud of dark cordite smoke which hid everything.

Wreckage was flung skywards, and as the *Tiger*, 400 yards astern, swerved aside and raced through the smoke at 22 knots, she received a heavy fall of débris on her decks. A few of the *Tiger's* officers saw the stern of the stricken vessel as they steamed by within a few yards ; but so thick was the pall that most of them were completely blinded.

The *New Zealand*, following astern of the *Tiger*, hauled out to starboard. The smoke had started to clear away, and, passing within fifty feet of the *Queen Mary's* remains, some of her people saw the after portion of the hull afloat, with the stern in the air and the propellers still revolving. Men were climbing up the after hatchway and up through the roof of the after turret, until the stern itself rolled over and disappeared with another explosion. The dense cloud of smoke rose 1,000 feet into the air like a pillar, and then spread laterally until it looked like some gigantic umbrella.

Out of the blackened, oil-strewn area in which the ship had disappeared, the destroyer *Laurel* rescued 2 officers and 4 men. Another man, Petty Officer E. Francis, captain of the *Queen Mary's* after turret, was rescued by the *Petard* and taken to the wardroom, where, being half blinded with oil fuel, he was attended to by the surgeon-probationer. Soon after midnight, in circumstances to be described later, the *Petard* was heavily in action, and a salvo of shell wrecked the after part of the ship and killed many officers and men. By some miracle, Francis escaped with his life.

One officer and one man of the *Queen Mary* were afterwards rescued by German destroyers; but in the wink of an eyelid 57 officers and 1,209 men had gone to their deaths.

The *Lion* herself had been hit again and again, and was only saved from blowing up by the gallantry of her mortally wounded Major of Marines. " The unnerving sights that occurred," wrote Captain Chatfield[1] in his report, " with the heavy casualties, which amounted to 95 killed and 49 wounded, mostly in the first two hours of the action, were a tremendous strain on the strongest discipline, yet there was never the least sign of wavering in the least degree from their duty. On visiting the mess-deck twice during the action while the ship was temporarily disengaged, I observed nothing but cheerful determination, zeal to succour the wounded, and thoughtfulness for the good safety of the ship and to keep her efficient."[2]

It had indeed been an unnerving experience, for the loss of the *Indefatigable* and *Queen Mary* was utterly unexpected.

During the run to the north the battle still raged, the *Lion* and her three consorts gradually drawing ahead of Hipper's squadron and pouring in a heavy fire whenever the German ships were visible. The enemy received severe punishment. The thick mist, however, still lay over the horizon to the north and east, and the haze of funnel and cordite smoke overhanging the calm sea added to the natural obscurity. It was rarely possible to see the enemy except by the red flashes of his guns in the pervading greyness, or when the sun occasionally broke through the clouds temporarily to show up the light grey hulls on the eastern horizon. As time went on, firing became intermittent so far as the *Lion, Princess Royal, Tiger,* and *New Zealand* were concerned. At about 5.10 it ceased altogether, the enemy being out of sight and Sir David Beatty having definitely established an overlap.

[1] Now Admiral Sir Ernle Chatfield, K.C.B., K.C.M.G., C.V.O. [2] *B. J. O. D.*, p. 146.

About two miles astern of the battle-cruisers, however, the four ships of the 5th Battle Squadron – *Barham, Valiant, Warspite, Malaya* – under Rear-Admiral Hugh Evan-Thomas, were still in hot action whenever the visibility permitted it. They were giving, and enduring, heavy punishment, the two leading vessels engaging the German battle-cruisers, and the *Warspite* and *Malaya* the van of the High Seas Fleet. At times they were literally hidden in shell-splashes. Spectators from a distance held their breath, expecting a repetition of what had already happened to the *Indefatigable* and *Queen Mary*. But, as often, the four ships re-emerged from the smoke and spray with their 15-inch guns flashing defiantly. They were hit repeatedly.

Between 5.12 and 5.30, runs one of the official reports of the *Malaya*, " enemy salvos straddled *Valiant* and *Malaya*. At this time we were outlined against a bright yellow horizon, but enemy were nearly obscured by mist, and we were under a very heavy constant fire from at least four ships of the High Seas Fleet. Only flashes were visible, and six salvos were falling round the ship per minute, and at one time, counting some which were probably meant for *Warspite, nine* salvos fell in rapid succession."[1] The same account states that the enemy had the range exactly, and between 5.12 and 5.35 the ship was hit by five heavy shell. Others were missing by feet.

In the " General Gunnery Remarks " of the *Valiant* there is the following note : " The range-finder glasses (especially those of the after turrets) became covered with cordite smoke, and in the case of ' Y ' turret a Boy 1st Class was employed sitting on the top of the turrets cleaning them."[2] What an experience for a lad of under eighteen !

Astern of the 5th Battle Squadron, keeping touch with the High Seas Fleet and reporting its every movement, were the four ships of the 2nd Light-Cruiser Squadron – *Southampton, Birmingham, Nottingham, Dublin* – under their gallant and imperturbable Commodore W. E. Goodenough.[3] At one time they had closed in to within 13,000 yards of the enemy's battle-fleet, and had come under very heavy fire. The distance had now opened out to about 16,000 – eight sea miles – and still they were mercilessly fired at. They steamed in line abreast, the salvos of heavy shell splashing into the sea all round them. But they zigzagged like snipe, and managed to avoid being hit. " We came under a very heavy

---

[1] *B. J. O. D.*, p. 218. [2] *B. J. O. D.*, p. 213.
[3] Now Admiral Sir William Goodenough, K.C.B. M.V.O.

fire from time to time until about 6.05 p.m.," Commodore Good-enough writes ; " no damage, however, resulted."

Personal feelings, perhaps, are out of place in an official des-patch ; but we know from other accounts what the officers and men of those lightly armoured cruisers felt as they saw and heard those great projectiles crashing and splashing into the sea all round them. One hit, and all might be over. But it was the Com-modore's task to report the enemy movements, and to keep on doing so. He obeyed his instructions to the letter.

Throughout the run northward the destroyers were on the disengaged side of the battle-cruisers, where they had an excellent view of all that went on. By 5.35 the *Lion* was gradually haul-ing round to the north-eastward to meet the approaching Grand Fleet. The enemy, at a distance of about 14,000 yards, were altering course to the east. The battle-cruisers re-opened fire, and the head of the German line received severe punishment.

The rumble of heavy gunfire from the east-north-east showed that other vessels were coming into action, and at 5.50 the *Lion* sighted British cruisers ahead – the advanced cruisers of the Grand Fleet. Six minutes later the leading battleships of Sir John Jellicoe's fleet were in sight about five miles to the north-ward, and Sir David Beatty swung round to the east and increased to full speed to take station ahead when the fleet deployed into line.

To those who had been in action it was a goodly sight to see that forest of masts and smoking funnels filling the northern horizon. It was more heartening still when Sir Jellicoe's mighty fleet deployed into line and opened a heavy fire upon any enemy ships visible in the rifts between the natural haze and the clouds of funnel and cordite smoke which lay over the surface of the sea in an ever-thickening canopy.

There was little or no breeze to dissipate the pall. Ship after ship of the Grand Fleet saw a grey smudge appearing through the mist, poured in salvo after salvo, saw her shell striking and her enemy battered and perhaps on fire, and then found herself baulked of complete success by the descent of an impenetrable curtain.

To those who had scoured the North Sea for twenty-two months hoping for this day it was a bitter disappointment. Except for occasional short sallies to sea, the High Seas Fleet had never ventured beyond its own waters. And now that contact had at last been made, complete triumph was wrested away by one of the immutable forces of nature – an abnormally low visibility.

It was exasperating, maddening.

2

The *Onslow*, foiled in her first torpedo attack at about 5 p.m., had taken station on the engaged bow of the *Lion*, Lieutenant-Commander Tovey's reason for doing so being because he " was in a most advantageous position for repelling enemy destroyers . . . or delivering an attack myself."[1] At about 6.5, after the British battle-cruisers had turned to a south-easterly course, he sighted an enemy light-cruiser with three funnels. This was the *Wiesbaden*, which, ten minutes before, had been damaged in action with the battle-cruisers *Invincible*, *Indomitable*, and *Inflexible*, of the 3rd Battle-Cruiser Squadron, sent on ahead of the Grand Fleet to join Sir David Beatty.

Dashing in to attack, Tovey fired 58 rounds of 4-inch shell at the *Wiesbaden* at ranges of between 4,000 and 2,000 yards, " undoubtedly," as he says, scoring a large number of hits, " as they were easily spotted at this range."   While closing this vessel the *Onslow* found herself on the port bow of the enemy battle-cruisers, and, steaming in to 8,000 yards, Tovey turned his ship and gave orders for all his torpedoes to be fired. One torpedo was actually got off, and at the very moment it left its tube the ship was struck by a large shell amidships.

There was a heavy escape of steam, and, thinking that all his torpedoes had gone, Tovey turned to escape " at greatly reduced speed."   While doing so, he passed the *Wiesbaden* at a range of 3,500 yards, and, being told that he still had three torpedoes left, took a shot at the German light-cruiser, which by this time had stopped.   It hit and exploded under her conning-tower.

Two torpedoes, however, still remained, when the *Onslow* sighted a line of enemy battleships at a distance of 10,000 yards. Already badly damaged and listing heavily, unable to steam more than 10 knots, Tovey turned towards them to attack.   He must have known he was courting instant destruction, but calculated that the loss of one destroyer and her ship's company was a small price to pay for the sinking of a German battleship. Sauntering in to a range of 8,000 yards, he fired his last two

<hr>

[1] *B. J. O. D.*, p. 237.

torpedoes, and then started to struggle out of action. The enemy must have turned to avoid them, for there was no hit.

It is a pity that so gallant an attack with a hopelessly damaged ship achieved no better result. But it is impossible to write of the incident without a thrill of pride, and Tovey's action will pass down to history as one of the unforgettable destroyer exploits of the war. In his official despatch, Rear-Admiral T. D. W. Napier, commanding the 3rd Light-Cruiser Squadron in the *Falmouth*, particularly drew attention to it : " Here I should like to bring to your notice the action of a destroyer (name unknown) which we passed close in a disabled condition soon after 6 p.m. She apparently was able to struggle ahead again and made straight for the *Derfflinger* to attack her. The incident appeared so courageous that it seems desirable to investigate it further, as I am unable to be certain of the vessel's identity."[1]

The *Onslow* was in a sorry condition. The after part of the ship was practically wrecked, and she was leaking badly. Two shell had burst in No. 2 boiler-room and had badly damaged the main feed tank, while all the water in the reserve feed tank was soon exhausted. Shortly before 7 o'clock the engineer officer came on the bridge to say that the ship could not steam for more than a few minutes. Even as he spoke she came to an automatic standstill – still within range of the enemy.

Before she became quite helpless, those on board had witnessed the *Warspite* turning circles under heavy fire. This was shortly after 6.20, when the cruiser *Defence*, attacking the still floating *Wiesbaden*, came under a hurricane of fire and blew up in a sheet of flame. The *Warrior*, severely damaged, limped off under heavy fire, and would have shared the fate of her flagship had not the *Warspite's* helm jammed during an alteration of course, due to injuries already sustained in action. Circling round the crippled cruiser, she drew upon herself most of the enemy fire, and to those in the *Onslow* the sight was an impressive one. " We observed near us one of our battleships stopped and surrounded with waterspouts, apparently about to be sunk, although she was replying to the enemy's fire with all her guns. . . . We afterwards discovered it was the *Warspite* doing her famous stunt at ' Windy Corner.' "[2]

The *Onslow* finally stopped. The fighting-ships disappeared in the haze to the east and south-east, and the roar of heavy gun-fire died gradually away to a growling like distant thunder. For

---

[1] *B. J. O. D.*, p. 186.   [2] *F. J.*, p. 173.

half an hour those on board had been deafened by an ear-splitting turmoil of sound – the whistle and whine of shell, and the crash of their explosion, the thudding reports of guns, the roar of escaping steam, the hum of flying splinters, and the clang of riven metal as they struck. The ship's machinery had stopped, and the sudden, unaccustomed silence, disturbed only by the lapping of the water alongside as the ship rolled uneasily in the heavy swell caused by the passage of many ships steaming at high speed, and that receding pulsation of gunfire, seemed eerie and oppressive.

The ship lay helpless. What would happen next? Would she be succoured by some friend, or would the grey shape of some enemy appear suddenly from the mist to sink her as she lay impotent?

They tried to stop the many holes in the side with shot and collision mats, though the jagged holes were larger than the mats. They made ready to be taken in tow, just in case a friend hove in sight to help them. But it seemed unlikely that any ship still capable of fighting would dally to help a stricken destroyer in the midst of a fleet action.

Then, at 7.15, appeared the welcome sight of the *Defender*.

This destroyer, commanded by Lieutenant-Commander L. R. Palmer,[1] belonged to the 1st Flotilla, and had been with the battle-cruiser force all day. At 6.30, when 200 yards on the disengaged side of the *Lion*, a ricochetting 12-inch shell struck the side in the foremost boiler-room, killed a petty stoker officer, put the boiler out of action, and started an oil fuel fire. The great projectile, failing to explode, lodged in the ashpit of the furnace. Had it exploded, the *Defender* would have been no more.

Turning out of the line, Palmer, still able to steam at slow speed, passed between the fighting battle-fleets until he reached " an area of comparative calm," and then set about repairing his damage. " The fire having been dealt with, it was found a mat kept the stokehold dry, my only trouble now being lack of speed. I looked round for useful employment, and saw a destroyer in great difficulties, so closed her."[2]

This was the *Onslow*. Ranging up alongside, the two captains hailed each other. We may, perhaps, imagine the joy with which the *Defender's* offer of a tow was received.

" Proceeded," writes Palmer, " to take her in tow," and the work was enlivened by a few large splashes falling round them. But the wire hawser was duly passed, and before long the *Defender*

---

[1] Now Captain, D.S.O.   [2] *B. J. O. D.*, p. 250.

was jogging westward at 12 knots, with the *Onslow* astern. They left the scene of their hair-raising adventures with the sound of occasional gunfire still coming from the southward. But their adventures were by no means ended.

Shortly after 9 o'clock they sighted a battleship coming up astern, and suffered a few minutes' anxiety until she was made out to be the damaged *Warspite*, making for Rosyth. " I will take station astern of you," the *Defender* signalled at 9.30, to which the battleship replied, " Am steering west 16 knots ; compass and steering-gear very erratic."

The *Defender* and *Onslow* were not 16-knotters, and the *Warspite* soon disappeared in the increasing darkness ahead. Once more the two crippled ships were in solitary occupation of their own small circle of sea.

A strong south-westerly breeze gathered strength during the night, and the sea rose fast. Very soon the ships were plunging and jerking heavily in the short, steep waves, and at 1 a.m. on June 1st the tow parted. By this time, using salt water for the boilers, the *Onslow* was able to steam slowly ahead, so for a time both vessels proceeded independently in company. At about 5 o'clock the *Defender* had to stop to re-secure the collision mat over her injury, and, having done this, took the *Onslow* in tow again. But the wind and sea had increased. The towed ship yawed and jerked heavily, and very soon the *Defender's* towing-slip carried away.

Palmer thereupon got up two shackles of chain-cable, secured it round his after gun-mounting and bollards, and managed to get the lame duck in tow again. " Proceeded at 8 knots," he says in his report. " Sea still rising continually. Had to reduce speed with very little headway on." The *Onslow's* pipe system had been damaged, and only the foremost oil tank had any fuel in it. By dint of transferring oil from one tank to another in every receptacle that could be found, however, they managed to raise sufficient steam in a boiler to enable the steering-gear to be worked.

All through June 1st and the following night they struggled on, with the haziest idea of their position. All the sextants belonging to the officers of the *Onslow* were in the after part of the ship, which had been damaged by shell fire, and water was finding its way into the officers' cabins. The wireless telegraphy was out of action, and throughout the day, far away to the eastward, signal after signal was being made by the commander-in-chief and Sir David Beatty to one ship or another asking for any news of the *Onslow*.

Finally, having struggled 350 miles across the North Sea in vile weather, the battered pair sighted the east coast of Scotland. Aberdeen was the nearest port, and thankfully they made their way towards it. At 1 p.m. on June 2nd, about forty-three hours after being damaged, the *Onslow* was handed over to tugs and taken into harbour.

The *Defender*, with the strange trophy of an unexploded German 12-inch shell still in the ashpit of her boiler, proceeded to Rosyth.

Both Tovey and Palmer received their D.S.O.s in the Jutland honours list – the first for his cool gallantry in action, and Palmer for the dogged pluck and determination, and remarkable display of seamanship, with which, in his own crippled ship, he had brought a hopelessly damaged consort home.

3

At 2.30 p.m. on May 31st, the 3rd Battle-Cruiser Squadron – *Invincible, Indomitable, Inflexible* – under the command of Rear-Admiral the Hon. Horace Hood, together with the light-cruisers *Chester* and *Canterbury*, and the four destroyers *Shark, Acasta, Ophelia,* and *Christopher* of the 4th Flotilla, were about twenty miles ahead of the Grand Fleet, and steering south-east. Seven minutes previously they had intercepted the *Galatea's* first signals reporting the enemy in sight, and at 3.13 the squadron increased to 22 knots. At 4 o'clock Rear-Admiral Hood increased to 24 knots, and, with his men at action stations, was steering south-south-east towards the scene of battle. He was, indeed, anticipating Sir John Jellicoe's order to support Sir David Beatty which was wirelessed to him at 4.5. At 4.12 the squadron was proceeding at full speed, with the *Canterbury* five miles ahead, the *Chester* the same distance on the starboard beam, and the four destroyers ahead of the battle-cruisers as an anti-submarine screen.

Soon after 5 o'clock the weather became misty. In certain directions it was possible to see seven or eight miles ; in others, no more than two-and-a-half. Half an hour later the *Chester* heard the sound of heavy firing to the south-west, and sighted gun-flashes in the same direction. Captain Lawson immediately informed the admiral by searchlight, and swung round to investigate. Six minutes afterwards he sighted enemy light-cruisers

and destroyers looming up out of the mist on the starboard bow
at a distance of no more than 6,000 yards. These vessels were the
Frankfurt, Wiesbaden, Pillau, and *Elbing,* stationed on the starboard side of Admiral Hipper's battle-cruisers, which were steering north and still in action with the 5th Battle Squadron and
Sir David Beatty's battle-cruisers.

Swinging round to starboard to bring her guns to bear, the
Chester opened fire. It was one against four. Almost immediately she became smothered in waterspouts and bursting shell.

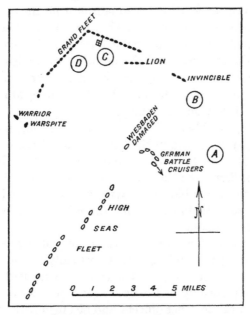

SITUATION AT ABOUT 6.26 P.M.

(Light-Cruiser Squadrons and Destroyer Flotillas
omitted)

(A) *Shark* sinking   (B) *Acasta* damaged
(C) *Defender* damaged.   (D) *Onslow* damaged.

Within a few minutes, severely damaged, with most of her guns
out of action, cordite fires blazing, and the upper deck a shambles
of dead and dying,[1] she turned to the north-east and made off at
full speed, zigzagging to avoid the salvos. The enemy turned to
pursue, and until she sighted the *Invincible, Indomitable,* and
Inflexible coming towards her at full speed, she had a most uncomfortable nineteen minutes.

[1] Her casualties amounted to 2 officers and 33 men killed, and 3 officers and
39 men wounded.

At 5.40, hearing heavy gunfire, Rear-Admiral Hood had turned to starboard, thus leaving his four destroyers on the port quarter. The *Chester's* four opponents were engaged, one, the *Wiesbaden*, being badly damaged. At about 6.20 Sir David Beatty's battle-cruisers, in hot action, were sighted on the port bow. Hood swung his ships into line ahead of them on an east-south-east course, and within three minutes the *Invincible*, *Indomitable*, and *Inflexible* were pouring in a heavy fire from their 12-inch guns on the leading German battle-cruisers at a range of about 8,000 yards. But the enemy shooting was unpleasantly good.

The admiral was fighting his squadron from the open bridge of his flagship, the *Invincible*. The ship had been hit several times by enemy shell with no appreciable damage. But she was giving more than she received, and the admiral had hailed the control officer in the control top over the bridge. " Your firing is very good," he shouted above the din of battle. " Keep at it as quickly as you can. Every shot is telling." [1]

They were probably the last words he ever spoke, for an instant later, at 6.34 p.m., a heavy shell struck one of the turrets, burst inside, and blew off the roof. Almost immediately there came a great flash of flame and the shattering roar of an explosion as the *Invincible's* magazine blew up. Wreckage was hurled a good 400 feet into the air. Again there came those billowing brown clouds of heavy cordite smoke.

The ship was broken in two. When the pall cleared away, her bow and stern were standing almost vertically out of the water to a height of seventy feet. Six survivors, who had miraculous escapes, were picked up by the destroyer *Badger* soon after 7 p.m. The rear-admiral, 60 other officers, and 965 men perished in a flash.

It was the fourth grievous calamity on that eventful afternoon – first the *Indefatigable*, then the *Queen Mary* and *Defence* ; now, the *Invincible*.

The battle raged on. The air shook and trembled to the rolling crash and thunder of heavy gunfire. The misty horizon to the north-west seemed filled with the blurred shapes of the battle-ships of the Grand Fleet deploying into line. The greyness was rent with the red flame of their guns as they fired at their enemies whenever the murk vouchsafed a fleeting glimpse of them. From the westward came the answering flashes of the Germans.

British light-cruiser squadrons, destroyer flotillas, and isolated ships were steaming in all directions at full speed as they took up

[1] *B. J. O. D.*, p. 168.

their stations ahead and astern of the battle-line. Their heavy, trailing smoke added to the natural obscurity. To any observer in the fleet itself the situation must have seemed utterly confused and haphazard. Yet, had the mist and smoke of battle rolled away and an all-seeing eye been overhead at about 6.30 p.m., just before the *Invincible* blew up, its owner would have seen that everything was developing according to plan.

The enemy battle-line, headed by Hipper's battle-cruisers, now badly battered, with his flagship, the great *Lützow*, little more than a sinking wreck, was advancing to the north-east. On the Germans' port bow, and ahead, the battle squadrons of the Grand Fleet, 28 ships in all if we omit the damaged *Warspite*, were swinging into line, the van, led by the *King George V*, moving eastward and enveloping the head of the German Fleet. Ahead of the *King George V*, Sir David Beatty's battle-cruisers prolonged the British line to the eastward.

The enemy fleet was having its " T " crossed, rendering itself liable to having its leading ships destroyed one after the other as they advanced. Only the low visibility, and Admiral Scheer's evasive " *Gefechtskehrtwendung*," or " Battle turn away," at 6.35, under the cover of a destroyer attack and a heavy smoke-screen, saved him from annihilation, as it did again about three-quarters of an hour later.

To this " turn away," which had assiduously been practised by the enemy, and in which every ship swung round together to an opposite course, the ablest tacticians had been unable to discover an effective counter-manœuvre. A pursuit from astern would have invited attack from the many German destroyers known to be present, which was a risk to which it was inadvisable to expose the British fleet at the opening stages of an action.

The German manœuvre had clearly been foreseen, and in his search for an effective antidote Sir John Jellicoe had come to the conclusion that " nothing but ample time and superior speed can be an answer, and this means that unless the meeting of the fleets takes place fairly early in the day, it is most difficult, if not impossible, to fight the action to a finish."[1] The evening was drawing on, the visibility was low, and Admiral Scheer, with remarkable skill, was deliberately and naturally avoiding action with a superior fleet. " It is difficult to see, even now," wrote Sir Julian Corbett, " how the action, so well begun, could have been pushed to a decision."[1]

[1] *N. O.* iii., p. 372.

But I have wandered into deep and stormy waters. This account does not pretend to be a full description and history of the much-debated Battle of Jutland. On the contrary, it is merely the tale of the doings of some of the destroyers during that hard-fought engagement.

4

We left the four destroyers *Shark*, Commander Loftus W. Jones ; *Acasta*, Lieutenant-Commander John O. Barron ; *Ophelia*, Commander Lewis Crabbe ; and *Christopher*, Lieu-tenant-Commander Fairfax M. Kerr, on the port quarter of the *Invincible* when, at 5.40, Rear-Admiral Hood swung round to the north-westward towards the sound of gunfire, was the means of saving the *Chester* from further severe punishment, dis-abled the *Wiesbaden*, and according to Admiral Scheer, severely damaged the *Pillau*.

At about 5.50 the destroyers were in company in the order named when, on the port bow, steering a southerly course, they sighted three or four enemy light-cruisers accompanied by de-stroyers, and, a few moments later, Admiral Hipper's battle-cruisers. The *Shark* at once led round at full speed towards the destroyers to prevent them from attacking Rear-Admiral Hood's squadron, and opened fire at a range which soon dropped to 5,000 yards. The accounts of the engagement are rather confused and contradictory ; but, shortly after 6 o'clock, both the *Shark* and the *Acasta*, by this time under very heavy fire, fired torpedoes at a light-cruiser and battle-cruiser respectively.

In a smother of bursting and splashing shell Loftus Jones turned 16 points – 180° – to escape. As he did so, his ship was badly hit, her oil suctions being damaged and the steering-gear being shot away. We know what happened through the statement of Petty Officer William Griffin, the *Shark's* torpedo-coxswain, who, wounded in the head and over the right eye, was eventually picked up with five other survivors.

Griffin reported the steering-gear shot away, whereupon Loftus Jones gave orders for the manning of the after steering position. The *Shark*, still under heavy fire, was apparently able to crawl, but it was now that a heavy shell hit the forecastle, killed every man at the foremost 4-inch gun, and blew the weapon overboard.

Seeing his sub-divisional mate practically stopped, Barron, in the *Acasta*, went close alongside the *Shark* and offered his assist-ance, being hit badly forward and aft as he did so.

" Don't get sunk for us ! " Loftus Jones hailed back, ordering Barron away.

The *Acasta* went off on other business, and the *Shark*, at her captain's own wish, was left alone, helpless and at a complete standstill. For a time she was left in peace, as the *Canterbury* – Captain Percy Royds – came up from the south-east, and enticed the German cruisers away.

Only the *Shark's* midship 4-inch gun remained fit for use. Nothing more could be done, and, realising that the sinking of his ship was a mere matter of time, Loftus Jones left his bridge and gave orders for the boats and life-saving floats to be lowered and got out, and the collision mats to be placed over the worst of the injuries. The boats, however, were already shot into splinters and utterly useless.

Then it was that two enemy destroyers, which had been sent to cover Hipper's retirement south, came upon the battered *Shark* and poured salvo after salvo into her at a range, according to one account, of only 600 yards. They were engaged with the only remaining gun, Loftus Jones himself controlling the fire. The gun's crew was very soon reduced to three men – Midshipman T. Smith, R.N.R., and two able seamen, Joseph Howell and Charles Hope. The commander was wounded in the leg ; but still continued to control the gun. Both German destroyers were hit by the *Shark's* fire and driven off to a distance.

The commander had given an order for all men not engaged at the guns to lie down on the deck. Very soon Howell, the gunlayer, was hit in the left leg. A minute later Loftus Jones himself had his left leg severed at the knee by a shell which did not explode. Hope left the gun and carried his wounded captain aft, attending to him as best he could.

Then it was that Loftus Jones, lying bleeding on the deck, noticed that the ensign was not showing clearly. Hope, who was with him, has described what occurred : " The gaff on which the ensign was flying was shot away, and Captain Jones, seeing the ensign was hanging down the mast, asked what was wrong with the flag, and appeared greatly upset as he lay on the deck wounded. Twice he spoke of it. Then I climbed up and unbent the ensign from the gaff. I passed it down to Midshipman Smith, R.N.R., who then hoisted it at the yardarm. Commander Jones seemed then to be less worried when he saw the flag was hoisted again."[1]

---

[1] Quoted in *N. O.* iii., p. 354

Then, from a distance of about 1,500 yards, the enemy destroyers fired two torpedoes, one of which took effect abreast of
the *Shark's* after funnel. The ship heeled over, and the gallant
commander gave orders for the men to save themselves. Two
Carley floats floated off with 14 or 15 men in each, a petty officer
helping the wounded captain into one of them. At about 7
o'clock the *Shark* went to the bottom with her ensign still flying.

The survivors in the water were between the opposing battle-
fleets. Five miles away to the westward they saw ten or more
German battleships or battle-cruisers being engaged by the
battleships of the Grand Fleet, which later passed within a mile of
their rafts. Steaming at full speed, they soon disappeared to the
southward.

The water was bitterly cold. One by one the survivors succumbed to exhaustion. At 10 p.m., when, by the mercy of
Providence, they were sighted by the Danish steamship *Vidar*,
only seven remained alive, and one, Chief Stoker Newcombe,
died soon after being rescued.

The survivors were Petty Officer William C. R. Griffin, Stoker
Petty Officer Charles Filleul, and Able Seamen Joseph O. G.
Howell, Charles C. Hope, Charles Smith, and Thomas W. Swan.

Their courageous captain, Loftus William Jones, who had upheld the finest traditions of the Service by fighting to the last in a
battered and sinking ship when surrender would have been no
disgrace, had gone to his death in the grey North Sea that he knew
so well. To that gallant soul surrender was unthinkable. He
desired no better death than to die in action. The posthumous
Victoria Cross subsequently awarded him was a fitting tribute to
the memory of one of the most heroic and intrepid officers bred
by the Destroyer Service.

5

The *Acasta*, ordered to leave the *Shark* to her fate, had already
been damaged. But, seeing the *Lützow* coming up on his port
quarter, Barron at once turned in to attack, instantly to come
under a storm of shell from the battle-cruiser's secondary armament. Pressing on to within about 4,500 yards, he fired the torpedo in his foremost tube, which appeared to hit. [1]

---

[1] It is now known that only one German battle-cruiser, the *Seydlitz*, was hit
by a torpedo, fired by the *Petard* earlier in the action. Those in the *Acasta* may
possibly have mistaken a shell explosion or a fire for the explosion of their torpedo,
for at this time the *Lützow* was badly damaged. Admiral Hipper left her soon

For twenty minutes the *Acasta* endured a withering fire from a battle-cruiser, light-cruisers, and several destroyers. Hit repeatedly, a shell burst in the engine-room, killing or wounding the engineer officer and 4 men, and cutting several steam pipes. The engine-room became filled with scalding steam and had to be evacuated. As the steering-gear was shot away, Barron was unable to steer or to stop his engines until 6.30.

It was an unnerving experience, for the ship was turning wild circles right in the path of the approaching Grand Fleet. More by good luck than by management, she " barged through " the cloud of destroyers ahead of the battle-line. Finally, managing to get the ship stopped, they hoisted the " Not under control " signal and the blue and yellow No. 6 flag, signifying " Am in danger of sinking of injuries received in action." As the *Acasta* lay stopped she was passed within a few hundred yards by division after division of battleships steaming at full speed into action. Some passed to port and some to starboard. " The men were very excited," an officer wrote, " and cheered each ship as she passed, particularly the commander-in-chief in the *Iron Duke*."[1]

" We passed a disabled destroyer on our starboard bow, very close to us," writes an officer in the *Marlborough*. " She was badly holed forward and aft, and was much down by the bows, but the crew were clustered aft cheering us and the other ships as we passed, and then she disappeared astern, rolling heavily in the wash of the battle-fleet, but with her ensign still flying, apparently not done for yet."[2]

The *Galatea* and *Fearless* stood by the *Acasta* for a time ; but she eventually managed to get moving at slow speed, and made off to the westward. During the night she twice sighted a German cruiser on fire to the south-west. At 9.45 on the morning of June 1st, however, she was fallen in with by the destroyer *Nonsuch*,

afterwards in a destroyer and transferred his flag to the *Moltke*. The *Lützow*, which was hit 40 times and had 111 killed and 54 wounded, was little more than a wreck. At 3.45 a.m. on June 1st, by which time her forecastle was under water and her propellers were in the air, she was finally sunk by a torpedo from a German destroyer after her crew had been rescued. The *Seydlitz*, torpedoed by the *Petard*, hit 24 times by heavy shell, and with 98 killed and 50 wounded, was in little better condition than the *Lützow*. Much damaged and down by the bows, she was barely got into harbour, and beached herself in the entrance to the Jade River. The *Derfflinger*, hit by 20 large shell, had 154 killed and 26 wounded. She had a huge hole in her bows, two turrets blown to pieces, and her fire control shot away. At one period she was ablaze from end to end. The *Moltke* and *Von der Tann* escaped with lighter injuries ; but only the stout construction of the *Seydlitz* and *Derfflinger* saved them from foundering like the *Lützow*. Had they had to be taken 300 miles across the North Sea they could never have survived.

[1] *F. J.*, p. 151.   [2] *F. J.*, p. 125.

Lieutenant-Commander H. I. N. Lyon, who reported she was escorting her damaged sister to Aberdeen at 10 knots. At noon the *Nonsuch* took the *Acasta* in tow, as the latter's oil fuel was practically exhausted and bad weather was coming on. Together they struggled on to the west, making good between 6 and 8 knots, both ships arriving at Aberdeen during the evening of June 2nd.

John O. Barron, who was promoted to the rank of commander in the next list after Jutland, was another of the destroyer officers who received his D.S.O. for services at Jutland.

The *Ophelia*, Commander Lewis Crabbe, had also been screening the 3rd Battle-Cruiser Squadron with the *Shark* and *Acasta*. This ship had only just been taken over from her builders, and, except for the passage from Sunderland to Scapa, had put to sea for the first time on May 30th.

When the *Shark* was put out of action, the *Ophelia*, dodging the salvos, ran back towards the British light-cruisers. A little later, however, Crabbe noticed that the enemy's battle-cruisers had turned to the south, and, dashing in at full speed, fired a torpedo at a range of 8,000 yards. His shot did not go home ; but these lightning attacks by even single British destroyers, whenever a chance presented itself, added no little anxiety to the already harassed minds of Admiral Hipper and his commander-in-chief.

CHAPTER XII

DESTROYERS AT JUTLAND: NIGHT, MAY 31st

I

FIRING died away as day gave place to twilight, and twilight deepened into night. The sky was heavily overcast, and the surface of the calm sea was shrouded in places by mist, which had gradually been thickening during the afternoon and early evening. The night came down intensely dark. Against the nebulous, indeterminate background the hulls of even the largest ships could not be made out at much more than three-quarters of a mile, sometimes less.

At 9.17, by which time it was nearly dark, Sir John Jellicoe turned his fleet to south at a speed of 17 knots. The battleships were in columns disposed abeam of each other and one mile apart, this compact formation being adopted to keep vessels in sight and to prevent them from mistaking each other for enemy ships. The fleet was between the enemy and his base, and destroyer attacks were expected.

" I rejected at once the idea of a night action between the heavy ships, as leading to possible disaster, owing, first, to the presence of torpedo-craft in such large numbers, and, secondly, to the impossibility of distinguishing between our own and enemy vessels. Further, the result of a night action under modern conditions must always be very largely a matter of chance,"[1] Sir John Jellicoe wrote in his despatch. Unwilling to lose the advantage of position which would have resulted from an easterly or westerly course, he steered south so as to be in a position to renew the engagement at daylight. On this course he would also be able to intercept the Germans if they elected to return to harbour by way of the swept channel past Heligoland, or through that leading past the Ems and South Frisian Islands.

At 9.27 the destroyers, or those that were present with the battle-fleet, were ordered to take station five miles astern. Here they would provide the fleet with a screen against torpedo attack during the night, and might also have opportunities for attacking

[1] *B. J. O. D.*, p. 21.

the enemy's heavy ships if they were steaming south with the intention of regaining their bases.

Five minutes later the *Abdiel*, Commander Berwick Curtis,[1] a flotilla-leader fitted as a minelayer, was ordered to lay her eighty mines in zigzags in a position near the Vyl Lightship, in the entrance to the German swept channel leading down from Sylt to the Jade River. Steaming off at 31 knots, she accomplished this mission by about 2 a.m. without sighting anything except a few fishing-craft in the low visibility caused by drizzling rain and overcast sky.

To the destroyers, ordered to take station five miles astern of the British battle-squadrons, the position was just about as obscure as it possibly could be. All most of them had seen of the actions before dark was their own ships firing heavily into the banks of mist and smoke on the horizon whenever enemy hulls loomed up through the haze. They had no clear conception of what was happening around them, in which direction their enemy had last been seen, or from which direction they might be sighted. Such snatches of wireless conversations between the squadrons of heavier ships that may have been intercepted by their over-worked telegraphists must have tended still further to confuse the situation, not to clarify it. Information of the enemy was what they needed, and information was what no senior officer seems to have been in a position to give them.

When Commander R. B. C. Hutchinson,[2] D.S.C., of the *Achates*, wrote in his report: " I respectfully submit that in future the maximum amount of information may be given to destroyers as to the disposition of our own forces, observing the difficulty of recognition at night,"[3] he was only voicing the general perplexity of many other destroyer captains. They knew their own battle-fleet was five miles ahead, steaming its southerly course at 17 knots. But few of them were aware of the whereabouts of the British battle-cruisers, two squadrons of cruisers, and four squadrons of light-cruisers—in all, thirty ships. Scattered during the daylight action, they might be anywhere. Yet, in the pitch blackness, with a visibility sometimes as low as half a mile, it was the duty of the destroyers to make certain before they attacked that they did not fire torpedoes at their friends. They knew full well that they would be fired upon if they approached their own ships at night, and were painfully aware that if they

---

[1] Now Rear-Admiral, C.B., C.M.G., D.S.O.   [2] Now Captain.
[3] *B. J. O. D.*, p. 309.

challenged an enemy with the usual flashing signal, it at once established their identity as British and would evoke an instant reply in the shape of a tornado of gunfire at point-blank range.

With ships steaming at high speeds, the darkness and low visibility did not give much time for thought if a vessel were suddenly sighted. Immediate action was necessary if a chance of making a successful attack was not to be missed. Yet how was immediate action possible if that blurred shadow *might* be a friend ?

Studying all the available records and narratives of the night fighting that followed, one realises that the task of the flotillas massed five miles astern of the British battle-fleet was as difficult, responsible, and dangerous as it possibly could be.

Difficulty and danger nobody minded, for they were used to it. Moreover, torpedo-attacks at night were one of the functions for which destroyers existed. But the prospect of sinking one of their own vessels was frightful to contemplate. Commander Hutchinson's remark was not made without good and sufficient reason.

As we know now, Admiral Scheer elected to take his fleet back to harbour by the quickest possible route, that which led him to the swept channel near the Horns Reef lightship. This course, to which he altered at about 9.30 p.m., led the High Seas Fleet, with its destroyers and cruisers ahead, and the battered battle-cruisers astern, diagonally across the track of, and through the British flotillas astern of the Grand Fleet.

At 9.45 p.m., receiving the commander-in-chief's signal made eighteen minutes earlier, the light-cruiser *Castor*, Commodore J. R. P. Hawksley, swung round to take station five miles astern. The commodore, besides commanding the Grand Fleet destroyers, was also Captain (D) of the 11th Flotilla, and with the *Castor* were the flotilla-leader *Kempenfelt* and fourteen destroyers. At 10.5, when she had altered to a southerly course, the *Castor*, then some distance on the starboard quarter of the battle-fleet, sighted three or more cruisers on her starboard bow. Being dark and misty, it was impossible really to make them out with certainty ; but very soon the strangers flashed the first two signs of the British challenge for the day, following it with two other flashed letters which were incorrect.

A moment later all uncertainty was dispelled by the two leading vessels switching on their searchlights and opening a heavy fire on the *Castor* from a distance of about 2,500 yards.[1] The *Castor* replied at once, and her 6-inch shell could be seen hitting. But she herself was struck repeatedly, losing about 12 killed and 23 wounded in the space of a few minutes. Considerable damage was also done to the ship, the bridge steering-gear and electric circuits being shot away, the wireless disabled, the voice pipes to several guns being destroyed, and the motor-boat being smashed into splinters and set on fire. The resulting blaze lit up the ship like a flaming beacon. The *Castor*, having fired a torpedo, turned away to port, and the enemy disappeared.

The two leading destroyers of those led by the *Castor* were the *Marne*, Lieutenant-Commander G. B. Hartford, and *Magic*, Lieutenant-Commander G. C. Wynter. Each fired a torpedo, but the effect of the gun-flashes and searchlights was so blinding that they were unable to fire more. The other destroyers, as says Commodore Hawksley in his official report, " were so certain in their own minds that a mistake had been made, and that we were being fired on by our own ships, that they decided not to fire their torpedoes."[2] A good opportunity of attacking was therefore lost, and the *Castor* was unable to signal to her destroyers through her wireless being temporarily out of action and her bridge flashing-lamps being demolished. Thus, very early in the proceedings, the risks and chances of night action were made manifest.

At 10.20, further to the eastward, the 2nd Light-Cruiser Squadron – *Southampton*, *Dublin*, *Nottingham*, and *Birmingham* – steering a southerly course after the fleet, sighted a line of five ships on the starboard beam on a slightly converging course at a distance of 1,500 yards. When first seen, one or two of them were silhouetted against a small patch of light sky which still lingered on the western horizon as the remains of the sunset.

The commodore, having seen the gun-flashes and blaze of the *Castor's* action, was fully aware of the enemy's proximity, and the guns and torpedo-tubes of his squadron were ready for instant action. The two lines of ships gradually closed in upon each other ; but beyond the fact that the strangers were light-cruisers, it was impossible at the time to make out their nationality. There was a discussion on the *Southampton's* bridge as to whether they might not be the British 3rd Light-Cruiser Squadron.

---

[1] Some accounts say only 1,500 yards.
[2] *B. J. O. D.*, p. 304.

Neither side wished to disclose its nationality by challenging and thereby to give its possible enemy an advantage.

The distance apart gradually diminished from 1,500 yards to 1,200, from 1,200 to 1,000, then to 800. Then the *Southampton* started to flash her challenge, which was replied to at once by strings of coloured lights from each ship in the enemy's line. A gun blazed out from the *Dublin*, and the shell was seen to strike home. Simultaneously, the *Southampton* and *Dublin* switched on their searchlights. The enemy did the same, and the guns opened a furious fire all down the opposing lines.

The next few minutes provided a roaring medley of gunfire – the crash and explosion as shell drove home and burst, the fiendish humming of splinters as they hurtled through the air like hail, and the horrible screech and splash of the few projectiles that passed overhead or struck short. In the blaze of gun-flashes, the glare of searchlights, the smoke, and shell-splashes, it was impossible to see. Both the *Southampton* and *Dublin* were smothered in close-range shell fire ; but the former, leading the line, suffered the worst.

The men serving the 6-inch guns on her open deck went down like standing corn before the reaper as the shell-splinters drove home in showers. Her after searchlight was demolished by a direct hit, and its fragments scattered. The flash of an exploding shell ignited some cordite cartridges on the upper deck, and in a moment a great gout of white flame rose from the upper deck between the second and third funnels. A second flared up from beside the foremast. Those on board, remembering the *Queen Mary*, thought that the *Southampton* was about to share her fate.

But the enemy had also been hardly treated. In spite of the storm of shell and splinters, the *Southampton's* torpedo-lieutenant, from the firing position on the bridge, discharged a torpedo at a group of hostile searchlights, which was all that he could see to aim at. In the noise and uproar, and the glare of lights and gun-flashes, it was impossible to note the result. But the searchlights were suddenly extinguished, the firing ceased as suddenly as it had begun, and the enemy disappeared to the westward and were no more seen. It was not until afterwards that it became known that the *Southampton's* torpedo had gone home on the *Frauenlob*, to send her instantly to the bottom with a loss of 342 officers and men.[1]

---

[1] Of this same squadron, the " 4th Scouting Group," the *Stettin* had 36 killed and wounded, the *Munchen* 27, and the *Hamburg* 39. Some of these may have been inflicted earlier in the day.

The action lasted little more than $3\frac{1}{2}$ minutes, during which the *Southampton* suffered 80 casualties – 35 killed or died of wounds, and 55 wounded. Hit 18 times, though luckily in no really vital spot, her starboard broadside was reduced from five 6-inch guns to two ; the four funnels were riddled with hundreds of small holes ; the deck and protective mattresses round the bridge were slashed and ripped with splinters ; there were several holes along the ship's side ; and the masts, boats, signal lockers, funnel casing – everything – was a mass of splinter holes. " The general effect," wrote an officer, " was as if handfuls of splinters had been thrown against the upper works of the ship."[1] It seemed a miracle how anyone in the open remained alive.

The *Dublin*, which had altered course 3 points to port on first being hit, was struck 13 times, and had 1 officer (her navigator) and 2 men killed, and 24 men wounded. One shell passing through her chart house had demolished most of the charts. Her wireless was temporarily out of action, and a fire was started between decks. The two rear ships, the *Nottingham* and *Birmingham*, though they poured in a heavy fire, did not switch on their searchlights and remained untouched.

2

To gather some idea of the desperate fighting that took place among the British destroyers from about 11.20 p.m. onwards it is necessary to visualise their disposition. To the westward (see diagram) came the flotilla-leader *Tipperary*, Captain C. J. Wintour, Captain (D) of the 4th Flotilla, with the flotilla-leader *Broke* and the ten destroyers named. About four miles away to the north-east, and about six miles astern of the main portion British battle-fleet was the light-cruiser *Champion*, Captain J. U. Farie, Captain (D) of the 13th Flotilla, with nine destroyers. Keeping station at one cable on the *Champion's* port beam, steamed the *Lydiard*, leading four other destroyers of the Harwich Force. A short distance astern of the *Lydiard* was the flotilla-leader *Faulknor*, Captain (D) of the 12th Flotilla, with the flotilla-leader *Marksman* and thirteen destroyers.

The *Tipperary* and other ships of the 4th Flotilla had seen the gun-flashes and searchlights, and had heard the gunfire, of the engagements fought by the *Castor* soon after 10 p.m., and the

---

[1] Commander Stephen King-Hall, *A Naval Lieutenant, 1914–18,* p. 156. (Methuen & Co.)

Southampton and the 2nd Light-Cruiser Squadron about a quarter of an hour later. They were, therefore, fully on the alert, and ready for instant action when at 10.35, the *Garland*, the fourth ship in the line, sighted an enemy light-cruiser on the starboard beam and reported it to the *Tipperary*. Ten minutes later, the *Unity*, Lieutenant-Commander A. M. Lecky, the last ship in the long line, saw three enemy destroyers conning up on her starboard quarter. Their leader fired a torpedo and immediately disappeared, Lecky avoiding the shot by going on at full speed and turning towards it.

At some time between 11.20 and 11.30 – individual accounts

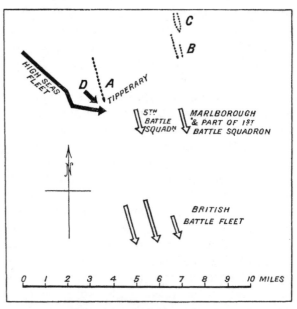

SITUATION AT ABOUT 11.20 P.M.

(A) 4TH FLOTILLA:—*Tipperary, Spitfire, Sparrowhawk, Garland, Contest, Broke, Achates, Ambuscade, Ardent, Fortune, Porpoise, Unity.*
(B) Light-Cruiser *Champion* with fourteen destroyers of 13th, 9th, and 10th Flotillas.
(C) *Faulknor* with fourteen destroyers of 12th Flotilla.
(D) German Light-Cruisers, *Elbing, Rostock, Frankfurt, Pillau.*
    Tipperary put out of action.
    Spitfire collides with *Nassau.*
    Elbing rammed by *Posen.*

vary – the leading vessels of the 4th Flotilla sighted a line of three ships coming up from abaft the beam and overtaking on a slightly converging course. They were seen to be light-cruisers with four funnels, and both the *Tipperary* and the *Broke*, and perhaps other ships as well, thought they might be one of the British Light-Cruiser Squadrons, which seemed all the more likely as a British light-cruiser had passed to port at 9.50 after replying correctly to the challenge.

For some minutes the strange ships were watched with uncertainty. Then the *Tipperary* started to challenge with her flashing-lamp, to which the instant reply was a blaze of searchlights from all three cruisers and a burst of heavy gunfire at a range of no more than 800 yards.

The very first salvo struck the ship forward, wrecked the bridge, cut the communications, and killed or wounded practically every soul in the forepart of the ship. Both the *Tipperary's* starboard torpedoes were fired, and the acting sub-lieutenant, N. J. W. William-Powlett,[1] opened fire with the after guns on his own initiative. A shell then severed a steam-pipe, and the ship became shrouded in clouds of steam.

Hit in the engine-room, the *Tipperary* was brought to a standstill. She was under fire for about three minutes, and when the steam died away William-Powlett found she was blazing forward, with the boxes of cartridges for the foremost guns exploding one after the other. Practically everybody forward or amidships had either been killed or wounded, the enemy fire having been concentrated on the forepart of the ship. Utterly helpless and stationary, she continued to blaze like a beacon.

The next ship astern of her, the *Spitfire*, Lieutenant-Commander C. W. E. Trelawny,[1] fired two torpedoes at the second ship in the enemy line which was a cruiser with four tall funnels. " The torpedo," Trelawny reported, " struck her between the second funnel and the mainmast. She appeared to catch fire fore and aft simultaneously, and heeled right over to starboard and undoubtedly sank."

After firing a number of rounds to distract the attention of the enemy from the blazing *Tipperary*, the *Spitfire*, under heavy fire, turned off to the west to reload her torpedo-tube with the spare torpedo. Unfortunately, this was impossible, as the davit had been hit in three places, and the gunner and 2 torpedo ratings wounded. Before he was aware of this, Trelawny turned back to attack a " cruiser "[3] which had a searchlight on the *Tipperary*. Unable to torpedo her, he satisfied himself by firing

---

[1] Now Lieutenant-Commander, and D.S.C.   [2] Now Captain.
[3] It was really a battleship.

at the enemy searchlight, which was promptly extinguished. Still closing the *Tipperary*, he suddenly sighted " two cruisers " very close steaming at high speed to the south-eastward. The nearest altered course to ram, opening fire as she did so. Two shells passed through the bridge-screens, one removing Trelawny's cap and inflicting a nasty wound, and the other killing everyone on the bridge except himself, the coxswain, and one seaman.

But things were happening in split seconds. A collision of some sort was inevitable, and, sooner than be cut in halves, Trelawny went on to full speed, put his helm hard over, and shouted over the bridge rails to " Clear the forecastle ! "

It was not a moment too soon. With a shuddering crash and the shrill screech of tearing steel the two ships, both travelling at high speed, met port bow to port bow. The *Spitfire* reeled bodily over to starboard under the blow until the edge of her upper deck was well under water. As they struck, the enemy opened fire with her bow guns immediately overhead. The weapons could not be depressed sufficiently to hit ; but their terrific blast utterly demolished the destroyer's bridge, and knocked down the mast and foremost funnel. Crashing and bumping along the *Spitfire's* side, the " cruiser " then wrenched out the boat's davits and did other damage before she finally drew clear.

With the remains of her bridge starting to blaze, the destroyer slid away from her big adversary into the darkness astern. Those on board expected that at any moment the fire would attract the attention of another ship, and that they would be demolished at point-blank range. But nothing happened, so they set about investigating their injuries.

The ship was little more than a wreck. Besides the damage to the bridge, mast, and foremost funnel, the forecastle was torn open above water for about sixty feet from the stem to well abaft the bridge, and below water from the stem to the second bulkhead. On the fore mess-deck a long, wide slice of the side had completely disappeared, and in the enormous rent the German had left about twenty feet of her side-plating. Surprising to relate, however, the *Spitfire* made comparatively little water forward.

Trelawny, who was lying stunned on the upper deck with the tangled remains of his bridge, was given up for dead, so the first lieutenant – Athelstan P. Bush – took charge of the ship and gave orders for the after steering position to be connected up. It was found that three of the four boilers were still fit for use, so that, if the bulkheads forward would stand the strain, the *Spitfire* could still steam.

It was while these preparations and investigations were being made that those on the quarter-deck suddenly saw a large ship on fire steering straight for them with, it seemed, the deliberate intention of ramming. Giving themselves up for lost, some of the men lay down flat and waited for the crash.

A few seconds passed in agonising suspense. Then the approaching vessel seemed to swerve. Missing the *Spitfire* by a few feet, she passed so close that her guns, trained out on the beam, reached out over the destroyer's stern. As one of the *Spitfire's* officers wrote afterwards : " She tore past us with a roar, rather like a motor roaring up-hill on low gear, and the very crackling and heat of the flames could be heard and felt. She was a mass of fire from foremast to mainmast, on deck and between decks. Flames were issuing out of her from every corner."[1]

This ship was probably one of the badly damaged German battle-cruisers, perhaps the *Derfflinger* or *Seydlitz*.

Bush managed to get the *Spitfire* under way, and steamed her off at slow speed on a north-westerly course. Then Trelawny, who had been hurled twenty-four feet on to the upper deck when the bridge was demolished, recovered consciousness, struggled free of the wreckage, and came aft. The others, thinking him dead, were overjoyed at seeing him. He was badly knocked about, but still capable of duty.

They discussed what they should do. As Trelawny says in his report, " The extent of the damage to the *Spitfire* seemed so great, and the possibility of steaming for long at any speed so small, that I decided not to endeavour to rejoin the fleet, but to make for port " – a distance, let it be said, of fully 260 miles.

Having destroyed all the confidential books and documents, lest the worst should happen and the ship should fall into the hands of the Germans, they set about shoring up bulkheads and filling up the great gashes in the bow with what scanty materials they had available. The *Spitfire* was anything but seaworthy by the time they had finished ; but, patching together the torn fragments of a chart, they shaped course to the westward at 6 knots.

I cannot stop to describe all the vicissitudes and anxieties of that dismal voyage home, at any moment of which the *Spitfire*

---

[1] *F. J.*, p. 205.

might have foundered. With her wireless demolished she could not call for assistance, and by dawn the next morning the wind was freshening from the south-west and the sea had started to rise. At 8 a.m. it seemed doubtful if the foremost bulkheads would stand the strain, and she was forced to turn head to sea and ease down. During the same afternoon – June 1st - the weather became worse, and she had to turn northward to keep the sea on the quarter.

The night came down, black, sullen, and full of wind, with a heavy, toppling sea. Their hopes of ever getting home fell almost to vanishing-point. Between 1 and 2 a.m. on June 2nd, thinking they were about sixty miles off the English or Scottish coast, they decided to fire distress signals on the off-chance of some ship sighting them and coming to their assistance.

Then the wonderful thing happened. They must have been under the lee of the coast without knowing it, for at 4.30 a.m. the wind and sea started to go down and they were able to steer west-south-west at 10 knots. Later on in the morning they met a patrol drifter, which informed them they were twenty-two miles from the Tyne. They reached the river at noon, thirty-six interminable hours after having been in action and collision with an enemy ship far away on the other side of the North Sea.

In this, one of the most amazing incidents of the battle, the *Spitfire* lost 6 men killed, and 3 officers and 16 men wounded. She returned to harbour with twenty feet of her enemy's side-plating, together with part of the anchor gear, wedged inside her mess-deck. " By the thickness of the paint," Trelawny wrote in his report, " 3-32nds of an inch, she could not appear to have been a very new ship."

But that plating did not belong to a light-cruiser. Trelawny's antagonist was the German Dreadnought battleship *Nassau*, a monster of about 20,000 tons.

The *Spitfire's* tonnage was no more than 935 !

3

Before describing the end of the *Tipperary*, which did not finally sink until about 1.45 a.m., it is as well to set forth the doings of other destroyers of the 4th Flotilla.

The *Sparrowhawk*, Lieutenant-Commander Sydney Hopkins,[1]

[1] Now Captain.

was the third ship in the line, astern of the *Tipperary* and *Spitfire*. When fire was opened, she discharged a torpedo at the third ship in the German line. Soon afterwards the *Tipperary* was blazing and the *Spitfire* had disappeared, so eventually, finding the *Broke* just clear of the line, Hopkins took station astern of her.

The *Broke*, Commander Walter L. Allen, the sixth ship in the line, had also fired a torpedo at the enemy, altering course to port to do so and increasing to full speed. A little later the ship was brought back to her original course of south and the speed reduced to 17 knots, it being Allen's intention to attempt another attack on the three cruisers. The *Sparrowhawk* was sighted and took station astern, when almost at once those on the *Broke's* bridge sighted a large ship before the starboard beam and not more than 800 yards away. The stranger switched on green and red recognition lights, which proclaimed her a German.

Allen instantly went on to full speed, ordered a torpedo to be fired, and then, after a pause, put his helm over to starboard. The sights of the tube never came on, and the torpedo was not discharged. At the same moment the hostile battleship switched on a blaze of searchlights and opened fire. The *Broke's* 4-inch guns replied, shooting at the enemy lights.

The German night defence organisation left nothing to be desired. In all the engagements on the night of May 31st—June 1st it was noticeable that the searchlights never wavered, but directed their beams straight on to their targets. And the guns opened fire immediately.

Like the *Tipperary*, the *Broke* was at once smothered in bursting shell. The lower bridge was struck, the helmsman and another man being killed, and the wheel and engine-room telegraphs demolished. Then the searchlights went out and the firing ceased.

The *Broke* was still going ahead at full speed with her helm to starboard. The *Sparrowhawk* was close to port, and, not realising his helm and engine-room telegraphs were useless, Allen ordered the helm to be put hard over the other way and the engines to go full speed astern. The order could not be obeyed.

An instant later the *Broke* struck the *Sparrowhawk* on her starboard bow abreast the bridge, her sharp bows cutting half way through the destroyer and pushing her bodily through the water until the two vessels crashed alongside each other. The impact was sufficient to bring the flotilla-leader up all standing, while the sub-lieutenant and three men of the *Sparrowhawk* were thrown on to the flotilla-leader's forecastle.

Lurching unpleasantly in the swell, the *Broke* seemed to be sinking by the bow. Steam roaring out of the foremost boiler-room through damage caused by enemy shell shrouded the ship in a cloud of misty vapour. Allen, having ordered his first lieutenant and another officer to go aft and connect up the after steering position, went into his sea-cabin on the bridge to dispose of the confidential books. The enemy had ceased firing, but

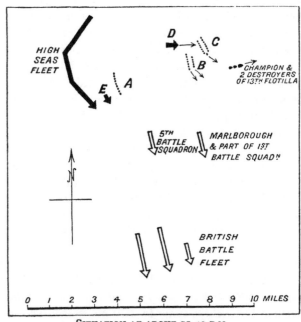

SITUATION AT ABOUT 11.40 P.M.

(A) 4TH FLOTILLA :—*Broke, Sparrowhawk, Garland, Contest, Achates, Ambuscade, Ardent, Fortune, Porpoise.*
    Broke, Sparrowhawk and *Contest* collide.
(B) Twelve destroyers of 9th, 10th, and 13th Flotillas.
(C) *Faulknor* with fourteen destroyers of 12th Flotilla.
(D) Two German light-cruisers, *Frankfurt* and *Pillau*, which foul rear of 12th Flotilla and cut off *Menace* and *Nonsuch* from rest of flotilla. *Nonsuch* never succeeded in rejoining.
(E) Light-cruiser *Rostock* torpedoed.

might reappear at any moment to complete the work of destruction.

The two officers found their way aft and met the engineer officer, who told them he had stopped the engines on his own initiative and that three boilers were still in working order. The after bridge was then manned, and the *Broke* went astern to clear the *Sparrowhawk*, against which she was bumping and crashing heavily. It was at this moment that the *Contest* suddenly appeared out of the darkness at high speed and crashed into the *Sparrowhawk*, cutting off five feet of her stern and jamming her rudder hard a-port.

The *Garland*, Lieutenant-Commander R. S. Goff, the *Sparrowhawk's* next astern, after firing a torpedo at a range of about 800 yards, narrowly escaped collision with the *Sparrowhawk* when she was struck by the *Broke*. She then lost touch with the flotilla, but later fell in with the *Contest*, who could still steam 20 knots without danger. The next destroyer in the line, the *Achates*, Commander R. B. C. Hutchinson, D.S.C., just avoided collision with the *Broke*, and then endeavoured to join up with the first half of the flotilla. " Firing at this time was general in the enemy's line on the starboard bow and beam and the range close," Hutchinson wrote in his report. " The order to fire was passed to the tubes as the sights came on. I subsequently cancelled the order to fire torpedoes, being under the impression that our cruisers were engaging the enemy between us and the enemy's line and fearing that my torpedoes would cross the line of our own ships."[1] This once more illustrates the hazards, chances, and uncertainty of destroyer actions at night, particularly when the destroyers have not been informed of the whereabouts of friendly squadrons.

The *Ambuscade*, Lieutenant-Commander Gordon A. Coles, the ship astern of the *Achates*, fired two torpedoes at the cruisers which had attacked the *Tipperary*, and the two remaining at a line of German battleships some twenty minutes later. Both this ship and the *Achates* were afterwards chased off to the eastward by enemy cruisers.

The *Ardent*, Lieutenant-Commander Arthur Marsden, astern of the *Ambuscade*, had been watching the other ships of her flotilla engaged ahead, when, just after midnight, she sighted four large ships on the starboard side closing in on a converging course. Their leader challenged with red and green lights, and almost immediately switched on searchlights, lit up the *Fortune* (Lieutenant-Commander F. G. Terry), the *Ardent's* next astern, and opened fire. Marsden fired a torpedo which seemed to strike, but the *Fortune*, heavily hit, was already in a sinking condition.[2]

---

[1] *B. J. O. D.*, p. 309.
[2] Ten of her survivors were picked up by the *Maenad* at 5 a.m.

Blazing like a bonfire, half shrouded in smoke and steam, she lay in a welter of shell-splashes.

The second ship in the enemy line then turned her searchlights on the *Ardent*, and opened up a furious fire. Marsden turned away to port and increased speed. A few minutes later he turned again to starboard to find his next ahead, and soon sighted what he took to be the *Ambuscade's* smoke. But it was not the *Ambuscade*. It was a line of four large enemy ships crossing the *Ardent's* bows from starboard to port.

Marsden attacked at once and fired a torpedo at the leading vessel. The usual thing happened. Two ships flashed on their searchlights, and in an instant the *Ardent* became the target for a withering fire. Her own little 4-inch guns replied until their crews were killed or wounded. Salvo after salvo struck home at point-blank range. The speed diminished – then the engines stopped altogether.

The bombardment lasted for about five minutes, after which the enemy switched off their lights and disappeared into the darkness.

Marsden himself had been badly wounded in the thigh by the first salvo. Most of his officers and men were killed or wounded, and his ship, gradually sinking, was a complete wreck. The boats and Carley floats were useless, the funnels perforated through and through with splinter holes, the deck and ship's side holed in many places, with smoke and steam rising through them. Marsden disposed of his confidential books by throwing them overboard, and then hobbled aft to try to get some rafts made with which to save the few survivors.

Overcome by his wound, which was hurting and bleeding a great deal, he sat down on the wardroom hatch. His servant and another man, with whom he had been shipmates for two years, came aft to help him. He sent them forward, and told them to pass the word for each man to look out for himself. Hardly had they left him when what remained of his ship was suddenly lit up by searchlights, and four or five salvos were poured in at point-blank range. Then darkness.

It was the end. The *Ardent* lurched over – started to sink.

Remembering his life-saving waistcoat, Marsden tried to inflate it. It had been shot through. Another sudden lurch and he was thrown on to the ship's side, so, snatching a lifebuoy, he slid into the sea. The stern of the ship remained in view for a few moments, and then disappeared. As the smoke and steam over the spot gradually thinned away, he could see the heads of forty or fifty men in the water, supporting themselves as best they could in lifebelts and lifebuoys, and any timber that floated. " I spoke to many men, and saw most of them die one by one. Not a man of them showed any fear of death, and there was not a murmur, complaint, or cry for help from a single soul. Their joy was – and they talked about it to the end – that they and the *Ardent* had ' done their bit,' as they put it."[1]

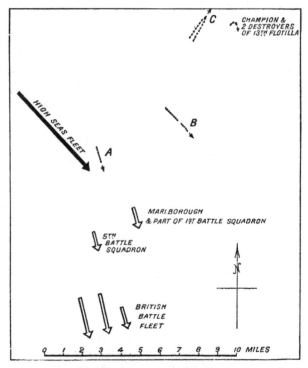

SITUATION AT ABOUT MIDNIGHT

(A) 4TH FLOTILLA :—*Achates, Ambuscade, Ardent, Fortune, Porpoise, Garland, Contest.*
(B) Thirteen destroyers of 9th, 10th, and 12th Flotillas.
(C) *Faulknor* and 12th Flotilla.
    Achates and *Ambuscade* driven off. *Ardent* attacks, turns to east and then to south, and is sunk about 12.15. *Fortune* sunk. *Porpoise* put out of action.

At one period a German ship came quite close and fired a star-shell. Marsden, who could see her distinctly, suggested hailing. But those men who were still alive said " No." They preferred

[1] For this and many of the details of the sinking of the *Ardent* I am indebted to Captain Arthur Marsden for permission to make use of his narrative printed in the *Britannia Magazine* of the R.N. College, Dartmouth, for Christmas 1916.

to take the remote chance of being saved by a friend, rather than find themselves in an enemy prison.

The long night wore on. Several times Marsden was nearly drowned by exhausted men clutching him, and once he was dragged right under water and separated from his lifebuoy. The men died without appearing to suffer ; " they just seemed to lie back and go to sleep."

After a long time the sun rose, and Marsden, who says he was feeling more comfortable than he had before, found a dinghy's oar, which he put under his arms. Then came periods of unconsciousness, from which he was brought to by little waves spluttering in his face. The sea was covered with oil. There was a swell, and once, coming to and hearing a shout, he saw the tantalising sight of ships in the distance, watched them disappear. Then, as he says, he " dozed off again."

Recovering consciousness again, he saw a flotilla-leader, the *Marksman*, close alongside. He was dragged on board without knowing much about it, and just in time. The time was just after 6 a.m. He had been in the water for over five hours.

Her captain, and two men rescued by the *Obdurate*, one of whom died on board, were the only survivors of the *Ardent*. All the rest of the ship's company – 4 officers and 74 men – had gone to their deaths.

The *Fortune*, the *Ardent's* next astern, had been sunk about midnight. Astern of the *Fortune* came the *Porpoise*, Commander H. D. Colville.

At the same time as the *Fortune* came under fire the *Porpoise* was also engaged, and was hit at the base of the after funnel by an 8-inch shell which did much damage, besides killing and wounding several men. The wheel and telegraphs on the forebridge having been demolished, and his ship lying stopped, Colville went aft and had the after steering position connected up. The boilers were damaged ; but the ship finally managed to limp home to the Tyne after falling in with the *Garland* and *Contest* on the way.

In the course of these various engagements, and the inevitable confusion at the head of the line, the *Unity*, Lieutenant-Commander A. M. Lecky, the rear ship of the 4th Flotilla, lost company with her consorts and joined up with the *Lydiard* and ten destroyers of the 9th and 13th Flotillas. She eventually arrived at Aberdeen without further incident.

4

We left the *Tipperary* at about 11.30 p.m., still afloat, but obviously a sinking ship, with her forepart blazing like a blast furnace. The bridge, or what remained of it, was alight. Long tongues of red flame and clouds of smoke rose from the foremost coal-bunkers. To add to the conflagration, the ready supply of ammunition for the foremost guns continued to explode at short intervals, to send showers of sparks and shreds of blazing cordite flying into the air. At any moment the flames might reach the fore magazine, to blast what remained of the ship into fragments.

It was impossible to get forward because of the fires. The deck was littered with dead and wounded, and all the boats were smashed to splinters. The only two serviceable floats that remained were got into the water. The many wounded were given what attention was possible, the worst cases being laid on the quarter-deck and covered over with bedding from the officers' cabins.

At about 1 a.m. two small ships appeared off the port beam. They looked like German destroyers, and hailed in English, " What ship is that ? " They did not open fire, and it is probable that one or other of these vessels rescued 8 men who had left the *Tipperary* in a Carley float and were afterwards reported to have been made prisoners of war.

At about 1.45 a.m. the first lieutenant[1] realised that the ship was about to sink, and ordered everybody aft. She started to heel over to starboard, and the bows went under. The order was given, " Everyone for themselves ! " and the survivors clambered over the side and into the icy-cold sea. A few managed to reach the one Carley float that remained ; but the rest jumped for their lives. After about a minute the bows disappeared completely, the stern shot up into the air until the propellers and rudder were out of water, and then disappeared.

There were about 30 men in the water and some more in, and holding on to, the Carley float. The sub-lieutenant describes how he swam away from the others, preferring to drown by himself. Then, thinking better of it, he swam towards the already overcrowded float, and was pulled up on to it. It was at about this time, or shortly before, that they were passed by the German pulling boats, filled with men. Some of the *Tipperary's* men shouted for help ; but were told, not unnaturally, to " Go to

[1] Apparently the Lieutenant (G), Lieutenant J. A. Kemp.

hell !" These boats came from the light cruiser *Elbing*, which had sunk shortly before, after having been in collision with the battleship *Posen* during the confusion created in the German line by the continuous destroyer attacks.

The *Tipperary's* survivors, utterly exhausted and half dead from exposure, tried to keep up their failing spirits by singing popular songs. A swell rose to add to their misery. Then the chilly dawn started to creep across the surface of the sea, and as the light grew they saw a small ship within a mile, apparently steaming in circles. This was the *Sparrowhawk*, with five feet cut off her stern, her rudder jammed, and her bows nearly severed in line with the bridge.

Those on board the *Sparrowhawk* at first took the Carley float for a submarine, for the swell had risen and they only saw it at intervals. Then, realising what it was, they tried to steam towards it, though with little success because of the jammed rudder. But by dint of using the paddles and extemporising a sail from a counterpane, the *Tipperary's* survivors, after almost an hour and a half, at last managed to work their way alongside the battered destroyer, singing as they did so, " It's a long, long way to Tipperary." The time was apparently between 4 and 5 a.m.

According to the sub-lieutenant of the *Tipperary*, 30 men were originally on the float, 4 of whom died from exposure, and 4 after reaching the *Sparrowhawk*. From the *Sparrowhawk's* account, however, 26 men from the *Tipperary* arrived alongside, 3 of whom were already dead. Sixteen collapsed after being hauled on board, and of these 5 died in the *Sparrowhawk*. [1]

The *Sparrowhawk's* own adventures had been thrilling enough. After being rammed forward by the *Broke* and aft by the *Contest*, efforts were made to work the ship to the westward with the still undamaged propellers. Progress, however, was desperately slow, which perhaps was just as well for the survivors of the *Tipperary*.

A little later an enemy destroyer suddenly steamed slowly up to the wreck and stopped within 100 yards. The after gun and after torpedo-tube were at once manned, all the spare men being ordered to lie down on deck. In the hope of saving the ship, however, Hopkins decided not to open fire unless the enemy fired first. For a few breathless minutes they awaited the expected flashes and the crash and explosion of driving shell. But nothing happened. The German captain, apparently satisfied that the

---

[1] Stoker Parkyn, of the *Tipperary*, was rescued by the *Dublin* at 5.30 a.m.

Sparrowhawk could fight no more, restarted his engines and disappeared in the darkness.

The engineers were trying hard to cut through the bolts of the damaged rudder and to drop it into the sea, which might have enabled the ship to steer a tolerably straight course with her screws while travelling stern first. But it was found to be impossible. Neither could help be summoned, for the wireless was demolished. A boy telegraphist of sixteen-and-a-half tried his utmost to produce a temporary set ; but it could not be made to function.

At about 2 a.m., when it was beginning to get light, the *Sparrowhawk* again saw the hull of a ship appearing through the mist. They watched it anxiously, hoping against hope that she might prove to be a friend. Then, as she approached, they saw to their horror that the stranger was a German light-cruiser with three funnels. Ammunition was got up from the magazines and shell-rooms. They prepared to fight to the last.

They waited anxiously for the flash of the enemy's guns. Nothing happened. The cruiser came closer and closer, until she was within a mile and a half. Then, as it gradually became lighter, someone with glasses noticed she was listing over and down by the bows. The heel increased. The strange ship's bows sank deeper and deeper in the water. Then the unforgettable thing happened – she " quietly stood on her head, and – sank."[1]

This vessel may have been either the *Elbing* or *Rostock*, the first-named having been in collision with the *Posen* during the night attacks at 11.30, and the *Rostock* being hit by a torpedo fired by one or other of the British destroyers at about the same time. From Admiral's Scheer's official report it was most probably the *Elbing*,[2] as the times seem to correspond.

[1] *F. J.*, p. 210.

[2] " At 1.30 a.m." (the German times are two hours in advance of the British) " the *Rostock* and *Elbing* became engaged with destroyers . . . and were at last compelled to turn away from the enemy's torpedoes and break through the line of the Squadron in order not to hamper the fire of our battleships. During this manœuvre the *Rostock* was hit by a torpedo, while the *Elbing* collided with the *Posen*. Both cruisers were unable to manœuvre. The *Rostock* remained afloat until 5.45 a.m., and was then blown up, a hostile cruiser being sighted, after the entire crew, including the wounded, had been transferred to boats of the III Flotilla. The crew of the *Elbing* were also taken on board a boat of the III Flotilla, only the commanding officer, the executive officer, the torpedo officer, and a cutter's crew remaining on board in order to keep the ship afloat as long as possible. On hostile forces being sighted at 4 a.m., the *Elbing* had to be blown up too. The crew who remained on board escaped in the cutter, were picked up later by a Dutch trawler, and returned home via Holland." (From Admiral Scheer's official report, a German copy of which was found in an officer's

The next incident was when the *Tipperary's* survivors arrived on board the *Sparrowhawk*, which has already been described. Wind and sea were rising fast, and very soon afterwards the bows of the damaged destroyer broke off from the hull and floated away.

Times are rather uncertain, but a little later the *Sparrowhawk* sighted a four-funnelled British cruiser in the mist on the horizon. She made the private signal, to which the destroyer could not reply – and then disappeared. A Dutch trawler next hove in sight at a distance of about two miles – possibly the trawler which had on board the captain and some other officers and men of the *Elbing*. The *Sparrowhawk* waved to attract her attention ; but the Dutchman took no notice, and steamed on out of sight. " We cursed her good and proper," one of the *Sparrowhawk's* officers wrote.

But salvation was at hand, for at about 6 a.m. there appeared the flotilla-leader *Marksman* and some British destroyers. The *Marksman*, Commander Norton A. Sulivan, was soon close alongside. Taking most of the men out of the *Sparrowhawk*, Sulivan succeeded in getting her in tow stern first with two 3½-inch wires. But, after towing for about half a mile at 3 knots, both hawsers carried away, due to the strain caused by the *Sparrowhawk's* stern being missing, and her rudder being jammed hard a-port. Salvage was impossible, and, the rest of the men having been transhipped, the remains of the ship were sunk by gunfire.

The *Sparrowhawk* went to the bottom at about 7.45 a.m. with her ensign still flying.

5

We left the *Broke* shortly before midnight, badly damaged by shell fire and after collision with the *Sparrowhawk*. She managed to steam off to the north at slow speed, soon afterwards sighting three enemy vessels which showed no signs of having seen her.

She had suffered terrible casualties, having been hit nine times by enemy shell. There were 42 killed, 6 missing, 14 severely, and 20 slightly, wounded – a total of 82 out of a complement of about 200. Most of the store-rooms and lower compartments in the forepart of the ship were flooded, the foremost boiler-room was leaking and the three foremost boilers were out of action, the

cabin of one of the ships afterwards scuttled in Scapa Flow. The report, translated, is printed in full as Appendix III of *Battle of Jutland*. *Official Despatches*, H.M.S.O.)

bridge was utterly wrecked and the foremost guns useless. The enemy fire, concentrated on the forepart of the ship, had been surprisingly accurate, so accurate that the ship had not been hit abaft the second funnel. By the mercy of Providence, the engines and after boilers were still in working order.

At about 1.15 a.m. on June 1st, two enemy destroyers – G.53 and G.88 – appeared on the starboard quarter, steaming towards the *Broke* at full speed. The only two serviceable guns that remained were aft, so, turning his stern towards them, Commander Allen increased to his best possible speed – 10 knots – and engaged them at a distance of about 500 yards. The enemy came up abreast of the damaged ship, fired about half a dozen rounds, two of which struck amidships, and then, to the amazement and joy of everyone on board, put their helms over and disappeared into the mist. The *Broke* was no longer a fighting unit.

All through June 1st she struggled on to the westward. During the ensuing night the wind and sea started to rise. At midnight the foremast rolled overboard, through most of its rigging being shot away, and by 4 o'clock on the morning of the 2nd it was blowing nearly a full gale from the north-west with a very heavy sea. The *Broke* was bumping so badly that she had to turn round and steam slowly to the south-east to prevent the foremost bulkheads from collapsing. Meanwhile, unable to get touch by wireless, the commander-in-chief had despatched cruisers to search for her. Their efforts were fruitless.

The weather moderated on the evening of the 2nd, and the *Broke* was able gradually to resume her course to the westward, eventually sighting the English coast at 5 p.m. on June 3rd, and reaching the Tyne about three hours later.

Thus ended the adventures of the gallant 4th Destroyer Flotilla.

As already described, the *Shark* and *Acasta*, of the same flotilla, had been sunk and seriously injured at about 6 p.m. while on detached duty with Rear-Admiral Hood's 3rd Battle-Cruiser Squadron. Of the two flotilla-leaders and ten destroyers present with Captain H. Wintour at nightfall on May 31st, four – the *Tipperary*, *Sparrowhawk*, *Ardent*, and *Fortune* – had been lost, and four more – the *Broke*, *Spitfire*, *Contest*, and *Porpoise* – more or less seriously damaged and out of action. Excluding the *Shark* and *Acasta*, the flotilla had lost 19 officers and 371 men killed or drowned, and 8 officers and 64 men wounded, a total casualty list of 462.

So far as can be discovered, they fired about 13 torpedoes,

possibly a few more. Though none of the enemy's battleships was hit, the light-cruiser *Rostock* was struck by a torpedo and afterwards sank, while the *Elbing*, though being forced to turn away to avoid the attack, came into collision with the *Posen*, and eventually foundered.

" Alone," as wrote the late Sir Julian Corbett in his account of the night fighting, " they had borne the brunt of the whole German battle-fleet, and not a man had flinched. Again and again, as a group of the enemy tore them with shell at point-blank and disappeared, they sought another, and attacked until nearly every boat had spent all her torpedoes or was a wreck. Such high spirit and skill had they shown that one thing was certain – the failure of the flotilla to achieve all that was generally expected from it was due to no shortcoming in the human factor. It was the power of the weapon itself that had been overrated."[1]

By " the power of the weapon " Sir Julian evidently refers to the power of the torpedo as a destructive agent, and the ability of destroyers to use it at night.

On various occasions at Jutland, both by day and by night, the torpedo proved its *tactical* utility by forcing fleets, squadrons, or even single ships, to turn away in the face of destroyer attacks. Nevertheless, there is no disguising the fact that as a means of inflicting destruction or severe damage it hardly came up to expectations. It showed itself to be a chancy, difficult weapon to use in the face of modern gunfire by day, and doubly difficult to use at night against modern methods of defence, with search-lights ably controlled.

Of all the mass of ships present on the British side, only the battleship *Marlborough* was struck and damaged by a torpedo, which eventually forced her to leave the line through loss of speed. On the German side, the battle-cruiser *Seydlitz* was torpedoed ; but was able to continue the action until incapacitated by gunfire. The by no means modern battleship *Pommern*, the light-cruisers *Frauenlob* and *Rostock*, together with one destroyer, were actually sunk by British torpedoes, while the *Wiesbaden* and one other destroyer were torpedoed after being badly damaged and stopped by gunfire.

Considering the number of torpedoes fired on both sides, the results actually achieved were surprisingly small.

But what the British flotillas most lacked during the night was INFORMATION. Beyond the fact that they were stationed

[1] *N. O.* iii., pp. 400 and 401.

about five miles astern of the British battle-fleet, most of them knew nothing of the whereabouts of Sir David Beatty's battle-cruisers, or the numerous cruiser and light-cruiser squadrons of the Grand Fleet. Moreover, apart from their own observation, which, in the low visibility, the stress and turmoil of a daylight action, and the preoccupation of their officers in keeping station and manœuvring at high speed, must necessarily have been very limited, they seem to have known little or nothing of the whereabouts of the enemy fleet, or where it had last been seen. In the strain and anxiety of the battle, nobody seems to have visualised the inherent difficulties of small craft at night, or to have realised the prime importance of telling them what to expect.

It is as well to remember that at nightfall the destroyers were NOT sent forth to attack the enemy's heavy ships. As the commander-in-chief wrote in his despatch, he was able to drop his flotillas astern – " thus at one and the same time providing the battle-fleet with a screen against attack by torpedo-craft at night, and also giving our flotillas an opportunity for attacking the enemy's heavy ships should they also be proceeding to the southward with the object of regaining their bases."[1] With a renewal of the engagement at daylight uppermost in his mind, Sir John Jellicoe would naturally wish to have his destroyers about him by dawn. This would have not been possible if the flotillas had been sent off in the night to search for and attack the High Seas Fleet.

Opportunities for attacking duly came ; but full advantage of them could not be taken. Time and time again destroyers were forced for a time to withhold their torpedo fire, lest the ships they sighted might be friendly. They could not fire on sight. Uncertainty meant delay, and delay at night, with potential attackers and attacked steaming at high speeds, meant the loss of chances which, in some cases at least, never came again.

Moreover, and probably unknown to most of the commanding officers in the British flotillas, the *Marlborough*, unable to keep up the speed of the fleet – 17 knots – because of her torpedo damage, had dropped a long way astern of station. With her were the *Revenge, Hercules* and *Agincourt*. At 10 p.m., Rear-Admiral Evan-Thomas turned his 5th Battle Squadron – *Barham, Valiant, Malaya* – back to look for the *Marlborough's* sub-division. Then it came about that at the time of the 4th Flotilla's action at 11.20 the 5th Battle Squadron was little more than a

[1] *B. J. O. D.*, p. 21.

mile on the *Tipperary's* port bow, with the *Marlborough* and her three other ships almost two miles farther to the eastward. (See diagram for 11.20.) If these battleships had been sighted in the darkness by the flotillas, which were supposed to be five miles astern of the main battle-fleet, there would have been more uncertainty as to whether they were friendly or hostile – possibly a regrettable incident.

CHAPTER XIII

DESTROYERS AT JUTLAND : NIGHT AND EARLY MORNING, JUNE 1st

I

THE light-cruiser *Champion*, Captain J. U. Farie, with nine destroyers of the 13th Flotilla, was roughly four miles to the north-eastward of the *Tipperary*. Keeping station on the *Champion's* port beam was the *Lydiard*, Commander M. L. Gold-smith, with four more destroyers, while a short distance astern of the *Lydiard* was Captain A. J. B. Stirling, in the *Faulknor*, with one other flotilla-leader and thirteen destroyers of the 12th Flotilla. (See diagram for 11.20.)

Most of these vessels had seen the glare of searchlights, the sparkle of gun-flashes, and the blaze of burning vessels during the *Castor's* and 2nd Light-Cruiser Squadron's engagement between 10 and 10.30. An hour later, however, the roar of a fiercer battle, with the usual searchlight rays, and the blaze of guns and ships on fire, broke out from nearer at hand to the west-ward, when the 4th Flotilla came into action against the German light-cruisers and battleships.

" Heavy firing was opened on our starboard beam, apparently at some of our destroyers between the 13th Flotilla and the enemy," Captain Farie wrote in his report. " I hauled out to the eastward, as I was unable to attack with any of our own flotilla, our own forces being between me and the enemy." [1]

The commanding officers of the *Nerissa* and *Nicator*, the fourth and fifth ships in the *Champion's* line, mentioned that at 11.30 salvos of shell were splashing into the water close to them, and Commander M. L. Goldsmith, of the *Lydiard* : " 11.30 p.m. Fire was opened on us by a line of large ships which we took to be our own." [2] The same observation was made by Lieutenant-Commander F. E. Hobart, of the *Landrail*, the third ship in the *Lydiard's* line. So once again there was this element of uncertainty, this suspicion that the ships firing might really be friendly.

The *Champion's* sudden swerve to the eastward at high speed

[1] *B. J. O. D.*, p. 225.   [2] *B. J. O. D.*, p. 255.

and without signal was unfortunate.   Only the two destroyers immediately astern of her, the *Obdurate* and *Moresby*, realised what was happening and managed to follow.   The third ship in the line, the *Nerissa*, lost touch, and, with the other six destroyers astern of her, the *Nicator*, *Termagant*, *Narbrough*, *Pelican*, *Petard*, and *Turbulent*, tailed on to the end of the *Lydiard's* line, until Goldsmith, without realising it, was leading twelve destroyers.   The *Unity*, of the 4th Flotilla, also joined him at midnight.   Soon afterwards, in order to get on the other side of the big ships, which were still firing spasmodically, Goldsmith increased to 25 knots and altered course to south-west.

But the *Champion's* unexpected movement to the eastward had another result, for Captain Stirling, leading his 12th Flotilla in the *Faulknor*, was driven off his course by Captain Farie steaming across his bows at high speed.   As the flotilla was turning, two enemy cruisers, afterwards ascertained to be the *Frankfurt* and *Pillau*, suddenly appeared at the end of the line.   (See diagram for 11.40.)   The *Menace* had to put her helm hard over to avoid collision, while the *Nonsuch* turned to the eastward, increased to full speed, and did not succeed in finding the flotilla again in the darkness.

The *Faulknor* was forced away until she was eventually steering north-east. (See diagram for Midnight.)   It was not until 12.15 a.m. that she was again able to steer south at 17 knots.   Captain Stirling estimated that his undesired détour put him five miles east of his original position and ten miles astern of the battle-fleet. In reality, it was about twenty-four miles.

The *Lydiard*, meanwhile, with a long line of destroyers behind her, was steering south-westerly at 25 knots.   Without knowing it, Commander Goldsmith was leading his ships almost at right angles across the line of advance of the van of the German battle-fleet.   The destroyers, travelling at high speed, must have been considerably spread out, for neither the *Lydiard* nor any of the eight leading vessels saw anything of the enemy.

At 12.30 a.m., however, the *Narbrough*, Lieutenant-Commander Geoffrey Corlett, the fourth destroyer from the end of the line, sighted " a large vessel making much smoke " crossing the rear of the flotilla from starboard to port at high speed.   He at first took her to be a British light-cruiser or an armoured cruiser, one of which had been in sight on the starboard quarter during the first watch.   It was not until she showed her recognition lights at a distance of about 1,000 yards, and, almost immediately, switched on her searchlights and opened a heavy fire on the rear of the line, that he realised she was hostile.

The *Pelican*, Lieutenant-Commander K. A. Beattie, immediately astern of the *Narbrough*, sighted two ships at much the same time, and also took them for British light-cruisers until they opened fire.

The ship astern of the *Pelican*, the *Petard*, Lieutenant-Commander E. C. O. Thomson, was in no doubt at all. At about 12.25 a.m., while still steering south-west, Thomson sighted the dark mass of a battleship about six points on his starboard bow at a distance of about 500 yards. She was steering about south-east, or at right angles across his bows. There was no doubt as to what she was. He could see her large crane derricks amidships silhouetted against a patch of clear sky, which at once proclaimed her as German.

There was little time to think. The course the *Petard* was steering would bring her very nearly into collision, and, as she had expended all her four torpedoes during the daylight action, Thomson increased to full speed and altered course to port to clear the battleship's bows. At much the same time the latter switched on recognition lights – two red over white – and, as some destroyer ahead showed her " fighting-lights," the German instantly recognised the destroyers as hostile. The *Petard*, steaming as fast as she could, cleared the battleship's stem by about 200 yards.

Immediately she had passed ahead, the enemy switched on a group of searchlights. They just missed the *Petard's* stern ; but then, training to the right, bathed her in their unearthly brilliance. The next moment the secondary armaments of the first two ships in the German line crashed into flame. At such a range it was nearly impossible to miss. A few projectiles splashed into the sea ; a few more whizzed overhead into the night ; but the destroyer could be felt to tremble as others hit her aft.

The *Petard*, struck six times in as many seconds, was soon out of range. It was sheer good luck that enabled her to escape without being seriously hit in the engine- or boiler-rooms and brought to a standstill. One shot had penetrated the deck over a stokehold and cut an oil fuel pipe, the contents of which shot up in a flaming geyser. The stern of the ship was also badly hit, the whole of the officers and crew of the after 4-inch gun being killed or wounded, all the officers' cabins being wrecked by a shell which made a hole about three feet by two feet in the ship's side, and the funnel and ventilating cowls being perforated through and through by splinters. Withdrawing out of range, they managed to quench the fire and to take stock of their injuries. In these few seconds the *Petard* had had 2 officers and 7 men killed, and 1 officer and 5 men wounded. One of the shell striking aft had killed the surgeon-probationer just at the moment his services were most urgently required.

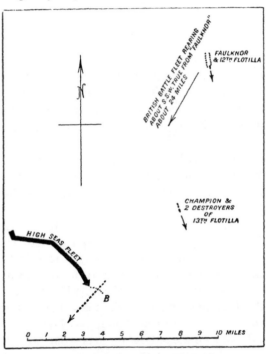

SITUATION ABOUT 12.30 A.M.

(B) *Lydiard* leading twelve destroyers of 9th, 10th, and 13th Flotillas :—*Lydiard, Landrail, Morris, Laurel, Unity, Nerissa, Termagant, Nicator, Narbrough, Pelican, Petard, Turbulent. Turbulent* sunk, *Petard* damaged.

" If only the *Petard* had had some torpedoes left," Thomson wrote in his report, " I am certain a successful torpedo-attack could easily have been made." [1] This seems likely, for the previous afternoon the *Petard* had already succeeded in getting home on the *Seydlitz* and a destroyer.

Next astern of the *Petard* came the *Turbulent*, Lieutenant-Commander Dudley Stuart. Illuminated in a blaze of search-lights, she was fired upon at point-blank range by every enemy

[1] *B. J. O. D.*, p. 233.

gun that would bear. There was no escaping. Spectators who saw her for one brief instant in the turmoil of smoke and shell-splashes describe her as rippling with fire from bow to stern as shell drove home and burst. Then, after a moment's horrible suspense, she was rammed amidships and cut in two by her huge antagonist. Thirteen survivors were afterwards rescued from the water by German destroyers. Five officers and 85 men perished.

2

The movements of the *Champion* had forced the 12th Flotilla to the northward of its proper position. Captain Stirling, in the *Faulknor*, as we have already seen, estimated he was ten miles astern of the British Fleet and about five miles east of his original station. He was actually about twenty-four miles north-north-east of the battle-fleet, with the *Champion* and the two destroyers that had remained with her further to the south. Thus it happened that the enemy fleet, steering its south-easterly course for the Horns Reef, crossed the tracks of both these British detachments.

Captain Stirling had with him his two flotilla leaders and twelve modern destroyers, and at 12.15 a.m. had resumed the course of south at a speed of 17 knots. The first gleams of daylight were appearing over the eastern horizon at about 1.30 ; but a swell had started to rise and the mist had thickened.

At 1.43 the *Faulknor* suddenly sighted a line of strange ships on her starboard bow, steering about south-east. It was still too dark and hazy immediately to make out who they were ; but, on approaching nearer, they were soon seen to be German battleships of the *Kaiser* class.

There was no time to be lost. Swinging round to a parallel course, Captain Stirling increased to 25 knots and ordered his first division, then on his starboard quarter, to attack. This division consisted of the *Obedient*, *Mindful*, *Marvel*, and *Onslaught*, led by Commander G. W. McO. Campbell in the *Obedient*. The division swung out towards the enemy, but almost immediately saw that they had disappeared in the mist. Sighting the destroyers, they had, indeed, turned away together to avoid the expected attack.

Leading on at 25 knots, with the enemy out of sight for the time, Captain Stirling got the destroyers with him into single line. At 1.52 he signalled to the commander-in-chief by wireless :

" Enemy battle-fleet steering south-east approximate bearing south-west. My position ten miles astern of 1st Battle Squadron."[1] This signal was sent off twice on power, as was another made at 2.12.

Neither message ever got through to Sir John Jellicoe, nor were they received by any other ship than the *Marksman*, in close company with the *Faulknor*. Probably the *Faulknor's* wireless was out of adjustment.

Certain in his mind that the enemy would resume their original

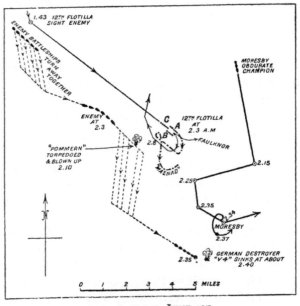

1.43 — 2.45 A.M. JUNE 1ST

(A) *Mænad, Narwhal, Nessus, Noble.*
(B) *Obedient, Mindful, Marvel, Onslaught.*
(C) *Marksman, Opal, Menace, Munster, Mary Rose.*
Faulknor's and *Obedient's* division turn to starboard and fire torpedoes at 2.8 a.m.
Mænad's Division turns a few minutes later, track shown— · — · — · —

course as soon as his destroyers had disappeared in the haze, Captain Stirling held on to the south-east for ten minutes. Then at about 2 a.m., with the *Faulknor* and four destroyers in single line, he led round sixteen points to starboard to north-west and dashed in to the attack. The enemy, five or six battleships in line, were sighted almost immediately on the port bow. The conditions for attack were excellent. It was too light for the use of searchlights, and sufficiently dark and misty for small craft travelling at high speed on an opposite course to make extremely difficult targets.

Very soon after turning, the *Faulknor* fired two torpedoes at the second and third ships in the line. The *Obedient* followed with two, and the *Marvel*, Lieutenant-Commander R. W. Grubb, and *Onslaught*, Lieutenant-Commander A. G. Onslow, D.S.C., with four each. The *Mindful*, Lieutenant-Commander J. J. C. Ridley, having two boilers out of action, was unable to make the speed, and attempted to attack the enemy before turning. Twice, however, she was foiled by other destroyers coming down on an opposite course, and had to turn away to avoid being rammed.

Almost as soon as the first torpedo was fired, the enemy battle-ships, together with some light-cruisers which had appeared at the end of their line, opened a furious fire with every gun that would bear – 12-inch, 11-inch, 5.9's, and 4.1's. The range, as the destroyers sped by in the mist, was little more than 1,500 yards. The sea spouted with shell-splashes, and the air was full of the roar of guns and the shrieking whistle of passing projectiles. More to keep their guns' crews employed than for any other reason, the attackers plastered the battleship with their little 4-inch shell as they drove by.

Then a torpedo went home on the third ship of the German line, the battleship *Pommern*. In the deafening turmoil of gunfire and bursting shell its detonation was inaudible. But right amidships, on the battleship's waterline, there appeared a splash of dull red flame. It immediately spread throughout the whole length of the ship, and then shot upwards in a gout of brilliant fire mingled with sparks and flying wreckage. Next came a column of dark smoke, at the base of which the bow and stern of the stricken vessel seemed to lift out of the water. Then the mist came down like a blanket to obliterate the scene of the disaster. [1]

She had suffered much the same fate as the *Indefatigable*, the *Queen Mary*, *Defence*, and *Invincible*, though from a torpedo, and not from gunfire. A magazine had exploded to shatter the centre portion of the ship, and in that moment 71 officers and 769 men of the *Pommern* were blown to destruction. Not a man was rescued.

---

[1] A German officer who witnessed the explosion from a distance wrote : " We saw a huge pillar of fire shoot up to the sky. It looked to us like the trail of a gigantic rocket. The ship must have been blown literally to atoms. . . . "

The *Faulknor, Obedient, Marvel,* and *Onslaught,* their attack completed, turned away under a withering fire. They put up a smoke-screen to make their escape ; but the *Onslaught,* the last ship in the line, was badly hit just after she turned away.

" Shell burst against the port side of the chart house and forebridge," wrote her sub-lieutenant, Harry W. A. Kemmis, the senior surviving officer, " igniting a box of cordite, causing a fire in the chart house, completely wrecking the forebridge, and destroying nearly all navigational instruments. At the time there were on the forebridge : the captain, first lieutenant, torpedo coxswain, two quartermasters, and both signalmen, and the gunner on his way up the bridge ladder. I had just been sent down to tell the engine-room to make black smoke, in order to screen our movements, and had only got to the bottom of the ladder from the forecastle deck to the upper deck. I went back to the bridge and, finding everything wrecked, the captain mortally wounded, and the first lieutenant killed, I assumed command and gave orders for the after steering position to be connected, which was done very smartly."[1]

Sub-Lieutenant Kemmis afterwards took the ship home. Her gallant Lieutenant-Commander, Arthur Gerald Onslow, who had won his Distinguished Service Cross in Somaliland as a midshipman, succumbed to his wounds on the way. In all, the *Onslaught's* casualties caused by that one shell amounted to 3 officers and 2 men killed, and 2 men wounded.

Commander J. P. Champion, in the *Mænad,* leading the 2nd Division of the 12th Flotilla, followed on in the wake of the others to the attack. Astern of him were the *Narwhal,* Lieutenant-Commander H. V. Hudson, and the *Noble* and *Nessus.* Thinking that Captain Stirling intended to pass round the head of the enemy line and to attack them from the other side, Champion had his torpedo-tubes trained to starboard. Discovering the *Faulknor's* intention when she put her helm over and swung sharply to starboard, Champion held on a little to give his men time to train the tube to port. Then he too turned to starboard and dashed past the enemy under heavy fire, discharging one torpedo as he went. The *Narwhal,* following astern, fired two. The *Nessus* and *Noble* were not vouchsafed a chance. The former, however, commanded by Lieutenant-Commander E. Q. Carter, was hit by enemy fire, losing 2 officers and 5 men killed, and 7 men wounded.

[1] *B. J. O. D.,* p. 337.

The other division of this same flotilla, led by the flotilla-leader *Marksman*, was apparently headed off by the German light-cruisers before it could reach a position whence to attack.

Commander Champion, of the *Mænad*, was not content with firing only one torpedo at so tempting a target. He decided to attack again, and, swinging his tubes round to starboard, turned, left his division, and went off at full speed after the Germans. He soon found them, and, steaming in alone, got in another two shots at a range of between 4,000 and 5,000 yards while under heavy fire. He thought at the time he had succeeded in hitting the fourth ship in the enemy line, though, in the light of after information, this was proved to be wrong. It was a pity that so bold an attack by a solitary destroyer did not meet with the success it deserved.

3

The light-cruiser *Champion*, Captain J. W. Farie, with the destroyers *Obdurate* and *Moresby*, was some little distance to the eastward when the 12th Flotilla made their attack. At 2.15 a.m. Captain Farie turned towards the sounds of gunfire, and at about 2.20 sighted the *Marksman*, to which he signalled by searchlight : " Where are enemy's ships ? "[1]

The *Marksman* replied : " Suspicious ships south." At the same time the *Marksman* remarked in her log : " Engaged enemy destroyers and light-cruisers (four destroyers and two cruisers)."[1]

At 2.25 the *Champion* altered course to the southward, and very soon sighted more ships in that direction. Signalling to the *Champion* by searchlight at 2.30, the *Marksman* asked, " What are ships bearing south ? " The *Champion's* reply was, " Germans, I think."[1]

For a few minutes Captain Farie steamed on towards the enemy, but at 2.34, " for some reason, started to make another cast to the eastward."[2] By this time the enemy were again steering direct for the Horns Reef, and at 2.35 the *Moresby*, Lieutenant-Commander Roger V. Alison, who was following the *Obdurate*, sighted four German battleships appearing through the mist to the westward at a distance of about 4,000 yards. They were steaming south-east at high speed.

" I considered action imperative," Alison wrote in his report,

[1] *B. J. O. D.*, Appendix II., p. 479.   [2] *N. O.* iii., p. 410.

" hoisted compass west, hauled out to port, firing a high-speed torpedo at 2.37 G.M.T. . . . This incident and opportunity was over very quickly, as the enemy was steaming 18 knots south-east. A concussion shook the ship about two minutes later. . . . Mist and smoke prevented the enemy being seen again, but I feel certain . . . that the torpedo hit something."[1]

" I find that the *Moresby* was in station with *Obdurate* astern of *Champion*," Sir David Beatty wrote in his despatch. " Some of the strange vessels were sighted by *Champion* and *Obdurate*, who took them to be some of our own light-cruisers."[2]

The despatch was written soon after the action ; but as the vessels referred to by Sir David were those about whom the signals had been exchanged between the *Champion* and *Marksman* between 2.20 and 2.30, there seems to have been little doubt that they were definitely recognised as hostile.

" It is very much regretted that *Champion* did not take steps to identify them," Sir David continued. " If, as was probable, they were the enemy, an excellent opportunity was missed for an attack in the early morning light. More important still, a portion of the enemy might have been definitely located."[3]

The *Moresby's* torpedo had found a billet ; but unfortunately not on a battleship. It hit and sank the enemy destroyer V.4 erroneously mentioned in Admiral Scheer's despatch as having run on " an enemy mine."

This was not quite the last shot fired in the Battle of Jutland. At about 3.25 a.m., when steering north in company with the *Marksman*, *Obdurate*, *Moresby*, and *Mænad*, which latter vessel had joined at about 2.45, the *Champion*, and some of the destroyers with her, sighted four destroyers on her starboard bow steering south. At first uncertain as to who they were, Captain Farie, at 3.30, made them out to be the enemy, and opened fire at a range of 3,000 yards. " Two torpedoes were fired at the *Champion*," he wrote in his report, " the first one passing under our bows, the second just missing close astern. Enemy passed on opposite course, and, when ship had been steadied after avoiding torpedoes, the enemy had disappeared in the mist, and I resumed my same course."[4]

This encounter is also mentioned in the report of Commander Champion of the *Mænad*, while another officer of the same ship observes that they sighted in the distance " a large ship screened

[1] B. J. O. D., p. 239.   [2] B. J. O. D., p. 239.   [3] B. J. O. D., p. 239.
[4] B. J. O. D., p. 225.

by many more destroyers."[1] It is possible that this may have been the badly damaged *Seydlitz*.

But it is to be regretted that the four destroyers sighted at 3.25 a.m. were not cut off and closely engaged. These vessels, G.37, G.38, G.40, and V.45, had on board 1,250 officers and men of the battle-cruiser *Lützow*, which had finally been sunk by a torpedo a short time before.

" On two occasions," says Admiral Scheer's despatch, " they encountered enemy cruisers and destroyers, and on both occasions they attacked under the leadership of the senior commanding officer . . . and successfully fought their way back to the German Bight. During the last action the engines of G.40 were hit, and she had to be taken in tow."[2]

Thus ended the Battle of Jutland. No units of the Grand Fleet now remained between the retiring Germans and the Horns Reef.

4

The Commander-in-chief had turned the Grand Fleet to the northward at 2.47 a.m., at which time the bulk of the High Seas Fleet was about thirty miles to the north-east and about an hour's steaming from the Horn's Reef. The morning was very misty, the visibility being no more than three or four miles. But hope ran high. With his fleet in line-of-battle, Sir John steamed north in the hope that one or other of his scattered cruiser squadrons or flotillas could give him news of the enemy.

He had not received Captain Stirling's signal reporting the enemy battle-fleet made at 1.56 a.m., or subsequent messages sent off at 2.8 and 2.13 reporting the fact that he was attacking, and that the course of the enemy was south-south-west.

No reports of being in contact with enemy heavy ships had been made by any of the flotillas engaged in the fighting of the night before ; but they could hardly be held to blame for this. At that time, the system of communication by wireless was by no means perfect. Moreover, it is beyond the capability of any man to dictate a signal, and, for another, to put it into code and to despatch it, when their ship is under a storm of fire at point-blank range. At such a time, the energies of the commanding officer are sufficiently absorbed in achieving his immediate object – that of fighting his vessel. It should be borne in mind, too,

---

[1] *F. J.*, p. 233.   [2] *B. J. O. D.*, Appendix III., p. 598.

that it was not the duty of every subordinate commanding officer to transmit such information to the commander-in-chief, but the task of the senior officer commanding detached units. The 4th Flotilla was in action with enemy battleships ; but within a few minutes its leader, the *Tipperary*, was a blazing wreck, while a little later the *Broke* also was out of action.

The German High Seas Fleet, steering south-easterly, passed diagonally under the sterns of the Grand Fleet battleships at a distance of no more than five miles. Indeed, at one period the van of the High Seas Fleet was no more than one and a half miles from the 5th Battle Squadron. (See 11.20 diagram.) Had Sir John Jellicoe been twenty minutes steaming astern of his 11.30 p.m. position, or Admiral Scheer twenty minutes ahead, the two battle-fleets would have met in the darkness, with a result that nobody can imagine.

It has sometimes been asked why, being aware of the actions that took place astern during the night, Sir John did not realise the High Seas Fleet was crossing under his stern. The question is simple to answer. He fully expected destroyer attacks on his rear, and at 9.55 p.m. a signal had been wirelessed from the Admiralty : " Three destroyer flotillas have been ordered to attack you during the night." When he saw the beams of search-lights and the flashes of gunfire, first on his starboard quarter and then astern, he had little doubt that what he expected was happening, and to guard against attack was one of the reasons that had caused him to mass his flotillas astern. When he was informed that the *Castor* and Second Light-Cruiser Squadron had been in action with enemy light-cruisers, it was a natural inference that these were supporting the enemy destroyers.

With the information as to the enemy's position and movements that Sir John Jellicoe had at his disposal, he could only guess at Admiral Scheer's course of action. Sir John hoped for a renewal of the battle the next morning, and chose what he considered the most likely course to achieve it. He knew his enemy was to the north-westward when the action terminated at daylight, and it was his object to remain between the High Seas Fleet and its base.

As we know now, the Admiralty intercepted no less than fourteen German wireless signals during the night, and successfully decoded them. It is unnecessary to go into details, but these signals indicated, without the least possible doubt, that Scheer was making for the Horns Reef, and had asked for an airship reconnaissance in that neighbourhood next morning. Certain of these messages were not wirelessed to Sir John Jellicoe exactly as received, but were summarised in one message sent off at 10.41 p.m., informing him that the High Seas Fleet was believed to be returning to its base as its course was S.S.E. ¾ E., and its speed 16 knots. The Horns Reef was not mentioned, probably because the course given was thought a sufficient indication of Scheer's intention.

But to the commander-in-chief it was not so clear. The Admiralty, at 9.38, had told him that the rear ship of the High Seas Fleet was in a position about ten miles to the south-west of his own leading ship at 9 p.m. This message was in Sir John Jellicoe's hands shortly before 11. He knew it to be wrong. At 9 p.m., when the Grand Fleet turned south, the German Fleet was well to the north-west.

So neither in the information received from the Admiralty, nor in that forthcoming from any of his outlying vessels, was there anything to warrant a change in his original plan of steering south.

For Admiral Scheer there was no alternative. His battle-cruisers were so badly mauled as to be incapable of further action. Some of his light-cruiser forces had been dispersed. His destroyers were to search in vain for the Grand Fleet during the night, and never to find it. With his battleships alone he was in no condition to resume the action next morning. He chose the shortest and quickest way home, where, on his return, he could have the first word and claim to be the victor because the British losses in ships and men had been greater than his own.

Led by the battleship *Westfalen*, commanded by the determined and gallant Captain Redlich, the High Seas Fleet hewed its way through the British destroyer flotillas astern of the Grand Fleet. As attack succeeded attack, the German line was flung into disorder. Stations were lost as ships altered course this way and that to avoid torpedoes. Even the squadrons became intermingled. So it was no organised fleet fit for immediate battle that steamed wearily past the Horns Reef Lightship at about 3.30 a.m. on the morning of June 1.

At that time Sir John Jellicoe was unaware of the Germans' retreat. It was not until about 4.15 a.m. that he was handed a message despatched from the Admiralty at 3.29, which gave him the momentous news that the High Seas Fleet was only sixteen miles from the Horns Reef Lightship at 2.30.

So while Admiral Scheer took his fleet homeward, congratulating himself upon a merciful escape, the Grand Fleet, compact and battle-worthy, remained upon the scene of the action.

An aerial observer with a clear view would have seen the sea dotted with ships – squadrons of battleships ; Sir David Beatty's battle-cruisers ; light-cruiser squadrons ; flotillas of destroyers ; a few isolated ships, and some sorely wounded vessels battling their way westward against the rising wind and sea. But every one of these ships was flying the White Ensign. There would not have been a glimpse of the white, black-crossed emblem of the German Empire.

Until shortly after 11 o'clock that morning, when he shaped course for Scapa Flow, Sir John Jellicoe swept to and fro over the battleground of the previous afternoon and night, calling for news of his lost and damaged ships, collecting the stragglers. A few survivors from vessels that had sunk were sighted and rescued from the water. They came across great smears of oil from sunken ships, Carley floats, splintered boats, mess-stools and tables, broken timber and wreckage, red German lifebuoys, and others marked *Black Prince*, *Ardent*, *Tipperary*, and *Turbulent*, together with numbers of dead seamen in lifebelts, friends and enemies – the pitiful flotsam of battle.

And all across the North Sea during the afternoon and evening of June 1st, as the detachments of the Grand Fleet steamed homeward, a trail of bodies was committed to the deep in their shotted hammocks. But of the 6,000 British officers and men who died at Jutland, more than half lay in and about the battered, foundered hulls of the ships in which they served and fought.

> By grassy grade or mead they shall not roam,
> Whose eyes are caught in sandy monochrome ;
> Nor watch the breakers whiten 'neath the Down,
> Nor march by Plymouth or in Portsmouth Town ;
> But surely bide at sea all mortal time,
> Till Arctic interchange with Tropic clime.
> Theirs ever be the under-Ocean calm ;
> Their name a Peace : their memory a Psalm. [1]

[1] From *The Epic of Jutland*, by Shane Leslie. Quoted by permission of the Author.

CHAPTER XIV

SOME RESCUES

I

ONE of the best-known destroyer characters of the war was Commander (afterwards Captain) Graham R. L. Edwards commonly known as " Daddy " or " Father." After his retirement in 1922, he became well known to the public as one of the speakers at the representation of the attack of Zeebrugge shown at the Wembley Exhibitions of 1924 and 1925, and also as a lecturer for the Navy League until his untimely death in 1930. His success as a popular speaker was only equalled by his skill as a seaman.

The early part of the war found him in command of the destroyer *Laforey* in the Harwich Force, and it was in this vessel, during some engagement or another, that he came under heavy fire from enemy cruisers. There was no chance of retaliation with the *Laforey's* little 4-inch guns, and the men, with nothing to do, were beginning to feel vaguely nervous. Edwards thought it time to distract their attention. Throwing off his uniform cap, he placed the brass binnacle top of the compass on his head, and looking over the bridge rails, observed to the gun's crew below, " It's all right, boys. Don't get the wind up ! Daddy's quite safe ! He's got his shrapnel hat on ! "

Edwards was always unconventional. When I knew him at Harwich and Dover during the war, he never made the usual flag signal, " Proceed in execution of previous orders," but merely semaphored " Follow Father " as he slipped from his buoy. On another occasion at sea, when one of his flock was badly out of station, he rather horrified the flotilla by signalling to the offender in broad daylight by semaphore, " If you don't keep better station, Daddy will come over when you are in your bath and smack your fat little —— ! " mentioning a portion of the anatomy which is not, as a rule, talked of in polite society.

Again, having hopelessly lost his way in a fog, and not having had sight of land or the sun for several days, he asked his next astern where they were. The next astern, however, was just as uncertain as Edwards himself, and did not hesitate to say so.

So Edwards instantly replied, " If you don't know where you are, how can you expect Father to lead you home ? " Perhaps it was this time that his charts were ruined by spray or washed overboard, and he afterwards declared that the best aids to successful war-time navigation in the North Sea were a bicycling map of the British Isles, a penny ruler, and a piece of string !

When he was in command of the flotilla-leader *Botha* at Dover, I remember one day going on board to see him, and quite inadvertently, in the wardroom, making a disparaging remark about " these beastly coal-burning ships," and what a nuisance they were to follow at night.

" Oh," said he, glaring at me with a mock ferocious expression, and beginning to roll up his coat-sleeves. " So that's what you think, is it ? " I suddenly realised what I had said. The *Botha* burnt coal. I retired hastily. " Daddy " had the build of a heavy-weight boxer.

One might go on for ever with stories of " Daddy " Edwards ; but as one never knew what he was going to say or do next, he certainly kept us amused whenever he was in company. Some people called him a " pirate," and senior officers were sometimes shocked by his queer signals. All the same, if he was a pirate, he was a very lovable one. His saving sense of humour forgave him much.

The most thrilling incident of his war career, however, was probably the sinking of the *Hoste*, a flotilla-leader in the 13th Flotilla of the Grand Fleet, which he had joined late in 1916.

On December 19th the entire fleet, consisting of anything up to 200 vessels of all types, from battleships to destroyers, had left Scapa Flow to carry out exercises between Norway and the Shetlands. The weather was none too good, and during the morning of December 20th, when battleships, cruisers, and destroyers were steaming at high speed to take up their preliminary stations for a tactical exercise, the *Hoste's* helm jammed at 25 knots, so that she narrowly escaped collision with several of her consorts. As a stud on the steering-engine had fractured, permission was asked and obtained for the ship to return to Scapa, accompanied by the *Negro* as an escort.

On clearing the fleet, she stopped and effected temporary repairs, afterwards shaping course for her base with the intention of arriving at 8 a.m. next morning. When darkness came, the *Negro* was ordered to take station two cables – 400 yards –

astern, both ships proceeding without lights. The weather, by this time, had hardened into a fierce south-easterly gale with a very heavy sea.

At about 9 p.m. a signal was intercepted to say that the Grand Fleet also was returning to Scapa Flow, expecting to arrive at 7.30 next morning. This meant that some 200 ships of all types without lights, would be overtaking the *Hoste* and *Negro* during the night.

" It was not a very pleasing prospect ! " Edwards observed.

At about 10 p.m. the *Hoste* and *Negro* were ordered by wireless from the commander-in-chief to switch on their navigation lights. Three hours later, when the light on Fair Island had just been sighted, a searchlight suddenly blazed out on the *Hoste's* starboard quarter. It was the commander-in-chief making the " Demand." " In other words," said Edwards, " the whole Grand Fleet was on top of us – then all was darkness again."

Wind and sea were on the port bow, with the gale blowing its fiercest, when, at about 1.30 a.m. the helm, which had been giving trouble for some time, suddenly jammed hard over to port. The *Hoste*, turning abruptly to starboard, sheered in towards the unlighted fleet. A moment later there came a thudding crash from aft as the *Negro*, not realising what had happened, collided with the *Hoste's* stern.

The shock knocked the depth-charges, each containing 300lbs. of T.N.T., off the *Hoste's* stern, and on reaching their set depth they both exploded in a huge upheaval of water. Specially designed to sink enemy submarines, they practically demolished the stern of the *Hoste* and blew in the bottom of the *Negro*.

The *Negro's* lights immediately became extinguished, and the *Hoste*, whose engines had come to an automatic standstill, was left with the waves breaking heavily over her, and the tangled mass of twisted plating which now formed her stern actually swaying from side to side as she rolled sickeningly to the great breaking seas.

Edwards and two officers were on the bridge, all the others being aft in their cabins very near the scene of the explosion. They were given up for lost, but one by one, very scantily clad, appeared on the bridge. The engineer officer, meanwhile, had inspected the damage, and presently reported that the entire stern portion of the ship, about a third of her total length, had been lifted bodily by the explosion, buckling the deck and splitting the ship's side from deck to waterline. The stern had then sagged downwards, to form a deep trench across the after part. With her broken bottom crumpled like a pierced concertina, and in the raging sea, it was doubtful if she could float for more than a few minutes. If she did live, however, it was possible that the engines might be used at very slow speed.

A signal was made by searchlight informing all ships in the neighbourhood what had occurred, and asking for help, and before long the destroyer *Marvel*, commanded by Commander Edwin A. Homan, popularly known as " Tip " Homan, arrived near the wreck of the *Hoste*.

Meanwhile, a signal was also made to the *Negro*, asking whether she required assistance. She replied that she was badly damaged forward. This was the last seen of her from the *Hoste*. As it became known afterwards, though, the two depth-charges had exploded under her engine-room, the largest compartment in the ship, completely blowing in the bottom and filling the compartment with water. The destroyer *Marmion* went to her assistance, but had no opportunity of trying to go alongside. In the fearful sea the strain on the *Negro's* bulkheads was more than they could stand. They collapsed suddenly, and the ship immediately sank.

The *Marmion*, steaming over the spot, rescued many of the men struggling in the water. Boats could not be lowered. The whole area was covered with a thick scum of oil fuel from the *Negro's* tanks, and many men, who might otherwise have been saved, slipped down the greasy ropes by which they were trying to climb on board their rescuer. In all, 5 officers and 45 men perished out of the total of 6 officers and 90 odd men which formed her crew.

The *Marvel* meanwhile, having joined the *Hoste*, was ordered to take station astern, but to be prepared to render assistance at any moment. Edwards, in fact, finding that his ship could still steam slowly, in spite of her broken back, attempted to take her back to the base.

The course towards home was south-west, with the wind and mountainous sea from the south-east on the port beam. And for a time, lurching and rolling through a right angle, the little vessel staggered on with her deck constantly swept by the waves.

" The agony," said Edwards, " lasted three hours, when suddenly a heavier sea than before broke over the after part, and there was an appalling crash of cracking, tearing metal." Everybody on board thought that this was the end. No human being, no boat, could live in such a sea, and it seemed utterly impossible that any vessel, let alone a lightly built destroyer, could come alongside to rescue the crew. If the two portions of the *Hoste* finally broke apart, the ship, and everyone in her, seemed doomed.

Her backbone was completely broken, the stern portion being only connected to the rest of the hull by the propeller shafts. The engine-room was rapidly flooding, and already the base of the third funnel was awash.

Edwards ordered his signalman to flash into the sky with his searchlight, " *Marvel* close and take off crew." This the man did twice, until the dynamos below became flooded and the lights were extinguished. " That signalman stands out in my memory," Edwards wrote afterwards. " When all hands were busy putting on their lifebelts, he went quietly on flashing his signal and making no attempt to touch his own until he had finished."

The *Hoste's* ship's company mustered on the forecastle, waiting for the ship to take her last plunge. Not a sound was heard from the men. They stood silent and waited for the end, their ship rolling 45° either way and the huge seas breaking on board in a succession of boiling cataracts. It was pitch dark. Nothing could be seen except the dim phosphorescence of the maddened water, and the white, red, and green of the *Marvel's* navigation lights bobbing about astern.

Then the *Marvel's* searchlight blazed out and illuminated the wreck, her captain steaming her close alongside, evidently thinking that the *Hoste's* crew would take to the water. But Edwards could see no reason for abandoning the ship until she sank beneath them.

The *Marvel* was then seen to be going astern, backing away against the seas until she literally buried herself in breaking water and swept away most of her deck fittings. Having given himself room, Homan then went straight ahead for the *Hoste* until the curving edges of the two ships' forecastles met with a shuddering crash. As she struck, the front rank of the *Hoste's* men jumped for their lives across the reeling gap.

The next sea carried the *Marvel* a hundred yards astern, but *thirteen* times did Homan bring his ship alongside, and on each occasion the leading rank of the *Hoste's* crew leapt to their rescuer's forecastle.

It was a terrible ordeal. Both ships were rolling heavily. At times the rise and fall between them was fully thirty feet. To make matters worse, the *Hoste's* torpedo-tubes had broken adrift

and had trained themselves outboard, with the torpedoes themselves half out of the tubes and waiting to crash through the
Marvel's thin side. Moreover, the explosive war-heads were
on them. Though nominally safe, something might bring about
their explosion. One never knew.

With the *Marvel's* thirteenth attempt, the last of the *Hoste's*
officers and men leapt across to safety, Edwards himself being
the final man. But not quite all of them had been saved. Two
poor souls had been crushed between the forecastles as the ships
crashed together ; two more had jumped across, only to slip on
reaching the *Marvel's* deck and to be hurled clean across the deck
into the raging sea on the other side. Others fell in between the
the ships and were dragged out with ropes, while still more
were injured in jumping.

Five minutes after the last man had left, the *Hoste* went to the
bottom.

If ever a destroyer captain handled his ship magnificently
in circumstances of extreme difficulty and danger, it was Edwin
Anderson Homan, of the *Marvel*. He had risked his own ship
and the lives of every soul on board her in gallantly rescuing
comrades who could do little to help themselves. One mistake,
one wrong order, might have caused another disaster – a disaster
which would have left nearly 200 men struggling in the raging
sea without any possible hope of salvation.

" At daybreak," Edwards concluded his account, " we arrived
at the base, and with the light we realised to the full the fight
the *Marvel* had made for us. Her forecastle was concertinaed,
her decks were swept of every article but her biggest fittings,
her men and her officers were swollen-eyed with their superhuman
endeavours to save their pals, but on their faces was a look of
perfect satisfaction that they had kept up the honour of the
Destroyer Service, and carried out to the letter the unwritten law
that a destroyer never leaves its mate."

We can agree.

2

In the early morning of October 28th, 1915, while on her way
up to Scapa Flow after a refit at Devonport, the cruiser *Argyll*,
Captain James C. Tancred, grounded on the Bell Rock, near
Dundee, in thick weather

It was blowing a heavy south-easterly gale, and was more than usually wet, cold, and cheerless. Luckily, not very far away, the destroyers *Hornet*, Commander the Hon. Barry Bingham, and *Jackal*, Lieutenant-Commander J. C. Tovey, were patrolling off the Firth of Forth. Receiving the signal, " Proceed at once and stand by the *Argyll*, aground on Bell Rock," the *Hornet* and *Jackal* steamed thither at full speed. They arrived just as daylight was breaking, to find the cruiser hard and fast on the north-west side of the reef, with her bows pointing in the direction of the gale. The extent of shoal-water was not sufficient to form any considerable lee ; but had she struck anywhere else the ship must have broken up almost immediately, and the rescue of her crew would have been extremely perilous, if not impossible.

The *Argyll* was firmly wedged on the rocks, with the sea breaking over her, and, hailing the *Hornet*, Captain Tancred shouted that she might break up at any moment and that there was no time to be lost. He suggested that the destroyer should make fast astern, and that the cruiser's officers and men should be ferried across gradually in boats.

But Bingham thought otherwise. With the heavy sea that was running, the transhipment of all the officers and men by boat would be slow and dangerous. Soundings showed that there was sufficient water for a destroyer half way along the *Argyll's* side, so he proposed steaming his forecastle alongside the cruiser's quarter-deck and allowing the men to jump across in batches.

It was easier said than done, for the *Argyll's* bows were bumping heavily on the reef, while the *Hornet*, pitching heavily, and with her engines jogging slowly ahead to keep her in position, was in constant danger of being dashed against the cruiser's quarter-deck. Helped by fenders lowered over the side, however, Bingham managed to keep his ship in position, and each time the two decks rolled together ten or twenty of the *Argyll's* men leapt across to safety.

At last, with 500 men on board, the *Hornet* was filled to her full capacity, and the rest of the *Argyll's* ship's company was transferred to the *Jackal* in boats.

Every soul on board the wrecked cruiser was saved, with no more damage than a few plates distorted and holed on the starboard side of the *Hornet's* forecastle. With men crammed into their stokeholds and engine-room to reduce the danger of capsizing, the two destroyers, rolling heavily in the full blast of the gale on the port beam, staggered off to the southward, and finally reached harbour in safety.

It is difficult to convey any real impression of the difficulty and danger of the task that had been successfully accomplished by those two 780-ton destroyers ; but had it not been for their efforts, and an exhibition of seamanship which called forth the praise, not only of the *Argyll's* captain, but also of the Commander-in-Chief of the Grand Fleet, Admiral Sir John Jellicoe, not one of the cruiser's men might have been saved.

Assuredly it was a good morning's work. We can picture those two little ships battling their way back to harbour with their officers and men glowing with satisfaction at the thought of duty well done.

3

Rather similar to the rescue of the *Hoste's* ship's company by the *Marvel* was that of the officers and men of the destroyer *Medusa* by the *Lassoo* – Lieutenant-Commander Vernon Butler [1] – on the night of March 25th, 1916. I have described the incident elsewhere more or less in the guise of fiction, but the story is worth telling again.

At dawn on the morning in question the Harwich Force arrived within a short distance of the island of Sylt. We consisted of four light-cruisers, headed by the *Cleopatra* flying the broad pendant of Commodore Reginald Tyrwhitt ; the seaplane carrier *Vindex* ; and a number of destroyers. The idea was that the seaplanes were to bomb the Zeppelin sheds at Tondern, on the mainland behind Sylt.

It was a bitterly cold morning, with a calm sea. There were bursts of sunshine ; but occasionally we had dense snow-flurries, which shut down the visibility to a few hundred yards.

Shortly before arriving at the spot where the *Vindex* would stop and hoist out her seaplanes, a German submarine fired a torpedo at the *Cleopatra*, which was avoided by a quick turn of the helm. Destroyers kept the U-boat down, and soon afterwards the *Vindex* stopped to hoist out her five machines. They were all away by 5.30 a.m. ; but the snow made flying very difficult. One seaplane, at least, found her objective, and under

[1] Now Captain Vernon Butler, D.S.O.

a withering fire dived down over the airship shed to release her bombs. The freezing snow, however, had clogged the releasing apparatus. Circling round, the pilot made another attack, shaking his machine to induce the bombs to drop. But it was useless. He was forced to return with his cargo intact.

Out at sea, meanwhile, we awaited the return of the seaplanes. The first arrived at 7 a.m., and a second soon afterwards, both being hoisted in. They were the only two of the five that did return.

After waiting for some time, we, the destroyers, were ordered to search down the coast to the south-east. We found nothing, but close in under the shore, within easy sight of Sylt, we sighted two enemy outpost boats to seaward of us making across our bows for their harbour at Lister Deep. It was chicken butchery ; but, as they opened fire upon us, we were compelled to reply, sinking them both.

We, in the *Murray*, rescued the survivors of the *Otto Rudolf*. There were 13 of them all told, including the skipper, a reserve warrant officer who spoke excellent English and had served as an officer in British ships. Of the survivors, 1 was badly, and 4 more slightly wounded, 9 having been killed outright.

We took all necessary precautions ; but the prisoners were very well behaved and gave us no trouble at all. They struck me as a fine-looking lot of men, and presently, when the wounded had been attended to, our men were filling them up with food and cocoa on the mess-decks. They seemed pleased enough to get it, for, from what we heard afterwards, they had evidently expected to be manacled, leg-ironed, and fed on biscuit and water. When they were given food, cigarettes, and clothing, they could hardly understand it.

I interviewed the commanding officer, Anton Frank, who seemed a good fellow. He was pleased to be congratulated on his plucky fight, and I certainly felt sorry for him.

" You came upon us so suddenly, and so near home," he said, looking wistfully at the island little more than five miles away. " We had no chance to do anything."

I could sympathise.

He told me he had been in the wheelhouse of his ship when the fight started. One of our first shells had passed through the glass windows within a foot of his head without bursting, while another exploded in the engine-room. He ran down there to see what could be done, and while he was away another 4-inch projectile burst in the wheel-house and put about twenty holes in his greatcoat, which was lying on the settee. His temporary absence saved his life. I saw the tattered garment when it came on board, and noticed in the buttonhole the black and white ribbon of the Iron Cross, and the red and white of some other decoration. On asking what the later was, he told me it was the Hamburg Cross, given by that city to all of its officers and men who carried the Iron Cross. I believe that Lûbeck, and the other Hanseatic towns, followed the same custom with their men.

One thing about Anton Frank that struck me very favourably was the great interest he took in his men. The poor fellow who was badly wounded had been hit in the back, and three or four pieces of shell were still inside him. He was in terrible agony ; but did not utter a sound. An operation was out of the question, and Lennon-Brown,[1] our R.N.V.R. Surgeon-Probationer, had him put in the hammock on the mess-deck and gave him morphia tablets to ease the pain. Soon afterwards Frank asked to be allowed to visit him, and when Lennon-Brown next went forward he found the *Otto Rudolf*'s captain swabbing the patient's brow with cold water to bring him to ! Our " Young Doc," as we called him, was rather peevish. He had given the poor fellow the morphia to deaden his agony.

While the little battle was in progress, however, two of our destroyers had collided, the *Laverock* ramming the *Medusa* at high speed. The *Laverock*, with badly crumpled bows, was able to proceed under her own steam and got safely home. Not so the *Medusa*. With an enormous hole in her engine-room, she had to be taken in tow.

The flotilla-leader *Lightfoot* set about doing this, and it was while the wires were still being passed across from ship to ship that many hostile seaplanes, stirred up like a wasps' nest by our aeroplanes earlier in the morning, came out and started dropping bombs all round us.

The snowstorms had finished. It was a bright, sunny morning, and it was uncomfortable to see the enemy machines hovering overhead. Our 2-pounder pom-poms got busily to work to keep them at a good height, and none of their bombs actually hit. A good many came very close, however, and I saw one string of five explode in the water practically alongside one of the destroyers. We heard afterwards that there had been a

---

[1] Now Surgeon-Lieutenant-Commander A. G. Lennon-Brown, D.S.C., R.N.

free fight among the men on her upper deck to secure the still hot splinters as trophies !

We were bombed off and on for four hours, the seaplanes going home for cargo after cargo of beastliness, which they showered upon us.

The *Medusa*, meanwhile, was in tow of the *Lightfoot*, and was being tugged slowly north-westward to rejoin the cruisers, while the rest of us protected them against possible submarine attack.

The project was not pleasant. We had heard the trawlers busy with their wireless before we sank them, and our prisoners told us their signals had been acknowledged. The glass had started to go down, and the look of the sky changed as the morning wore on. A swell started to set in from the west. Before nightfall it would be blowing hard, and we had a crippled ship to tow back to England, if possible. Heligoland was a bare forty miles distant. We should not be allowed to escape without molestation.

As we learnt afterwards, urgent wireless messages had been received from the Admiralty ordering the commodore to withdraw with all speed. Intercepted signals showed that enemy ships were putting to sea.

We crawled on to the northward, rejoined the cruisers, and steamed on to the north. There was a large mined area to the west ; but, instead of taking the most obvious course home along its southern side, the commodore steamed north along its eastern side, with the intention of turning to the west along its northern edge. This was to avoid the enemy if his intercepting force searched for us along our most likely route home.

The weather got worse as the afternoon wore on. It started to blow hard from the south-west, with a heavy, toppling sea. Violent rain-squalls alternated with snow-flurries, and before long our speed was reduced to barely more than 6 knots, the greatest speed at which the *Medusa* could be towed. Even so, with the seas breaking heavily over her as she lay over at an appalling angle, she looked more like a half-tide rock than a ship. We could see the towing-wire sagging under water at one moment, while the next it came dripping out of the sea, vibrating like a harp-string. Both the *Lightfoot* and the *Medusa* were pitching and rolling heavily. If the wire parted, it would be an almost impossible task to take the cripple in tow again.

At about 4.30 p.m. we saw Sir David Beatty's battle-cruisers to the westward. At first, when we sighted their upperworks over the windy horizon, they looked strangely unfamiliar. For a moment or two we thought they were Germans, and it was not until the *Lion's* searchlight winked out a message to the commodore, telling him they would stand by us during the night, that we really breathed again.

The situation, as we discovered later, was decidedly serious. Had all gone well, we should have been well to the westward of the battle-cruisers by 9 a.m. Now, nearly at sundown, we were still to the eastward. The enemy light-cruisers and destroyers were at sea, and the battle-cruisers were to cover our leisurely retirement. It was running a risk to expose these vessels to torpedo-attack during the night; but the risk had to be accepted. Their presence certainly gave us a great feeling of security.

The weather grew steadily worse. Wind and sea were on the *Medusa's* port quarter, causing her to override frequently, and putting a great strain on the towing-hawser as it tautened out. Some time after dark the inevitable happened. The wire carried away, leaving the *Medusa* helpless. The sea was too heavy for boatwork. She could not be taken in tow again, and at about 10 o'clock orders were given for the ship to be abandoned and scuttled. In pitch darkness, and the heavy sea running, it was easier said than done.

But it was done, and the *Lassoo*, Lieutenant-Commander Vernon Butler, was responsible for saving the *Medusa's* ship's company. I have by me an account written by one of the *Lassoo's* officers.

" The weather was pretty filthy," he says, " and both ships were chucking about a lot. The *Medusa* had a good length of cable out, and was yawing considerably. It was very difficult to see her in the dark, and the bow lights had to be used to assist us in going alongside.

" The *Lassoo* lay off the *Medusa's* port quarter for about five minutes, waiting for the yaw, and, when the yaw towards us appeared to be about three-quarters of the way through, we made a dart and got alongside, forecastle to forecastle, quite nicely. We passed in plenty of wires forward, and one aft, while lifelines had been rigged along the *Lassoo's* near side, fenders put over and men lined up and down the ship to help men clambering across. On arrival alongside our people were greeted with a hail of bundles of clothing hurled across ᵣᵒm the *Medusa*, and within two or three minutes three-quarters of her crew had jumped across to us.

" By that time her yaw had reached its limit, and she started to go back. The stern wire promptly parted, and a steward from the *Medusa* managed to fall overboard between the two ships. He was luckily fished out with a rope's end before being squashed. Meanwhile, the ships had been grinding heavily, and the *Medusa's* whaler at the davits had been smashed to matchwood by the davits of our motor-boat. Most of the foremost wires had parted, and, with the heavy rolling, the grinding, and the crashing, it was very difficult for the men to stand up on our forecastle. I noticed one officer lying flat on his stomach as he hauled in another wire from the other ship.

" We couldn't remain alongside without breaking things up, so had to back away. We made another attempt to go alongside, but couldn't stay there, though a few venturesome spirits hopped across as the ships came together. The captain and about 15 men were still left in the *Medusa*, so our captain told them to muster on the forecastle and that he would save them somehow."

After the second attempt, Lieutenant-Commander Butler realised that if he made a bad shot at going alongside he might do serious damage to the *Lassoo*, so this time he turned his ship until she was pointing straight at the *Medusa*, and steamed slow ahead into the after end of her forecastle from a distance of about twenty-five yards. By working the engines and helm he managed to keep her there, enabling the remaining people in the *Medusa* to jump across to safety and to bring their dog with them.

" I may say," the account continues, " that the gunner of the *Medusa* arrived with the first batch of rescued men complete with yards of connected electric cable and a firing-key. This he assured us was connected to a charge secured to the *Medusa's* engine-room bulkhead, which was to be exploded to sink her when all the men had been rescued. As we were close alongside, I wasn't altogether unhappy at seeing the electric leads carry away when we had to back astern."

Having rescued all the men and got clear, " we found our leading telegraphist with a huge sheaf of intercepted German wireless signals. ' Please, sir,' he said, ' there seems a good few 'Uns knockin' about ! ' "

Reading of this episode long afterwards, it sounds comparatively simple. But with the two little ships rolling, pitching, and grinding together in the heavy sea, and in pitch darkness, it required cool judgment and consummate nerve. Had the *Lassoo* and *Medusa* come into really violent contact, the former might also have found herself a sinking wreck. As it was, the only damage to the *Lassoo* was a slight bulge on the stem just below the forecastle, which did not in the least impair her seaworthiness.

It was an excellent display of seamanship on the part of Lieutenant-Commander Butler, and one which earned him the official commendation of the Admiralty.

At much the same time that the rescue work was being done, the four light-cruisers, headed by the *Cleopatra*, were a few miles ahead of us. Soon after 10 p.m., Captain Loder-Symonds, of the *Cleopatra*, on board of which was also Commodore Tyrwhitt, sighted a vessel steaming fast on his port bow. Realising from the showers of sparks coming from her funnels that she was burning coal, and not oil fuel, he rightly assumed her to be German. Increasing to full speed, he put his helm over to starboard, and in a few seconds saw two destroyers steaming across his bows. Steadying the helm, he rammed the second destroyer full amidships, and nearly at right angles. There was a violent explosion, a rush of escaping steam, and the crash of tearing steel as the *Cleopatra* cut her enemy in two.

It was the German destroyer G.194, and her stern portion sank on one side of the *Cleopatra* while the bow part, in which men could be heard shrieking, rushed on into the darkness at 30 knots. Not a soul survived.

The *Cleopatra* then altered course to attack the other destroyer, both she and the *Undaunted*, her next astern, opening fire with their 6-inch guns. But the enemy escaped in the pitch blackness of the night. During the sudden alterations of course, however, the *Undaunted*, Captain F. G. St. John, rammed the *Cleopatra's* stern and was seriously damaged forward. She was ordered to part company and to steam to the Tyne, and, in the bad weather that followed, barely succeeded in reaching England. Most of the time I believe she was making good about 3 knots against a terrific sea, and at one period there was a prospect of her having to be abandoned.

Nothing else occurred during the night, except that the weather became worse and worse. By daylight next morning, when we had turned to the west along the top of the minefield, we could steam no more than 8 knots against the sea. The motion was dreadful, with the ship crashing and bumping against the short almost perpendicular lop. We were all wet through and miserable. The galley fire having been put out by the water, there was no hot food.

It lasted for something over twenty-four hours, until we reached the shelter of the English coast, and eventually reached Harwich with 15 tons of oil fuel left in our tanks. A few more hours' steaming and we should have exhausted every gallon.

The prisoner who had been badly wounded died on the way home. He might have lived if the weather had been good, but the motion killed him.

It was a mournful little party that gathered on deck in oil-skins and sea-boots to commit the remains to the deep in a hammock with two 4-inch projectiles at the feet. The ship was crashing into a head sea and burying herself in flying spray. The gale howled dismally, and the heaving grey sea was flecked with white horses and wisps of flying spindrift. The heavily overcast sky was streaked with white storm-wrack, and overhead our dingy, tattered White Ensign flapped and strained at its halliards. Out of respect for the dead, we had lowered it to half-mast from its usual position at the gaff on our little mizzen-mast.

The German officer recited what he could remember of the burial service, while we stood by bareheaded, our faces unshaven, our eyes red and sore for want of sleep, our bodies swaying tiredly from the knees to the violent motion of the ship.

The corpse, sewn up in its hammock – we had no German ensign – lay on a mess-table, its end on the ship's side. The officer ceased to speak, and looked at me. I nodded. He said something in his own language. The bearers lifted the inboard end of the mess-table. Its shotted burden slid overboard with the sound of canvas rasping against wood, and curved through the air to disappear with a little splash.

The deceased was our enemy, but we had done our best to save his life, had shown what respect we could to his mortal remains. One could feel no animosity.

Before he finally left the ship at Harwich under a guard of marines, Anton Frank thanked us for what we had done for him and his men. Most of them went away with little bundles of spare clothing given them by the seamen, and Anton Frank with some thick undergarments and a muffler of mine. I noticed, however, that many of their uniform buttons were missing – bartered away to our men as mementoes in exchange for cigarettes.

" How long will this war last ? " asked Frank, just before he left the ship. " When shall I see my wife again ? "

It was more than I could tell him.

" Well, if you are ever made a prisoner by our Navy, I hope they will treat you as you have treated us," he said.

I hoped so too.

4

Here is a tale of another exploit by a destroyer, probably one of the most remarkable rescues at sea that has ever taken place.

On the morning of Sunday, October 6th, 1918, a convoy of transports carrying American troops were approaching the north coast of Ireland. It was blowing a full gale, with a very heavy sea, when, at about 9 a.m., the steering-gear of the S.S. *Kashmir* broke down and the ship became unmanageable. Swerving out of her course, she crashed heavily into the armed mercantile cruiser, *Otranto*, Captain E. G. W. Davidson, R.N., on the port side, making an enormous hole. At the time the incident took place the ships were about eight miles off the Irish coast.

Immediately after the collision had occurred, Captain Davidson realised there was very little prospect of saving the ship, and, including officers, crew, and American troops, he had on board over a thousand men, for whose lives he was responsible. A wireless signal of distress was made the moment the crash occurred, while everyone on board went to their boat stations. In the conditions of wind and sea, however, no boat could possibly have lived.

The weather was hazy, and before long the *Kashmir* drifted out of sight and the *Otranto* was left alone. For an hour she managed to steam slowly ; but at the end of that time was forced to stop by the large amount of water that had entered the ship and flooded the stokeholds. She had drifted close inshore, apparently, and Captain Davidson was looking for a suitable place on which to beach her. The coast-line, however, was composed of sheer, precipitous cliff, with the great waves rioting and bursting in spray along the water's edge. There was no sheltered beach at hand. To have ventured close inshore was to court destruction in the breakers.

According to the account of one survivor, the ship had anchored but was dragging, when, at about 10 a.m., the destroyer *Mounsey* appeared in answer to the distress signal. In the huge seas the destroyer rolled and plunged violently as she approached, at times all but hidden from the sight of those in the *Otranto* as she fell into the troughs of the waves. But, circling round the *Otranto's* stern, she came up on her starboard side.

Captain Davidson advised the *Mounsey's* captain, Lieutenant F. W. Craven, not to attempt to come alongside. To do so seemed to be risking almost certain disaster. But Craven replied that it was the only chance of saving life, which was the simple truth.

The *Otranto* lowered two of her lifeboats almost to the water's edge to act as fenders, and the *Mounsey*, unable to come alongside in the ordinary way because of the sea, lay off close to the liner's lee side and allowed the larger ship to drift down on top of her. On board the *Otranto*, all the men were still fallen in at their boat stations wearing lifebelts, and word was passed advising them to take off their heavier clothing and overcoats. Many, realising they would have to jump for it, also removed their boots.

The *Otranto* was heeling over considerably. Nearer and nearer the *Mounsey* drifted, staggering, rolling, pitching in the sea, borne high on the back of a great comber at one moment, and the next sliding into a watery valley. It seemed impossible that so frail and so lightly built a ship, with plating no stouter than thick cardboard, could withstand the shock of meeting a larger vessel broadside on in such weather conditions. She might beat in her side, become hopelessly disabled, perhaps sink alongside.

Fenders were lowered, and with the splintering of wood as the suspended lifeboats took the weight and collapsed, the two ships met with a crashing, grinding shudder. On board the *Otranto* there was no confusion or panic. The men in the first line were ordered to jump for their lives when the opportunity came. They did so as the destroyer was lifted on a sea, and though a few missing their footing, fell between the ships and were crushed to death, many more landed on board the *Mounsey*, where willing hands were waiting to receive them. Some, jumping too late as the destroyer fell into a hollow, broke their arms or legs as they landed on her steel deck.

After being alongside for some time, it was reported to Craven that the *Mounsey* was damaged, and that there was a large amount of water in the engine-room. He was forced to abandon the work of rescue for a time, and, managing to claw his way clear of the *Otranto* with the greatest difficulty, found that the damage was not so serious as he expected.

So he took his ship alongside again – in all, four times – saving many men on each occasion. Altogether, he rescued 596 officers and men, of whom 300 were American soldiers. Then, with his little ship crowded as she had never been crowded before, and without room on board for another soul, he was forced to steam away.

The gale persisted, and the helpless *Otranto* eventually drifted ashore on Islay, where, in the raging sea, she became a total loss. Of the 447 officers and men who remained on board, only 16 were saved when the vessel struck, Captain Davidson and most of his officers being numbered among the drowned.

The *Kashmir*, it may be added, managed to make a Scottish port, where she landed her troops.

Craven's action in rescuing 596 lives that would otherwise have been lost was a magnificent feat, for which he was afterwards awarded the D.S.O. and, by the President of the United States, the American Distinguished Service Medal. No man deserved these honours more. " His performance," in the words of the *London Gazette* of March 17th, 1919, " was a remarkable one, and in personal courage, coolness, and seamanship ranks in the very highest order."

It is difficult to write of such an episode in cold blood, more difficult still to write in such a way that a reader may realise something of the awful difficulty and danger of taking a fragile little ship of 1,000 tons alongside a vessel more than ten times her own size in a howling gale and a raging sea. Craven risked his ship, his own life, and the life of every man on board the *Mounsey*. Moreover, he knew the risk he was running. But it was justified, and his cool judgment and seamanship brought him out triumphant.

There are many tales of heroic rescues at sea ; but for calm determination and gallantry there are few that I have come across that equal Craven's saving of those men from the *Otranto*. Even in the Royal Navy, which sets a high standard upon personal merit and regards as an everyday occurrence an incident which would provide a " scoop " story for a popular newspaper, the *Mounsey's* feat is not forgotten.

It is all the more to be regretted, then, that Francis Worthington Craven retired from the Navy as a lieutenant-commander soon after the war, and, while serving with the Auxiliary Division of the Royal Irish Constabulary, was killed on duty in Ireland on February 2nd, 1921.

LITTERA SCRIPTA MANET

CHAPTER XV

THE DOVER PATROL

I

THERE were never really enough destroyers at Dover to do
the work of the Dover Patrol, and most of the Harwich
Force destroyers, the *Murray* included, occasionally found themselves detached thither from time to time to eke out the numbers.
Even so, though we sometimes had our little excitements, we
were only allowed to be used for work on the Belgian coast barrage
in 1916–17.

In 1917–18, with other minelaying destroyers, the *Telemachus*,
when I was in her, also did occasional operations from Dover.
These I have described elsewhere in this volume.

It always struck me that the regular Dover destroyers of the
6th Flotilla were very hardly worked and insufficiently recognised
when it came to the question of honours and awards. As Admiral
Sir Reginald Bacon says in his book, " The routine of the Dover
destroyers was to have steam on the engines, either at sea, or in
harbour, for seventeen days in succession ; then to spend three
days laid up for boiler-cleaning, and once every four months
they had twenty days in the dockyard and for coating the ship's
bottom, and making defects good. During the seventeen days,
when in harbour, officers and crews remained on their vessels
ready to slip instantly. . . . "[1]

During the dark periods of the month, when German destroyer
raids were likely, the destroyer captains got " only one good
night's rest in four, and, if lucky, one day's rest in four also.
. . . None of the captains ever broke down, although, as their
three days' stand-off for boiler-cleaning approached, they also
approached their limits of endurance, and I could see by their
pinched faces that they were badly in need of rest."[2]

There were certainly periods when the Dover destroyers were
badly overworked, and although officers and men never com-
plained, and never reported sick through overstrain, there is no
doubt that living in a constant state of physical exhaustion was

[1] *The Dover Patrol*, pp. 328–9 (Hutchinson & Co.).   [2] *Ibid.* pp. 330–1.

not conducive to efficiency. " Had we had three times the destroyer force, I could have arranged for an easier routine, but as numbers stood, this was impossible. . . . The principle that I acted on was that we were at war. War happened only once in a lifetime, and therefore everyone had to be prepared to expend the energy of a lifetime during the war."[1]

This is all very well ; but there is a limit to human endurance. Considering the nature of their work, the rest periods allowed to the Dover destroyers were definitely insufficient. Moreover, having regard to their many losses, and the many ships damaged by mines, torpedo, and gunfire, it is all the more surprising to think that for the first two years of the war the 6th Flotilla were given only one D.S.O. and one D.S.C.[2] At that time decorations in the Navy seem only to have been granted to the more junior officers and men for what one may call lucky incidents, such as the sinking of a submarine, not so much for prolonged and arduous service in a zone where vessels were constantly in touch with the enemy. One would not cheapen decorations to the point of absurdity ; but the paucity of awards to destroyers in the earlier days of the war showed a great lack of imagination on the part of those responsible for advising His Majesty. Much meritorious work was suffered to pass unnoticed.

2

I had no personal experience of the " tip and run " raids, when the German destroyers from Zeebrugge, choosing their own time at night, broke through the mine-net barrage between the Goodwins and Dunkerque, and proceeded to attack the patrol drifters lying at their anti-submarine nets in the Straits, to bombard Calais, or to try to raid the cross-Channel traffic line between Folkestone and Boulogne. They inflicted considerable losses on the drifters, and also upon the destroyer patrols ; but the shore bombardments were singularly ineffective. Moreover, in the course of the whole war, enemy destroyers succeeded in destroying only one cross-Channel transport, and that an empty one. This was the *Queen*, lost on the night of October 26th-27th, 1916.

Sometimes the enemy varied their plans by bombarding

[1] *The Dover Patrol*, p. 329.
[2] *Keeping the Seas*, by Captain (now Rear-Admiral) E. R. G. R. Evans, C.B., D.S.O.

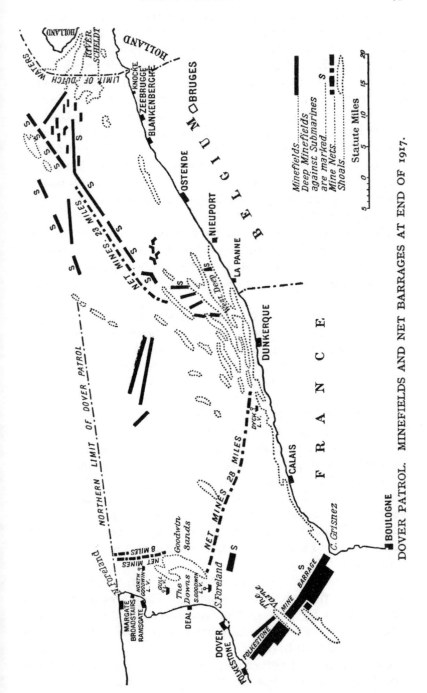

DOVER PATROL.   MINEFIELDS AND NET BARRAGES AT END OF 1917.

Ramsgate or Broadstairs, or threatening the mass of shipping in
the Downs. But they never really pushed these attacks home.
Had they done so, they might have reaped a rich harvest.

But all night and every night, in fogs and vile weather, the
destroyers of the Dover Patrol had to guard that twenty-seven-
mile stretch of water between the South Foreland and France.
Those who have crossed between Dover and Calais, and Folkestone
and Boulogne, during a blow will realise the conditions of wind
and sea that sometimes prevailed in the Straits. Except for the
Pentland Firth, I know of no short expanse of water that can be
more uncomfortable for small craft when a strong tide is flowing
against a snorting south-westerly gale beating up-Channel. And
how frequent these gales were !

The destroyers were not on their stations for a night or two
at a time ; but for seven, eight, and ten nights in succession,
sometimes more. I knew of one T.B.D. captain who was *nineteen*
nights at sea, without any sleep except an occasional afternoon
in his bunk.

They were working, too, in an area where all the shore lights
had been extinguished, and where the abnormally strong tides
and network of shoals made accurate navigation a matter of
difficulty. In addition, they had the added dangers of a complicated system of anti-submarine nets and mines laid here and
there across the Straits and in the passages among the shoals, and
the frequent minefields deposited by hostile submarines. Hardly
a day passed after July 1915 that some area or other in the
Straits was not mined, the favourite spots being those most used
by mercantile shipping – off the North and South Forelands, off
Folkestone, between Dungeness and Beachy Head, off Boulogne,
and between Calais and Gravelines. In all, 1,200 mines were
swept up and destroyed in the Dover area from July 1915 to the
end of 1917, most of them in the latter year. They were laid in
little bunches of seven, or eight, or a dozen at a time by the U.C.
boats from Zeebrugge.

The enemy destroyers, choosing their own night and time,
might come through at any moment. They need only keep a
rigid look-out for three or four hours, and could open fire with
guns or torpedoes on any vessel they saw in the absolute certainty
that she was British.

Our patrols, on the other hand, were working in an area fairly
populated with their friends. Consequently, they had to establish the identity of any strange vessel seen in the darkness before

they opened fire. If the ship challenged were German, the inevitable reply was a torpedo, or a burst of close-range gunfire. It was generally the former, a torpedo being more likely to sink an opponent immediately. In the circumstances, geographical and otherwise, it was unavoidable that the initiative should lie with the enemy. Our patrols were acting on the defensive. The vice-admiral at Dover was forced, very largely, to dance to the German piping.

So much for the night.

During the day, the destroyers had to protect the endless flow of transports plying between Folkestone and Boulogne and vice versa. The average number of sailings in any one year was about 700, and, up to the end of 1917, 5,614,500 troops had been ferried to and fro without the loss of a single man. Another 198,000 troops were embarked or disembarked at Dover during the same period, while 810,000 wounded or sick were landed there. In the three years 1914–1917, the arrivals and departures of store-carriers, troop-transports, and ambulance-ships at Dover numbered over 14,800. The only casualty was the mining of the ambulance-ship *Anglia* while sailing under the Red Cross.[1]

About 120,000 steamers passed through the Dover area in the years 1915, 1916, and 1917, on their way up- or down-Channel. These also had to be escorted by the Dover destroyers, assisted by trawlers, between Beachy Head and the North Foreland.

And in the brief leisure that the destroyers were supposed to enjoy in harbour at Dover, a harbour where, as likely as not, they were rolling heavily at their buoys, they were frequently sent to sea at five minutes' notice to hunt submarines in the Straits. Sometimes, while supposed to be " resting," they had also to be detailed to take distinguished officials across the Channel. As Sir Reginald Bacon wrote afterwards, " Perhaps these gentlemen can now understand why requests for a destroyer were not received with overflowing cordiality, but rather grudgingly."

The destroyer strength of the Dover Patrol at the outbreak of war was twelve vessels of the *Tribal* class completed between 1905 and 1908, steaming a nominal 33 knots. The five earliest were armed with five 12-pounder guns, and the others with two 4-inch guns. With them were twelve of the old " 30 knotters," ships of between 350 and 400 tons, completed between 1897 and 1901, and carrying one 12-pounder gun, five 6-pounders, and the usual two torpedo tubes. Even in 1914, most of the " 30

[1] For these figures and statements I am indebted to *The Dover Patrol*, pp. 315–16.

knotters " were really due for the scrap-heap, though many of them survived until the end of the war, by which time some had reached the very respectable age of twenty-two. At Dover, as elsewhere, they did yeoman service.

From time to time, the destroyer force at Dover was considerably augmented. Here are the strengths for January 1917, and August the same year.

	January 1917	*August 1917*
Flotilla-leaders.	3	6
Tribal class.	11	10
Modern destroyers	7	19
Older destroyers (small)	13	10
Patrol-boats.	7	6
Torpedo-boats.	3	2

What with casualties and refits, not more than three-quarters of these numbers could be expected to be present on the patrol at any particular time.

Yet, in spite of their many sleepless nights, the Dover destroyers managed to amuse themselves. Someone even found time to produce a magazine, known as *Nubian Nonsense*, after the ship in which it was produced.

On one occasion a newcomer to Dover made rather an alarming wireless signal : " Am sinking. German mine." Hurrying to the spot expecting to find nothing but shattered remains, his would-be rescuers found him firing at an enemy mine with rifles. The mistake had been made by the wireless operator, who had inserted an unnecessary fullstop. The incident evoked the following verses[1] in a composition entitled " The Laws of Patrolling," produced by the flotilla poet :

> When you see a horned object that's floating,
>   And you've got all your rifles in line,
> Please don't make a wireless signal
>   " Am sinking " – full stop – " German mine."

> If you sink it or burst it, just say so ;
>   That certainly cannot do harm ;
> But to make the above stupid signal
>   Causes panic and useless alarm.

[1] Quoted by Rear-Admiral E. R. G. R. Evans, C.B., D.S.O., in *Keeping the Seas*.

Another verse in this same effusion, referring to the difficulty we sometimes had in obtaining permission to enter Dover harbour, a necessary formality in wartime which involved a good deal of signalling and occasional delay in thick weather, ran as follows :

> If you find yourself close to the entrance
> In fog or in mist or in rain,
> Take permission to enter as granted ;
> Get inside, where the guns cannot train.

Destroyers entering *without permission* were liable to be fired upon as hostile. On one occasion, H.M.S. *Lookout*, from Harwich, commanded by Lieutenant-Commander Maurice B. R. Black-wood,[1] had to wait a considerable time off Dover in a fog, before being given leave to enter. Losing patience, he made up his mind to enter. As he steamed in through the narrow eastern entrance between the breakwaters, the ship was hailed by an officer and men of the Royal Garrison Artillery.

" What ship is that ? " they shouted.

" *Lookout,*" Blackwood replied.

" Ship ahoy ! What ship ? " again.

" *Lookout !* " went back, *fortissimo.*

To Blackwood's intense astonishment, the khaki-clad gunners and their elderly major took to their heels and disappeared.

Instead of recognising the *Lookout* as a British destroyer, they thought her an enemy whose captain was giving them a friendly hint to take cover before he opened fire !

3

Beyond a good deal of monotonous patrol work across the Channel, an occasional submarine hunt, and much escort work, little in the way of actual fighting came the way of the Dover destroyers until October 17th, 1914, when, Antwerp having fallen, the German army reached the Belgian coast. From then until November 8th, when the French and Belgian armies were established along the line of the Yser, stretching inland from Nieuport, the 6th Flotilla had their full share of excitement in bombarding the enemy positions and trenches in company with a motley armada of other vessels.

From time to time the bombarding squadron, under the

[1] Now Captain Maurice Blackwood, D.S.O.

command of Rear-Admiral Hon. Horace Hood, comprised the old battleships *Revenge* (afterwards *Redoubtable*) and *Venerable* ; the monitors *Severn, Mersey,* and *Humber,* building at Barrow-in-Furness for a foreign Government and taken over when the war began ; a couple of light-cruisers ; various destroyers ; two old cruisers, the *Sirius* and *Brilliant* ; the sloops *Vestal, Wildfire,* and *Rinaldo,* which had been serving for years as tenders to the gunnery schools at Portsmouth, Chatham, and Devonport ; and the two ancient " flat iron " gunboats, *Excellent* and *Bustard*, one of 508 and the other of 254 tons, built no less than forty years before and barely able to stem the tide.

These ships, aided by French destroyers, poured in a furious bombardment on the shore positions, and the British T.B.D.s came in for their share of excitement and were often under heavy fire. On October 20th, the destroyer *Amazon*, flying the flag of the rear-admiral, was hit on the waterline by a shell which blew in a hole eight feet square. Three days later it was decided to examine Ostend, so at about 11 a.m. the destroyer *Crusader*, Lieutenant-Commander George L. D. Gibbs, flying Admiral Hood's flag, steamed at high speed up the coast and went close off the town, rounding the quay just off the entrance to the harbour. A good deal of excitement was noticeable ashore ; men running about and horses dragging guns into position. Fire was presently opened, and the *Crusader* replied.

Read what was written of this incident by the Swedish writer and explorer, Dr. Sven Hedin, who was with the German army as an observer. He describes the scene in the Hotel Majestic, on the sea front at Ostend, where the dining-room was crowded with hungry officers of the German General Staff, who had just marched in. Then he continues :

" A destroyer had just detached itself from the rest and was making at full speed for Ostend, parallel with the coast, as close as possible to the shore. Presently another destroyer appeared, following in the wake of the first. What could they want, these ruffians ? Strong language was heard – it was a piece of con-summate impudence to come steaming right under our noses like this. Evidently they were reconnoitring – but what insolence ; they must have known that we had occupied Ostend ! Aha ! they suspect that there are submarines and destroyers in the inner harbour, and want to see whether they can detect anything from outside ! . . . Astounding insolence. Two small German guns are hurried up. " Are they going to shoot ? " I asked.

" Oh, yes, they are going to shoot all right." . . . The first shot rang out. . . . Directly the German shots had been fired, the two destroyers swung round to port and at the same moment opened fire. Their guns seemed to flash out straight at us. . . . "

" The results," as says Mr. Winston Churchill in *The World Crisis*, " were instantaneous. The restaurant, which had been one of the most elegant in Europe, was blasted into a smoking shambles of ruin and death."

What a glorious opportunity! From my heart I envy the captains of those two destroyers. It has been vouchsafed to few to shell a restaurant full of feasting enemies at point-blank range. Imagine steaming past Brighton and bombarding the Grand or the Metropole at a few hundred yards!

From their bridge and decks, as they patrolled the Belgian coast at night, the destroyers had a good view of the fighting ashore – the red flashes of exploding shell, the burning houses, the flames that showed through the shattered windows of the little seaside villas at Westende and Mariakerke. " It was all un-utterably weird and sad to watch the devastation of the Flanders seaside health resorts," wrote Captain E. R. G. R. Evans, who at that time commanded the destroyer *Mohawk*.

The enemy soon mounted 8-inch guns, which made things very unpleasant for the flotilla working inshore. On October 28th the battleship *Venerable* was in action, and, as it was absolutely necessary to protect her against possible submarines, the de-stroyer *Falcon* was sent to patrol the North-East Channel off Ostend. She was a 375-ton, 30-knot destroyer dating from 1899, commanded by Lieutenant Herbert Wauton. At 12.30 p.m., while carrying out this duty, she came under very heavy fire from the shore. Increasing speed, Wauton held his position, returning the fire with lyddite shell from his tiny guns. At 2 p.m. an 8-inch shell burst on the muzzle of her foremost 6-pounder, killing the captain and 7 men, and wounding the gunner and 15 men, 10 of them very seriously – this out of a total complement of about 60. Severely damaged, the little *Falcon* was steamed out of action by her sub-lieutenant, Charles J. Du Boulay, with the shell splashing into the sea all round her. Herbert Wauton was the first destroyer captain of the 6th Flotilla to lose his life in the war.

The bombarding squadron was withdrawn from the Belgian coast on November 8th, and for many months the Dover destroyers had the arduous and increasing work of patrolling, and of escorting the cross-Channel troop transports, alleviated by frequent submarine hunts. It was not until the late summer of 1915, by which time Vice-Admiral (afterwards Admiral Sir) Reginald Bacon had succeeded to the Dover command, and the first of the war-built monitors had arrived, that the destroyers' work was further varied by their use as anti-submarine screens for the monitors in their occasional bombardments of Zeebrugge at a range of about 20,000 yards.

It is easy to be wise after the event, but even during the war I remember wondering to myself what real purpose these monitor bombardments served. They were carried out with the idea of destroying lock-gates and so forth, and so making Zeebrugge and Ostend harbours untenable by enemy torpedo-craft and submarines. It is true that, in the circumstances, they were the only *offensive* action we could take on the Belgian coast, apart from landing troops or actually blocking the harbours. Moreover, the threats of bombardments and landings made it necessary for the enemy to fortify the coast with heavy artillery and to retain a large number of troops to repel a possible landing.

On the other hand, the bombardments from the sea entailed a vast expenditure of time and material and money for very little direct result. Firing from a very long range, the mathematical chance of hitting a lock-gate at Zeebrugge, assuming absolutely accurate aiming, was once in sixty-seven rounds. On September 22nd, 1917, the monitor *Terror*, with her 15-inch guns, actually obtained three hits on Ostend dockyard, and damaged the floating dock and lock-gates, draining the basin to low-water mark, which doubtless caused the Germans some inconvenience.

Sir Reginald Bacon claims that the bombardments " obliged the enemy to abandon the use of Ostend as a harbour, and had practically limited his use of Zeebrugge as a base and driven him up to Bruges."[1] If this was so, the abandonment was merely temporary, for at the time of the St. George's Day blocking expeditions, April 23rd, 1918, both Zeebrugge and Ostend were still in use by German naval forces.

The number of submarines based on the Flanders coast grew from 7 in May 1915, to 14 at the end of the year. By December 1916 the number had risen to 25, and in March 1917, after the institution of the unrestricted submarine campaign, to 38. Thereafter, it remained at 30 or more until February 1918, and at 20 or more until the following August. One is tempted to

[1] *The Dover Patrol*, p. 107.

wonder what would have been the effect on the losses of Allied shipping if Zeebrugge had *not* been available as an enemy submarine base.

Apart from their indirect results, the British bombardments achieved little in combating the submarine menace. How much simpler it would have been to have destroyed the harbour facilities at Zeebrugge and Ostend *before* the Germans reached the coast. One understands this was not done for two main reasons – first, because the Belgian Government objected ; second, because it was hoped to use Ostend and Zeebrugge harbours as bases *if* the Allied troops succeeded in pushing along the coast.

One can only imagine that the bombardments from the sea were carried out *faute de mieux* in the search for some form of offensive.

I have rather wandered from the point, but on the ships being withdrawn from the Belgian coast in November 1914, the destroyers reverted to their normal duties. It was on May 7th following that the first destroyer loss occurred, when the *Maori*, Commander B. W. Barrow, and the *Crusader* were ordered to approach Zeebrugge to sketch some of the salient landmarks. They were told not to go within 10,000 yards of the shore. While carrying out their work, the *Maori* unfortunately struck a mine and sank, her officers and crew being made prisoners by two enemy armed trawlers which came out from Zeebrugge.

In another chapter of this book I have described the laying of the anti-submarine barrage laid off the Belgian coast in April 1916. Here I will continue by telling the stories of some of the enemy's " tip and run " raids on the patrols in the Dover Straits.

4

On the night of October 26th–27th, 1916, the 30-knot destroyer *Flirt*, a 370-ton vessel completed in 1897 and commanded by Lieutenant R. P. Kellett, was in the eastern area of the Channel, ready to assist the little flotilla of drifters on patrol in case a submarine should be sighted, or become involved in the mine-nets stretched across the Straits.

Aerial reconnaissance on the 26th had shown that there was considerable train activity and movement of barges at Ostend, to which place additional enemy destroyers had already been sent. As there were no night movements of British troops on the transport route between Folkestone and Boulogne, a fact of which it was considered the enemy must have full knowledge, the German preparations seemed to point to an attack on that portion of the Belgian coast still in Allied hands, together with a possible raid on the merchant shipping anchored in the Downs. To guard against these eventualities, four Harwich Force destroyers, together with four " 30-knotters," were lying with steam ready at Dunkerque; four more Harwich destroyers were in the Downs ; and five destroyers of the *Tribal* class were in Dover harbour with steam at ten minutes' notice.

The raid was apparently carried out by twelve large enemy destroyers, which arrived off the eastern end of the net barrage, and there separated.

Half steered for Cape Grisnez, and, steaming up the Boulogne-Folkestone route, came across the empty transport *Queen*, which they shelled after removing her papers. She was reported by her crew to have been definitely sunk, though, as a matter of fact, she did not founder until she had drifted near the South Goodwin, nearly three hours later.

The remaining six Germans steered for Dover, being sighted in the darkness by the *Flirt*, which took them for British destroyers returning to Dover from Dunkerque. Soon afterwards the *Flirt* heard heavy firing to the westward, and steamed at full speed in the direction of the flashes. The gunfire was also heard at Dover, whereupon the five *Tribal* destroyers there were ordered to sea.

The enemy had attacked the drifter patrols, sinking 6, and damaging 3 others and 1 trawler. The *Flirt* very soon arrived upon the scene, saw men swimming in the water, and stopped and lowered her whaler in charge of her first lieutenant. She then switched on her searchlight. The moment she did so she was attacked by two enemy destroyers, who riddled her at close range until she sank. Not one of her officers or men, except those away in the boat, lived to tell the tale. Even the boat's crew, pulling about looking in vain for their shipmates after the *Flirt* had sunk, had an unnerving experience. Mistaking the boat for a submarine in the darkness, a British destroyer dropped a depth-charge close alongside, which nearly destroyed her. A little later, moreover, they sighted an enemy U-boat on the surface, which, also taking the whaler for a submarine, dived to escape destruction.

The destroyers from Dover, meanwhile, soon appeared on the

scene, and the enemy made off. In the engagement that followed, the *Amazon*, Lieutenant Guy L. Warren, sustained some casualties and was severely damaged by gunfire. The *Nubian*, Commander M. R. Bernard, had become detached from the others, and came across the enemy a little later. She did her utmost to ram one of her opponents during the fierce engagement that ensued ; but, before she could effect her purpose, was hit by a torpedo, which practically blew off her bows. What remained of her was finally taken in tow, and brought close to Dover harbour. Bad weather coming on, however, the towing-wire parted and the ship drifted ashore on a reef near the South Foreland. Here she shed the remains of her bow, and was driven up under the cliff at high water. After enduring the two heavy gales, a cutting was blasted through the rock and the after part eventually refloated. Being joined in a dockyard to the bow of the *Zulu*, which had been mined some time before, the composite vessel was christened the *Zubian*.

So the first German " tip and run " raid was a distinct success for the enemy, a decided encouragement to try again. It had resulted in the loss to us of 2 destroyers, 1 transport, 6 drifters, and damage to a number of other vessels. The casualties in personnel had amounted to over 100 officers and men killed or drowned, many wounded, and 10 prisoners.

These raids were particularly difficult to counter with the small number of destroyers at Vice-Admiral Bacon's disposal, and the next occurred on the night of November 23rd-24th, when six large enemy destroyers tried to attack the Downs. Engaged by our patrol drifters off Ramsgate, little vessels armed with nothing larger than 6-pounder guns, the enemy damaged the *Acceptable*, and disappeared in the darkness before our destroyers could overtake them.

On March 1st, 1917, again, the L class destroyer *Laverock*, on patrol in the Channel, was attacked by five enemy destroyers who hit her with a torpedo which luckily failed to explode. Three other enemy destroyers fired a few shell into Broadstairs. Another raid was delivered on the night of March 17th-18th, when, at 10.50 p.m. the British destroyer *Paragon*, on the usual patrol line near Calais, was attacked by three or four enemies. On sighting the strangers, the *Paragon*, commanded by Lieutenant R. T. Bowyer, made the usual challenge, the instant reply to which was a torpedo, which struck and exploded with deadly effect. The *Paragon*, a modern destroyer of 928 tons armed with three 4-inch guns, returned the fire, and herself fired a torpedo without result. Seriously damaged, she sank in eight or nine minutes.

Arriving on the scene about ten minutes later, the *Laforey* switched on her searchlight to rescue survivors. She was joined soon afterwards by the *Llewellyn*, which did the same. The enemy were still in the vicinity, and at 11.15 p.m. the *Llewellyn* was torpedoed, presumably by the same destroyer who had sunk the *Paragon*. Badly damaged but still afloat, she reached Dover harbour at 4.30 a.m. in tow of a tug; but only two survivors from the *Paragon* seemed to have been rescued.

Meanwhile, between 0.44 and 1 a.m., three or four other German destroyers approached the North Foreland from the north-east-ward, torpedoed the steamship *Greypoint* at anchor in the North Downs, fired at the drifters, hitting the *Paramount* in several places, and then decamped at full speed after throwing a few shell into Ramsgate. Three houses were hit, but there were no casualties.

Again, from the German point of view, the raid had been a success.

It was easy for some of the newspapers to fulminate, and for people to write abusive and anonymous letters to the admiral – as they did – demanding to know what the Navy was doing; why people living in the coast towns could not sleep peacefully in their beds; and why, when the raiders came, they were not immediately intercepted, brought to action, and destroyed.

But the wiseacres knew nothing of the conditions in which the defending destroyers had to work; did not seem to realise that on dark nights the visibility was little more than a quarter of a mile, and that, with craft steaming at 30 knots – one sea mile in two minutes – they were in sight at one moment and gone the next. The initiative, as I have pointed out before, lay almost entirely in the hands of the Germans, and they had a choice of several promising objectives. With the small number of destroyers available for defence, it was not possible to guard every vulnerable point of attack in sufficient strength to ensure success against a concentrated attack. "The enemy can choose the night and time, and which part of the coast he wishes to attack," Sir Reginald Bacon wrote. "I must cover the whole breadth of the Straits. The enemy can attack at a point."

To put the matter in a nutshell, raids were largely a matter of luck. But even the worst of luck usually turns in time.

5

The night of April 20th, 1917, was fine, but heavily overcast, with no moon – altogether a likely night for another German raid. The usual destroyer patrols were out in the Channel, while the flotilla-leaders *Swift*, Commander Ambrose M. Peck, and *Broke*, Commander E. R. G. R. Evans, C.B., were patrolling off Dover.

At 11.10 p.m. there was a sharp outburst of firing off Calais which lasted for seven or eight minutes. Twenty minutes later there came a short bombardment off Dover from a position about three miles to seaward. The *Swift* and *Broke*, increasing to full speed, immediately steered towards the gun-flashes. They had some miles to travel, and, reaching the spot without meeting anything, returned to the eastward with the idea of preventing the enemy from attacking the shipping in the Downs through its southern entrance.

As it afterwards appeared, the raid had been undertaken by six large German destroyers, two of which bombarded Calais, doubtless to draw the patrols to the eastern end of the Channel while four had shelled Dover twenty minutes afterwards. These latter then steered north-east along the eastern edge of the Goodwins, and then came back to rejoin the detachment from Calais.

At 0.50 a.m., when the *Swift* and *Broke* were in a position about seven miles east of Dover and steering about west-north-west, a line of six vessels steaming fast on an approximately parallel and opposite course were sighted on the port bow. The Germans immediately opened a heavy fire, to which the two British ships replied. At the same time, they increased to full speed, the *Swift* putting her helm hard over to starboard with the intention of ramming one of her opponents.

The vessels on both sides were now a blaze of gun-flashes, which made it very difficult to see what was happening, and Peck, in the *Swift*, was temporarily blinded by the flame of the 6-inch gun on the forecastle. Losing sight of the enemy for several seconds, and now travelling at full speed, he passed astern of the German line, though not before firing a torpedo at the fifth ship in the opposing line, which probably took effect.

Altering course out of the wake of the *Swift*, Evans, in the *Broke*, held his fire for a moment to bring the sights of the torpedo director on the bridge on their target. Despard, the first lieutenant, actually fired it, and after an interval it, or the *Swift's* torpedo, fired at much the same time, struck the fifth ship in the enemy line full amidships, to explode in an upheaval of smoke and whitened spray which glowed redly in the blaze of gun-flashes.

Both sides were steaming fast. Things were happening in seconds, and once more the *Broke's* foremost guns had opened fire. Evans had been steering to ram ; but, seeing the ship he was aiming for – G.85 – struck by the torpedo, realised it was now unnecessary, put his helm to port, and swung outwards for a few seconds to give himself room to swing back again and ram the destroyer astern of G.85.

" If you put the helm over now, sir, you'll get this next one all right, sir," said Hickman, the *Broke's* navigator, to his captain, who himself was conning the ship.

Under heavy fire, and in a coruscation of gun-flashes and the sparkle and smoke of exploding shell, Evans put his helm over and drove straight for his enemy at 27 knots. There was hardly time to breathe, let alone to think coherently.

The German, G.42, increased speed, smoke and showers of sparks pouring from her funnels as she strove to escape. But it was too late. With a grinding thud, and the screech of tearing steel, the *Broke's* bow crashed into her opponent's port side abreast the after funnel. The terrific impact hurled the German practically over on her beam-ends as the *Broke's* ram pushed her bodily through the water.

It is impossible to describe the sensations of those on board both these ships as the collision occurred – the *Broke's* grimly triumphant ; the Germans filled with terror-stricken amazement and horror. It was a dreadful moment ; but worse was yet to come.

Men were screaming and shouting for help as the *Broke's* guns, at their maximum depression, pumped shell after shell at a few yards' range into the mass of men huddled on the deck of her stricken enemy. One of the German's torpedo-tubes had stuck into the *Broke's* side and was torn off its mounting. The anti-aircraft 2-pounders added to the din with their stuttering uproar, while the British seamen that remained alive in the forepart of the ship, with rifles and fixed bayonets, and revolvers and naked cutlasses, headed by Mr. Midshipman Donald Gyles, R.N.R., already wounded by a shell splinter in the eye, swarmed forward on to the *Broke's* forecastle to repel boarders.

They were taking no chances. No quarter was given. Every German who clambered over the bows was shot or bayoneted. A deadly small-arm fire was poured from the forecastle into the terrified men on G.42's deck. Even the officers on the *Broke's* bridge used their automatic pistols. Few of their enemies survived the storm of lead and nickel.

But the *Broke* did not escape unpunished. When things were happening every second, it is impossible to describe events in their strict chronological sequence ; but early in the action, which cannot have lasted more than a few minutes, a shell explosion on the forecastle had hurled a box of 4-inch cartridges into the air to scatter them round about the bridge, where they burnt with the fierce red glow and leaping flames of consuming cordite. She was also blazing amidships. Illuminated like a beacon, she made a conspicuous target. A hostile destroyer slammed in salvo after salvo until she disappeared into the night. It was nearly impossible to miss at so short a range.

In the space of a few moments the *Broke* was converted into a smoking shambles. In places, her decks were literally running in blood. She sustained 57 casualties, of whom 21 were killed outright, and no part of the ship was immune. Two shell had hit the bridge structure, to kill a signalman, and seriously to wound the helmsman and a man at the engine-room telegraphs. But the former, Able Seaman William George Rawles, who afterwards received the Conspicuous Gallantry Medal for his bravery, continued to steer the ship until G.42 had been rammed. Then he collapsed from loss of blood.

Many casualties had occurred among the guns' crews of the forecastle through two enemy shell, one of which had detonated projectiles in a ready rack. All the electric cables and voice-pipes from the bridge had been shot away, while the after compass, after wireless-room, and searchlight were demolished. The foremost funnel was pierced through and through by splinters until it resembled a huge nutmeg-grater. A shell passing in through the side above the waterline had penetrated a coal-bunker, to explode in the boiler-room beyond, killing or wounding every man in the compartment and severing the main steam-pipe, from which the steam escaped with a deafening roar. And, besides the damage from enemy shell, the British flotilla-leader had a badly bent and crumpled bow, and two huge gashes forward above the waterline. Dead and wounded lay everywhere.

With her bows locked in G.42, she still steamed ahead, her speed gradually diminishing. Every man in sight on the German's deck had been killed or wounded. Her stern portion was gradually sinking. Finally, it disappeared altogether as the *Broke* ground her way clear.

For a time Evans and his officers thought their ship was about to sink ; but, once clear of G.42, they set about trying to inflict further damage upon the flying enemy. Two were still in sight, one ahead and one to starboard, with the *Swift* in chase, long flames pouring from the funnels of all three as they steamed at full speed.

But the *Broke's* speed was dropping fast, and presently an engineer-officer arrived on the bridge with the sad news that the loss of feed-water was so great that she could not steam more than half-speed. He also pointed out that the ship must eventually come to a standstill. Evans accordingly turned and steamed slowly back towards the two sinking destroyers.

About a mile from the spot, they passed through a number of German seamen in the water, who cried " Save ! Save ! " But at any moment the enemy might return to continue the fight. The *Broke* could not afford to stop to lower her boats.

A little later they saw the phosphorescent wake of an approaching destroyer, which flashed the usual challenge. The *Broke*, hit in thirty-two places on the bridge by shell, splinters, and bullets, had had all her electric circuits shot away and could not reply. For a moment it seemed as though the stranger might open fire, until the yeoman of signals produced an electric torch and spelt out the name of the ship. The other vessel was the *Swift*, which had pursued the flying Germans until, badly damaged by shell fire, she could pursue no more. Hit many times, her wireless was out of action, and she had four feet of water on the lower mess-deck. The two British ships cheered each other in the darkness.

The *Broke* then closed one of the sinking Germans, G.85, which was badly holed forward and was ablaze amidships. Men on her battered forecastle shouted " *Kamerad ! Kamerad !* " and Evans replied through a megaphone, " All right. We will pick you up ! "

But other Germans in the stern of G.85 thought otherwise, and opened fire with the after 4.1-inch gun, a shell from which passed through the *Broke's* bridge. She instantly retaliated with four rounds of 4-inch shell, while Acting-Sub-Lieutenant L. W. Peppe fired a torpedo from aft at a range of 200 yards. Set to run at six feet, it struck G.85 near the stern.

The *Broke* was then compelled to stop through the damage

to her boilers. She was gradually drifting nearer G.85, which was still blazing. It was a matter of uncertainty whether the German would sink before the flames reached her magazine. If she blew up with the *Broke* close alongside, the latter might also be sunk by the explosion. By the efforts of those in the engine-room, however, she was able to go astern sufficiently to prevent collision. It was 1.20 a.m., thirty-five minutes from the time when the enemy had first been sighted, and a few moments later the destroyer *Mentor*, Lieutenant-Commander A. J. Landon, came alongside, and managed by good seamanship to take her in tow.

The *Swift*, meanwhile, were rescuing the survivors of G.42.

The *Broke* anchored for what remained of the night, and at daylight next morning was towed into Dover harbour amid the cheers of the men clustered on the decks of the other ships present. She had sustained more damage and more casualties than the *Swift*, though for this very gallantly fought engagement equal credit was due to the officers and men of both vessels. If I have dealt more with the doings of the *Broke* than those of the *Swift*, it is because there is more information available from the former ship upon which to write an account of the action.

For this remarkable and timely action Commanders Peck and Evans were both awarded the D.S.O., and promoted to the rank of captain. The engineer-lieutenant-commanders of both ships, James Hughes and Thomas George Comber, received a step in rank; while Lieutenants R. D. King-Harman and H. A. Simpson; Surgeon-Probationer J. S. Westwater ; and Mr. Henry Turner, Gunner (T), all of the *Swift*, received the D.S.C. The same decoration was awarded to Lieutenants G. V. Hickman and M. C. Despard ; Surgeon-Probationer C. T. Helsham ; Mr. F. Grinney, Gunner (T), and Midshipman Donald Gyles, R.N.R., all of the *Broke*. Four other officers were also " noted for early promotion." One man, Able Seaman Rawles, of the *Broke*, received the Conspicuous Gallantry Medal for an act of bravery already described, while 24 petty officers and men in both ships were awarded Distinguished Service Medals. Thirty-four officers, petty officers, and men were " mentioned in despatches," among these latter being Lieutenant-Commander A. J. Landon, of the *Mentor*, whose good seamanship in taking the damaged *Broke* in tow had been specially mentioned by Commander Evans.

The enemy had been taught their lesson. Thereafter, except for ineffectual sorties on April 26th and May 2nd, no further raids were made by German destroyers upon the Dover Straits for nearly a year.

6

At nightfall on March 20th, 1918, a combined Anglo-French force of torpedo-craft was lying in the roadstead off Dunkerque. It consisted of the flotilla-leader *Botha*, Commander Roger L'E. M. Rede ; the destroyer *Morris*, Lieutenant-Commander Percy R. P. Percival ; and three French destroyers, the *Capitaine Mehl*, *Magon*, and *Bouclier*. The latter were all fairly modern vessels of 800 tons, with trial speeds of 31 knots or more, and armed with the usual four torpedo-tubes, a couple of 3.9-inch guns, and four 9-pounders.

For a considerable time it had been usual to station a few destroyers off Dunkerque during the dark moonless nights when enemy destroyer raids were most likely. Indeed, less than five weeks before, at 1 a.m. in the morning, an attack on the Channel patrols had been made by a force of large destroyers from Zeebrugge, in the course of which they had sunk a trawler and seven drifters with heavy loss of life. Twenty-four hours later, moreover, in the early morning of February 16th, an U-boat had shelled Dover from the sea for three or four minutes to kill 1 child, and to wound 3 men, 1 woman, and 3 children.

The *Botha*, *Morris*, *Capitaine Mehl*, *Magon*, and *Bouclier* lay as usual with slips on their cables, steam on their engines, and everything ready for instant action. At about 3.45 a.m. heavy firing was heard to the northward, and gun-flashes were seen out at sea, which made it evident that the enemy had come down the coast from the direction of Ostend and were shelling the Belgian or French coast between La Panne and Dunkerque. The batteries ashore immediately opened a heavy barrage fire, and the star-shell began to burst overhead.

Slipping her cable, the *Botha*, followed by the others as soon as they were ready, steamed off at full speed to the north-west in the direction of the gun-flashes. They ran considerable danger from the barrage put down by the guns ashore, the shell from which could be heard hissing and whining overhead ; but passing over the banks to seaward of the anchorage they hauled up to a course parallel with the coast. The *Botha* then began to fire star-shell to light up the enemy, whereupon the firing from the sea ceased as suddenly as it had begun.

The night was calm and very dark, with a clear sky overhead, but a mist that shut down the visibility to about three-quarters of a mile. And very soon a lucky star-shell from the *Botha* showed up a line of blurred shapes on the port bow. Overhauling them fast, the *Botha* made her recognition signal, which was answered by a series of red lights from the strangers. This at once identified them as Germans. They were at close range, little more than 600 yards, and the next moment the British and French destroyers burst into a furious fire, the " poom-poom-poom " of the 2-pounder pom-poms and the sharp crackle of Lewis guns mingling with the deeper notes of the 4-inch.

A night action between fast-moving ships is always something of a mêlée and very difficult to follow, but, coming up fast, the *Botha* fired two torpedoes at the enemy line, which seemed to consist of five or six vessels. She herself was under heavy fire, and one shell, passing in through the side of the ship, had burst and cut an auxiliary steam-pipe. The speed started to drop, and, realising that he must act at once, Roger Rede put his helm hard over and steered straight for the fourth ship in the line.

Travelling at between 26 and 27 knots, it was a matter of a few seconds before the *Botha* had covered the few hundred yards necessary. Rede timed his stroke well. His ship's sharp bows took the enemy full amidships and nearly at right angles, to carve through his hull with nothing more than a slight tremor. The torpedo-boat was completely bisected, the two halves floating past with the men in them screaming for help.

Swinging round with the helm hard over the other way, the *Botha* then tried to repeat her *coup* on the next ship in the enemy's line. Speed, however, was failing, and the German succeeded in dodging the thrust, though she did not escape a heavy fire from every gun of the *Botha* that would bear as she sped by at point-blank range. It reduced her to little more than a blazing wreck.

In another moment the British vessel found herself blinded by a dense smoke-screen put up by the flying enemy. Then the cloud suddenly lifted, and a French destroyer[1] passed down

---

[1] The French destroyer was the *Capitaine Mehl*. The French contingent were somewhat astern of the British, and, emerging suddenly from the smoke screen, the *Capitaine Mehl's* commanding officer sighted a ship lying damaged. His challenge not being replied to, as the *Botha's* lights had been put out by gun-fire and the effects of the collision, he naturally fired a torpedo at close range. The incident shows the inevitable hazards of a close-range destroyer action fought at high speed in pitch darkness, with the additional obscurity caused by smoke screens.

the *Botha's* port side at full speed, firing a torpedo as she went. It struck with a crash, exploding in a huge upheaval of spray and a gout of blinding flame.

With a large hole in her port side, and her port torpedo-tube blown overboard, the *Botha* lay stopped and helpless, the steam escaping with a bellowing roar in which even shouted orders went unheard. For the time those on board thought she was about to sink, and one eye-witness describes how he blew up his life-saving waistcoat, and watched someone else putting on a lifebelt and removing his boots preparatory to swimming for his life.

The smoke and steam cleared away. The dawn came, and except for one enemy torpedo-boat, stopped and blazing fiercely, not a German was in sight. All that remained of her was promptly shot to pieces by the *Morris* and the French destroyers, and finished off with a torpedo.

Daylight came, and, while the French picked up the few Germans that were seen in the water, the *Morris* went alongside the *Botha* and took her in tow. Progress towards Dunkerque was very slow, as the damaged ship had a heavy list through the water pouring in through the great gash in her port side. What saved her from sinking was the fact that the torpedo had exploded in a full coal-bunker, which cushioned the shock of the explosion. Immediately above the spot where the torpedo struck were the port torpedo-tubes, the torpedoes from which had been fired earlier. It was actually being trained fore and aft when the explosion came, and, hurled backwards through the air, the lip of the twin tube hit the top of the after-funnel before sliding overboard. Not a man of those who were working about it was hurt, though they had a startling experience. One astonished petty officer was left with the large training-handle in his grasp as the tubes disappeared into the sea.

" Well, sir, it's like this," he explained. " We had just fired both torpedoes, and I was training the tubes fore and aft, when 'e came along, and the next thing I knew was that I nearly had me photograph took."

One may imagine that the flash of the explosion in the dark reminded the petty officer of a photograph by flashlight.

The *Botha* was eventually taken to Dunkerque and temporarily repaired before being taken to an English dockyard, and for this action, which resulted in the sinking of the German torpedo-boats A.7 and A.19, Rede and Percival, of the *Botha* and *Morris*, received their D.S.O.s. Their first lieutenants, D. G. H. Bush and

B. R. Willett, were awarded D.S.C.s, and several of the men D.S.M.s and mentions in despatches. One is pleased to see that the artificer-engineer of the *Botha*, Mr. E. G. Wellman, was not forgotten, for he also received the D.S.C. for his " exceptional coolness and initiative "[1] when a shell damaged the auxiliary steam-pipes. Escaping steam prevented the watchkeepers from leaving the boiler-room affected, but Mr. Wellman " isolated the compartment by closing stop-valves from the upper deck, the ship being under heavy fire at the time. By this action he saved the lives of the men and assisted them to escape."[2] Stoker John Darrock, also of the *Broke*, received the Conspicuous Gallantry Medal, second only to the Victoria Cross, " for most conspicuous gallantry and devotion to duty. He entered the damaged boiler-room, from which steam was still escaping, and assisted watchkeepers to get on deck under heavy fire."[3]

The sister ships *Broke* and *Botha* were building in this country for Chile when the war started, and were taken over by the Admiralty. Both distinguished themselves, the first serving at Jutland as well as in the Dover Straits. They were reconditioned, and returned to Chile in 1919, and now appear in the Chilean Navy List as the *Almirante Riveros* and *Almirante Williams*. A third ship of the same class, the *Faulknor*, also served at Jutland, and is now in the Chilean Navy as the *Almirante Uribe*. They are flotilla-leaders of about 1,700 tons, with a nominal speed of $31\frac{1}{2}$ knots, now armed with two 4.7-inch and two 4-inch guns and 4 torpedo-tubes.

[1] *London Gazette*, 21 /6 /18.
[2] *Ibid.*
[3] *Ibid.*

CHAPTER XVI

DESTROYERS AND U-BOATS

I

NOBODY seemed to treat submarines with much respect at the beginning of the war. Indeed, in August 1914, when serving in the *Patrol*, the light-cruiser serving as Captain (D)'s ship of one of the patrol flotillas, I remember we anchored off the Tyne and piped " Hands to bathe." It was not until after September 5th, when the *Pathfinder* was torpedoed off the Firth of Forth, and September 22nd, when the *Aboukir*, *Cressy*, and *Hogue* were sunk with terrible loss of life in the " Broad Fourteens " – south of the Dogger Bank – that we came to realise that submarines were a real menace, and it was not advisable to take any liberties.

At the beginning of the war, destroyers in general had no method of fighting submarines except by ramming or gunfire. The first submarine actually sunk by the ram was U.15, which was sighted by the light-cruiser *Birmingham* at dawn on August 9th, 1914, in the northern part of the North Sea. It was a very misty morning, and the cruiser was scouting ahead of the British battle-fleet, when she saw the U-boat lying stopped on the surface at close range, evidently repairing some damage. Opening fire, the *Birmingham* swung round to ram, and succeeded in cutting the U.15 completely in two and sending her to the bottom.

The first submarine rammed by a destroyer was U.19, which was run down at night off the Dutch coast by the *Badger* – Commander C. A. Freemantle – on October 24th, 1914. The submarine was badly damaged and had to return to her base, where she was repaired. After an exciting career in the Baltic, North Sea, Channel, and Atlantic, and sinking 36,000 tons of shipping in the Irish Sea in February 1918, U.19 was one of the 176 submarines surrendered at the end of the war.

On November 23rd of the same year, U.18, while reconnoitring Scapa Flow, was located and rammed by the armed trawler *Dorothy Grey*, which damaged the U-boat's periscope and hydroplanes. After diving to the bottom, the submarine broke surface, to be rammed again by the destroyer *Garry*, Commander

W. W. Wilson. She sank for the time, but again managed to come to the surface, drifting helplessly with her crew firing signals of distress. The *Garry* came alongside and rescued all her crew but one, and U.18, scuttled by her own men, sank off Muckle Skerry.

Soon after the outbreak of war, certain destroyers were fitted with a complicated invention known as the "modified sweep." When we commissioned the new destroyer *Murray* in October 1914, we were supplied with this apparatus, and most heartily we cursed it.

It consisted of a loop of wire about 200 feet long fitted at intervals with explosive charges. The upper leg of the loop was floated near the surface by a line of wooden floats, while the lower leg was kept well down beneath the surface by means of a wooden water-kite. The arrangement, which was extremely cumbersome and difficult to handle, was supposed to be towed astern of a destroyer when hunting for a submarine which had already been sighted. So far as I recollect, however, it could be towed at no more than 8 or 10 knots without carrying things away. It took at least twenty minutes to get out, and double that time to get in, and the complicated system of wires and floats and charges were for ever becoming hopelessly tangled. When once out, moreover, it very much restricted our manœuvring power.

If any obstruction fouled the sweep, the fact was announced by a needle flicking over, when the man stationed at the firing apparatus pressed his electric key and fired the whole series of explosive charges.

Altogether, it was a much anathematised contrivance, and deservedly so, an invention which seemed beautiful in theory, but was hopeless to use in actual practice. Five enemy submarines were supposed to have been destroyed by explosive sweeps, though as far as I know only two were actually sunk by "modified sweeps."

On March 4th, 1915, soon after midday, in calm, foggy weather in the Dover Straits, U.8 was sighted by the destroyer *Viking* – Commander E. R. G. R. Evans, C.B. – five miles east-north-east of the North-east Varne Buoy. The destroyer opened fire at a range of about 1,000 yards without hitting, and the submarine disappeared.

The *Viking*, calling other destroyers to the spot by wireless, got out her modified sweep. Sighting the U-boat's periscope, she fired her sweep over the spot without success. For an hour nothing happened, and then the *Maori* – Commander B. W.

Barrow – again saw the periscope farther down-Channel. The *Ghurka* – Lieutenant-Commander R. W. Richardson – towed her modified sweep across the track which the submarine appeared to be taking. At 5 p.m. it caught in an obstruction, and the operator pressed his firing-key.

The result was dramatic in its suddenness. Hardly had the explosions subsided than the stern of a submarine appeared on the surface, followed by the conning-tower. The *Maori* and *Ghurka* at once opened fire, some of their shell driving home just as the submarine's captain appeared with his hands up in token of surrender.

The 4 German officers and 24 men were rescued, and U.8, as she turned out to be, was taken in tow by the destroyer *Ure*. The crew, however, had opened the sea-cocks, and the submarine was sinking fast. Within a quarter of an hour she went to the bottom in sixteen fathoms.

Quite early in the war all destroyers were supplied with " lance bombs " – bombs weighing between 20 and 30 lbs. – mounted on a stout ash staff and supposed to be thrown on to the hull of a submarine close alongside. Elsewhere in this book[1] I have described how on April 24th, 1916, while a barrage of nets and mines was being laid off the Belgian coast, the German submarine U.B.13 fouled the cable of the little drifter *Gleaner of the Sea* and was disabled, if not destroyed, by a lance bomb. To make quite certain, however, she was later finished off by the destroyer *Afridi*, which fired her modified sweep over the spot.

Of the 178 German submarines sunk in the war, only 5 were destroyed by high-explosive sweeps, as against the 44 sunk by mines, 38 by depth-charges, 17 by torpedoes from British submarines, 16 by gunfire, 14 by ramming, 12 by Q-ships, 6 by aircraft, and 6 by mine-nets.[2]

Any form of towed sweep was obnoxious to those who had to use it, and was not a very potent weapon. The " paravane," used in the later stages of the war, was very effective for protection against mines, for, towed from the bows, it afforded a ship almost complete immunity when passing through mined areas. The " high speed submarine sweep," however, which consisted of two explosive paravanes towed from either quarter, was a very different matter. With many other destroyers, my own ship, the

---

[1] See chapter " Running the Gauntlet."
[2] Appendix III., *The German Submarine War*, by R. H. Gibson and Maurice Prendergast. (Constable & Co., 1931.)

Murray, was fitted with this apparatus during 1915. It involved the fitting of special winches, and small revolving gallows on each side of the stern to carry the paravanes themselves, which were rather like small torpedoes with lateral fins.

They could be set to run at any depth below the surface, and were supposed to enable a destroyer to attack a submarine whose position was only approximately known. They could either be exploded by means of a hand switch, if the ship wished to get rid of them in a hurry, but exploded automatically if any obstruction fouled the wires or the paravanes themselves.

We hated the contrivance, which was difficult to use and always going wrong. Moreover, one had to ease down when getting the sweep in or out, which was always a risk with a submarine anywhere in the vicinity. Added to this, no commanding officer feels really happy with two explosive fish towing about under his stern. There was always the danger that one might forget them in an emergency, go full speed astern to avoid a collision, and find the paravane wires wrapped inextricably round the propellers and the explosive fish themselves bobbing up alongside.

So far as I can discover, only two U-boats were destroyed by this particular form of attack – U.B.18 by the destroyer *Ariel* off the Bishop's Rock Lighthouse on December 6th, 1916, and U.C.16 by the destroyer *Melampus* off Selsey Bill on October 23rd, 1917.

As time went on, all the later destroyers were fitted with steel rams at the bottom of the stem, and very efficacious they were as tin-openers.

But, apart from acoustic for locating submerged submarines, which were supplied to numbers of destroyers and patrol craft from 1917 onwards, by far the most potent weapon was the depth-charge. It was merely a steel canister containing 300 lbs. of T.N.T. or amatol, which could be set to explode at any distance under water by means of a hydrostatic device. Kept in chutes at the stern, the charges could be released from the bridge by means of an arrangement like a pump-handle. They rolled overboard into the water and detonated on reaching the depth for which they had previously been set.

Contrary to popular belief, which credits a depth-charge with being able to sink a submarine at a hundred yards or more, it was necessary to explode it within 14 feet of a submarine to ensure destruction. Up to 28 feet the explosion might be expected to disable a submarine to the extent of forcing her to the surface, where she could be rammed or sunk by gunfire ; while up to

60 feet the moral effect on the crew was considerable and *might* force the submarine to the surface. [1]

First supplied, as far as I can recollect, towards the end of 1916, the output was only sufficient to maintain four on board each destroyer, though many trawlers and patrol craft were supplied as well. In July 1917 the average weekly output of depth-charges was only 140, though it had become 500 a week in October, and 800 a week in December, and was still increasing. [2] As a consequence, it was possible to provide as many as 30 or 40 depth-charges to those destroyers engaged in anti-submarine and escort work. The expenditure mounted rapidly. During 1917 between 100 and 300 depth-charges were used a month. From May 1918 until the end of the war they were being used at the average rate of 2,000 a month. [3]

The introduction of depth-charge throwers, like mortars, which hurled the charge to a distance of about 100 yards on the beam of the attacking destroyer, was another innovation.

Officers of British submarines who were attacked by mistake by our own destroyers paid full testimony to the unnerving effect of depth-charges, even when exploding at a comparative distance. A German submarine commander, Lieutenant Hersing, of U.21, describes his sensations when depth-charged after firing two torpedoes at a convoy off the south-west coast of Ireland. He was forty metres under water, and every ten seconds charges detonated at depths of ten, twenty-five, and fifty metres in all directions. After a shattering explosion from ahead, all U.21's electric light went out, and for five hours the Germans in their steel hull could hear the explosions of the " water bombs " all round them, and the hollow roaring sound of the destroyers' propellers overhead.

The first submarine actually to be sunk by depth-charge was U.C. 7, which fell a victim to the motor-boat *Salmon* on July 6th, 1916, off Lowestoft. The first British destroyer which successfully used the same method was the *Llewellyn*, which destroyed the minelayer U.C. 19 in the Straits of Dover on December 4th, 1916.

2

It is impossible to describe all the encounters between destroyers and U-boats which took place during the war. So far as I can

[1] *The Crisis of the Naval War*, Lord Jellicoe.
[2] *Ibid.*
[3] *The German Submarine War*, Gibson and Prendergast.

ascertain, destroyers and P-boats, which latter were virtually small destroyers, sank, or were concerned in the sinking of, 33 submarines. How many more were attacked it is quite impossible to estimate. A brief description of a few typical successes must suffice for many more.

On March 6th, 1915, a patrol trawler sighted a U-boat steering west-north-west off Aberdeen, and pursued her. Having no wireless, the trawler was unable to transmit the news until next morning. Hunting flotillas were called out, and on the morning of March 8th the submarine was located off Buchan Ness, and in the evening south of Aberdeen. Sighted again the next day off Stonehaven and Montrose, the submarine, U.12, was evidently making her way south towards the Firth of Forth, right into the arms of a destroyer flotilla sent out to search for her.

After a hunt lasting four days, U.12 was eventually sighted on the surface off Fife Ness on the morning of March 10th by three destroyers of the 1st Flotilla from Rosyth – the *Acheron*, *Attack*, and *Ariel*. They approached at full speed, the *Attack* opening fire. The submarine dived instantly, the destroyer passing over her. Some little time later, however, the *Ariel* – Lieutenant-Commander J. V. Creagh – sighted the periscope about 200 yards to starboard of his ship. Putting his helm over and swinging round, he rammed U.12 amidships just as she was coming to the surface. Fire was at once opened, and the crew of the stricken U-boat tumbled up the conning-tower hatch, ten of them being rescued before she finally sank.

Destroyers were concerned with not more than half a dozen of the 47 German submarines sunk from the outbreak of war until the end of 1916. Their most prolific years were 1917 and 1918, and the tale of successes was by no means confined to the more modern craft.

On February 8th, 1917, U.C.39 was sighted by the twenty-year-old, 395-ton, 30-knot destroyer *Thrasher*, Lieutenant Ernest M. Hawkins, R.N.R., while in the very act of sinking a ship off Flamborough Head. The submarine immediately dived; but too late. Approaching the spot at full speed, the *Thrasher* let go a depth-charge, the explosion of which burst in U.C.39's conning-tower and flooded it and the control-room. With his crew in a state of panic, the German captain decided to come to the surface and surrender. The moment the conning-tower appeared, however, the *Thrasher* opened a heavy, close-range fire with her 12-pounder gun and 6 pounders. The submarine's captain was killed as he climbed out, and, had it not been for an English prisoner on board the U-boat, the master of a ship who had been captured some days before, who climbed up the conning-tower and waved a white handkerchief, it is probable that U.C.39 would have been sunk outright by gunfire. Seventeen men of the crew were rescued, while U.C.39 was taken in tow by another destroyer. Shortly afterwards, however, she sank. For this spirited action Lieutenant Hawkins received his D.S.O., while other awards were made to some of his officers and men.

In April and May 1917, enemy submarines from Zeebrugge were busily laying mines in the Channel, and, on April 30th, U.C.26 sailed from Ostend and duly laid her " eggs " off Havre, Cherbourg, and other French ports. She then steered along the route to Southampton, in the hope of finding some shipping. There was little or nothing to be seen, and, baffled in his attempt, the submarine's captain decided to return to Zeebrugge.

At dawn on May 9th (some accounts say about an hour after midnight) U.C.26 was suddenly sighted on the surface north-west of Calais by the destroyer *Milne*, Commander V. L. A. Campbell, D.S.O. The submarine attempted to dive ; but delayed a few seconds too long. Campbell, as quick as his look-outs, had instantly altered course and increased to full speed, steadying his ship for her target. U.C.26 was gradually getting lower and lower in the water as she strove to escape. The moments seemed interminable. Would the *Milne* reach her before she disappeared ?

She did, striking her just before the conning-tower, when the latter was still clear of the surface. The steel ram at the bottom of the destroyer's stem crashed through the submarine's hull like cardboard. Overwhelmed by a torrent of water spurting in through the great gash, U.C.26 sank in a rush and struck heavily on the bottom, where she was depth-charged by two other destroyers. There was, however, still a chance of escape for the 28 officers and men inside her. As the water rose within the hull, the pressure of the air increased and formed various air-locks. Seven men actually managed to open the engine-room hatch, 5 of whom seemed to have come to the surface. But only 2 were picked up alive.

The *Milne* came back into harbour with pieces of the submarine's plating still sticking to her ram, and for this smart piece of work Commander Campbell received a bar to the D.S.O. he had already earned with the Royal Naval Division in Gallipoli.

Lieutenant Pearson, the officer of the watch, who had first seen U.C.26, was awarded the D.S.C., while the coxswain, Frederick Robinson ; a leading signalman, Leonard Pearson ; and two men of the engine-room department, Ernest Pike and John Reason, were all granted the D.S.M.

Another exciting encounter took place off Bergen on August 12th, 1917. A sweep of the Norwegian coast was being carried out by three light-cruisers spread in line abreast at visibility distance apart. Each cruiser was screened against submarine attack by a couple of destroyers, and the *Oracle*, Lieutenant-Commander A. G. Tippet, happened to be on the port bow of the port wing cruiser, the *Birkenhead*. Strong enemy wireless signals having been intercepted from somewhere close on the evening of the 11th, Tippet kept his men at action stations throughout the night.

Nothing happened until after daylight next morning, when, at 6 a.m., the *Oracle's* officer of the watch, Lieutenant Claude Butlin, sighted a strange ship far away on the horizon, which was reported to the captain. Shortly afterwards the vessel was seen by others on the *Oracle's* bridge. She had a sail hoisted, and was thought to be a trawler.

A few minutes later, Butlin, still peering through his glasses, saw a bow and stern rise out of the sea on either side of the sail. He at once realised the stranger was a submarine, and the *Oracle* increased to full speed and dashed towards her. At a distance of about seven miles the sail was taken in. They saw in its place the unmistakable conning-tower of a U-boat, which disappeared at 6.7 as she dived.

Tippet, evidently not wishing to overrun his adversary, slowed down. Six minutes later the submarine suddenly broke surface three miles away on the port bow, with her conning-tower moving fast through the water in a flutter of spray. She disappeared again in a few seconds, and the *Oracle* altered course to cut her off. Two minutes afterwards, at 6.15, as though unable to remain submerged, the U-boat again appeared about half a mile ahead of the *Oracle* with her bows well out of water. The *Oracle* steered straight for her, opening fire with her foremost 4-inch gun.

At 6.17 the destroyer's sharp stem crashed into the submarine midway between the conning-tower and the stern at a speed of 27 knots. The *Oracle's* bows were badly damaged from the waterline downwards. The bows of U.44 appeared for a moment at an angle of 45°, and then vanished for ever in a depth of 137 fathoms.

For this exploit Lieutenant-Commander Tippet was awarded the D.S.O., and Lieutenant Butlin the D.S.C. Nine of the *Oracle's* men were also decorated or mentioned in despatches.

The peculiar feature of the encounter was that the submarine made desperate efforts to submerge, but constantly broke surface. It is possible she was not able to submerge, which might also account for the ruse of a sail being hoisted when she was first sighted.

It is known that the Q-ship *Bracondale* engaged a U-boat 125 miles north-west of the Donegal coast on August 5th, during which the submarine was hit at 800 yards range, but the Q-ship herself was sunk after being three times torpedoed. Was this the same submarine that was despatched by the *Oracle*? It seems more than likely. Damaged in the *Bracondale* action, she may have been forced to make her way homeward on the surface.

What is certain, however, is that the *Oracle* sank U.44, commanded by Kapitän-Leutnant Paul Wagenführ, who on July 31st had committed a detestable crime against humanity after torpedoing the British steamer *Belgian Prince* 175 miles off the north coast of Ireland.

Having made the master of the ship a prisoner, he lined up the crew of the steamer on the deck of his submarine, removed their lifebelts and belongings, and then gave orders to dive. Thrown into the sea, a few men managed to remain alive for a time by clinging to wreckage. Wagenführ, doubtless, expected they would all be drowned, leaving no trace; but, of the total crew of 43, three were eventually picked up by a British destroyer. They told the story of the crime.

So little sympathy can, or need, be felt for Paul Wagenführ, in his rusting steel tomb 137 fathoms deep off the coast of Norway. The only pity is that the master of the *Belgian Prince* perished with him.

Unhappy was the lot of those made prisoners by U-boats, dragged out of their sinking ships to perish, in some cases, through the depth-charges, rams, or guns of vessels manned by their own compatriots or allies.

3

The "P-Boats," or "Patrol Boats," of which 54 were built during the war, were not, strictly speaking, destroyers. Yet, being largely used for escort and convoy work, as well as for submarine hunting and patrol duties, their function was the same as that of many destroyers.

Having less speed and armament they were cheaper to build, while the general simplicity of their design allowed of their construction by firms who had never specialised in torpedo-craft. Their time of completion varied between nine and eighteen months. They were light-draught vessels of 573 tons, with speeds of about 22 knots, and driven by turbines and oil fuel boilers. They were provided with the usual depth-charges for anti-submarine work, one 4-inch gun, one 2-pounder anti-aircraft pom-pom, and a couple of 14-inch torpedo-tubes. A few of the later craft had two 4-inch guns.

In appearance, with their sharp bows, low mast and bridges, peculiar cut-away funnels built into the superstructure, and strange-looking sterns sloping almost to the water's edge, they looked very like large submarines on the surface. This was intentional.

Ten of the last 30 P-boats to be ordered were built up to give them the appearance of merchant-ships. Known as " P. C. Boats," these were designed to work with convoys and to act more or less as submarine decoys, a purpose for which they were particularly suited by reason of their speed and hidden armament. Being of light draught, they were also less likely to be hit by enemy torpedoes.

Here is the story of P.C.61, which, on September 26th, 1917, while escorting the oiler *San Zeferino* in the St. George's Channel, met and destroyed the German submarine minelayer U.C.33.

The little ship was commanded by Lieutenant-Commander Frank Worsley, R.N.R., well known as the captain of Sir Ernest Shackleton's *Endurance*, which was lost in the ice of the Weddell Sea in 1915 during his abortive Imperial Trans-Antarctic expedition of 1914–16. Worsley, indeed, was the navigator of the boat in which Shackleton made his 800-mile journey across a tempestuous sea to South Georgia to summon help after the remainder of the party had found their way to Elephant Island nearly six months after the loss of their ship. Another Antarctic navigator on board P.C.61 was her first lieutenant, Lieutenant J. R. Stenhouse, R.N.R., who had served in the *Aurora*, in the Ross Sea, during the same expedition.

At daylight on September 26th, P.C.61 was zigzagging across

the *San Zeferino*'s bows at 17 knots. There was a slight sea, and the weather was thick, with a visibility of no more than three-quarters of a mile. At 5.57 a.m. those on P.C.61's bridge noticed that the oiler seemed to be settling by the stern, though nobody had heard an explosion, or seen signs of any submarine. Circling round, Worsley asked the *San Zeferino* if she had been torpedoed. The reply came back that she had, also that the U-boat had been sighted.

Seeing that the oiler had her boats turned out and was in no immediate danger of sinking, Worsley reduced speed so as not to betray his presence to the enemy, and steered off to the north-west to find him. Very soon he lost sight of the oiler in the haze, and turned again towards her to keep her in sight. Crossing her bows, he steamed down her port side and under her stern. The moment P.C.61 was clear, Stenhouse, on her bridge, sighted the submarine barely 1,000 yards away on the starboard beam, heading west at about 9 knots.

Opening fire with a 12-pounder gun, one shell from which hit the submarine just before the conning-tower, Worsley increased to full speed and steered straight for his enemy, which seems to have made no attempt to dive. Just before he reached her he stopped his engines, with the idea of bringing the ship's bows deeper into the water and to make a better hit.

The two vessels met with a shuddering crash, P.C.61's steel ram striking the submarine just abaft the conning-tower at a speed of about 20 knots. The U-boat rolled over and disappeared, a violent explosion taking place as P.C.61's stern passed over the spot.

The submarine was U.C.33, a minelayer, and it seems probable that some of her mines detonated. For some time the sea boiled with foam in the spot where she had gone down, while huge air-bubbles came to the surface in rushes. Oil presently appeared, and in the midst of it two men could be seen struggling. Boats were lowered to pick them up, and one of them turned out to be Ober-Leutnant Alfred Arnold, the U-boat's captain. The remaining 24 men of her crew had gone to the bottom in 47 fathoms.

Taken in tow by P.C.61, the *San Zeferino* was eventually brought safely into harbour after twelve hours' arduous work. Worsley received the usual reward of the D.S.O., Stenhouse the D.S.C., and two of the petty officers D.S.M.s for good steering and gunlaying.

On November 18th of the same year, P.57, Lieutenant-Commander H. C. Birnie,[1] R.N.R., was patrolling off Flamborough Head. At about 6 o'clock in the morning, when it was still dark, she had just challenged a ship by searchlight and had ascertained her to be a friend, when the man on the look-out reported a buoy on the port bow. As no buoy was known to be in the neighbourhood, the patrol-boat altered course towards it. Almost immediately, Birnie and his officer of the watch, Lieutenant Isdale, R.N.R., saw that the supposed buoy was really the conning-tower of a submarine.

It was only 200 yards away, and there was no time to be lost. P.57 swung sharply round to port to ram, and her engines leapt to full speed. The crash came in fifteen seconds or less, the patrol-boat's armoured stem driving through the U-boat's hull just before the conning-tower, and nearly at right angles. A depth-charge was dropped as the submarine passed astern, but, to make quite certain, Birnie turned, came back over the submarine and let go another, marking the place with a buoy when the turmoil had subsided.

Half an hour later, after verifying his exact position, Birnie found oil coming to the surface within fifty yards of his buoy. He let go a third depth-charge and another buoy, and patrolled in the vicinity for the rest of the day and throughout the night. The wreck was located with a chain bottom sweep in thirty fathoms, and was destroyed with another explosive charge. Thus ended the career of U.C.47, Ober-Leutnant Wigankow. Lieutenant-Commander Birnie, one of his officers, and two men received the usual rewards.

There is a certain similarity between most of the attacks carried out by destroyers upon submarines – perhaps the explosion of a torpedo against some ship of a convoy, or a whitened track seen in the water ; occasionally, the sighting of a U-boat's conning-tower, or the tip of a periscope fluttering through the sea. Then the rush at full speed to the spot in the hope of ramming before the enemy could dive, followed, in the event of failure, by the release of depth-charges. Next, the muffled thuds of their detonation, the dome-shaped hummocks of whitened water rising up astern, and their bursting upwards in great fan-shaped upheavals of spray and smoke fully seventy feet high. Occasionally, very occasionally, the sight of the grey bow, or conning-tower,

[1] Now Captain H. C. Birnie, D.S.O., R.D., one of the Elder Brethren of Trinity House.

or stern of a stricken U-boat rising to the surface, to be greeted with a sudden burst of gunfire.

More often than not, however, the submarine managed to escape. Twenty-eight feet is the greatest distance at which the explosion of a depth-charge can possibly bring a submarine to the surface. For every success there must have been a hundred or more attacks.

But I feel that no apology is needed for telling the story of the *Fairy*, a 370-ton destroyer of the old " 30-knotter " type completed by Fairfields' in 1896. Had it not been for the war, this little vessel would have found herself on the scrap-heap some years before her name finally disappeared from the Navy List.

As it was, 2 o'clock in the morning of May 31st, 1918, discovered the *Fairy*, under the command of Lieutenant Geoffrey Howard Barnish, R.N.R., escorting a convoy of thirty-odd merchantmen, with an average speed of 7½ knots, in the vicinity of Flamborough Head. The escort force consisted of one armed " whaler," six armed trawlers, and the *Fairy*, the last-named being the only destroyer present, and Barnish being in charge of the convoy.

His official account of what happened, supplemented by a private letter, lies before me. " I always considered that when only one destroyer was present with the escort, her position should be to seaward and a little abaft the beam of the rear ship of the convoy," he writes. " Whatever emergency then arose, one did not have to waste time by turning round."

It was calm, with a very smooth sea, the night dark, and the sky heavily overcast, with no moon or stars to be seen. The visibility was reasonably good, and the convoy, as usual, was steaming without lights. " To be in full charge of a valuable convoy always filled me with a certain amount of anxiety," Barnish goes on to say. " And it was with a feeling of great relief when, after rounding Flamborough Head, I left our small bridge in order to have a walk on the after deck. It was generally considered that a German submarine was not likely to attack south of Flamborough Head, because of the proximity of shoals."

At 2.5 a.m., while still walking up and down to stretch his legs, he heard a heavy thud from the direction of the convoy. It sounded suspiciously like the detonation of a torpedo. Rushing forward to the bridge, he found that the officer of the watch, Mr. Arthur James Bennett, Gunner, R.N., had sounded the alarm gongs, increased speed, and was heading for the spot whence the crash had come. Full speed was immediately ordered. The men poured up on deck, and a few seconds later a submarine was sighted on the surface one point on the port bow at a distance of 300 yards. It was at this exciting moment that Barnish found himself in something of a quandary. He had every justification for engaging a submarine on sight : but there was a doubt in his mind. " In the past," as he writes, " we had all had one or two scares over our own submarines suddenly appearing on the surface after their patrol in the Bight, and wanting the bearing and distance of Middlesbrough or the Tyne. I couldn't understand a German submarine being in this position, so you can well imagine my extreme anxiety. We made challenge after challenge, while all the time we were rapidly approaching our friend or foe. Then I decided we must cripple her, so that, if she did turn out to be British, our own unfortunate fellows would have a chance to save their lives. With that object in view, I ordered the torpedo coxswain (William James Spinner) to steer for her stern, or what I thought to be her stern.

" We were very close to her by now, and I cannot express to you my relief when I heard a voice from her conning-tower calling ' Kamerad ! Kamerad ! ' I knew exactly what to do now, and quickly ordered the coxswain to port the helm in order to hit her in a more vital spot. But we were too close for the helm to have any effect, and quickly passed over the stern of our enemy. I don't remember feeling any considerable force of impact at this time, and we probably damaged ourselves more than we did him. However, on passing over him, I determined to renew the attack by ram, and, sending the gunner aft to open fire with our after gun, proceeded to turn the Fairy round."

The submarine fired her gun ; but Mr. Bennett ran aft and proceeded to enjoy himself by pumping shell after shell into her from the after 6-pounder at point-blank range. In all, forty rounds were fired, and there were many direct hits.

We know nothing of the sensations of those in the submarine as they felt the Fairy crashing over them, and saw her open fire as she circled round to renew the attack. What we do know is that the thud Barnish had first heard was caused by the U-boat colliding with a ship in the convoy. A few minutes later she was rammed in the stern by a destroyer. Two collisions were all very well ; but when the Fairy opened fire and swung round for another attack, those men of the submarine's crew who happened to be on deck took to the water. One can hardly wonder.

" It was a very simple job this time," says the Fairy's captain.

" We came on again with our ram, and I always remember wondering how far back our bows would be pushed in, and with these
feelings I backed to the wheel and kept my hand on the coxswain,
probably deriving a feeling of comfort, as well as knowing that the
coxswain would do what I wanted him to do with my hand
directing."   The destroyer's bows struck the U-boat with an
appalling crash close beside the gun.   " We on the bridge found
ourselves all mixed up on the deck.   How far we pushed our stem
in I don't really know, for the next thing I realised was that our
fore-deck was under water and the submarine had disappeared,
leaving two Germans calmly standing on our submerged forecastle with their hands held up.   We picked up three more
later."   One of these was Ober-Leutnant W. Schmitz, the
U-boat's captain.

Anybody who knew the old " 30-knotters " is aware of their
flimsiness, and the comparative ease with which their bows could
be bent or squeezed into folds like the sides of a concertina.   They
were not built for collisions, as many young destroyer officers
found to their cost, and the *Fairy* had charged full tilt at the
German minelayer U.C.75, a vessel considerably larger than
herself.[1]   In doing so, she paid the usual penalty.   It was
lucky, moreover, that there were no men in the fore part of the
ship, the hands being at their action stations.

" Signals were sent off reporting our damage.   Boats were
put over the side, and the prisoners were taken charge of and
searched.   The artificer engineer, Mr. Charles Palmer, reported
on the extensive damage to the hull, and it was decided to steam
very slowly towards the beach.   However, this was too much
strain for the bulkhead forward, and efforts were then made to
steam her stern first.   This was very soon useless, as both propellers were out of water.   Engines were then stopped, the crew
embarked into the boats, and ordered to lie off at a safe distance.

" A last message was sent to Captain (D) by wireless informing
him we were about to abandon the *Fairy*, and then, as we could
do no more and the ship had taken a very dangerous angle, I
told the two signal ratings, who had remained with me, to swim
across to one of the boats.   I then hitched my binoculars to the
bridge rail, took off my coat, stepped off the bridge, and swam to
the nearest Carley float.   I think I should mention that I wore
one of those life-saving waistcoats throughout the war, but when

[1] U.C.75 was a vessel with a surface displacement of 420 tons.   She carried 3
torpedo-tubes, 18 mines, 1 gun, and a crew of about 26.

I took to the water I never thought of blowing it up. Reaching the float, I watched the *Fairy's* screws getting higher and higher out of the water until she gracefully disappeared, leaving everything very quiet. The time was 3.5 a.m.

" It was extremely cold in that Carley float, and we were very thankful when a drifter came along at about 5 a.m. and picked us up. Soon afterwards the destroyer *Greyhound* arrived, and, transferring to her, we were all back in Immingham by about 8 a.m."

For this action Lieutenant Barnish received the D.S.O., and Mr. Palmer, his artificer engineer, the D.S.C. Five of his men were awarded the D.S.M., and nine officers and men were " mentioned in despatches."

" Lieutenant G. H. Barnish," said an official letter from the Admiralty of July 5th, " acted with great promptness, determination, and judgment, and showed great skill and judgment in the manner in which he handled his ship, although he had not the satisfaction of bringing her safely into port before she sank. The conduct of the ship's company throughout was also worthy of high praise, and testifies to the state of discipline and organisation on board."

In view of what had occurred, the *Fairy's* officers and men must have been rather amused at an announcement that was issued by the Admiralty to the newspapers on June 4th. " One of His Majesty's destroyers was sunk on the 31st May after being in collision," it said. " There were no casualties ! "

One of the most remarkable features of this little engagement was Lieutenant Barnish's deliberate decision first to ram the submarine in a non-vital spot, in case she afterwards turned out to be British. In the inevitable flurry and excitement of the moment it showed commendable presence of mind.

But I am glad the *Fairy* died gamely in sixteen fathoms of water instead of ending her days in a shipbreaker's yard, for once, years before the war, I served in command of her.

AVE ATQUE VALE

CHAPTER XVII

THE CONVOY SYSTEM

I

THE unrestricted German submarine campaign against all British, Allied, and neutral shipping approaching the British Isles recommenced on February 1st, 1917, with immediate results. In October 1916, before it began, 148,000 tons of British and 164,000 tons of foreign shipping were destroyed by enemy submarines.

The following table gives the losses in ships and tonnage from December 1916 to April 1917 inclusive, and shows the enormous increase after February 1st, 1917.

NATIONALITY	Dec. 1916		Jan. 1917		Feb. 1917		Mar. 1917		April 1917	
	Ships	Gross Tons	Ships	Gross Tons	Ships	Gross Tons	Ships	Gross Tons	Ships	Gross Tons
BRITISH	39	110,000	51	112,000	114	260,000	146	287,000	196	522,000
ALLIED	58	67,000	63	58,000	77	77,000	114	115,000	108	145,000
NEUTRAL	70	99,000	66	115,000	69	132,000	78	122,000	126	185,000
TOTALS :	167	276,000	180	285,000	260	469,000	338	524,000	430	852,000

From the outbreak of war up till the end of 1916, Britain had lost through enemy submarine action 519 merchant vessels, and the Allies 420, while 49 submarines had been destroyed in the same period. From the great increase of losses after February 1st, 1917, however, it appeared that the submarines would win the war for Germany. They were being built faster than they could be destroyed, their number increasing from 110 on February 10th to 127 on April 10th. On April 19th, the worst day of the blackest month in the history of the war, 11 British merchantmen and 8 fishing-craft were sunk by submarines. One out of every 4 merchant ships that left the British Isles during that month never returned.

The figures, as says Admiral of the Fleet Earl Jellicoe in his book *The Crisis of the Naval War*,[1] " made it clear that some method of counteracting the submarines must be found, and

[1] Messrs. Cassell & Co. Ltd., 1920.

found quickly, if the Allied cause was to be saved from disaster."
Elsewhere, he describes the submarine campaign as " the gravest
peril which ever threatened the population of this country, as
well as of the whole Empire."

Those words are literally true. Starvation, together with
cutting off of reinforcements and essential supplies from oversea,
stared us in the face, and was likely to bring the Allied cause
crashing down in ruin.

During the first thirty months of the war, transports carrying
troops were almost invariably escorted by destroyers or other
craft, while, when the submarine war increased in intensity, oil-
tankers and other vessels with important Government cargoes
were escorted within the danger-zone. Traffic up and down the
east coast of England, and to Rotterdam, also received some
degree of protection from comparatively early in the war.

But although the question of putting all mercantile traffic
approaching the British Isles into convoy had been considered at
the Admiralty at various stages of the war, the general consensus
of opinion was against it. It was condemned as impracticable
and undesirable – impracticable because there were insufficient
cruisers, destroyers, and other craft to provide escorts, and the
difficulties of station-keeping in merchant steamers of varying
types and speeds were considered insuperable ; undesirable for
the reasons that delays would be involved in unloading cargoes
through the faster ships in any convoy being restricted to the speed
of the slowest, and because the protection afforded by an escort
was considered to be more than counter-balanced by a large target
spread over several miles of sea being offered to submarine attack.

There was also the perfectly justifiable fear that there would
be a tremendous loss of confidence in the system if, through some
unhappy chance, a convoy blundered into an enemy minefield
and incurred heavy casualties.

Early in 1917, with the beginning of the unrestricted submarine
warfare and its increasing toll of losses, something clearly had to
be done, not merely to protect the ocean-going trade, but also to
increase the vigour of the Allied anti-submarine measures.

It is impossible to give the credit for the introduction of the
convoy system to any single person, though the application of
convoy to ocean traffic was persistently being urged both within
and without the Admiralty in the earlier months of 1917. There
is no doubt, however, that American opinion had much to do with
its introduction.

By February 1917, war between the United States of America
and Germany was inevitable, and on March 31st, at the suggestion
of Mr. Walter Page, the American Ambassador in London, an
admiral of the United States Navy was sent to England to co-
operate with the British Admiralty " in a full and frank naval
interchange of information " and the discussion of methods of
combating the submarine menace with the assistance of the
American Navy.   The officer chosen was Admiral William Sowden
Sims, who, in 1910, during a visit to England as commander of the
battleship *Minnesota*, caused something of a sensation at a
dinner at the Guildhall in London when he said in a speech,
" Speaking for myself, I believe that if the time ever comes when
the British Empire is menaced by an external enemy, you may
count upon every man, every drop of blood, every ship, and every
dollar of your kindred across the sea."

A semi-official protest against this utterance having been made
by the German Government, Sims was severely reprimanded by
the President of the United States.   Nevertheless, his speech
made him *persona grata* in Britain.

On March 31st, accordingly, Admiral Sims, travelling incognito
as " S. W. Richardson," and accompanied by an A.D.C. also
masquerading under another name, embarked for England in the
steamship *New York*.   Reaching Liverpool on April 9th, three
days after the American declaration of war, the ship was mined
outside the Mersey.   With the other passengers, Sims and his
A.D.C. were transferred to another vessel and taken ashore.
Here the two American officers were welcomed by Rear-Admiral
Hope of the British Navy, and went to London in a special train
provided by the Admiralty.   On arrival, they at once conferred
with the American Ambassador and the British naval authorities,
Admiral Sir John (afterwards Earl) Jellicoe being then the First
Sea Lord.

In his book, *The Victory at Sea*, published in 1920, Sims describes his first interview with the First Sea Lord.

" ' It looks as though the Germans were winning the war,' I
remarked.

" ' They will win, unless we can stop these losses – and stop
them soon,' the Admiral replied.

" ' Is there no solution for the problem ? ' I asked.

" ' Absolutely none that we can see now,' Jellicoe announced."

In a letter to Mr. Josephus Daniels, Secretary of the United
States Navy, Sims wrote on April 19th, " After trying various

methods of controlling shipping, the Admiralty now believes the best policy to be one of dispersion."[1] The British Admiralty, he went on to say, were being blamed and criticised " for not taking more effective steps." One of the chief demands was for " convoys of merchant shipping, and more definite and real protection within the war zone."

" The Admiralty," Sims went on to write, " has had frequent conferences with merchant masters and sought their advice. Their most unanimous demand is : ' Give us a gun and let us look out for ourselves.' They are also insistent that it is impracticable for merchant vessels to proceed in formation, at least in any considerable numbers, due principally to difficulty in controlling their speed and to the inexperience of their subordinate officers. With their view I do not personally agree, but believe that with a little experience merchant vessels could safely and sufficiently well steam in open formation."[2]

Admiral Sims was perfectly correct.

Although the convoy system that was presently put into force may not have been entirely due to the American suggestion, the month of May saw the establishment of a Special Committee at the Admiralty to draw up a convoy scheme for the ocean trades. In the same months experimental convoys sailed from Gibraltar and Hampton Roads across the Atlantic. Both arrived without the loss of a single ship, and the experience went far to disprove the difficulty of station-keeping.

The intense anxiety for the safety of these first convoys arose from the fact that upon their success hung the justification of the decision. (See p. 348.)

Further investigations showed that the difficulty of providing escort vessels would not be so great as had originally been imagined. The situation was further eased by the arrival of American destroyers, the first six of which reached Queenstown, Ireland, on May 4th.[3]

Regular convoys were inaugurated from Hampton Roads in June ; in the following month from Sydney (Cape Breton), New York, and Gibraltar ; while in August the system was extended to the South Atlantic trade routes and traffic outward bound.

From the very first the convoy system was a triumphant

---

[1] *Our Navy at War*, by Josephus Daniels (George H. Doran & Co., New York), 1922.
[2] *Our Navy at War*.
[3] For the number of American destroyers and other vessels which served in European waters during the war see the chapter " American Destroyers."

success, due in no small measure to the willing and cheerful co-operation of those who had hitherto condemned it, the officers of the Merchant Navy. The grouping of ships lessened the number of targets offered, while the threat of instant retaliation by the escort, and the danger presented to a submarine by a number of vessels zigzagging on a broad front in fairly close formation, undoubtedly acted as a deterrent to successful torpedo attack. The routes were also varied and carefully chosen, the convoys being deflected by wireless from areas known to be occupied by U-boats.

A total of 16,693 ships were convoyed from May, 1917, up till the end of the war. Of these, 16,539, or 99.08 per cent., were safely escorted ; 102, or 0.61 per cent. were torpedoed in convoy ; 16, or 0.09 per cent., were lost through the ordinary perils of navigation, while 36, or 0.22 per cent., were lost after parting company from their escorts.

Outside the submarine danger-zone – that is, 300 or 400 miles clear of the coast – the homeward-bound convoys were escorted by old battleships and cruisers of the British and American navies, and by the armed merchant-cruisers of the 10th Cruiser Squadron which had hitherto been employed upon blockade duty in the northern part of the North Sea. As, however, there was still a considerable shortage of suitable escorts, some of the faster cargo-vessels themselves were provided with 6-inch guns to act as convoy cruisers. The protection afforded by these various ships outside the actual area of submarine activity was designed principally to guard the convoys against attack by German raiders like the *Wolf* or *Moëwe* disguised as ordinary merchant-men.

Each convoy, it should be said, was in general charge of a commodore, who hoisted his broad pendant in one of the merchantmen, and acted under the orders of the captain of the ocean escort vessel when the latter was in company. The commodores were either naval officers of flag or captain's rank on the active or retired lists, or experienced masters of the Merchant Navy. Their work, as Lord Jellicoe says, was " arduous and responsible."

Through the submarine danger-zone the convoys were escorted by destroyers or sloops. Indeed, by September 1917, outward-bound convoys were accompanied by destroyers or sloops 300 or 400 miles out into the Atlantic, where the merchant ships were dispersed and allowed to steam on to their destinations un-attended because of the insufficiency of ocean escort vessels to accompany them. The destroyers or sloops then steamed off to another predetermined rendezvous, where they met the home-coming convoy and escorted them through the submarine danger-zone.

This meeting at a rendezvous in the broad Atlantic sounds easy enough on paper. In practice it was often extremely difficult, bad weather sometimes causing the convoys to be delayed in their passage across the Atlantic, and their wireless not being sufficiently powerful for the commodores to inform the Admiralty in time for the outward-bound convoy, with the anti-submarine escorts, to be stopped from sailing. Destroyers and sloops had, sometimes, to hang about near a rendezvous for a day or more before picking up a homecoming convoy. Any considerable delay meant that there was always a risk of running short of fuel.

The convoys themselves were usually classed as " slow " or " fast," the slow containing ships of between 8 and $12\frac{1}{2}$ knots, and the fast those of between $12\frac{1}{2}$ and 16. Ships of more than 16 knots did not as a rule sail in convoys, but trusted to their speed and to darkness for safety within the submarine danger-zone. It must be remembered, however, that the speed of a convoy is the speed of its slowest ship, and some of the vessels sailing in convoy from Gibraltar could do no more than 7 knots, which largely increased the responsibility of the escorts.

In spite of the co-operation of the Americans, who sent practi-cally every destroyer they possessed, as well as a large force of sloops, yachts, torpedo-boats, revenue cruisers, tugs, etc., to Europe ; of the Japanese,[1] who helped with the escort work in the Mediterranean ; of the French, and a few Greek destroyers, there was always an insufficiency of small craft for convoy and escort work.

Anybody who knows destroyers, and the average state of the wind and sea in the Chops of the Channel, and between 300 and 400 miles out at sea off the west coast of Ireland, and between Finisterre and Cape Clear, will realise that even in peacetime there can be little real rest for the personnel of these small ships in anything approaching really bad weather. But add to this the responsibilities of war, day in, day out, for weeks on end, with only a short interval for a refit once every four months.

Imagine the difficulty of finding a convoy late in arriving at its

[1] In February 1917 the Japanese Government had offered to send eight destroyers to the Mediterranean under a Japanese rear-admiral. In June 1917 two British destroyers, the *Minstrel* and *Nemesis*, were also lent to the Japanese and com-missioned by them. They were renamed the *Sendan* and *Kanran*.

rendezvous, with perhaps never a sight of the sun or stars for two or more days wherewith to verify one's position in the wild grey waste of heaving, windswept water. Think of the constant strain of watching for the momentary, tell-tale splash of a periscope, or the whitened track of a torpedo lengthening out across the sea at 35 knots towards a fleet of merchantmen, which might first betoken the presence of an enemy submarine. All through the daylight hours, and on moonlit nights, the convoys would zigzag at irregular intervals according to a predetermined plan – one of many – laid down in a book. The attendant destroyers steered their own serpentine courses independently ahead and on either flank.

The zigzagging was designed to make it more difficult for a submarine to attack, the alterations of course being carried out by all ships of the convoy at the same moment. Though none of the ships were fitted with engine-room revolution telegraphs and the like to help them to keep close station, though their deck officers were unused to manœuvring in close formation, and their engine-room personnel unaccustomed to frequent alterations in speed by a revolution or two, they very soon picked it up.

Zigzagging sounds complicated, but it was not really so. The signal might be made, " Carry out zigzag No. 17." When the flags came down, each vessel would start her stop-watch, altering course the number of degrees to port or to starboard at the time stated in the plan.

A page in the book would read approximately as follows :

Time : Mins.			Course
00	.	.	Steady
09	.	.	15 degrees to Starboard.
18	.	.	30 ,, ,, Port.
26	.	.	40 ,, ,, Starboard.
32	.	.	35 ,, ,, Port.
39	.	.	30 ,, ,, Starboard.
45	.	.	50 ,, ,, Port.
53	.	.	45 ,, ,, Starboard.
60	.	.	15 ,, ,, Port.

and so on.

At night, too, especially on dark and stormy nights, constant vigilance was necessary in the destroyers to enable them to keep touch with a large collection of merchantmen steaming without lights, and to make certain that the inevitable stragglers were encouraged to keep closed up. It was arduous, unceasing work, deadly monotonous, and carried on, as often as not, in the vilest of weather. There was not even the hope of a fight with an enemy which could be seen, merely the possibility of plastering with depth-charges an area from which some hidden submarine had fired a torpedo and perhaps bagged one of the ships of the convoy.

Official returns showed that some of the destroyers working in the western approaches to the English Channel averaged 60 or 70 per cent. of their time at sea. By November 1917, when the convoy system had been in force for about six months, the strain and lack of regular sleep was beginning to tell on the health of many of the officers and men. Engines and boilers, too, were beginning to give trouble, for, unlike a big ship, destroyers' machinery requires nursing and constant attention, which, in these conditions, it was impossible for them to be given.

" However," as Lord Jellicoe says, " the destroyers held on here as elsewhere, but it is only just to the splendid endurance of the young officers and the men who manned them to emphasise as strongly as I can the magnificent work they carried out in the face of every difficulty."

CHAPTER XVIII

THE AUSTRALIAN DESTROYERS

I

NO story of the work of the British destroyers in the war can be quite complete without some mention of their sisters of the Royal Australian Navy. It is seldom realised in Great Britain what these craft did, and how, after months of arduous service in the Bismarck Archipelago during the Australian occupation of New Britain, New Guinea, and a host of outlying islands, they spent some time on the Australian coast, and then were despatched to the South China Sea for patrol work in the enervating heat of the tropics. In 1917, when the submarine menace became acute in Home Waters and the Mediterranean, the Australian destroyers steamed to Malta and were eventually used for work on the Adriatic Patrol. After the collapse of Turkey they saw service in the Sea of Marmora and Black Sea. In January 1919 they came to Plymouth, and, sailing the next month for home, eventually arrived back in Australia in April.

Like the greater majority of the British destroyers, there was little in their work that was spectacular. They had no exciting affrays in the Heligoland Bight or the Dover Straits, no Battle of Jutland. Their task consisted of day after day of monotonous patrols, with a few incidental excitements thrown in to prevent officers and men from becoming too utterly stale and weary of the incessant drudgery. I cannot hazard a guess at the number of days spent at sea during the war by the Australian destroyers, or the thousands of miles that they must have steamed. Both were prodigious.

But they did their job, and a bit more than their job, when one recollects that their officers and men were serving far away from their homes, and could not enjoy the short spells of leave vouchsafed to the ships' companies of British destroyers serving in Home Waters.

NOTE.—For most of the details in this chapter I have drawn upon the *Official History of Australia in the War*, vol. ix., *The Royal Australian Navy*. I am indebted to the author, Arthur W. Jose, Esq., and to the publishers, Messrs. Angus & Robertson, of Sydney, for their permission to make use of a book without which this account of the doings of the Australian destroyers could not have been written.

2

When war broke out, Australia's navy was an infant Service. It was only in 1908 that a unit system had finally been decided upon whereby Australia should provide 1 battle-cruiser, 3 light-cruisers, 6 destroyers, and 3 submarines. The Commonwealth Government had loyally fulfilled its obligations. Actually in Australian waters in August 1914, or under construction or projected at the same time, were the following vessels :

The battle-cruiser *Australia*.

The light-cruisers *Melbourne* and *Sydney*, with the *Brisbane*[1] under construction, and the *Adelaide*[2] projected.

The destroyers *Parramatta*, *Yarra*, and *Warrego* completed, the *Huon*[3] and *Torrens*[4] building ; and the *Swan*[5] about to be laid down.

The submarines A.E.1 and A.E.2.

A destroyer depot-ship and repair-ship, and a fleet oiler, were also being built in England before the end of 1914.

In addition to these vessels the Commonwealth had the light-cruiser *Encounter*, lent by the Admiralty until the completion of the *Brisbane* ; the smaller old cruiser *Pioneer* ; two old gunboats ; and a couple of old torpedo-boats still suitable for local defence. Australia had also arranged for the entry and training of her own officers and men, had established a branch of the Royal Naval Reserve, and had provided its own supply depots and dockyards.

The seagoing Australian Squadron at the outbreak of war was under the command of Rear-Admiral Sir George E. Patey,[6] K.C.V.O., an officer of the Royal Navy, with his flag in the *Australia*.

The *Australia*, built in England, had arrived at Sydney in October 1913. In less than a year, with the other ships of the Australian Navy, she had helped to capture the German colonies in the Pacific, and had caused Admiral Von Spee's two armoured cruisers *Scharnhorst* and *Gneisenau* to proceed from the Western Pacific to the coast of South America. On November 9th, 1914,

[1] *Brisbane* Laid down 25/1/13.   Commissioned 31/10/16.
[2] *Adelaide*   ,,   ,, 20/11/17.   ,,   5/8/22.
[3] *Huon*   ,,   ,, 25/1/13.   ,,   14/12/15.
[4] *Torrens*   ,,   ,, 25/1/13.   ,,   3/7/16.
[5] *Swan*   ,,   ,, 22/1/15.   ,,   16/8/16.
[6] Vice-Admiral, September 14th, 1914 ; Admiral, January 1st, 1918 ; K.C.M.G.

the *Sydney* destroyed the *Emden* off the Keeling-Cocos in one of the few single-ship actions of the war.   By February 1915 the Australian Squadron was scattered over the oceans – the *Australia* in the North Sea ; the *Sydney* in the South Atlantic ; the *Melbourne* in the North Atlantic ; the *Encounter* in the Pacific ; the little *Pioneer* on the east coast of Africa ; the *Warrego*, *Parramatta*, and *Yarra* in New Guinea ;   and the submarine A.E.2 in the Ægean.   Her sister vessel, A.E.1, had disappeared without trace on September 14th, 1914, while on patrol duty off Rabaul, New Britain.

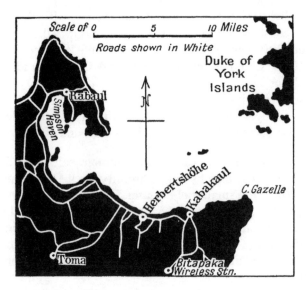

3

The three Australian destroyers in service at the beginning of the war, the *Warrego*, *Parramatta*, and *Yarra*, like the *Huon*, *Torrens*, and *Swan*, completed during hostilities, were specially designed, turbine-driven, oil-fired craft of 700 tons, armed with one 4-inch gun, three 12-pounders, and three torpedo-tubes. The little flotilla was under the command of Commander Claude L. Cumberlege,[1] an officer lent from the Royal Navy.

The main objective of the Australian Squadron was Admiral Von Spee's squadron from Tsingtau, of the whereabouts of which very little was known.   But as it was considered likely that the *Scharnhorst*, *Gneisenau*, and the German light-cruisers might be used for attacking Australian trade, Simpsonhafen, in the German

[1] Now Rear-Admiral.

colony of New Britain, seemed a probable base for such operations.

It was determined to attack it, so at 10 a.m. on August 9th part of the Australian Squadron met at a rendezvous off the south-east coast of New Guinea. It consisted of the *Australia*, flying the flag of Vice-Admiral Sir George E. Patey, the light-cruiser *Sydney*, and the three destroyers.

The orders were simple. As indications pointed to the probability of the German ships being at Simpsonhafen or in Matupi Harbour, within a mile or two of it, it was the admiral's intention to " make an attack on these ports with the object of torpedoing any ships which are there and destroying the wireless station. . . ."

On arriving in the neighbourhood after dark, the *Sydney* was to take charge of the destroyers, and to go on at 20 knots. If the enemy ships were met under way outside, the destroyers were to attack at once. If they were not sighted, the *Sydney* was to remain off the harbour in support, and the destroyers were to steam inside, search the bay, and attack any men-of-war found there. If no men-of-war were discovered, the destroyers were to land a party to demolish the wireless station reported to be at Rabaul.

In the light of our present knowledge this operation may seem to have been easy and without risk. At the time, however, the presence of the German ships in Simpsonhafen was regarded as all but certain. So it was with the nerves of every officer and man on board keyed up to concert pitch, and their torpedoes and guns ready for instant use, that, at 9 p.m. on August 11th, the *Warrego*, *Parramatta*, and *Yarra* parted company with the *Sydney* and shipped off on their mission with all lights extinguished. We need not describe their search. Luck was against them. They found – nothing.

Meanwhile, the German wireless station somewhere in the neighbourhood had been heard sending off signals, and at about 7 a.m. next morning the destroyers appeared off Rabaul to carry out the second part of the programme. But it was easier said than done. No news of any wireless station could be discovered from the inhabitants, while a search of the coast from the sea disclosed nothing resembling wireless masts.

At 9 a.m., Cumberlege landed with an armed party at Rabaul and interviewed the local German district officer. The information derived from this official, who was a loyal son of the Fatherland, was purely of the negative kind.

The wireless station, meanwhile, was despatching further

messages reporting the presence and movements of the Australian ships, to which Admiral Patey retaliated by threatening to open fire on the settlement unless they were stopped at once. The district officer, while protesting against any bombardment of the settlement as contrary to the usages of war, disclaimed all responsibility, and stated the wireless station was neither in or near Rabaul, nor under his jurisdiction.

Searches were made in other likely spots and people were questioned; but still no information was forthcoming. The admiral was therefore forced to the conclusion that the offending station was some distance inland in the bush. To find it and silence it might take several days. The German squadron,

meanwhile, was still unlocated, and the Australian ships were running short of fuel. On August 12th the *Warrego* landed an armed party at Rabaul which demolished the post-office and destroyed all the telephonic and telegraphic communications that could be found. The next day the squadron withdrew to refuel, the flagship going to Port Moresby and the *Sydney* and destroyers to Rossel Island.

From August 17th until early in September the admiral, with the *Australia* and *Melbourne*, was engaged in convoying the New Zealand Expeditionary Force to Samoa for the capture of that German Colony. New Britain and Rabaul were left for a time to their own devices, the destroyers being sent to Port Moresby – British New Guinea – to keep watch over a transport.

On September 9th, however, Samoa having been occupied, a force assembled off Rossel Island for an expedition to Rabaul. It consisted of the *Australia, Encounter,* and *Sydney,* the three destroyers, and two submarines. With them were an oiler, three colliers, and a P. & O. steamer serving as an auxiliary cruiser and transport carrying troops and a landing-party of 500 men of the Royal Australian Naval Reserve. The combined naval and military landing-force was under the command of Colonel William Holmes.

It had been decided that the two most important coast towns in New Britain, Rabaul and Herbertshöhe, should be occupied and garrisoned, the first by the military contingent, and Herbertshöhe by the Naval Brigade. From the latter place naval detachments would be sent inland to search for wireless stations. Comparatively little opposition was expected.

Early in the morning of September 11th, the *Sydney* and destroyers searched the various anchorages in the neighbourhood of the landing-places and found them clear, and at 6 a.m. a party of 25 petty officers and men were transferred from the *Sydney* to the *Warrego* and *Yarra.* Reinforced by 2 warrant officers and 10 men from the destroyers, this little detachment, under the command of Lieutenant Bowen, R.A.N., landed at a jetty at Kabakaul Bay, about fifteen miles east of Simpsonhafen. It had been directed to push inland to search for the wireless station.

It is unnecessary here to describe the little expedition which resulted in the discovery of the wireless station five miles inland the same evening. The landing-parties, however, had to push their way through the bush while avoiding a road which had been mined and entrenched. There was considerable opposition from parties of armed natives led by Germans, and the original force of 40 men or so had to be considerably reinforced. Indeed, at one time Commander Cumberlege had to send ashore all the available men from the *Warrego* and *Yarra,* 59 in all, 14 armed with all the rifles that remained on board, and the rest with cutlasses and revolvers.

The wireless station was duly seized, the instruments removed, and the naval parties returned to the coast with the loss of 2 officers and 4 men killed, and an officer and 3 men wounded. It was the first time that officers and men of the Royal Australian Navy were under fire. The raid was attended by a good deal of luck ; but if it did nothing else it showed pluck and level-headedness on the part of all concerned which were happy auguries for the future.

On September 13th the *Warrego* found the little German Government yacht *Nusa* at Kawieng, in New Ireland, and escorted her back to Rabaul. Further operations ashore in New Britain, however, had been handed over by the admiral to Colonel Holmes with his combined force of soldiers and naval reservemen. The occupation of the German portion of New Guinea was accomplished without opposition on September 24th, while the outlying German islands passed into Australian hands, and wireless stations were destroyed. Thus all the German possessions in the Pacific that were administered from Rabaul – which

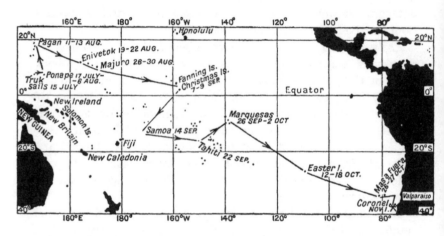

SKETCH MAP SHOWING TRACK OF " SCHARNHORST " AND " GNEISENAU."
JULY 15th – NOVEMBER 1st, 1914.

included a portion of New Guinea, together with New Britain, New Ireland, and Bougainville Island – now flew the British flag.

This first important operation of the Royal Australian Navy was marred by only one unhappy accident, which was the loss of submarine A.E.1 on September 14th. This vessel, with one of the destroyers, had been sent out on patrol from Rabaul. When evening came she did not return, and, in spite of a prolonged search, no traces of her could be found. Her loss, with Lieutenant-Commander H. F. Besant, R.N., 2 other officers, and 32 men – about half of them Australians – remains to this day one of the mysteries of the war. Neither a morsel of wreckage nor a trace of oil ever came to the surface.

Admiral Von Spee's squadron was still unlocated, and the situation in the Pacific altogether uncertain.

On September 7th, one of the German light-cruisers, the Nürnberg, had raided the British cable station at Fanning Island, in mid-Pacific, and had sailed again after cutting the cable, destroying the instruments, and taking £720 2s. 6d. from the office safe.

Four days earlier, however, Von Spee had heard of the capture of Samoa by the New Zealand Expeditionary Force. He knew he could not retake it; but at dawn on September 14th the *Scharnhorst* and *Gneisenau* appeared off the island in the hope of surprising transports and men-of-war at anchor in Apia harbour. They found nothing except an American sailing-ship, and the two cruisers sailed again without opening fire. No doubt Von Spee wished to husband his valuable ammunition, which could not be replaced; but he was also actuated by humanitarian principles. As he himself wrote, " I refrained from ordering a bombardment of the houses by which there were a few groups of people – conjectured to be soldiers – or of the three tents, because natives with women were everywhere standing among them."

The *Emden*, meanwhile, had started her predatory career in the Indian Ocean, and on September 15th, after the capitulation of German New Guinea, Admiral Patey sailed for the south with the *Australia* and *Sydney*, it being the intention that the battle-cruiser, and the two Australian light-cruisers, should escort the Australian and New Zealand Expeditionary Forces across the Indian Ocean from Albany, in Western Australia. Subsequently diverted to Egypt, and thence to the Dardanelles, where they earned undying fame, these troops were at one time destined to be landed to deal with the insurrection in South Africa. Von Spee's appearance off Samoa, however, indicated that he might be contemplating a break back to the westward to attack Australian trade. On the 17th the *Australia* was therefore recalled to Rabaul to cover the Australian occupation of New Guinea with the French cruiser *Montcalm*, after which both ships were to go in search of the *Scharnhorst* and *Gneisenau*.

Friedrich-Wilhelm Harbour, in German New Guinea, was occupied on September 24th without resistance, and on October 1st, the *Sydney* having destroyed the wireless station at Angaur on September 26th, Admiral Patey, with the *Australia*, *Montcalm*, *Encounter*, and *Sydney*, with two of his three destroyers, was at sea ready to intercept Von Spee if he should double back and try to enter the Indian Ocean.

On October 2nd the admiral heard that the French island of Papeete (Tahiti) had been bombarded by the *Scharnhorst* and *Gneisenau* on September 22nd. There was still a chance that Von Spee might carry out similar attacks at Samoa or in New Zealand, and on October 3rd Admiral Patey sailed from Rabaul for Suva, Fiji, with the *Australia, Montcalm*, and *Sydney*. They were followed next day by the *Encounter, Warrego, Parramatta*, submarine A.E.2, and four supply ships. The third destroyer, the *Yarra*, having damaged her propellers, returned to Sydney for repairs.

The *Australia* arrived at Suva on October 12th, but within a day the *Sydney* was detached to the south for convoy duty, leaving Admiral Patey with his flagship, the *Encounter*, two destroyers, A.E.2, and the French *Montcalm*.

For nearly four weeks this force remained based on Fiji, while the *Australia* " made darts into neighbouring waters and was pulled back before any results could be obtained. She visited Samoa on October 20th ; later in the month she did three-legged cruises in the waters between Fiji and New Caledonia."[1]

On November 1st the *Sydney* and *Melbourne*, with the *Minotaur* and the Japanese cruiser *Ibuki*, sailed from Albany, Western Australia, to convoy the 38 transports carrying Australian and New Zealand troops for service oversea. Eight days later the *Emden* was destroyed off Keeling-Cocos Island by the *Sydney*.

On November 8th, three days after the disaster at Coronel, the *Australia* finally left Fiji for the eastern Pacific, not again to be seen in her own home waters until the end of the war. Finally, passing through the Straits of Magellan, she arrived at Plymouth on January 28th, 1915, and subsequently joined the Grand Fleet. In little more than eighteen months she had steamed 59,514 miles, the greater portion of this distance being covered after the outbreak of war.

The destroyers returned to the westward to scour the Bismarck group and the New Guinea coast for any small German craft that might still be in hiding among the scattered islands, or in the various creeks and rivers. Commander Cumberlege made a systematic search, and in December proceeded some distance up

[1] p. 124 of *Official History of Australia in the War of 1914-18*, vol. ix., *The Royal Australian Navy*, by A. W. Jose.

the little-known Sepik River, where, with small parties of Australian troops, he hoisted the British flag and established defensible posts at various settlements, rounded up a party of German native police with their white officers, and generally introduced the natives to British rule.

During January 1915 they visited various little ports along the New Guinea coast and in the outlying islands, and on February 5th, after two more months of work at high pressure, left Rabaul for Sydney. This, as says the *Official History of Australia in the War*,[1] " probably more than any other single factor, established British dominance in the huge area of scattered island groups so recently taken from Germany. It was no light task to occupy with scanty forces, and administer with inexperienced officials from southern climates, the valued possessions of a great Power which was a bitter enemy. That such intrigues as were attempted by German colonists during the subsequent period of occupation produced so little effect on the natives whom they had previously ruled was the effect, no doubt, of several causes – but high among them, it can safely be claimed, was the excellent work of Cumberlege's destroyer flotilla in the summer of 1914-15."

We can agree. For seven months the Australian destroyers had never been idle. They had had little in the way of real excitement to keep them up to the mark – merely mile upon mile of rather monotonous cruising over long distances, and equally dreary patrol work far out of the limelight of publicity and in a vile climate. Destroyers, as those of us who have served in them are aware, are among the most uncomfortable of craft for work in the sweltering heat of the tropics a few degrees south of the Equator ; but the *Warrego*, *Parramatta*, and *Yarra*, like their sisters in British waters, more than justified their existence.

They were at Sydney from February 1915 until the end of April, when they left that port for an extended cruise up the eastern Australian seaboard. September, however, saw them back at Sydney for docking and refitting, and by the middle of October they were on their way to a new scene of activity.

4

It had long been known that one of the German war schemes was to stir up trouble in India. So early as in 1911 Von Bernhardi, the well-known German soldier and writer, had suggested

[1] p. 145, vol. ix., *The Royal Australian Navy*, by A. W. Jose.

that the union of the disaffected Bengali population with the up-country Mohammedans might shake the British Empire to its foundations.

A revolution in India was always a grave danger while the British Empire was engaged in a world-wide war, and in 1914–15 a revolutionary Indian organisation of German origin known as " Ghadr " actually had its leader in Berlin, attached to the German General Staff.   It was the aim to create trouble in Persia

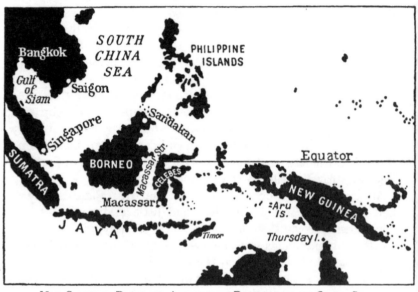

MAP SHOWING BASES OF AUSTRALIAN DESTROYERS IN CHINA SEA.

and on the North-West Frontier ; to smuggle seditious literature and arms across the frontier between Burma and Siam ; and to import large quantities of arms and munitions from America by sea into Bengal.   The second of these schemes was directed from Bangkok, and the third from Batavia, though both were generally in charge of the German Consul-General at Shanghai and were ultimately controlled by the German Embassy at Washington, unknown, of course, to the Government of the United States.

Various ships had been chartered for gun-running across the Pacific ; and, in spite of the strict neutrality of the Dutch officials, the Dutch East Indies, where there existed small but influential and energetic German colonies, were hotbeds of enemy intrigue.

As a counter-measure, a regular system of patrols was established in the Bay of Bengal by men-of-war detached from the Mediterranean, the Cape of Good Hope, and China, assisted by the small cruiser *Psyche* and the sloop *Fantome* from Australia. On August 6th, 1915, indeed, the Admiralty had officially informed the Australian Naval Board that " an extensive German conspiracy is on foot to cause a rising in Burma and India, involving smuggling in very large numbers of rifles." On October 14th another message was received from the commander-in-chief of the China Station to say it was rumoured that " a German base for munitions exists either off Java, Timor Island, or in the vicinity of Celebes Island."

The Naval Board was requested to arrange for a watch between the southern end of the Macassar Straits and the Aru Islands off Dutch New Guinea, and thither, on October 19th, the three destroyers sailed from Sydney. Six days later, at Thursday Island, in the Torres Straits, they were joined by the captured German armed yacht *Una*, and, sailing again on the 28th, proceeded to Dilli, in the Portuguese portion of Timor. Little information could be discovered there ; but the islands in the vicinity were searched for possible arms depots. Nothing was discovered, so Commander Cumberlege took his flotilla on to Macassar. The ships then separated, the *Una* and *Yarra* proceeding up the western side of the Macassar Straits, and the *Warrego* and *Parramatta* up its eastern shore. They rejoined at Sandakan, in British North Borneo, on about November 20th, and were at once taken over by the commander-in-chief of the China Station for patrol work between Borneo and the Philippines. The work was dull and monotonous ; but if it did nothing else it taught possible enemy agents and others interested in gun-running that the Navy's watch was world-wide.

At the end of December the destroyers were ordered to Singapore to assist in a scheme of patrols which embraced practically the whole expanse of sea between Siam and Java. January 1916, indeed, found the *Warrego* and *Parramatta* cruising off Bangkok, during which they were based on the French port of Saigon. Their task was strenuous enough. In eleven days they boarded and examined 48 ships of various nationalities. " The steamers seemed to come out in batches of half a dozen," wrote Captain Cumberlege, who had been promoted to that rank on June 30th, 1915. " What with others inward-bound, and yet others plying between the rivers and the island, it means chasing at full speed, sometimes for long distances, to get through them all."

They had little luck, only one German subject being discovered and sent to Saigon for internment ; but a great many more remained shut up in Bangkok because they feared capture.

Another similar patrol was carried out in February, after which it was reported that the movement of enemy subjects by sea in the Gulf of Siam had completely stopped, which was, of course, the result desired. The work, carried out in small ships in the heat of the tropics, told hardly on the crews of the destroyers. But occasional landings on good bathing-beaches in French territory, with the advantage of good fishing and a consequent change in diet, brought them through without heavy sick-lists. Towards the end of January, Captain Cumberlege was appointed to the cruiser *Encounter*, and Lieutenant-Commander W. H. F. Warren, R. A. N., of the *Parramatta*, succeeded him in command of the destroyers.

During March the *Parramatta* and *Yarra* patrolled the Java Sea between Banka Island and Batavia ; but at the end of this month they were transferred again to Sandakan, with orders to patrol the waters round about the Philippines. It was difficult work. The United States were then neutral. It was easy for small vessels to slip into territorial waters ; easier still for the destroyers to be tempted to follow them and to be charged with a violation of neutrality.

The searching of ships was also a delicate matter. Enemy subjects might disguise themselves as natives, the destroyer officers were told, and it was therefore necessary to check the ship's articles very carefully, and to examine any officer or man who had joined recently. Suspicious cases might be tested by suddenly rolling up the suspect's sleeves, to make certain he was the same colour all over. Moreover, it was tolerably certain that the Germans were everywhere attempting to arm ships for use as commerce destroyers. There were many German merchantmen sheltering in neutral ports, which could leave at any time. They might embark substantial gun armaments at secret bases. " It is not probable that they would court an action," the destroyers' orders ran, " although if sufficiently armed they might even do so with destroyers. It is more likely they would steam away, and on being overhauled would hoist a neutral flag to allay suspicion, and draw the destroyer into such a position that they could successfully deal with her when she was lowering her boarding-boat."

And so the weary work went on in the heat of the tropics,

intermingled with gunnery practices at sea between patrols, and spells in harbour, with route marches and exercise ashore to keep officers and men healthy and fit.

The three new Australian destroyers, however, the *Huon*, *Swan*, and *Torrens*, were completing. The first-named reached Sandakan towards the end of July, and the two others in September, allowing the *Warrego* to return to Sydney for refit. The *Parramatta* and *Yarra* went to Albany, Western Australia, where they might be required to deal with possible enemy raiders or minelayers escaping from German waters and coming across the Indian Ocean to prey upon the Australian coastal trade. This actually occurred when the heavily armed *Wolf*, disguised as an ordinary merchant-ship, succeeded in escaping from the North Sea in December 1916, and, between March and August 1917, was working in Australasian and East Indian waters. During this period she sank or captured five merchant-ships and laid four minefields.

The *Swan*, *Torrens*, and *Huon* continued to be based upon Sandakan and to cruise in the Celebes-Philippines area. In accordance with a new arrangement, it had been intended to relieve them with the *Warrego*, *Yarra*, and *Parramatta* in or about February 1917. But the expected relief never came. The unrestricted German submarine war intervened, and on May 9th the British Government asked if the three destroyers mentioned could be spared for service nearer home. Three days later the Australian Government " gladly agreed " to the proposal, and even hinted at the despatch also of the *Swan*, *Huon*, and *Torrens*, then at Singapore. This offer was gratefully accepted.

The six little ships were refitted at Sydney and Singapore, and on July 7th met at the Cocos Islands in the Indian Ocean. " A notable event in the H.M.A.T.B.D. Flotilla," wrote one of the *Parramatta's* men. " For the first time in its existence the six destroyers came together," under the command of Commander Warren, R.A.N.

We need not describe the voyage westward, but, proceeding by way of Diego Garcia, the Seychelles, and Aden, the flotilla passed up the Red Sea and through the Suez Canal. By August 9th they were at Port Said, and three days later came orders from the Admiralty to proceed to Malta. Thither they escorted a convoy of merchantmen, and at noon on the 16th, when within 100 miles of Malta, the *Parramatta* sighted the wash of an enemy periscope. She chased it at full speed, saw the wake of " some large object moving under the surface of the water," ran ahead, and dropped a depth-charge. There came the usual heavy explosion, followed by bubbles and a trickle of oil. At about the same time the *Torrens* sighted another periscope, and opened fire on it with her 4-inch gun. Neither of these attacks was successful ; but, as says the *Official History of Australia in the War*,[1] " the effect of this small action on the flotilla was great. After the weary years of tropical patrol, so important in reality but so meaningless to the crews engaged in it, here was active service indeed, actual fighting, a hard hit at a definite enemy. From that time forth, it is believed, no man in the flotilla hankered after land service."

After refitting, carrying out gunnery and torpedo exercises, and some convoy work, the early part of October found the six Australians based on Brindisi, to back up the patrols of drifters with the anti-submarine nets stretched across the forty-mile gap of the Straits of Otranto between the heel of Italy and Albania.

From the Adriatic ports of Pola, Trieste, and Cattaro came most of the submarines engaged in sinking merchantmen in the Mediterranean. The destroyers frequently sighted the tracks of submarines and attacked with depth-charges, though, according to the records, they never enjoyed the satisfaction of a definite " kill."

But other adventures sometimes came their way. At 11.10 a.m. on November 16th, for instance, when four of them were on patrol, the *Parramatta* – Commander W. H. F. Warren, R.A.N. – intercepted an S.O.S. signal from the Italian transport *Orione*, which, with 400 troops on board, had been torpedoed by a submarine. Racing to the spot at full speed, Warren arrived at 12.10 p.m. to find the transport still afloat ; but that the explosion had blown away her rudder, counter, and upper portion of the stern. Something very like a panic had occurred among the troops when the torpedo hit, and numbers of them had taken to the water.

The *Warrego* was already alongside taking off the remainder of the troops and crew, while the *Huon* was picking up survivors, most of them being in the last stages of exhaustion in the bitterly cold water. The *Warrego* was soon forced to cast off because of the heavy swell, and, while she and the *Yarra* circled round to prevent another attack, Warren rescued some more men from

[1] p. 313, vol. ix., *The Royal Australian Navy*.

the water, and picked up the transport's boats containing the master of the ship, the crew, and some soldiers.

He then sent Lieutenant C. J. P. Hill, R.N., with Engineer-Lieutenant C. W. Bridge, R.A.N., and a signalman on board the *Orione* to examine her condition and report. She could neither steam nor steer ; but, as she was making no water, Warren, as he wrote in his report, " prevailed upon the master to return to his ship and take his crew." A few men went with him, when, at 1 p.m., the track of a torpedo was seen approaching the *Parramatta*. It luckily passed underneath the destroyer and missed the transport. Destroyers were sent off to keep the submarine submerged, while the *Parramatta* proceeded to take the *Orione* in tow, with the *Yarra* secured to another hawser astern of the transport for steering purposes.

At 2.30 p.m. some French destroyers appeared on the scene and were asked to circle round to prevent further attacks. The *Warrego* at much the same time was sent into Brindisi with the rescued men. The towing of the damaged ship, however, was no easy task. A portion of her rudder remained, and was jammed hard over to port. The *Orione* yawed badly from side to side, and twice during the afternoon the *Parramatta's* hawser parted. At 5 p.m., too, the *Yarra's* after-hawser carried away. Half an hour later an Italian tug which had been asked for by wireless took the *Orione* in tow. Warren, after transferring his rescued men to the *Huon*, sent her into Brindisi and resumed his patrol with the *Yarra*. As the *Orione* was being towed at 6 knots and everything appeared satisfactory, he decided to leave his two officers and signalman on board her with orders to rejoin next morning when the *Huon* came out from Brindisi.

Hill and Bridge, on board the damaged transport, had anything but an enviable time. At 9.30 p.m. the wind started to freshen and the sea increased. The French and Italian torpedo-craft escorting the *Orione* lost her in the darkness, and at about 11 p.m. the towing hawser broke and the Italian tug also disappeared. By midnight it was blowing a gale, and the transport, quite help-less, was rapidly drifting in towards the Italian coast. To save the ship from driving ashore, Hill was forced to let go both anchors in the middle of a minefield.

She rode safely during the night ; but when the dawn came a mine was discovered close to the cables and within six feet of the ship's bows. There was no rifle on board with which to sink it, no boat in which to escape before it touched something and

exploded. Sighting a shore lighthouse, however, Hill hoisted a
distress signal, and the Italian tug again came out. She carried
a small gun, and the master of the *Orione* suggested that he and
his crew and the three Australians should be transferred to the
tug, after which the mine should be sunk by gunfire. He promised
that he and the six men with him would return with Hill and his
party to the transport to bring her into harbour after the mine
had been sunk. But the tugmaster thought otherwise. When
once the people from the *Orione* were on board, he headed for the
shore at full speed. Nothing that Hill could do would induce him

SKETCH MAP OF STRAITS OF OTRANTO, 1918

1. Allied submarines
2. Advanced day patrol of destroyers
3. Advanced night patrol of destroyers
4. Trawlers and destroyers
5. Trawlers and drifters
6. Fixed barrage and patrol
7. American submarine chasers

to fire upon and sink the mine. And so, for two or three days,
the *Orione* remained at anchor in the minefield without a soul on
board until the Italians finally towed her into Taranto for repairs.

The regular patrol of the Straits of Otranto continued, though
early in 1918 it was reconstituted and greatly strengthened. A
fixed barrage of submerged nets and mines over thirty miles long
was laid across the narrows, an allied submarine diving patrol
was established off Cattaro and Durazzo, while the numbers of
destroyers, trawlers, drifters, and motor-launches watching the
area were greatly increased. The force eventually comprised 35

destroyers, 4 torpedo-boats, 8 submarines, 6 sloops, 52 trawlers, 74 drifters, 31 motor-launches, and 36 American " submarine chasers " based on Corfu. The Straits of Otranto, indeed, had become a second Straits of Dover, except that the former was about double the width, with depths of between 300 and 50c fathoms as against a maximum of thirty off Dover.

So far as can be discovered, only two German and two Austrian submarines were actually destroyed in or about the Straits of Otranto during 1918. The main object of a broad belt of patrol vessels, however, was to force submarines to dive soon after leaving Cattaro, and to remain submerged until they were well clear of the Straits, a distance approaching 200 miles. Owing to the great depth, submarines could not remain on the bottom as they could in the North Sea. Moreover, if they stopped their engines, they must either rise to the surface or sink below a safe depth, according to their buoyancy at the time. They must remain under way, and at their lowest speed of about 3 knots could not stay under water for more than thirty hours. It was, therefore, hoped that the U-boats would exhaust their batteries before covering the extensive patrol area, and so be forced to come to the surface to recharge them.

But though the Otranto barrage undoubtedly lessened the enemy submarine activity in the Mediterranean, it did not achieve the results expected of it, and never became impassable like the Straits of Dover. This was partly because the great depth made it possible for submarines to dive under the nets, partly because resolute officers were able to proceed on the surface at night and dodge the patrols. In the Mediterranean, as elsewhere, it was really the convoy system which saved the situation.

With the reconstitution of the patrol the six Australian destroyers became absorbed into the 5th Destroyer Flotilla and co-operated with the British. Their patrol and convoy work was sometimes varied by the usual excitement of war. On April 10th, 1918, for instance, the *Torrens*, with the British destroyer *Redpole*, was sent off to the rescue of the Italian destroyer *Benedetto Cairoli*, which had been rammed by a consort. It was blowing the best part of a gale, with a very heavy sea ; but, as it was a matter of urgency, both ships had to increase to 23 knots.

" On board the *Torrens*," wrote an officer, " it seemed as if we were moving in a sort of travelling Niagara, and every moment I expected the bridge to be carried away. . . . Twenty-three knots was ordered, and I held my breath to see what would happen. I did not wait long, for the next moment the bridge was smashed in and the quartermaster and myself were flung flat. . . . We eased her down, repaired the damage as best we could, and went on again. Five minutes later she shipped a beauty, which swept away the foremost gun-shelter, broke the anchors adrift . . . twisted a lot of shot racks . . . flung the shells overboard . . . and sent the youngest and smallest rating on board to his death. He was swept over the side in a torrent of foam which nothing could resist, and . . . was never seen again."

On April 13th, Commander Warren was unfortunately drowned in Brindisi harbour, and Commander A. G. H. Bond, R.N., of the *Swan*, took over the control of the Australian Flotilla. He was only in command so far as " personnel, pay, medical treatment, and general responsibility for the good organisation and conduct of the vessels " were concerned, and, though he took charge of the patrols when he happened to be senior officer, he rarely had any Australian ship other than his own under his direct command or found more than one Australian in harbour at the same time as himself. Here, as elsewhere, the Australian Navy had become absorbed into the British. In many ways it was an advantage ; but Bond alone was responsible for his Australian personnel, who served under different conditions to the British and drew different rates of pay. He could not rely on obtaining from the depot-ship the spare ratings for filling vacancies, with the consequence that the Australian destroyers were often undermanned.

On April 22nd, when five Austrian destroyers attacked the *Jackal* and *Hornet* on patrol, inflicting casualties and severely damaging both, the *Torrens* was one of the destroyers which chased them back to Cattaro. On May 14th, the British destroyer *Phœnix* was torpedoed by a submarine. The *Warrego* took her in tow and tried to get her into Valona ; but, though all the crew were saved, the *Phœnix* sank. On August 8th the *Yarra* and *Huon* were in collision. Both ships had to be docked for repairs, and while at Genoa five of the *Huon's* men died of Spanish influenza. On October 2nd the *Swan* and *Warrego* were present at the bombardment of Durazzo by an Allied force. . . . And so, with hydrophones, and kite balloons, and guns, and depth-charges, and numbers of men on the sick-list, through the unhealthiness of Brindisi as a base, the weary work went on.

But a change was coming. Turkey was on the verge of collapse. The Germans, in April 1918, had penetrated to the Crimean peninsula, and there was a danger that some of the Russian battle-ships at Sebastopol might fall into their hands. The Allied Squad-ron in the Ægean was therefore strengthened by four French battleships, two British dreadnoughts, and various destroyers, among which were the *Torrens* and *Yarra*, which left Italian waters for Mudros on October 17th.

Bond was left behind at Brindisi for a few days with the *Swan* and *Warrego*, but on the 25th was ordered to Port Said to assist in escorting troops to Salonika. The *Warrego* was left at Salonika, the *Swan* rejoining the 5th Flotilla in the Sea of Marmora after the Armistice.

The *Yarra*, *Torrens*, and *Parramatta* patrolled for a time off Suvla Bay and Imbros, but on November 12th accompanied the Allied Fleet, led by the British battleship *Superb*, through the Dardanelles into the Sea of Marmora, and to Constantinople. While the destroyers in line ahead were steaming through the narrows, the commander of the *Parramatta* requested permission to fly an Australian blue ensign presented by the people of Parra-matta before the war, as a tribute to the men of Australia killed on the Gallipoli Peninsula. The reply was, " The Commonwealth blue ensign may be flown at the port-yard in honour of Australia's glorious dead." So the *Yarra*, *Torrens*, and *Parramatta* hoisted their Commonwealth ensigns, and kept them flying until they arrived at Constantinople early next morning.

We cannot describe all the comings and goings of the various Australian destroyers in the Black Sea in November and Decem-ber, 1918 – Batoum, Sebastopol, and Novorossiisk, together with Kertch and Marioupol in the Sea of Azov. On Boxing Day, how-ever, the *Swan*, *Yarra*, *Parramatta*, and *Huon* left Ismid, in the Sea of Marmora, for Malta, where they were joined by the *Torrens*. The *Warrego* met them at Gibraltar, and, leaving that port on January 3rd, 1919, the flotilla, once more complete, sailed for Plymouth.

They had very bad weather on the way and became separated, the *Torrens* and *Warrego* being forced to put into the Tagus, and the *Huon* and *Parramatta* into Ferrol. In February they sailed again from Plymouth, and on March 17th, accompanied by the light-cruiser *Melbourne*, the flotilla left Malta for home.

Port Said – Aden – Colombo – Malacca – Singapore – and Port Darwin, in the Northern Territory of Australia, on April 26th.

And so, as unostentatiously as they had shipped away on the

outbreak of war, these Australian destroyers came home. " Primarily Australian, and persistently Australian," as says the *Official History of Australia in the War* when referring to the Royal Australian Navy as a whole, " they had taken their full share of Imperial tasks, and everywhere had upheld the honour of the country which gave them being and owned them."

We can agree. The British Navy was proud to be associated with the Australian, and though the *Warrego, Yarra, Parramatta, Swan, Huon,* and *Torrens* have gone the way of all good ships, and their names no longer figure in the list of the Royal Australian Navy, their services in the war are never likely to be forgotten.

CHAPTER XIX

THE DOG " BOOSTER "

HERE is a story of another kind – the tale of the dog "Booster," a large Norwegian elk-hound which, with 16 Swedish officers and men of the sailing-vessel *Esmeralda*, we found in an open boat during a howling gale of wind in the middle of the North Sea.

In October 1917, with a few drifters and some other destroyers, we, the *Telemachus*, were engaged in watching a long line of anti-submarine explosive mine-nets stretched for about twenty or thirty miles across the North Sea about midway between Scotland and Denmark.[1] The weather was disgusting, blowing a full gale from the north-north-west, with the great seas rolling down upon us. And such seas they were – huge grey monsters, each tipped with frothy white, which literally blotted out the horizon when we sank into the hollows between them.

From 15 knots we were compelled to ease to 12, and finally to 8, to avoid damage. Even so, we were constantly swept from end to end, while the bows bumped badly as they fell into each watery abyss. The motion at times would have been horrifying to one unused to it – a heavy roll up to forty degrees either way, combined with a violent pitching and lurching, sliding and thudding, which nearly flung us off our feet. It certainly caused all but our most seasoned sailors to retire to their stuffy, water-logged mess decks, there to lie, comatose, white-faced, and utterly dejected, in the throes of acute internal discomfort. One of our signalmen, whose name was a byword on board, appeared as usual on the bridge with the bucket that rarely left him. Poor wight, on this particular occasion he was long past caring for anything else.

Going aft along the upper deck, which was constantly swept by the seas, was an undertaking of no little danger. We were battened down fore and aft, though even the chart house under the bridge – my invariable home at sea when I was not on the bridge – was wet and horrible, its floor littered with the remains of a broken tea-cup, some sodden woollen garments, the relics of

[1] These operations resulted in the loss of the German submarines U.50 and U.66.

my afternoon meal hurled off the chart-table, together with several saturated charts, a bottle of ink with the cork out, and many bound volumes of Sailing Directions, all sliding from side to side in several inches of filthy water as the ship rolled. Even the bridge, swept though it was by heavy spray which left us breathless and gasping, was preferable to the chart house. Moreover, hot food was not to be had. The seas had long since put out the galley fire, while poor " Cookie " was beyond caring whether it was Christmas or Easter. Our diet had been the same as usual – corned beef sandwiches and cocoa out of vacuum bottles tasting strongly of cork.

The night came down very dark, with a young moon, all but obscured by the wisps of wind-flung cloud streaming across the sky. When full darkness came, the fury of the gale seemed to have increased. It boomed and screeched and howled, until we had to shout to make ourselves heard.

We continued on our weary patrol, up and down, to and fro, rolling and pitching, longing only for the time when we could return to harbour.

It was soon after 9 o'clock, when we had nearly reached the southern end of our beat, that we sighted a flickering glare reflected on the undersides of the low clouds far away to the southward. Sometimes it shone redly like a blazing bonfire, sometimes ebbed away to an orange glow. It was a ship on fire ; it could be nothing else. And who but an enemy submarine could have set a ship on fire a full 200 miles away from the nearest land ? Even now the wretched crew must be in open boats, battling for their lives against the fury of the storm.

Turning to the southward, we steered towards the blaze. Wind and sea were now astern, and, increasing speed, we were soon driving along at 20 knots, with a sensation rather like surf-riding as the seas lifted us and held us poised before dropping us dizzily into the next hollow.

We had not gone very far before we sighted another blaze on the horizon, perhaps eight miles from the first. Fritz had certainly been busy.

We approached the first ship, reduced speed, and circled round to investigate. She was a large, barque-rigged sailing-vessel with a deck cargo of timber – pit-props, if I remember rightly. With her fore- and main-topsails set, she still sailed on before the wind yawing wildly as she travelled. Her hull was ablaze from end to end, so that her masts seemed to be standing erect out of a sea of fire. The flames danced about her, roaring and crackling loud above the booming of the wind and the crash of breaking seas. Sometimes they streamed madly to leeward, for all the world like the blazing tail of a comet.

Trails of fire mounted higher and higher, until masts, yards, sails, and rigging were outlined in brilliant scarlet. Then the mainmast swayed drunkenly, tottered, and tumbled with a crash and a shower of sparks. The foremast and mizzen-mast came down a few minutes later, to leave the blazing hull vomiting forth smoke and flame like a small volcano.

Her boats were gone ; but, steaming round, we swept our searchlights to and fro looking for boats which might contain survivors. Had they been anywhere within a mile we must have seen them, for sea and sky alike were dyed a flaming orange.

Within 200 yards of the burning ship the heat was so great as to be uncomfortable. In any case it was inadvisable to tarry long in her vicinity, for German submarines had the knack of remaining by their victim on the chance of slipping a torpedo into the would-be rescuers.

Satisfied, then, that there were no men left on board, and no survivors in boats in the immediate vicinity, we were about to return to our patrol to the north when, far away in the opposite direction, we suddenly saw a feeble flicker of light. It shone out for a moment and then disappeared. But in that instant some-one, standing by the compass, had managed to take its bearing. We increased speed – steered in its direction.

The light never showed again, but at last, fifteen miles to leeward, and after steering in a series of short zigzags to cover more ground, we came across a large open boat crowded with men. There was only one way to rescue its occupants, and that was by putting the *Telemachus* bows on to the sea and to windward of the boat, and then allowing the ship to drift slowly down on top of her. The moment we touched, seamen waiting ready with ropes would fling them down and whip out the shipwrecked men. It was a risk, for with wind and sea on the bow the ship would roll and plunge madly, so that the boat might be capsized and every soul in her flung into the water and drowned alongside. But it was that or nothing. The risk had to be taken.

The helm went over, and the port engine went astern to circle the ship on her heel. Broadside on to the sea she rolled more than I knew she could roll without capsizing. On the bridge we could not stand without holding on, while the lee edge of the deck went under water as she heeled over and three enormous seas broke waist-deep over the weather side and cascaded to leeward in torrents.

Still turning, I managed to get the ship with wind and sea on her bow, holding her there with the propellers. We drifted slowly to leeward, and presently the boat was close alongside, at one moment carried aloft high above our upper deck on the crest of a breaking wave, and the next sinking almost out of sight under our bottom as she fell into the trough and the ship rolled away from her.

I do not know to this day how our men managed to save the sixteen men on board her – sixteen men and one large dog. I expected every moment that she would be capsized, or else carried inboard as she was lifted on a sea and the edge of our deck went under water. But it was done somehow. They even salved the boat's compass, which I possess to this day, and two bottles of very potent spirit called " Aquavit " belonging to the Swedish captain. The waterlogged boat, a heavy craft fitted with a motor, was allowed to drift astern. We could not salve her.

Having long since given themselves up for lost, the Swedes were grateful enough at being rescued, – embarrassingly grateful. Perished and blue with cold, exhausted, wet through to the skin, they were taken below, officers and men providing them with dry clothing, giving them what food and hot drink could be provided.

Theirs was the usual story. Their ship, the barque *Esmeralda*, was on her way to the Tyne with a cargo of pit-props. At noon a German submarine had appeared on the surface a couple of miles away and opened fire. The Swedish skipper hoisted out and provisioned his boat, abandoned ship, and pulled away. Some little time later the submarine ceased firing and came close alongside the boat, her crew pointing rifles and revolvers. The captain and mate were ordered on board, where the German commanding officer demanded to see the ship's papers and asked many questions, evidently thinking that the *Esmeralda* might be a British Q-ship disguised as a neutral.

Finally, after four men had been ferried across to the *Esmeralda*, where they commandeered all the food they could find, the sailing-ship was set on fire and the Swedish captain and mate were allowed to get back into their boat.

" You can think yourselves lucky I spared your lives," the German officer said in English.

" Spared our lives ! " the Swede retorted. " There's a gale coming up. We shall never see land."

" Then get your own damned Navy to help you ! " the U-boat officer retorted. " This is war ! My ship is not an hotel ! "

The submarine made off on the surface, presently to disappear.

The weather grew rapidly worse. Realising the seriousness of his position, the Swedish captain rigged a sea-anchor and put canvas round the gunwale of his boat to increase her freeboard. With sixteen men and the dog on board she was already very low in the water. And before long, when the seas started to break, they were baling for their lives.

They gradually drifted to leeward away from their burning ship, and when darkness came down there was nothing in sight except that blazing beacon adrift upon the waters. The wind increased and the sea rose. By about 6 p.m., in spite of their efforts, the boat was full to the thwarts. Then the rope to the sea-anchor chafed through, due to the violent plunging, and they started to drift helplessly to leeward.

" We started to say our prayers then," the captain told me.

Finally, after what seemed an eternity, they saw our search-light playing round their burning ship miles away to the north-ward. They had no flares, no fireworks in the boat. How should they attract our attention ?

Cutting off a bit of rope, they teased it out into spun-yarn, soaked it in oil, and lashed it to a boathook stave. Between them they had only one box of matches, already sodden with sea-water. Time and time again they struck a match while in the troughs between the waves, but as often the damp oakum either refused to ignite, or the little flame was extinguished the moment the boat lifted on a crest and the driving spray and wind beat down upon them.

Finally, after exhausting nearly every match in the box, the flare was induced to burn for a moment and was held aloft. Fifteen miles away to the north we saw its flickering light.

Those sixteen men and their dog were saved by a box of Swedish matches !

The men were landed in due course at Leith, full of Navy rum, ship's biscuit, corned beef, and gratitude. But since his master, the *Esmeralda's* skipper, could not take him with him, " Booster," the dog, remained with us as a living memento of a not unexciting episode. He soon settled down to life in a destroyer in wartime.

He was an enormous creature, weighing, at a guess, well over

100 pounds. He had a heavy, lupine head, a pair of the gentlest eyes I ever saw, a curling, bushy tail, and a thick coat, dark grey on the outside and cream-coloured beneath. He was altogether a very engaging person, though, in the earlier days of his naval career, he rather developed a passion for desertion. Indeed, on one occasion he absented himself from the ship for fully a week, during which we spent no small portion of our time and considerable money in sending reply-paid telegrams to the police and inserting advertisements in the local newspapers. Finally we received a belated reply. It came from a sergeant of Scottish police, and was not altogether satisfactory. " Re dog Booster," he wrote, " I beg to state that, in accordance with your telegrams and letters, Dog Booster was discovered wandering at large in this town at 7.30 a.m. on the 17th inst. He was conducted to the police station and secured with rope. After partaking of a hearty breakfast he *slipput* his collar and escaped. This circumstance is much regretted, but the police are on his track. Yours faithfully, — P.S. – The collar may be obtained on application at this police station."

With the help of a friend, who knew someone who knew the Assistant Provost-Marshal, the truant was finally run to earth by the military police, whereupon we received a telegram : " Dog now in custody. Please send escort as soon as convenient." So the escort, consisting of one midshipman and a stout sailor with a chain and a coil of rope, was duly sent off and the deserter brought back to the fold in triumph. We were pleased to see him, though he himself, unaware of the trouble and anxiety he had caused us, had not even the manners to look ashamed of himself. Grinning all over his face, he yawned, wagged his bushy tail, and then sat himself down on deck to scratch behind one ear.

In the wardroom, " Booster " usually occupied the best arm-chair, and would rouse himself and scramble up the steep ladder leading to the upper deck at the time when he knew that the butcher was due to cut up and serve out the meat to the different messes. He was an honorary member of every mess in the ship, and had meals in most of them. His was a gargantuan appetite. But he never went short, not even during the drastic food rationing at the end of the war. He was wise, too, and when the liberty men sometimes went ashore in the afternoons, " Booster " accompanied them. Going into the nearest town involved a forty-minute journey in a tram, and " Booster," though he occupied a seat, was never asked for his fare. Neither was he charged for his seat at the local cinema patronised by our seamen.

He was a faithful, intelligent creature, with a heart of pure gold, though he fought like a devil when really roused. Coming into harbour and alongside the jetty, he would take his stand on the forecastle in the eyes of the ship, sniffing the air and barking defiance at any dog he saw. His pet aversion was a bulldog from one of the minesweeping trawlers, and one morning, after some impertinence or other, the pair of them had it out on the jetty abreast the ship. The fur literally flew. Men came with buckets of water and threw them over the combatants. Somebody else appeared with a pepper-pot. But nothing would stop them. It was a long and bloody battle – a drawn battle, for, while the bulldog retired with a torn face and many scars, '' Booster '' left the field with a damaged hind leg from which he never properly recovered. For ever afterwards there was a distinct coolness between our two ships' companies.

For eighteen months or more he served in the Navy, taking part in many minelaying operations in enemy waters in the Heligoland Bight and off the Belgian coast. Even in the stormiest winds that blew I never knew him to refuse his food. And after the Armistice, when the *Telemachus* went to the Baltic with her flotilla, he was in action against German troops in the Dvina River, in what is now Latvia.

Then the ship paid off at Devonport, and '' Booster,'' the veteran of many gales and various adventures, retired ashore to a farm on Dartmoor, where, for all I know, he may be still. But it is unlikely. He was two years old at the time we rescued him, so that would make him sixteen now, and one year in a dog's life, they say, is equivalent to seven years of a man's.

But '' Booster '' is not forgotten. His photograph is on my mantelpiece. Though of alien birth, he was our true friend and a great-hearted gentleman – a prince among dogs to those of us who loved him.

CHAPTER XX

THE SCANDINAVIAN CONVOY

I

THE story of the Scandinavian convoys across that stormy stretch of sea between Lerwick, in the Shetland Islands, and various points on the Norwegian coast, a distance of about 180 miles, dates back to the autumn of 1916, when a system of " protected sailings " was inaugurated to guard Norwegian and Swedish shipping against submarine attacks. These attacks against Scandinavian vessels were gradually increasing, and in October 1916, when they still sailed unescorted, their losses were more than three times as large as the previous highest monthly casualties. As there was a danger that the Scandinavian Governments might refuse to take the risks and prohibit sailings, some degree of protection had to be afforded. Special alternative routes were therefore laid down, which were patrolled by destroyers and auxiliary vessels from the Orkneys and Shetlands.

By April 1917 the heavy losses still being inflicted showed that some further measure of protection was needed. The only solution of the difficulty was to run all merchantmen using the route in regular convoys.

Lerwick acted as a junction for the whole system, from which convoys for Scandinavia sailed in the late afternoon under the escort of two or three destroyers from the Grand Fleet, accompanied for a certain distance by armed trawlers. Reaching the Norwegian coast some time the next day, the convoy then dispersed, while the destroyers picked up a westbound convoy at dusk and accompanied it homeward. At dawn the next morning they were met by armed patrol vessels, which accompanied them to Lerwick for additional protection during daylight. From Lerwick, further convoys were escorted down the east coasts of Scotland and England.

The Scandinavian convoy system was always a matter of some difficulty. There was frequent congestion at Lerwick and in Norwegian ports, while bad weather and the slow speed of some of the merchantmen considerably lengthened the time on passage and increased the risks. Moreover, there were very few destroyers available for the work, while the greatest difficulty was always found in keeping a hybrid collection of neutral merchant steamers in tolerably compact formation during the night. With vessels pounding along at their best speeds, which varied, dawn frequently found the convoys scattered over many miles of sea.

The destroyer and trawler escorts were mainly designed as a protection against submarine attack. Attacks by enemy surface ships, which, at 20 knots, could cover most of the distance from German waters in the fifteen hours' darkness of a winter's night, had always been regarded as a possibility. A partial deterrent against such attacks, however, lay in the frequent presence to the southward of the convoy route of light-cruiser squadrons from the Grand Fleet.

2

At about 6 p.m. on the evening of October 16th, 1917, a convoy of twelve merchantmen – two British, one Belgian, one Danish, five Norwegian, and three Swedish – left Lerwick as usual under the anti-submarine escort of the destroyers *Mary Rose*, Lieutenant-Commander Charles L. Fox, and *Strongbow*, Lieutenant-Commander Edward Brooke. With them went two armed trawlers, the *Elsie* and *P. Fannon*. Well to the southward of the convoy route, though not actually in touch, were four or five light-cruiser squadrons, a total of not less than sixteen vessels.

The convoy became rather scattered during the night, and in the grey half-light of the misty dawn the destroyers were apparently engaged in hurrying on the laggards. There was a south-westerly wind, a heavy swell, and a visibility of not more than 4,000 yards, when at 6 a.m., just at daylight, the *Strongbow* sighted two cruisers to the southward. Uncertain of their nationality, she challenged twice without being answered. At her third challenge the strangers bluffed a reply.

Realising they were hostile, Brooke increased to 24 knots, with the intention of trying to save the convoy, but at 6.15 the Germans opened fire. Their first salvo hit and burst in the destroyer's engine-room, while almost immediately afterwards another cluster of 5.9-inch shell struck her forecastle, started a fire, put the foremost gun out of action, and killed most of its crew. The *Strongbow*, lying stopped, was then heavily shelled at a range of little more than 2,000 yards, the coxswain and a telegraphist being killed, the commanding officer severely wounded, and the bridge, steering-gear, and wireless demolished. The two cruisers, leaving her sinking, then sheered off towards the convoy.

The *Mary Rose*, meanwhile, heard the sound of gunfire and sighted gun-flashes ahead. Going on to full speed, Fox, her commanding officer, made towards the scene of action to investigate, presently to sight two cruisers which were obviously German.

No reply being received to his challenge, he steamed at full speed towards them with the intention of attacking with torpedoes, his three little 4-inch guns being no match for the 5.9's carried by the enemy.

Steaming at something like 30 knots, the distance dwindled rapidly to 3,000 yards – practically point-blank range for naval guns.

The cruisers burst into flame, and the salvos started to splash down into the calm sea all round the *Mary Rose*. The destroyer replied. For a moment or two the gallant little ship steamed on, only to be brought to a standstill at a range of little more than a mile by a salvo of shell which hit and burst amidships.

Crippled, little more than a blazing, battered wreck, she still fought on, the great spray fountains leaping out of the water all round her. But it was practically impossible for the German guns to miss altogether. Firing at a motionless ship was like shooting at bottles at a fair. Shell after shell drove home with the clang of riven metal, to burst in gouts of bright red flame and puffs of acrid smoke. Splinters shrieked and whined through the air. Their sound, and the screech of hurtling projectiles, all but drowned the noise of the heavy gunfire.

Wreathed in flame and smoke and steam, smothered in shell-splashes, the *Mary Rose* still fought – fought against overwhelming odds until all her guns except one were out of action, and everyone on the upper deck except Fox himself, two other officers, and a few men were either killed or wounded.

We know what happened from the ten survivors. Leaving the bridge with the intention of going to his cabin to throw overboard the confidential books which must not fall into the hands of the enemy, Fox noticed that the after gun was not firing.

" God bless my heart, lads ! " he shouted, seeing a few unwounded men. " We're not done yet ! "

They managed to get the after gun going again, even fired a

torpedo at the enemy, after which Fox went below to dispose of the confidential books. From all accounts he seems never to have reappeared.

The first lieutenant told the gunner to sink the ship with explosive charges. But before the intention could be carried into effect the *Mary Rose* was hit by another full salvo.

Shattered, she sank to the bottom with her White Ensign still flying. Of her ship's company of 98, all but 10 perished. No men could have done more. They had fought to the very last, had upheld the finest traditions of the Royal Navy.

The enemy then proceeded to attack the convoy, sinking all except two vessels, the British and Belgian, which succeeded in escaping undamaged. Having done their worst, the two cruisers then returned to the crippled *Strongbow*, whose men had placed their wounded captain on to a raft. Shelled at close range, most of the men on deck being killed, she gallantly returned the fire with guns and torpedoes, but was overwhelmed by the deluge of 5.9-inch shell poured in upon her. Leaving her afloat, but sinking and ablaze from end to end, the enemy made off to the southward at 8.20. In rather more than two hours they had sunk 2 destroyers and 10 merchantmen, and had killed 135 British officers and men and about 40 neutrals.

The *Strongbow* foundered at 9.30, her survivors being most gallantly rescued by the armed trawler *Elsie*, which had also done good work in picking up survivors from the sunken ships of the convoy while under fire. All the survivors spoke in terms of the highest praise of the bravery of the Royal Naval Volunteer Reserve surgeon-probationer of the *Strongbow*, L. M. Thomson, a young medical student, who, with one leg shattered above the knee, continued to attend to the wounded. His heroism saved many lives. Both the trawlers subsequently reached Lerwick.

It has sometimes been said that the captains of the *Mary Rose* and *Strongbow* should have used their speed to keep out of effective range while employing their wireless to tell the British light-cruiser squadrons to the southward what was happening, for, had they done so, there was a good chance of the raiders being brought to action.

I believe it to be a fact, however, that the *Strongbow*'s wireless was demolished at the very first salvo. Whether or not the *Mary Rose* tried to make a signal, and whether her wireless was disabled before she could do so, I do not know.

But suppose they had made off at full speed? Here was a case where two British destroyers were guarding a neutral convoy against submarines. The convoy was attacked by two cruisers, more than a match for the two destroyers. Should the latter fight on the off-chance of damaging their large opponents, or should they run, leave the convoy to their fate, and trust to their wireless signals enabling British cruisers to the southward to intercept the raiders on the way home?

What would the neutrals have thought of the British Navy and its prestige if the *Mary Rose* and *Strongbow* had left them?

It is easy to be wise after the event, to say that people should have done this, that, and the other on the spur of the moment when faced by a hideous uncertainty. The convoy was theirs to protect if they could. They gallantly took their chance, and failed through no fault of their own. Wireless signals apart, I consider that the captains of the *Mary Rose* and *Strongbow* did what every British naval officer should hope to do in similar circumstances.

They upheld the honour of the British flag and the honour of the Service to which they belonged. And they did not sacrifice themselves, their men, and their ships in vain.

At this distance of time I cannot remember whether it was on this particular occasion that, in the *Telemachus*, with one other destroyer in company, we happened to be at sea from the Firth of Forth with a squadron of light-cruisers. For the earlier part of the trip we had vile weather – a fierce gale from the eastward with a very heavy sea. At noon on the day after our departure we were somewhere in the neighbourhood of the North Dogger Bank Lightship, well over towards the Danish coast. The weather had moderated, though there was still an evil swell.

The cruisers, which had been spread in line abreast, started to concentrate on their flagship, and at much the same time our number went up at the flagship's yardarm. We closed in to read his semaphore.

"Take your other destroyer," she said. "Remain in the vicinity of North Dogger Bank Lightship, but out of sight of it. Keep a good look-out for enemy minelayers, and report if sighted. Cruisers will be spread fifteen miles apart on a line between North Dogger and Hantsholm.[1] Four other destroyers have been ordered to join you."

I asked for further news of the enemy – what sort of minelayers; how many?

---

[1] A point on the Danish coast about eighty-five miles south-west of the Skaw the northern point of Denmark.

" Have given you all the information I possess," came the answer from the rear-admiral.

Soon afterwards, when the lightship had been sighted, the cruisers disappeared over the horizon and left us to our own devices. The weather was none too bad, and at about 5 o'clock in the afternoon we received the wireless signal " Return to base," which we did at a fair 23 knots, with the wind and sea astern.

It was not until some time afterwards that we discovered that the enemy minelayers were the *Brummer* and *Bremse*,[1] German light-cruisers fitted to carry mines, armed with 5.9-inch guns, and capable of a speed of 36 knots. Our speed, " all out," was perhaps 34 and a bit.

But the *Brummer* and *Bremse*, the fastest light-cruisers the enemy possessed, were the very two ships which sank the *Mary Rose* and *Strongbow* some 350 miles north of where we had been told to keep a look-out for them.

3

On yet another occasion the Scandinavian convoy was raided, when, on December 12th, 1917, four large enemy destroyers attacked an eastbound convoy in a position about twenty-five miles west of the Norwegian coast.

It consisted of six vessels, one British and five neutrals, and was escorted by the destroyers *Partridge*, Lieutenant-Commander Reginald H. Ransome, *Pellew*, Lieutenant-Commander J. R. C. Cavendish, and four armed trawlers.

The destroyers were ahead of the convoy, when, at 11.45 in the morning, the four enemy destroyers suddenly appeared from the north-west. The *Partridge* and *Pellew* tried to save the merchant-ships by drawing the enemy away ; but one German was detached to deal with the convoy, while the other three engaged the escort.

The *Partridge*, with a shell in her main steam-pipe, was very soon disabled, but returned the enemy's fire and discharged a torpedo, which actually hit one of the Germans but failed to explode. Fighting to the last, she was set on fire, blown up, and sunk with her colours flying, 3 officers and 21 men being rescued by the enemy and landed at Kiel.

---

[1] Curiously enough, I saw the *Bremse*, which was one of the vessels scuttled at Scapa Flow on June 21st, 1919, and afterwards salved, being demolished bottom-up alongside Messrs. Cox and Danks's jetty at Lyness, Orkney, in June 1931.

The *Pellew* hit one of the enemy rather heavily, but was herself struck in the engine-room by a shell which killed all the engine-room complement. By a happy chance, the turbines continued to run for twenty miles with nobody attending them. The Germans broke off the action, and did not attempt to pursue. Badly holed and partially disabled, and helped by the misty weather and rain squalls, the *Pellew* reached Norwegian waters with a loss of 4 killed and 2 wounded.

The four trawlers and the whole of the convoy were sunk, 115 of their crews managing to reach the Norwegian coast in their boats after great suffering. Eighty-eight men were rescued by British destroyers which arrived on the scene after the Germans had disappeared.

At the time of the attack the cruisers *Shannon* and *Minotaur* with four destroyers were at sea, acting as a covering force for the two convoys in transit. They were about thirty miles to the westward when the attack took place, and, receiving a wireless signal from the *Partridge* before she sank, steamed at full speed for the spot, arriving in time to rescue survivors ; but not to save the convoy.

Another British light-cruiser squadron was at sea eighty-five miles to the south-eastward when the raid occurred ; but neither this force nor the *Shannon's* was able to intercept the enemy before he steamed home at full speed, apparently by way of the Skager Rack. The enemy's escape was hardly to be wondered at. His destroyers had an ample start, and could steam a full 30 knots in the calm weather prevailing, added to which the weather was misty, and in those high northern latitudes there are very few hours of daylight in winter.

The escape was due to no fault on the part of the covering forces. It was the general arrangements that were inadequate, for on both the occasions that the Scandinavian convoy was raided the escorting destroyers were overwhelmed before reinforcements could arrive on the scene of action.

4

The subsequent adventures of the damaged *Pellew* are not without interest.

Arriving in Norwegian waters, she entered Brandersund Inlet, inside Gisö Island and about one mile from Slottero, where she managed to shut off steam and anchor. There she was spoken by the Norwegian torpedo-boat *Hvas*, which was on patrol, and was informed that she was in an exposed anchorage and advised to go farther up the fiord.

The *Pellew* explained her difficulty about steam, whereupon the friendly Norwegian offered to tow her to a safer anchorage. The offer was accepted ; but while the towing-wire was being passed from ship to ship the *Hvas* got it foul of her propeller and became temporarily disabled. The *Pellew* then contrived to get steam on her engines, and in her turn towed the *Hvas* into shelter, where the latter cleared her screw. The *Pellew* then went on and anchored in Bekkevig Sound, about seven miles farther up the fiord.

During the night of December 12th the covering force, after rescuing the survivors of the convoy, proceeded to the southward, and at 2 a.m. the next morning the destroyer *Sabrina*, Lieutenant-Commander Vernon S. Butler, was detached to find the *Pellew*, to tow her home if possible, but, if not, to remove the crew, etc., and leave the ship to be interned.

Slottero was then distant about eighty miles, and, steaming thither at full speed, the *Sabrina* arrived soon after 7 a.m. and was lucky to find the *Pellew* almost at once, with the Norwegian torpedo-boat *Brand* lying alongside her. The *Sabrina* went alongside the *Pellew* at 7.50 a.m., and what occurred is set forth in the words of one of the *Sabrina's* officers.

" Repair work on the *Pellew* was commenced at 8 a.m. Wireless offices of both ships had to be locked and keys given to C.O. *Brand*, as no W/T was permitted in Norwegian waters to a belligerent. About 11 a.m., Lieutenant Evensen, the commanding officer of *Brand*, informed us that he had received a signal from the Norwegian Admiral in *Heimdal* that ' in view of *Pellew* being helped into harbour by *Hvas*, it was possible that the decision of Christiania might be that the ship must leave by 3 p.m. that day.' This message was presumably sent under the impression that *Hvas* had assisted *Pellew* into territorial waters, in which case, unless she left within twenty-four hours, it might have been interpreted by a hostile power as an unfriendly act, damage or no damage. A protest was at once made to Lieutenant Evensen stating that *Pellew*, as a damaged ship was justified in remaining over twenty-four hours to repair that damage in accordance with Hague Convention, paragraph 14.

" Lieutenant Evensen then very kindly escorted the C.O.s of *Pellew* and *Sabrina* ashore, and took them to a farmhouse, where the latter were able to get into touch with the British Vice-Consul

at Bergen and explain the situation. This, however, had to
be done by Lieutenant Evensen on their behalf, as it was stated
that, at the time, no English was permitted over the Norwegian
telephone system. However, he appears to have done it very
faithfully and accurately. About 1 p.m. the following message
was communicated by Lieutenant Evensen :

" ' From :   *Norwegian Foreign Office via Department of War,*
West Coast of Norway.

" ' The towed-in T.B.D. *Pellew* is at any rate to be detained
until later on. The question of her final internment is to be
decided when all details are present. The *Sabrina* must leave
territory within twenty-four hours after arrival in same.'

" Lieutenant Evensen, during the course of lunch in the *Pellew*,
stated that there were two destroyers hanging about just outside
territorial waters at the entrance to the fiord, but would not
say what was their nationality. Were they enemy destroyers
waiting for us to emerge ? Repairs to the *Pellew* were being
pushed on continuously, but in view of there being only two hours
left before *Pellew's* twenty-four hours was up, and the doubtful
question of ultimate internment, an immediate decision as to
what was to be done with her crew, stores, guns, etc., became
imperative. If *Pellew* was to be interned, it would have been
necessary to take her crew on board *Sabrina* before the twenty-
four hours was up, namely 3 p.m. This would have been legal,
and also, up to this time, guns, stores, etc., could have been
transferred, although the transfer of torpedoes and ammunition
would probably have been objected to on the grounds that
Sabrina was increasing her military force in neutral waters.

" In view of the Norwegian message at 1 p.m., the question of
whether men and material could have been transferred after the
twenty-four hours had elapsed, and in the event of a decision to
intern the *Pellew*, was a doubtful one. It was decided to maintain that the damaged ship clause covered the issue and therefore
no transfer of men, or material was made, and this decision
proved, in the end, to have been the correct one.

" It was desired to get in touch with the British Vice-Consul
again, but Lieutenant Evensen stated that the telephone ashore
had become temporarily out of order. He, however, offered to
try to obtain a T.B. to take the C.O. of *Pellew* to Bergen to see
the British Vice-Consul. This did not materialise, as, at about

3.20 p.m., Captain Robinson, a convoy pilot, arrived in Wilson Liner *Princess Dagmar* from Bergen, sent down by British Vice-Consul. He produced written orders to tow *Pellew* to sea within twenty-four hours of her arrival. This was impracticable, as *Pellew* was not yet seaworthy.

" Repairs to *Pellew* to make her seaworthy and able to be towed were completed by 5.30 p.m. *Princess Dagmar* was sent back to Bergen at 5.30 p.m. with a report in writing from C.O. *Pellew* concerning the circumstances of his arrival in territorial waters, and was instructed to ask the British Vice-Consul to communicate with the British Ambassador at Christiania, stating that *Pellew* was ready for sea, and to ask him to obtain permission from the Norwegian Government for her to proceed under Hague Convention, 1907, paragraph 14, and Norwegian Royal Proclamation of 1912 referring to stay of damaged ships.

" All repairs to *Pellew* were completed by 9.30 p.m. Ship had steam and was ready to sail by that time. Two additional Norwegian T.B.s arrived during the course of the evening and secured alongside *Brand*. Lieutenant Evensen dined in *Sabrina*, and a discussion took place after dinner between the C.O.s on the feasibility of proceeding to sea during the night and without waiting further for the decision of the Norwegian Government. The C.O. of *Brand* was asked what action he would take in the event of our doing this. Would he try to restrain us by force of arms ?

" He deprecated the idea, saying that the Norwegian Government was friendly towards the British and he thought that this would be flouting them and would lead to protests and complications. He did not consider his forces strong enough to attempt to restrain us by force of arms, and would not do so. All preparations were made for silently slipping cables and the Norwegian T.B.s. However, about 12.30 a.m., 14th, C.O. *Brand* sent over the following message he had received from Bergen : ' English Consulate reports through *Heimdal* that decision will be taken during the night and probably given us early to-morrow morning 14th.' In view of this and what was felt to be the impregnability of our position, it was decided to remain where we were and await this.

" *Sabrina* would have to sail at 6.30 a.m. in any case, to be clear of territorial waters by 7 a.m., and it was arranged that she should wait outside territorial waters for *Pellew*, who, if the decision was unfavourable, should again represent to C.O. *Brand* that she held herself bound by the damaged ship rule only, and should proceed to sea and join *Sabrina* outside. The British Ambassador must have put in some hard work during the night with Norwegian Ministers, as, at 6.20 a.m., a message was received from C.O. *Brand* saying that *Pellew* might proceed.

" This was a blessed relief, and a suitable ending to an anxious and hectic period. The ten minutes just sufficed to get back our W/T office keys, say good-bye, thank Lieutenant Evensen for his help, good sense, and courtesy, and get off to sea together, where we were picked up by an infuriated *Shannon*, who greeted us by demanding why the —— —— we hadn't answered about thirty W/T signals she'd been making to us for the last twenty-four hours. However, a soft answer about the keys turned away the wrath.

" The repairs to *Pellew* were extensive as regards machinery. It was necessary to use a floor plate from *Sabrina's* engine-room to bolt over the hole about one foot in diameter in *Pellew's* side which was just above the water-line, and to use another plate to put over another hole in her upper deck. The work of drilling out the old rivets in the side and making new holes for bolts was heavy, and particularly so when done against time. The engineer officer of *Sabrina* was on leave in Scotland at the time, and the work devolved on the Chief E.R.A. of *Sabrina*, assisted by five others of her engine-room complement, all the senior ratings of *Pellew* having been killed except the chief stoker.

" The chief E.R.A. of *Sabrina* was sent in charge of *Pellew's* engine-room for the return journey, and the fact that she steamed back to Scapa Flow in the teeth of a heavy north-west gale testified to the excellent work done. The ship was, in fact, sent on to Glasgow as she was. I am glad to say that special recognition of this work carried out by the engine-room staff was made by the Admiralty, the Chief E.R.A. being offered Warrant rank, and the remainder being advanced in rating, or other suitable recognition."

Both the *Partridge* and the *Pellew* had fought gallantly until they could fight no more, and at the official investigation subsequently held at Scapa Flow, Lieutenant-Commander Cavendish, of the *Pellew*, was congratulated upon his conduct in most trying circumstances. In his crippled ship nobody could have done more against such overwhelming odds.

CHAPTER XXI

AMERICAN DESTROYERS

I

A T 9.30 p.m. on April 14th, 1917, eight days after the United States of America had declared war upon Germany, the six destroyers of the 8th Destroyer Division of the American Atlantic Fleet received orders from their flagship to fit out for long and distant service. Sailing at daylight next morning, they went to the naval yards at New York and Boston, where they were placed in dry-dock, underwent repairs, and embarked three months' stores and provisions.

Sailing on April 24th under sealed orders, they opened their confidential envelopes at midnight when fif+y miles out at sea. What orders they contained had probably already been guessed. Briefly, they were told to proceed to Queenstown, Ireland, there to co-operate with the British Naval Authorities.

The names of those six destroyers were the *Wadsworth, Conyngham, Porter, McDougal, Davis*, and *Wainwright*, under the command of Lieutenant-Commander J. K. Taussig in the *Wadsworth*.

After a week's bad weather in a strong south-easterly gale and a heavy sea, the *Wadsworth* and her consorts were nearing the Irish coast. On their ninth day out they were met by the British destroyer *Mary Rose*, which, about six months later, was to be sunk with her colours flying by a German cruiser while gallantly attempting to save the vessels of her Scandinavian convoy.

On board the *Mary Rose* on May 3rd, 1917, was Captain (now Rear-Admiral) E. R. G. R. Evans, C.B., D.S.O., of the *Broke*, who, less than a fortnight before in the English Channel, and in company with the *Swift*, had added to his fame as an Antarctic explorer by being largely instrumental in sinking two enemy destroyers in close conflict at night. On sighting the Americans the *Mary Rose* hoisted the signal, " Welcome to the American colours."

" Thank you," the *Wadsworth* replied. " We are glad of your company."

On the brilliant sunlit morning of May 4th the newcomers

steamed into Queenstown Harbour and started to replenish with fuel. Their arrival was an open secret. The Stars and Stripes flew from many of the public buildings and the ships in the harbour. Cheering crowds lined the waterfront.

It was an historic occasion. Those six grey four-funnelled destroyers afforded the first outward and visible sign that the Government of the United States had thrown in its lot with the Allies in their struggle against the Central Powers.

American help was sorely needed. April 1917 was the blackest month of the whole war, not merely for Britain, but for the Allied cause. During that month, 430 British, Allied, and neutral merchantmen had been sent to the bottom by submarines, an average of over fourteen a day, exclusive of fishing-craft. It was before the institution of the convoy system. Few, miserably few, British destroyers and other craft were available for the task of commerce protection. In an area of about 25,000 square miles to the western approaches to the English Channel, an area through which passed an enormous volume of trade, there were sometimes as few as four British destroyers available for patrol work. Never were there more than fifteen.

The Germans, with the institution of their unrestricted submarine campaign on February 1st, hoped to beat the Allies to their knees in five months, to force them to sue for peace. If things went on as they were, there was every prospect of the enemy winning the war.

In command at Queenstown at the time the American destroyers arrived was Vice-Admiral Sir Lewis Bayly, an officer who in the British Service was rather feared by his subordinates as a dour and taciturn martinet. Fiercely energetic, he was a man of few words, who believed in doing rather than in talking. He is one of the few British admirals whose photograph I never recollect having seen in any newspaper.

" When will you be ready for sea ? " was almost the first question he asked Taussig, the senior American officer.

After a stormy 3,000-mile voyage across the Atlantic lasting nine days, it was to be expected that some of the Americans would want time for making good defects. Taussig's answer, however, was characteristic.

" We shall be ready as soon as we have refuelled, sir," he replied.

" I'll give you four days from the time of arrival," said the admiral. " Will that be enough ? "

" Yes, sir," Taussig answered. " That will be more than ample."

And four days later the *Wadsworth, Conyngham, Porter, Mc-Dougal, Davis,* and *Wainwright,* were at sea helping their hard-pressed British comrades in searching for enemy U-boats. They were merely the forerunners, the pioneers as it were, of the large collection of American men-of-war of all types which subsequently saw service during the war in European waters.

Soon after their arrival at Queenstown the few British destroyers were detached elsewhere. Within a month two American depot-ships and twenty-two destroyers had either arrived in the Irish harbour, or were on their way thither. Seven additional destroyers arrived after they had convoyed the first American troop convoys to Saint Nazaire. By July 5th there were thirty-four American destroyers working from Queenstown, some meeting the convoys of American reinforcements for France far out at sea, others the ordinary convoys of merchantmen coming to the British Isles.

The number of American destroyers working from Queenstown varied from time to time according to circumstances, but some were based there until the end of the war.

Before they had been at Queenstown a month, Admiral Bayly was referring to their commanding officers as " my boys," while sometime in May the American Admiral Sims was invited to hoist his flag at Admiralty House, Queenstown, while Sir Lewis Bayly was absent on a few days' leave. " So far as exercising any control over sea operations was concerned, this invitation was not particularly important," Admiral Sims wrote. " Matters were running smoothly at the Queenstown station. . . . The British Admiralty merely took this way of showing a great courtesy to the American Navy, and of emphasising to the world the excellent relations that existed between the two Services."

It was not the only occasion on which the blue, white-starred flag of an American admiral has been flown in a British man-of-war or naval establishment. In September 1917, the American Admiral Mayo, together with Admiral Sir John Jellicoe and three other British flag officers, embarked in the flotilla-leader *Broke* at Dover to witness a bombardment of the enemy positions on the Belgian coast by a British monitor. The *Broke,* on this occasion, flew the flags of Admirals Jellicoe and Mayo side by side.

The Germans returned the monitor's fire with considerable

accuracy, and a heavy shell fired at range of something like twenty miles splashed into the sea about 300 yards off the *Broke*. It would have been nearer if the ship had not just altered course.

Vice-Admiral Sir Reginald Bacon, who was in charge of the operations, apologised to the American Chief-of-Staff for having hauled out, and not bringing the shell closer.

" Don't mention it, admiral," the American officer answered. " By the time we get to New York that shell will have been close alongside right enough."

2

Before going on to describe a few of the many incidents that befell American destroyers during the war, it is desirable to give some idea of America's naval effort from the date on which she finally decided to throw in her lot with the Allies, April 6th, 1917.

Eighty-five of her destroyers saw service in European waters during the war. Most of them were modern ; but six, old and under 500 tons displacement, made the long journey of 12,000 miles from the Philippines to Gibraltar.[1]

But destroyers were not all. Some 400 American men-of-war, and 81,000 officers and men of the United States Navy, served in Europe. Three hundred and seventy-three ships were present at the time of the Armistice – 8 battleships ; 3 cruisers ; 70 destroyers ; 12 submarines ; 10 minelayers ; 13 mine-sweepers ; 10 gunboats and revenue cutters ; 120 submarine chasers ; 27 armed yachts ; and the remainder repair and depot-ships, colliers, tugs and the like.

Five of the American battleships were serving with the British Grand Fleet, and three more at Berehaven. The cruisers served at Gibraltar and Murmansk, and the destroyers at Queenstown (24), Brest (38), Gibraltar (6), and Plymouth (2). Submarines were stationed at Berehaven and the Azores, and submarine chasers at Queenstown (30), Plymouth (36), Gibraltar (18), and Corfu (36). The ten minelayers were based on Invergordon, and the various other vessels wherever needed – Queenstown having a total of 59 American ships at the time of the Armistice ;

[1] For most of the detail in this section, I am indebted to information contained in *Our Navy at War*, by Mr. Josephus Daniels, American Secretary of the Navy, 1913-21. (George Doran & Company, New York, 1922.)

Brest, 85 ; Cardiff, 57, of which 55 were naval colliers taking coal to France for the American troops ; Gibraltar, 45 ; Plymouth, 39 ; and Corfu, 37.

Forty-four American naval or marine corps aviation stations were established in England, Ireland, France, Italy, and the Azores, with a record of 5,691 war flights covering a distance of 791,398 miles.

Of the rather more than 2,000,000 American troops sent to France before the Armistice, 911,047 were transported in American Naval transports ; 41,534 in other American ships ; and 1,075,333 in British ships or vessels chartered and manned by us. About 557,788 of the soldiers ferried across the Atlantic by the N.O.T.S., otherwise the American Naval Overseas Transportation Service, were accommodated in 20 ex-German and ex-Austrian ships, large liners for the most part, interned in American harbours since 1914 and taken over by the United States Government when war was declared against Germany.[1]

The N.O.T.S., manned entirely by officers and men of the American Navy, the greater number of whom were entered and trained after the outbreak of war in 1917, had 378 vessels of all kinds in operation when hostilities ceased. It not only transported the troops, but kept up the constant supply of the vast amount of stores, ammunition, and food required for the American armies in France and elsewhere. It was reckoned that five tons of supplies were needed a year for every American soldier abroad. Fifty-five colliers of the N.O.T.S. also took coal from Cardiff to various ports in France for the use of the American Expeditionary Force.

When war was declared there were in the regular American Navy 4,376 officers and 64,680 men. Including the reserves, the naval militia, and the coastguard, the total strength was about 95,000. To man the large number of additional ships, including the transports of the N.O.T.S., large numbers of additional officers and men were needed. They were sent to sea after a few months' intensive training, until, at the time of the Armistice, the strength of the naval personnel stood at :

[1] " Admiral Sims, U.S.N., testifies that, of the 1,500,000 troops brought over during the summer of 1918, 1,000,000 were embarked in British bottoms. . . . Of the escorts necessary for the troop movements, 70 per cent. of the vessels were British ; of the destroyers, only 14 per cent. were American ; and of the auxiliary craft, just 3 per cent. were American. Out of the vast auxiliary patrol force of 3,000 vessels, American ships numbered 160." *The German Submarine War*, by R. H. Gibson and Maurice Prendergast, p. 298. (Constable & Co., 1931.)

	Officers	*Men*
REGULARS	10,590	218,251
RESERVE	21,618	278,659
COAST GUARD	688	6,101
	32,896	503,011

or a grand total of 535,907, which is probably the largest strength a navy has ever had.

The American building programme, embarked upon immediately the rupture came with Germany, included 275 destroyers, 447 submarine chasers, 99 submarines, 112 " Eagle boats," and 54 minesweepers, not all of which were completed by November, 1918, by which time there were 2,000 United States naval vessels in commission.

The speed with which some of the new destroyers were built constituted a world's record. The pre-war time for completion was between twenty months and two years ; but one, the *Ward*, was launched 17½ days after her keel had been laid, and was commissioned in 70 days. The *Reid* was actually commissioned in 45½ working days from the time she was laid down.

The " Eagle boats," designed especially for submarine hunting, were built by Mr. Henry Ford, of motor-car fame, at a special plant on the River Rouge, near Detroit. He volunteered to build any number between 100 and 500, working on a mass production principle, and estimating that when he got going he would turn out twenty-five a month. One hundred were actually ordered, besides twelve for the Italian Government. The completion of twenty-three in one month showed that Mr. Ford was not far wrong in his original estimate, but, though sixty were actually built, very few were in commission by the time the war ceased. " Eagle-boats " did, however, steam across the Atlantic to Scotland, while others were employed in North Russia during the post-Armistice operations. Not unlike the British P-boats built during the war for anti-submarine work, the " Eagles " were craft of 500 tons with a speed of 18 knots, armed with a couple of 4-inch guns, anti-aircraft and machine-guns, together with depth-charges for destroying submarines.

The submarine chasers were built in large numbers, 355 being ordered before war was declared, and 441 being finally completed. They were built at the naval dockyards at New York, New Orleans, Norfolk, Charleston, Mare Island, and Puget Sound, and were craft 110 feet long with a speed of 14 knots ; armed with 3-inch and machine-guns, together with the usual depth-charges. As there was a shortage of labour and of steel, they were built of wood. Fifty of these little craft were acquired by the French, crossing the Atlantic under their own motor power. Others served at Queenstown, Plymouth, Gibraltar, and Corfu.

" Sub-chaser " 28, manned by the French, broke down in the Atlantic 700 miles from the Azores and was given up for lost. The boat was leaking badly, and, though rockets and distress signals were fired, no help was forthcoming. All lubricating oil was expended, so all the salad oil and butter on board were used in an attempt to start up the engines. But the motors refused to function, whereupon table-cloths, blankets, sheets, and bed-spreads were made into sails. Rationing the food and water that remained, the commanding officer, Alexis Puluhen, steered his little ship eastward under her motley rig. With a favouring breeze they found they could make good about 4 knots.

For a month they crawled on. Four steamers in all were sighted during that period, though only one came close enough to see the broken-down " chaser." And when the latter fired guns as a signal of distress, the steamer, no doubt taking her for an enemy submarine, promptly ran away at her best speed. S.C.28 eventually sighted Fayal, in the Azores, on the thirty-third day after disablement, and was towed into Horta by a tug.

3

Accounts of a few exciting adventures that befell the American destroyers serving in European waters must serve as examples of many others.

On October 15th, 1917, the *Cassin* – Lieutenant-Commander W. N. Vernou – was patrolling off the Irish coast twenty miles south of Mine Head, Co. Waterford. There was considerable wind and sea when, at 1.30 p.m., she sighted a submarine at some distance. The U-boat dived before the *Cassin* could reach her. Half an hour later, while still continuing his search, Vernou sighted the white wake of a torpedo approaching the ship. He promptly rang down for full speed, and put the helm hard over. For a moment it seemed as if the torpedo might pass astern. About fifteen feet away from the destroyer, however, it suddenly broke surface and sheered to the left, striking well aft above water on the port side, and practically blowing away the stern.

Gunner's Mate Osmond K. Ingram, stationed at his gun, had seen the torpedo approaching. Realising that if it struck among the depth-charges in the stern the resulting explosion might wreck the ship, he at once ran aft to put them to " safe." Whether or not he had time to do this will never be known, for he was blown to pieces when the torpedo exploded. It was an act of wonderful heroism, to commemorate which one of the new destroyers was afterwards christened the *Osmond Ingram*. She was the first man-of-war ever to be named after an American bluejacket.

The *Cassin*, meanwhile, badly damaged and with her rudder gone, could only steam in circles. About 850 lbs. of T.N.T., in the torpedo and depth-charges, had detonated above water in the stern, thirty-five feet of which was blown completely away. All the living compartments and store-rooms in the after part of the ship were demolished, and the twenty men below at the time had a miraculous escape with their lives.

Her captain tried steering her with the propellers, but had to give it up as hopeless, as the starboard turbine was out of action. The ship then fell off into the trough of the sea, and became unmanageable, with the dynamo useless and all the lights below extinguished. The ordinary wireless being destroyed, help had to be summoned by rigging an auxiliary set and aerial. At 2.30, while this work was still in progress, the conning-tower of the submarine broke surface. The *Cassin* opened fire. Two shells struck close to the enemy, who dived and did not attack again.

At 4 o'clock the American destroyer *Porter* arrived on the scene, and five hours later the British sloops *Jessamine* and *Tamarisk*. The sea and wind had risen, and it was not until 2.30 next morning that the *Tamarisk* managed to get a wire hawser into the *Cassin* and started to tow her towards the land. At 3.30 a.m. the hawser parted, and the damaged destroyer was again helpless.

Two trawlers, a tug, and another sloop had meanwhile appeared and they made desperate efforts all through the night to get her in tow again. It was not until after 10.30 a.m. on the 16th, twenty and a half hours after being torpedoed, that the *Cassin* was finally in tow of the British sloop *Snowdrop* and was brought safely into harbour.

On November 17th, 1917, the two destroyers *Fanning*, Lieutenant A. S. Carpender, and *Nicholson*, Lieutenant-Commander B. A. Long, were in company with a convoy just off Queenstown when, at 4.10 p.m., the coxswain of the first-named suddenly saw the top of a periscope, a thing no larger than a broomstick, appear momentarily out of the sea 400 yards on the port bow. Heading in that direction at full speed, the *Fanning* dropped a depth-charge as she crossed the supposed track of the submarine.

The 300 lbs. of T.N.T. exploded at its set depth, to fling up its dome-shaped hummock of whitened water, which burst upwards in a great plume of spray and smoke. The *Nicholson* was approaching at full speed to drop another depth-charge when the conning-tower of a submarine suddenly broke surface. She steered straight for it, the *Fanning* turning in her wake to make another attack.

Dropping a depth-charge close alongside her enemy, the *Nicholson* opened fire. The submarine's bow broke surface. With her stern well down, she seemed badly damaged, but was still moving ahead. The *Fanning* gave her three rounds from her bow gun, and at the third the German crew came on deck in their lifebelts, holding up their hands in token of surrender and shouting " *Kamerad !* "

She surrendered at 4.28, only eighteen minutes since the *Fanning's* coxswain, David D. Loomis, had first sighted the periscope.

As the submarine, U.58, was still afloat, the destroyers tried to take her in tow. But it was not to be. Two of the crew disappeared below to scuttle her, and as she sank the Germans took to the water and swam across to the *Fanning*. Only one man of U.58's crew was drowned, and him the American seamen jumped overboard to save, only to find that he was beyond recovery when they got him on board.

The U-boat's commander, 3 other officers, and 35 men were made prisoners, and the *Fanning* and *Nicholson* returned triumphantly to their convoy, presently to decorate their funnels with the white, five-pointed star which, in the United States Navy, was the badge of honour denoting a submarine " kill." This was the only submarine sunk by the United States forces unaided. American ships contributed indirectly to the sinking of three others.

It is impossible to mention a tithe of the sightings of, and subsequent depth-charge attacks upon, enemy submarines ; but here is the story of the American destroyer *Jacob Jones*, Lieutenant-Commander D. W. Bagley.

During September 1917, with two other destroyers, she was credited with a successful encounter against a U-boat. On October 19th, when the British armed merchant cruiser *Orama*, acting as escort ship to a convoy, was torpedoed and sunk, the

Jacob Jones, with the *Conyngham*, also helped to save the 478 persons on board.

On the afternoon of December 6th the *Jacob Jones* was on passage alone from a position off Brest to Queenstown when, at 4.21 p.m., a torpedo was seen approaching. It had been fired at a range of over 3,000 yards by U.53. The destroyer's helm was put hard over, and she increased to full speed.

Jumping clear of the water, the torpedo dived again within about fifty feet of the ship, eventually to strike and explode in the oil-fuel tank three feet below the waterline.

About twenty feet of the deck was blown up, several men were killed instantaneously, the auxiliary machinery room was wrecked, a torpedo-tube hurled into the air, and the mainmast and wireless aerial were carried away. The ship immediately started to settle by the stern, and the after part of the deck was soon awash. An officer, Lieutenant J. K. Richards, realising that the depth-charges would explode at their set depth when the ship sank, rushed aft to set them to " safe," but was unable to do so as the stern was already under water. Realising that the ship was doomed, and knowing the wireless to be out of action, Lieutenant-Commander Bagley gave orders for two guns to be fired, in the hope of attracting the attention of some ship. But no vessel was within sight or hearing.

Boats were lowered and life-saving rafts thrown overboard, together with the large circular Carley floats and all the timber that could be found. The ship sank in eight minutes, the captain, officers, and men taking to the water just before she disappeared. Foundering stern first, the *Jacob Jones* turned upside down as she swung upright, the depth-charges at her stern detonating at the same time and killing or stunning the men in the water near by.

Twenty minutes afterwards the submarine broke surface about two miles off, and then gradually closed and picked up two men from the water, whom she made prisoners. Then she disappeared.

All the survivors in sight were collected, and the rafts and boats brought together. There seemed little hope of rescue unless help could be obtained from the shore, so, leaving a lieutenant in charge of the rafts, Bagley, with one other officer and four men, started to row for the nearest land.

It was soon pitch dark. The month was December, and, shivering with cold, many still dazed after their experience, the survivors huddled together for warmth, those with thick clothing dividing it with those more scantily dressed. One raft, which had separated from the others, was picked up the same evening by a steamer. The others remained all night in their perilous position, being finally picked up at 8.30 next morning by the British steamer *Camellia.*

One officer, Lieutenant Stanton F. Kalk, died of exposure and exhaustion before rescue came. Though suffering from the effects of the depth-charge explosions, and weakened by his efforts after the ship sank, he had spent some time swimming from raft to raft to equalise the weight in them. Anxious for the safety of his men, he overtaxed his strength and died – died, as said some of the survivors, " game to the last." In recognition of Kalk's gallantry, one of the new destroyers was named after him.

In this disaster 2 officers and 62 men lost their lives. " Bagley's handling of the situation after his ship was torpedoed," wrote Admiral Sims, " was everything that I expected in the way of efficiency, good judgment, courage, and chivalrous action."

Perhaps the most curious feature of this incident was that the commanding officer of U.53, taking pity on the survivors in their open boats in bad weather, actually signalled into Queenstown by wireless, gave the latitude and longitude of the *Jacob Jones's* boats, and then made off as fast as he could. But this particular officer, Hans Rose, was noted as a humane enemy. Sometimes he would collect a ship's boats and tow them in towards the land to give them a chance of saving their lives.

On the night of April 17th, 1918, an American convoy, escorted by three destroyers and four armed yachts, was nearing the French coast in the vicinity of Quiberon Bay. The night was very dark, with an overcast sky and a calm sea, when, at 10.45 p.m., a searchlight was seen flashing from the bridge of the *Florence H.*, a ship laden with munitions. A moment later she suddenly burst into a great gout of flame, which shot 100 feet into the air in a cloud of smoke, and projected masses of blazing wreckage skywards. From the accounts of survivors, it afterwards transpired that a sudden explosion in No. 2 hold had lifted the deck and blown out the ship's starboard side.

The dense smoke and flame prevented those in the other ships from seeing what had happened. Rescue, however, seemed utterly hopeless. The water round the burning ship was soon littered with blazing powder-cases and wreckage, so tightly packed that they floated away to leeward like huge rafts. The sea was covered with flaming oil-fuel. Ammunition was exploding in all directions.   The ship had split open amidships and was vomiting tongues of flame like a volcano.

The moment the fire was seen, the three destroyers made for the wreck to save life, the *Stewart*, Lieutenant-Commander H. S. Haislip, leading, followed by the *Whipple*, Lieutenant-Commander H. J. Abbett, and the *Truxton*, Lieutenant-Commander J. G. Ware. As they approached, the ammunition on the deck of the munition ship started to explode, to shoot up in showers of sparks and flame like fireworks. For the wooden yachts to have ventured into the blazing sea surrounding the *Florence H.* was to court almost certain destruction. It was dangerous enough for the destroyers, their sterns being laden with depth-charges.

As the *Stewart* approached the wreck she was cautioned by the senior officer to be careful. It seemed impossible that any of the men from the *Florence H.* could be left alive ; but Haislip, pushing on, heard men shouting in the water. There was only one way to rescue them, and that was to plough a way through the blazing ammunition cases and oil which littered the sea in patches. The *Stewart* moved on, clearing a way for her consorts close behind.

Lines were thrown to those of the men in the water who could help themselves. Seamen jumped overboard to rescue others who were blinded or drowning. Boats were lowered, and pushed their way through the burning flotsam to get at men beyond. All the time, the flames from the *Florence H.* lit up the sea until it was almost as bright as day. Still blazing like a torch, she finally sank a quarter of an hour after the first explosion.

Many gallant deeds were performed on that dreadful night. Two men, who had jumped overboard to save a drowning man at great risk to themselves, were awarded the Medal of Honor, the American equivalent of the V.C. Others were officially commended, while Haislip, decorated by the United States Government, was praised by the French Vice-Admiral for his " super-contempt of danger " and " remarkable qualities of seamanship."

Forty-five of the officers and men of the *Florence H.* lost their lives in the fire and explosions. Thirty-two were saved. Had it not been for the work of the destroyers, not one of them could have escaped alive.

On May 31st, 1918, the American Naval Transport *President Lincoln* – an ex-German liner – was on her way back to the United States in company with three other transports. At 9 o'clock in the morning, when 500 miles from the nearest land, she was torpedoed three times by a submarine. The other vessels, obeying their orders to avoid attack, steamed off at full speed when the *President Lincoln* was hit.

On board the sinking ship there were 715 officers and men, many of them invalids. It was realised at once that she was doomed, so the boats were lowered and life-saving rafts thrown overboard. At the same time an S.O.S. was made by wireless. A quarter of an hour after being torpedoed, all men except a few of the officers and the guns' crews were ordered into the boats.

Every time the submarine appeared fire was opened. It was kept up until the water was over the main deck, and all on board were ordered to save themselves. The ship finally sank twenty five minutes after being struck, taking with her 3 officers and 23 men.

Thirty minutes later a large submarine broke surface close to the boats and rafts, and went in among them to make prisoners of the captain – Commander P. W. Foote – and senior officers. Unable to identify him, the submarine, U.90, took one of the lieutenants. After remaining in the vicinity until the afternoon, she eventually disappeared.

Darkness came, the boats and rafts being lashed together to prevent separation during the night. Lanterns were hoisted and signal flares burned every few minutes ; but nobody knew when help would come. The distress signals had been answered by the American destroyers escorting another convoy 250 miles away, the *Smith*, Lieutenant-Commander Kenyon, and the *Warrington*, Lieutenant-Commander Klein. But it was possible, if submarines were known to be in the vicinity, that they might not be detached.

Five hundred miles out at sea in their boats and rafts, the *President Lincoln's* survivors spent the early part of the night singing and cheering to keep up their spirits. The hours passed in terrible anxiety, until, shortly before 11 p.m., the lights of two vessels were seen in the distance.

They were the lights of the *Smith* and *Warrington*, which, with only the 9 a.m. wireless signal to guide them, had steamed at their fastest possible speed to the rescue. They had travelled 250 miles. In the interval the boats and rafts had drifted fifteen miles.

The 618 rescued were crowded on board the destroyers, which

remained in the neighbourhood until daylight searching for other survivors. Then they steamed on for Brest, sighting on their way the flutter of a periscope, which they attacked with twenty-two depth-charges. It is as well, perhaps, that they did not succeed in destroying the submarine underneath it, for she was U.90, the very vessel which had sunk the *President Lincoln*, and on board of which was a prisoner in the shape of Lieutenant E. V. M. Isaacs, of the United States Navy.

A few months later the *Smith* again distinguished herself when, on August 15th, 1918, a vessel called the *West Bridge*, one of a convoy 400 miles from the French coast, stripped her main turbine and lay helpless. She sent off a wireless signal to Brest asking for help, and hardly had she done so when a submarine made her appearance and torpedoed the *Montanan*. The latter ship sank, whereupon the U.boat turned her attention to the *West Bridge* and torpedoed her twice. She seemed on the point of foundering when the destroyer *Smith* arrived and sent on board a volunteer crew under Lieutenant R. L. Connolly.

The turbines being damaged, there was no chance of steaming the *West Bridge* under her own power. Nor could she be steered except by hand. Connolly and his men, indeed, had the greatest difficulty in keeping her afloat. The holds, engine-room and stokeholds were flooded. The well-deck before the bridge was awash, and great seas constantly broke over her in a welter of spray and foam.

Eventually she was taken in tow by four tugs, which started to pull her towards Brest. During the whole of the five days of the passage the volunteer crew struggled to save the ship. She finally reached Brest, where she was beached. The officials who examined the damage declared that she had had no more than a hundred tons of positive buoyancy to keep her afloat. A leaking bulkhead, another compartment flooded, and the *West Bridge* must have foundered.

Here is another story of an American destroyer.

On October 9th, 1918, in the English Channel, the *Shaw* was escorting the huge Cunarder *Aquitania*, carrying nearly 8,000 men in officers, ship's company, and troops. The destroyer was just completing the leg of a zigzag which brought her close to the convoy, when her helm suddenly jammed. As the *Aquitania* turned, the *Shaw's* bows were aimed straight at her great wall side.

There was no room to manoeuvre. The commanding officer of the destroyer, Commander William Glassford, realised at once that nothing could avert a collision. Either his own ship or the *Aquitania* must be sacrificed. If the *Shaw's* sharp bows carved their way through the liner's comparatively thin side, she might be ripped open, and sink with heavy loss of life.

Glassford determined to sacrifice his own ship, and, unable to turn, gave the order " Full speed astern," with the intention of taking the blow as far forward as possible.

I have been in a few destroyer collisions ; but never have I had the misfortune to be rammed by a larger ship. The few seconds that passed before the vessels struck must have been like a ghastly nightmare for those in the *Shaw*.

Imagine being twenty feet above the water on the bridge of a 900-ton destroyer, a thin, fragile thing with sides the thickness of stout cardboard, to see approaching one nearly at right angles, at a speed of something over 20 knots, the sharp stem of a great liner, with the twin plumes of the bow-wave playing round the forefoot. And beyond that stem the huge wall sides, with their rows of scuttles, towering to the sky like the wall of some great building – a glimpse of the masts and smoking funnels and a few excited faces peering over the bow, a dead weight of 45,000 tons travelling at the speed of a suburban railway train.

No power on earth could avert a collision ; but imagine, or try to, the few horrible moments of waiting for the crash, with that great wedge-shaped bow coming nearer and nearer, remorselessly, relentlessly. Think of the dreadful uncertainty of not knowing where the blow would come, and with the possibility that in a few more ticks of the clock one's body and those of some of one's shipmates might be dismembered and bleeding like the joints in a butcher's shop, or, with broken limbs, pinned or jammed beneath a tangle of twisted steel.

The two ships met with a crashing, shuddering impact which nearly flung the *Shaw* on her beam-ends. Then the sound of tortured, tearing steel as the destroyer rasped along the liner's side.

Colliding just forward of the *Shaw's* bridge, the *Aquitania* sliced her in two, cutting off ninety feet of her bows, killing 2 officers and 10 men, injuring 3 officers and 12 seamen, tearing open the foremost boiler-room, completely wrecking the bridge, and bringing down both masts with a crash. The mainmast, in falling, fouled the starboard propeller. Before long, sparks set fire to the oil fuel in the foremost tanks and the *Shaw* burst into flame.

Two destroyers came to her help, one rescuing the survivors

from the bow, which was still afloat two hundred yards away from the rest of the hull.

Then, as the *Shaw's* men worked to put out the fire, the flames reached some of the ammunition, which started to explode. But they laboured on, finally managing to put out the blaze. They then set about getting the engines and steering-gear into working order.

That the ship remained afloat at all is remarkable. Most of her bow had vanished, and a photograph of the damage shows a great heap of shapeless, crumpled steel extending as far as the foremost funnel, with, on top of it, the circular bridge structure canted over to port at an angle of nearly eighty degrees.

That what remained was safely navigated into Portland harbour that afternoon is more remarkable still, but got in she was. Temporary repairs being effected, she was presently taken to a dockyard and a new bow constructed.

There were many occasions during the war when British destroyers, or even light-cruisers, had their bows or sterns removed by mine, torpedo, or collision, and had new ones built on. But no British vessel that I ever heard of during the war had the honour of being collided with by a ship the size of the *Aquitania*, which perhaps was just as well.

I might go on for a long time writing of the adventures of American destroyers in the war. Enough has been said, however, to show that Admiral Sims's speech at the Guildhall in 1910, quoted in Chapter XVII, was not altogether exaggerated.

We may be paying back the dollars, with interest, but the fact remains that the British and American Navies worked in the greatest amity and co-operation from May 1917 until the Armistice and after.

Here is an order issued by Admiral Sir Lewis Bayly, the commander-in-Chief at Queenstown, in May 1918, to the American destroyers working under his command.

" On the anniversary of the arrival of the first United States men-of-war at Queenstown, I wish to express very deep gratitude to the United States officers and ratings for the skill, energy, and unfailing good nature which they have all consistently shown, and which qualities have so materially assisted in the war by enabling ships of the Allied Powers to cross the ocean in comparative freedom. " To command you is an honour ; to work with you is a pleasure ; to know you is to know the best traits of the Anglo-Saxon race."

Speaking of American naval co-operation in the war and of Admiral Sims, reminds me that the United States Naval Headquarter offices in London were in Grosvenor Place. But, before this location was chosen, certain American naval officers had been looking for suitable houses. One solved the matter to his own satisfaction by deciding upon the Athenæum Club, in Waterloo Place.

"Say, Admiral," he is reputed to have said to Sims, "I guess I have found *the* place for us. There's that Club A-theneum that's good and central, and near to the British Admiralty. It sure can't matter if the old boys and old books there go elsewhere for the rest of the war, and we take over the residence."

Sims, who knew his London, was aghast at the idea.

" My boy," he is supposed to have said, " I guess I'd as soon ask for the Houses of Parliament or Buckingham Palace as your Club A-theneum ! "

CHAPTER XXII

TORPEDO-BOATS[1]

I

THOUGH torpedo-boats were really obsolete, there were still over one hundred of these craft in the Navy when the war began. Thirty-six of these, vessels of between 250 and 300 tons, were built between 1906 and 1909 as " coastal destroyers," and finally received numbers instead of names. They were turbine-driven, oil-fired vessels of 26 knots, armed with two 12-pounder guns and three 18-inch torpedo-tubes. Numbered from 1 to 36, they were generally known in the Service as the " oily wads."

About twenty-four of them formed the local defence flotilla in the Firth of Forth on the outbreak of war, while the remaining twelve were based on the Tyne, Sheerness, and Portsmouth. Later on, when convoy and escort work became general and the flotillas became mixed up, these torpedo-boats became more or less scattered. Some worked on the Dover Patrol, while a few went as far east as the Dardanelles.

Six of these vessels were lost during the war, numbers 9, 10, 11, 12, 13 and 24 – three being mined, two sunk in collision, and the sixth being wrecked off Dover breakwater.

The torpedo-boats immediately before the so-called " oily wads " were the craft of between 180 and 200 tons, built between 1901 and 1903. Their numbers ran intermittently from 98 to 117, and they were 25-knot, coal-burning, single-screw vessels armed with three 3-pounder guns and three torpedo-tubes. They also were used for local defence purposes, principally at Portsmouth, and one, No. 117, was sunk in collision in the Channel in 1917.

The next torpedo-boats in order of age were those of the " 90 " class, with numbers running from 90 to 97. They dated from 1894, had a tonnage of 130, and a nominal speed of about 24 knots. These eight vessels, with T.B.s Nos. 83, 88, and 89, formed the local defence flotilla at Gibraltar throughout the war. I am indebted to Captain W. W. Hunt, D.S.O., Royal Navy, who

[1] War losses of torpedo-boats will be found in Appendices III-VI.

commanded the flotilla throughout the war, for an account of their work.

At the outbreak of war, the naval force kept at Gibraltar consisted of the eleven torpedo-boats and three " B " class submarines. For years past the torpedo-boats had been kept in commission with reduced complements, being commanded by commissioned warrant officers, with a lieutenant-commander in charge of the flotilla. Their crews were made up to full complement four days before the war began, when they took up their patrol stations. They did the night patrol across the Straits of Gibraltar, and the submarines the day patrol.

Actual war conditions, however, gradually modified the duties of the torpedo-boats. When, with the retirement of the *Goeben* and *Breslau* to Constantinople, the threat of the passage of the Straits by enemy surface vessels no longer had to be provided against, the torpedo-boats maintained a day and a night patrol. Six boats were used at night and three during the day, the entrance to Gibraltar Bay being swept for mines each morning by the boats returning.

Their duties were sufficiently onerous, for every merchantman passing through the Straits had to be identified, examined, and, if necessary, sent in to Gibraltar for search. As the number of vessels passing amounted to over sixty a day during the earlier part of the war, the work of the flotilla in dealing with this number was very heavy.

Moreover, the weather conditions in the Straits are bad for small craft. Gales are of frequent occurrence, not only in winter, but also in summer, when the " Levanter " sometimes blows hard for a week on end. Blowing dead against the current, which runs at between 3 and 5 knots, it raises a steep, nasty sea which incommodes even cruisers.

For the first months of the war, from August until November, the torpedo-boats maintained their patrol unaided. At that time, as Italy was not yet in the war, there were opportunities for contraband to reach enemy destinations by way of the Mediterranean ports. Cargoes consigned " To order " to Italian ports often had ultimate enemy destinations, and many ships so laden were intercepted by the flotilla, sent into Gibraltar, and their cargoes unloaded. Large numbers of enemy reservists also attempted to return to Europe from the United States in Italian mail steamers. Their identification was a matter of great difficulty and not without its humorous side ; but upwards of

600 enemy reservists were discovered and interned at Gibraltar.

" I sometimes wonder," writes Captain Hunt, " whether the Gibraltar Patrol might not rightly claim to have committed the first act of war at sea. At 12.20 a.m. on August 4th, 1914, an hour and twenty minutes after the declaration of war, Torpedo-Boat 92, which I commanded, met the German Ost Afrika Liner *Emir*, stopped her, put a party on board, and sent her into Gibraltar as a prize. She brought nearly a million sterling into the Prize Fund. Not long afterwards the Hansa liner *Schneefels*, also with a valuable cargo, was captured, and two smaller ships within the next twenty-four hours. After that, however, all German ships on the High Seas when war was declared had put into neutral ports."

The strain on the personnel, and the impossibility of obtaining proper intervals of rest for the repair of machinery and cleaning of boilers, occasioned by the necessity of keeping practically the entire flotilla always at sea, caused the eleven torpedo-boats to be augmented by three armed boarding-vessels in November 1914. They took the day patrol, which made things slightly less onerous.

In the spring of 1915 there were repeated rumours that German U-boats were about to attempt the passage into the Mediterranean to interfere with the operations in the Dardanelles. Early in May the information was more definite, and it became known that a U-boat had been given a rendezvous at Alboran Island, about 115 sea miles east of Gibraltar. For some time the neighbourhood was patrolled by the torpedo-boats, until at dawn on May 9th a submarine was sighted by Torpedo-Boat 92, Lieutenant-Commander Hunt.

" She was five or six miles off when first seen, and did not dive until we were within three miles of her," this officer writes. " She unwarily came up to have another look a few minutes later, and we sighted her barely a cable away. Luckily for her, we did not have depth-charges in those days ; but she only avoided our attempt to ram by a very narrow margin. Though she got down in time to save her hull, her periscope must have suffered, as it cut a deep score along the T.B.'s bottom. The U-boat fired a torpedo in the agony of collision, and this was the last we saw of her."

This submarine was U.21, commanded by Kapitan-Leutnant Otto von Hersing. She was the first enemy submarine to enter the Straits, and her definite appearance caused Lord Fisher, then the First Sea Lord, to recall the new battleship *Queen Elizabeth* from the Dardanelles, his action being much resented by Lord Kitchener, the Secretary of State for War. But after events proved Lord Fisher's wisdom. On May 25th, after a visit to Pola, U.21 appeared among the fleet off Gallipoli. She attacked the *Swiftsure* and *Vengeance* without success; but torpedoed and sank the old battleship *Triumph* off Gaba Tepe. On May 27th she also sank the *Majestic*, and arrived at Constantinople amid scenes of tremendous enthusiasm on June 5th.

Several more enemy submarines passed through the Straits of Gibraltar into the Mediterranean during the summer of 1915. The deep water, with the easy navigation, the neutral territorial waters on either side, and a constant east-going stream of 3 to 5 knots, made the passage comparatively easy for U-boats, so the torpedo-boat patrol was stationed between 50 and 100 miles to the eastward, in the hope of catching them on the surface after their passage. In almost every case they were sighted and attacked in this area ; but were invariably able to escape damage by diving in plenty of time.

It was not until 1916 that the U-boats attempted any definite operations against merchant-ships in the western Mediterranean, when a few attacks were made on ships in the Gibraltar area. To cope with this situation, the Gibraltar Patrol was strengthened by twenty motor-launches. A base for small craft was also established near Cape St. Vincent, in Portuguese territory, nearly 200 miles to the westward of the Straits, and at Tangier, forces from these two bases patrolling the western approaches. Various submarines were sighted and attacked from time to time ; but, though they may have been damaged, I cannot discover from the records that any were actually sunk until April 21st, 1918, when U.B.71 was sighted by Motor-Launch 413 near Almina Point, Ceuta, on the African coast opposite Gibraltar.

It was still early in the morning and dark, with the weather rather thick, when M.L.413 heard the sound of approaching propellers on her hydrophones. Soon afterwards she saw a submarine steering east on the surface at high speed. The U-boat altered course, crossed the bows of the motor-launch at a distance of about ten yards, and then dived. But M.L.413 dashed after her at full speed, followed on in her wake, and dropped a string of depth-charges. After the explosions had subsided the M.L. listened on her hydrophones, but could hear nothing of her enemy. Then the dawn came, and the sea was seen to be covered with a scum of thick oil, in which floated several pieces of woodwork and part of a steel-lined mahogany door, pitted with splinters. Submarine U.B.71 had been well and truly disposed of.

In the main, the U-boats avoided the Gibraltar area for offensive action. This, in view of the volume of traffic converging from both sides on the bottle-neck of the Straits, and the huge collection of vessels usually congregated in Gibraltar Bay, was somewhat surprising.

It was in April 1917 that one of the experimental convoys that initiated the whole convoy system, assembled at Gibraltar and sailed for England. It was escorted by all the available torpedo-boats, which finally left the convoy to its ocean escort about 100 miles west of the Straits. " It was a very anxious time," Captain Hunt writes. " The convoy straggled for miles, and it was not until it was fifty miles west of the Straits that our anxiety in any way abated. If my memory is correct, that convoy of about twenty-four merchantmen reached England without casualty, and the adoption of the convoy system was assured."[1]

In the latter period of the war all merchant-ships entering the Mediterranean called at Gibraltar as a matter of routine. The armed boarding vessels were quite able to deal with this traffic, which left the torpedo-boats free for anti-submarine duties. They had a wide area to cover, most of it in open water, for which they were hardly suited. It was very bad weather which caused Torpedo-Boat 90 to capsize and sink on April 25th, 1918, with the loss of all but five of her officers and men. Torpedo-Boat 96 had also been lost with both officers and most of her crew in bad weather on November 1st, 1915, after colliding with a merchant-ship at night with no lights.

The war had a dramatic ending for the Gibraltar Patrol. After Austria's collapse it was augmented by about seventeen trawlers and twenty American " sub-chasers " released from the Otranto Barrage. " We were able," Captain Hunt writes, " to form a very effective screen across the Straits to stop the German submarines from leaving the Mediterranean, which was a different proposition for them to that of passing to the eastward with the strong current in their favour, as it meant they had to come through on the surface. Two submarines in company made the attempt on the night of November 8th-9th, 1918."

They were heard by the hydrophone patrol off Almina Point, Ceuta, and M.L.155 sighted one just after midnight and gave

[1] See p. 283.

chase. A Very light fired by M.L.373 showed the submarine to be diving, whereupon 155 let go a depth-charge. The U-boat was damaged and forced to the surface, and presently a reinforcement arrived in the shape of the decoy ship *Privet*. She sighted and fired on the submarine, hitting her on the conning-tower with her 12-pounders, and finishing her off with depth-charges. By 12.30 a.m. the last German submarine to be sunk in the war had gone to the bottom. She was U.34. " So phosphorescent was the water," says one account, " that U.34 could be seen, quite distinctly, moving under water, glowing and outlined by sea-fire."[1]

The other submarine, U.B.50, profiting by the distraction caused by the mêlée, passed on unobserved, and managed also to get through the western patrol line of American " sub-chasers." At daylight the next morning she encountered the *Britannia* off Cape Trafalgar, and succeeded in torpedoing her in one of the 9.2-inch magazines. After another torpedo the 16,350-ton battleship lay down to die. She took between three and a half and four hours to founder, and luckily the weather was calm and practically all the officers and men were rescued. The contents of the 9.2-magazine, however, burnt without detonating, which, as says Captain Hunt, " produced results which were both deplorable and unique. Upwards of 50 of her men died from some obscure form of gas poisoning during the next twenty-four hours, many of whom had shown no signs of illness when landed at Gibraltar. Indeed, some were found dead in their hammocks, though perfectly well when they turned in."

2

Various of the old " 80 " class torpedo-boats of 85 tons dating from 1889 were used for harbour services at home, as were also about twenty-four still older and smaller craft dating from between 1885 and 1888. Six of these veterans – Nos. 043, 044, 046, 063, 067, 070 – formed the local defence flotilla at Malta on the outbreak of war, and were sent to Egypt when the Turks were massing for the attack upon the Suez Canal.

" During the spring of 1915," writes the commanding officer of this flotilla, Captain G. B. Palmes, D.S.O., who was then a lieutenant-commander, " I had two T.B.s at Port Said, two at

---

[1] *The German Submarine War, 1914–1918*, by R. H. Gibson and Maurice Prendergast, p. 277.

Suez, and two on the Bitter Lakes, based at Ismailia. The
Turkish Army attacked at Toussoum, so only one boat, 043,
got into action."

This happened to be Palmes's own command, and his little
vessel particularly distinguished herself on February 5th, 1915,
when the Turkish attack was delivered. She used her 3-pounders
and machine-guns at close range, and with devastating effect,
on the enemy troops massed on the canal bank and trying to
cross in lighters.

Her work is thus described by a French author[1]: " Torpedo-
Boat 43 (British), hardly larger than a picket-boat, frisks about
everywhere, seeking for a prey. She demolishes the abandoned
Turkish rafts and pontoons one by one, then returns and goes
alongside the *D'Entrecasteaux* to have her wounded commander
and second-in-command seen to." According to this same
writer, " Lieutenant-Commander Palmes and his sub-lieutenant,
having noticed a pontoon that had been overlooked, landed in
the dinghy to blow it up. Palmes, having reached the top of
the sand-dune, rolled suddenly to the bottom of a trench, wherein
were fifty Turkish soldiers awaiting the turn of events. General
stupor ; not a soul budges. Palmes first mistakes the Turks for
Indians, then, perceiving his mistake, scales the parapet and
makes off with his second-in-command under a hail of bullets,
which, however, do not hit them until they are just on board
again."

Captain Palmes tells me nothing of this incident in his letter ;
but the fact remains that his aged torpedo-boat did excellent
service in the Canal, and he himself received the D.S.O.

" After that," he goes on to say, " the flotilla went up together
under their own steam to Mudros," off the Dardanelles, " where
one ran out of coal and was wrecked on Lemnos." This was
Torpedo-Boat 046, which is down in the official " Navy Losses "
as having been " Wrecked by heavy weather while in tow in the
Eastern Mediterranean " on December 27th, 1915.

" The other five did boom patrols and submarine hunting,"
writes Captain Palmes. " With reference to a T.B. which capsized in tow in the Mediteranean," he adds, " I have reason to
remember this grim incident, as during the two years I was at
Malta in charge of the torpedo-boats I could never induce the
Admiral to let me go for a cruise round Sicily. He always quoted

[1] Commandant Paul Chack in *On se bat sur Mer*, translated from the French
by Commander L. B. Denman, R.N. as *Sea Fights, 1914–1918*.

the above case to show that these ancient T.B.s were unseaworthy. The incident happened, I believe, some five or six years before 1912. The boat was being towed, and broached to and capsized, drowning several of the crew. These T.B.s were very bad sea-boats, long, and of narrow beam. My own ship, 043, nearly foundered off Crete on the way from Malta to Egypt – and, indeed, would have been lost but for the good seamanship of the captain of a storeship, who poured oil to windward and saved me."

But the fact that they were bad sea-boats and dangerous did not prevent these twenty-five to thirty-year-old veterans from playing their part in the Great War. All honour to those who manned and built them.

CHAPTER XXIII

BAD WEATHER

I

I HAVE sometimes been asked what it is like to be in a real gale of wind in a destroyer. It is rather a difficult question to answer. So much depends upon the strength of the gale, the height of the sea, the size of the destroyer, and whether one is steaming with the sea or against it.

In the days before the war, serving in the old 27- and 30-knotters of something under 400 tons, we had our fair share of bad weather. These little ships, with their sharp bows and low turtle-back forecastles, used sometimes to dive through the seas, bringing them green and solid on to the bridge, and drenching us with spray in anything approaching a stiff breeze. They were lively, too. On the other hand, none of our cruises were really long. We were generally going from port to port in the British Isles, and, if the weather was really bad, we could usually run for shelter. If we did have to weather out a gale at sea, we could choose our own speed.

The average destroyers of the war period were ships of about 1,000 tons, craft far more weatherly and roomier than the older ones built between 1894 and 1899 in which most of us had served our early apprenticeship in the destroyer service.

In war, however, we could not run for shelter when things became really uncomfortable. We were generally in company with battleships and cruisers as an anti-submarine screen, and if they could stick the weather, we had to. Moreover, we could not choose our own speed, but had to steam the speed of the fleet or squadron.

It was no unusual thing for destroyers to have their bridges knocked flat, and most of us suffered damage at one time or another. Read what Captain the Hon. Barry Bingham says in writing[1] of the 780-ton *Tigress* – he himself was serving in her sister ship, the *Hornet*: " To steam 20 knots with the battle-cruisers in practically all weathers was no sinecure, and, while these enormous ships were slipping along comfortably, the unhappy destroyers were having a bad time of it. One could

[1] *Falklands, Jutland, and the Bight.* (John Murray.)

only marvel at the way they jumped and dodged the waves of a long head sea. But every now and then you would catch a huge wave in the wrong stride, and a sheer wall of green sea would fall over the whole ship. When the bridge started carrying away, we thought it was time to 'submit' this fact to the admiral, requesting permission to ease down a few knots.

"The *Tigress*, one of the destroyers in my division – in fact, my sub-divisional mate [1] – encountered one of these enormous seas, which struck her fair and with sufficient force to drive the bridge rails about four feet aft on the compass and to pin her captain, Lieutenant-Commander Paul Whitfield, [1] between the two. He broke two ribs and sustained some internal damage, yet nevertheless continued in command."

But even when alone it was not advisable for destroyers to be too leisurely. "Fritz," the ubiquitous German submarine, used sometimes to slam in a torpedo at anything he saw provided he had a fair chance of hitting. I remember one of the Harwich Force destroyers, the *Moorsom*, being torpedoed off the Maas Lightship, a favourite lurking-ground for U-boats. The *Moorsom* was steaming 20 knots when hit, and the torpedo duly exploded in an upheaval of smoke and spray. But nobody can have been more surprised than the submarine's commander when the destroyer steamed off at 15 knots until she was out of harm's way. The torpedo had exploded against her rudder, detaching the A bracket of one propeller from the hull, and loosening the other. Her escape was one of the many lucky ones of the war. Had it struck amidships – indeed, almost anywhere else – she must have been brought to a standstill, when another shot would have finished her.

Apart from one or two expeditions to the Skager Rack, when we had a severe pounding, I think the worst trip I ever experienced in a destroyer was in January 1918, when, in the *Telemachus*, we were ordered to proceed north-about from the Firth of Forth to Avonmouth for our biennial refit. Avonmouth was at the very opposite end of the British Isles – 690 miles if we went round the north of Scotland and through the Irish Sea; about 60 miles more via the east coast of England and the Channel.

[1] Captain (then Commander) the Hon. Barry Bingham, V.C., O.B.E., and Captain (then Lieutenant-Commander) Paul Whitfield, D.S.O., O.B.E., were also sub-divisional mates at Jutland, the first in the *Nestor*, and the latter in the *Nomad*. Both these ships were sunk after making a gallant attack upon the enemy battle-cruisers, their surviving officers and men being afterwards rescued by the Germans. The incident has been described elsewhere in this volume.

Having arrived in harbour at 7 a.m. after three days' buffeting at sea, we received orders a few hours later to sail at 5.30 p.m. The weather was vile, with a strong north-easterly breeze and occasional flurries of snow and sleet, so thick that they shut out all view of the Forth Bridge, about half a mile downstream. It was a filthy day. The needle of the aneroid had been travelling anti-clockwise for thirty-six hours, and still continued to fall. I heard the quartermaster of the forenoon watch, a hoary-headed mariner, sucking his teeth with astonishment when he gazed at it at about noon to enter the reading in the deck log.

" What's the matter, Jevons ? " I asked him.

" I can't make it out no'ow, sir," he replied, tapping the glass with a gloved finger. " I've never seen the likes of it – goin' backwards all the time. Maybe it's out of order, sir."

I shook my head. The aneroid was telling a dismal tale ; but it was a true one.

We were in for a dusting.

We got it.

2

By 5.40 p.m., at which time it was dark, we were steaming under the great arch of the Forth Bridge with the white, red, white lights glimmering high overhead to show that the inner anti-submarine net had been lowered for our benefit. Steaming on past a line of lighted buoys to starboard, we came to the inner boom, its southern entrance marked by trawlers showing red and green lights. We passed on through the outer gate, increased speed to 20 knots, and were soon abeam of Inchkeith, whose searchlight promptly demanded our name. There were still the outer anti-submarine defences to be negotiated, the heavy boom and nets between Elie and Fidra Island, almost at the entrance to the Firth.

Getting in or out of the Firth of Forth in wartime was not particularly easy. Four separate systems of anti-submarine defences had to be passed through. It was as well. On September 2nd, 1914, late at night, the German submarine U.21, commanded by Lieutenant Hersing, had crept up as far as the Forth Bridge before she was detected. Unable to attack the men-of-war above it, she was forced to retreat, and three days later sank the first man-of-war ever destroyed by a torpedo fired from a submarine. This was the light-cruiser *Pathfinder*, torpedoed off St. Abb's Head on the afternoon of September 5th, 1914.

About two hours after leaving our buoy we were passing May Island, the light on which was shown for our especial benefit.

We fixed our position accurately, switched off navigation lights, steamed on for a mile or two, and then altered course to the northward up the Scottish coast.

Shore lights were not ordinarily displayed in wartime as they helped enemy submarines. There were no outlying dangers, however, beyond the Bell Rock, off which we were steering well clear. We had asked for the lights at Girdleness, near Aberdeen, and Rattray Head and Kinnaird Head, farther north, to be shown between certain stated times, allowing for a speed of 20 knots. The wind, still blowing very hard, was in the north-north-west. We were anxious to make good going while under the lee of the coast. Once past Kinnaird Head and into the open stretch of water off the Moray Firth, we might expect a heavy sea. I was aiming to make Duncansby Head, at the eastern end of the Pentland Firth, soon after daybreak.

For over a hundred miles the going was good, for there was nothing really vicious about the sea. But the cold was uncomfortable. The thermometer was well below 32°, with the spray freezing as it fell. Moreover, we had frequent snow squalls, until the bridge and mast were well covered in ice.

We duly sighted Girdleness, Rattray Head, and Kinnaird Head lights, and at about 1.20 a.m. altered course to the north-north-west for Duncansby Head, about eighty miles on. Almost as soon as we left the shelter of the land the sea became heavier and steeper, and the old ship began to tumble about with a violent corkscrew motion as only a destroyer can. We had eased to 14 knots; but, even so, the ship was pitching heavily into the head sea, flinging her bows dizzily into the air at one moment, and under water the next. Occasional green seas smashed over the forecastle and thudded against the bridge, while the spray drove over in sheets and stung our faces like hail.

It was bowling really hard, with the wind booming and shrilling through our scanty rigging. Ahead, the sea was faintly phosphorescent. I could see nothing but a confused maelstrom of leaping white, and the foaming summits of the nearer waves as they drove towards us. The upper deck was constantly buried in breaking water as they surged on board and went racing madly aft. The ship was bumping badly, sometimes flinging her stern out of water until the propellers raced madly in air. There was nothing for it but to ease down.

We tried her at 12 knots; but even this was too much. We eased to 10, at which she no longer crashed and threatened to break herself in halves. She rode easier, though the motion was still frightful.

Pyke, the pale-faced, seasick signalman, was crouched over a bucket in the tail of the bridge. He was never happy at sea, poor fellow, and, glancing at him, I thought of what it must be like on the fœtid, sloppy mess-decks under the forecastle.

Contrary to popular belief, a good many sailors are still seasick, even destroyer sailors.

Turning the ship over to the officer of the watch, I retired to the chart house below the bridge, to find the usual scene of desolation. The violent rolling and pitching had unshipped every movable fitting from its place and had hurled it on to the deck. A trickle of dirty water from a faulty pipe connection in the roof dripped steadily on to the cushioned settee which served as my bed. The two steel doors, normally watertight, admitted streams of water every time a sea broke on board.

It was cold and damp and miserable. The drawers under the chart-table containing the chart folios were slowly disgorging their contents on to the already littered deck covered with six inches of dirty water swishing dismally from side to side. It was a gruesome sight.

I salved some books, some bound copies of Sailing Directions, an unbroken cup, a tin of biscuits, my spare sea-boots, the sub-lieutenant's sextant, a pair of parallel rulers, and a tin of cigarettes. But no sooner had I wedged them in what I fondly imagined were safe positions than they fell down again. Rather than wedge the books in the bookshelf over the settee, where, as likely as not, they would work themselves loose and descend in an avalanche on my head as I tried to sleep, I let them lie.

Taking off my dripping oilskins and sodden muffler, I arrayed myself in a tolerably dry " lammy coat " and tapped on the little window of the wireless-office behind the chart house.

It flicked open, to display the red face of Biddle, the leading telegraphist, with a pair of telephone receivers clipped over his ears. Biddle enjoyed what is popularly known as a " fug." His cubby-hole was perhaps six feet square, littered all over with the mysterious instruments of his calling, and with just sufficient room on the deck for a chair, a desk, and a box of confidential books. With all his ventilators tight shut, the electric light blazing, the radiator full on, and the ship rolling and pitching drunkenly, he was literally stewing in his own juice. Biddle had a hardened stomach, and was even smoking. But the wave of heated air which smote me in the face caused me to step back hastily. It smelt of overhearted humanity, damp serge, acrid cigarette smoke, and the stench of hot metal.

" Aren't you rather hot in there ? " I asked him.

Biddle laughed. Indeed no, he replied, it was just nice and snug.

" Has anything been coming through ? " I enquired.

" Nothing much, sir," he answered. " Some of the destroyer patrols in the Pentland Firth have been reporting very bad weather, that's all. They've been ordered to return to base."

I groaned inwardly. In eight hours or so we should be in the Pentland Firth ourselves. If the patrols had been withdrawn, it meant we were in for a real snorter.

3

When daylight came at about 7.30 land was in sight on the port bow. It was not until two hours later, however, that we rounded Duncansby Head and altered course to the westward through the Pentland Firth.

It was a grey morning, with a few stray gleams of wintry sunlight flickering through the dark snow-clouds scurrying down from windward on the wings of the gale. The sea, with the wind blowing against the tide, was very confused. The waves rose and fell in no regular cadence, rearing themselves up perpendicularly to topple in yeasty white. At times, charging furiously together, the spray of their impact went hurtling to leeward in sheets of flying spindrift. The wind, if anything, had increased.

We staggered on through the Firth. Land lay on both sides. On the starboard bow, within a mile and a half, was the rocky islet of Swona, veined with the snow lying in its gullies and its low summit covered with a mantle of white. Beyond, from right ahead to well abaft the starboard beam, lay Hoy, Flotta Island, and South Ronaldshay, the southern islands of the Orkney group guarding the great expanse of Scapa Flow. Looking through glasses, one could see masts just showing over the distant hills, for inside, in the landlocked anchorage, lay the Grand Fleet.

The hills and mountains looked very bleak and barren, tier upon tier of white-capped hummocks fading into the dim distance, their lower slopes streaked with lying snow. The mountains of Hoy, fine on the starboard bow, shone intensely white when touched by the errant gleams of sunlight, then disappeared altogether as the dense snow flurries drove down from the northward.

On our port bow lay Stroma with its lighthouse, and beyond, terminating to the west in the bold mass of Dunnet Head, was the mainland of Scotland, Caithness. It was a forbidding-looking shore, the wind-driven water surging madly against the rocks off the sheer cliffs.

The Pentland Firth had always had an evil reputation among seamen. Its tides are strong; its eddies and whirlpools uncertain. Even great battleships, for no apparent reason, have been suddenly swirled through a right angle or more out of their course. But in a gale of wind its dangers are magnified a hundred-fold. The tide sometimes runs at 10 knots, and the wind, blowing against it, is apt to raise a toppling sea sufficient to overwhelm an ill-found vessel. Many a light-cruiser or destroyer has limped into Scapa Flow with her bridge beaten flat, and boats, and possibly men, washed overboard. Even a battleship, steaming westward against a gale, had her bridge completely removed by an enormous sea which broke on board in a liquid avalanche and flooded the ship with hundreds of tons of water.

So it behoved us to be careful.

It would be dark by 4.0 p.m. I had no wish to struggle on during the night through the Minch and Little Minch, between the Outer Hebrides and the west coast of Scotland. Lights were few and far between, and the Shiant Islands lay right in mid-channel. If we did ask for the lights to be shown, we might never sight them if it really came on to snow. What we had in mind was to push on as fast as possible during the day, so as to arrive before dark at Loch Ewe, some fifty miles down the coast from Cape Wrath. There we would spend the night.

Alas for our good intentions!

Once out of the lee of the Orkneys the sea rapidly got worse. We were steaming along towards Cape Wrath with the gale on our starboard beam and nothing between us and Iceland. Seldom have I experienced such motion. Yawing wildly in her course, the ship was rolling as much as fifty degrees to leeward. We had to lash ourselves on to the bridge rails to remain upright.

One is accused of exaggeration if one describes a sea as " mountainous," though mountainous, compared with ourselves, this sea certainly seemed to be – great hills of grey water streaked and topped with white which seemed to reach as high as our masthead as we sank into the valleys between them. The ship, borne skywards on a crest, leant drunkenly over on her side and seemed to slide down the next watery abyss. Occasionally, as a comber caught her bows and drove her off her course, the forecastle buried itself in the water and the stern was well in the air, with the rudder and propellers useless, while her midship portion, straddled awkwardly across the back of the wave, would be overwhelmed in a boiling cataract eight feet deep. Then, as the sea drove on and the bows lifted, the stern fell into the next hollow, and another watery avalanche broke over our tail.

We were battened down, with life-lines rigged along the deck. Even so, it was only possible to get from aft forward, or vice versa, by watching for a lull and taking a chance of being washed overboard. If anyone had gone, no boat could have been lowered to rescue him. We should have had to try picking him up from the ship.

The sea had already made a clean sweep of the canopies over the wardroom and cabin hatches in the stern. I had no wish to see the flimsy circular hatches beaten in, and the stern compartments flooded.

But what could one do?

The helmsmen did their utmost to keep the ship on her course. If they could keep her from yawing, things were more or less satisfactory beyond the rolling, and we took no heavy water on board. The wheel was never still; but there was no holding her within thirty or forty degrees of her course as she was buffeted alternately on bow and stern. She was here, there, and everywhere. Wet through and numb with cold, the quartermasters were soon tired out. We had them relieved every half-hour.

We were moving along in a sort of zigzag crawl. It was manifestly impossible to reach Loch Ewe before dark. What should we do?

I made up my mind to anchor in some sheltered anchorage that we could reach before dark, and to sail again next morning. Whatever happened, I was determined not to attempt the Minches by night.

Going down to the chart house and hanging on by our eyelids, the first lieutenant and myself hauled out a chart or two and examined the Sailing Directions. The nearest anchorage was twelve miles down the coast from Cape Wrath, and its name was Loch Inchard. It was a narrow fiord about four miles long, "little used by shipping," said the Sailing Directions, "partly in consequence of the entrance being difficult to make out from seaward." Moreover, it seemed that the average width of the loch was little more than 600 yards, while within half a mile of the entrance lay the unmarked Bodha Ceann na Salie, a submerged rock with a least depth of twelve feet. The *Telemachus* drew fourteen and a half feet of water to the tips of her propellers.

On the whole, Loch Inchard did not sound particularly inviting, though it did afford a sheltered anchorage farther up which should be unaffected by any wind that blew. But it was literally the only port in a storm – Hobson's choice. We made up our mind to go there.

We staggered on towards Cape Wrath – rolling, lurching, and pitching, flung about like an empty cask in the great seas. The snow seemed to be increasing, for frequent squalls shut down the visibility to a few hundred yards. In the intervals we could see the coast to port. Its snow-covered mountains, dark cliffs, and welter of breaking water looked grim and menacing, altogether horrible.

The distance from the Pentland Firth to Cape Wrath is a bare sixty miles. It was the longest sixty miles I have ever travelled !

The galley fire had long since been put out by a sea, so that hot food was impossible. When I sent for the coxswain to enquire as to what had been done about the men's dinner, he grinned sadly and replied that most of them required no nourishment at all. They wished to lie down and die, and that speedily. For those who were strong enough to eat, we contrived hot cocoa and thick bully-beef sandwiches – that and their rum ration. My own lunch, eaten on the bridge, consisted of slightly thinner sandwiches well flavoured with sea-water.

It was not until 2.30 that we saw the irregular hummock of Cape Wrath with the lighthouse on its summit. Seldom have I seen a spectacle to compare with the sight of the huge seas breaking against that wall of dark cliff. Great hillocks flung themselves at its rocky base, to burst in upheavals of spray a full seventy feet high. The body of each wave, recoiling seaward after its fruitless effort to breach the solid rock, impacted against its successor, so that the coast was fringed with half a mile of whitened, leaping water which rioted in all directions, tumbling, playing madly. It was fascinating to watch. I began to realise then why some mediæval mariner, clawing his way round that promontory in his crazy sailing-ship, had christened it Cape Wrath.

Passing it by, we gradually hauled round to the southward. I looked anxiously aft as we turned, for the alteration of course would bring the stern swinging into the sea. For a few moments all went well. Then, as luck would have it, the bows lifted on the back of a huge wave, and the stern sank into the next hollow.

A hillock of grey water, steep and sheer like a wall, white capped and foaming, towered up astern and started gradually to overtake us. I watched it, fascinated. For a few breathless moments it hung there, its crest overhanging the quarterdeck by fully twenty feet. It came nearer – nearer. Would the stern never rise ?

Then the after part of the ship started to lift ever so slowly. But it was too late. The curling summit of the sea tottered, fell on board with a crash which made the whole ship tremble.

For what seemed an eternity the after part of the ship remained buried in the heart of the sea. All I could see was the mizzenmast standing up out of the whitened water. We had sent down a message for nobody to remain on the upper deck before we altered course, and I prayed fervently that no man was on the quarterdeck when that wave overwhelmed it. Then the stern rose, the water cascading forward and overboard in a miniature Niagara.

We increased speed to 15 knots. The ship yawed wildly ; but the increase certainly saved us from being " pooped " again.

The shore, composed of peculiar reddish cliff, was only a couple of miles or so to port. We sped by a ten-fathom patch upon which the seas, suddenly checked in their deep-water stride, burst furiously. We passed a rocky little island, its rounded summit almost obliterated in sheets of flying spray.

But half an hour later we had steered in towards the land and were steaming by Eileen an Roin – the Island of the Seals – at the entrance to our harbour. Once under the lee of the land the sea started to go down, and a few minutes later we were travelling up the narrow inlet of Loch Inchard with the snow-covered hills on either side. The gale, whistling round the gullies, sent the powdery snow flying. But in the sheltered loch the water was flat calm. The ship was on an even keel again.

We steamed on, hugging the shore to port to avoid the rocks in mid-channel, and passing two little clusters of houses which looked more like Esquimau *igloos* than civilised habitations. The ship's company, rubbing their eyes, came on deck and looked about them. Their cigarettes and pipes appeared.

A boatswain's pipe twittered :

" Ha-ands bring ship to our anchor ! "

Five minutes later the engines were stopped, and the anchor went to the bottom with the cheerful rattle of cable.

I fixed the position of the ship on the chart by cross-bearings, waited until she had " got " her cable, and then left the bridge. Half-way down the ladder I had an inspiration, and called to the coxswain.

" Sir ? "

" Issue an extra rum ration at supper-time."

" Extra rum ration, sir ! " he started to object. " We can't——"

" We will ! " I cut him short. " If the powers that be ask you why, refer them to me."

" Aye, aye, sir," he replied, not at all displeased.

I went to my cabin to change into something dry, perhaps to have a bath. But the moment I saw the stern at close quarters I knew the worst. Practically everything except the after gun had been swept overboard, even the after binnacle.

The wardroom, two feet deep in water, was a scene of chaos. I swallowed some raw whisky, and retired to my cabin, to find it even worse. My steward, busy with a bucket and my bath sponge, was trying to compete with the flood. All my most treasured possessions had been hurled to the deck. Books, boots, and clothing had joined forces on the floor with my typewriter, all the contents of the drawers in my writing-table, and the half-finished manuscript of a book whereof all the typing had run.

It was a grisly scene.

I got my bath two hours later.

The thermometer was still below freezing.

I did not escape a raging cold in the head which lasted the whole of my ten days' leave.

My typewriter was never quite the same afterwards. Undoubtedly it was our worst journey.

4

At eight next morning, fortified after a night's rest, we resumed our journey southward. The gale still raged furiously, but the wind and sea were astern. In the intervals between the snow-squalls the sun shone out in a pale blue sky.

We went on at 20 knots, and by 11.30 were steaming down the Inner Sound between Raasay and the mainland, with the hills on either hand. Far away to starboard the snow-clad mountains of Skye shimmered silver-blue and gold, as if cast in solid ice. Through the Kyle of Loch Alsh and the narrows of Kyle Akin to Sleat Sound. Then on through a stretch of open water, past the islands of Rum and Eigg and Muck – delicious names – to Ardnamurchan Point.

At 2.30 we were abreast of Tobermory on our way down the Sound of Mull. At anchor inside the little harbour was a convoy of colliers, oilers, and storeships on their way up to the Grand Fleet, escorted by a couple of destroyers, with whom we exchanged signals. They had been ordered to wait, partly because of the gale, partly because enemy submarines, driven from the open sea by the weather, had been reported in the more sheltered waters of the Minches farther north.

The rest of our journey was practically uneventful, and by 9.30 in the evening we were passing Rathlin Island. Steaming down the Irish Sea was strange after the North Sea. All the shore lights and lightships were in full operation, and one by one they hove in sight over the horizon on both sides, winked at us in friendly fashion, and then, having served their purpose so far as we were concerned, faded away astern. It was quite like peace.

Soon after 11 p.m. we exchanged signals with a solitary destroyer, the *Racoon*, battling against the sea on her way back to Buncrana, Lough Swilly, while the next morning we were rounding Pembrokeshire on our way up the Bristol Channel to Avonmouth, where we arrived in the afternoon.

In the newspapers a few days later we read an Admiralty *communiqué* – " *Early in the morning of January 9th one of H.M. destroyers was wrecked off the north coast of Ireland. It is regretted there were no survivors. All the next of kin have been informed."*

It was the *Racoon*, commanded by Lieutenant George L. M. Napier, the very ship we had passed and with whom we had exchanged signals. Little did we think when we saw her that within three hours every soul on board her would have perished.

In the pitch darkness and driving snow she struck the rocks within a few miles of the entrance to Lough Swilly. Nobody will ever know the exact circumstances of her loss. But the northerly gale was still raging, and one can imagine that little ship, reeling and lurching, groping her way towards the land in the midst of a blinding snow-squall, with the officers and men on her bridge endeavouring to see ahead. It was anxious work ; but those on board were probably optimists, with little doubt in their minds that within one hour or two they would be safely at anchor and asleep in their bunks or hammocks.

Imagine the black shadow of a wall of rock suddenly looming

up out of the darkness close ahead, and the fringe of leaping, whitened water surging round its base. An agonised scream from the men on the look-out, the clang of the engine-room telegraphs as they were rattled over to " Full astern " – for the last time. Too late.

A crashing, rending thud, which tore the bottom out of the ship as she drove ashore, lifted on a giant sea, and crashed again. Wave after wave breaking on board, to sweep men and deck fittings into the sea. Then a sickening lurch as she was lifted again and hurled broadside on to the rocks, to be battered to pieces, disintegrated.

We do not know the end of her officers and men, or of how, with their ship breaking up beneath their feet, they were torn one by one from their hand-holds to be drowned in the pitiless sea, or dashed to death among those cruel rocks. It is a mercy we do not.

5

It was three days after the loss of the *Racoon*, on January 12th, 1918, that the destroyers *Narbrough* and *Opal* were wrecked on the Pentland Skerries while returning to Scapa Flow in the midst of a gale of wind and a blinding snowstorm.

" Bartimeus " – otherwise Paymaster-Commander L. A. da C. Ricci, R.N. – has told the story under the title of " The Survivor " in one of his books called *The Navy Eternal*.[1] He wrote it in the form of fiction ; but as at that time he had access to the official reports, and was permitted to write subject to the usual censorship, his tale is substantially a true one.

The two destroyers had accompanied a cruiser to the eastward from Scapa Flow, but had been ordered to return to the base on account of the weather. Shuddering as they clove their way through the mountainous seas, they thankfully put their helms over and altered course to the westward, surveying their battered bridges and streaming decks, thinking of hot food, warm bunks, and hammocks, and all the creature comforts so dear to those who go down to the sea in small ships. It was bitterly cold, with the spray freezing as it fell. It blew a howling gale from the westward, and the dark clouds banked up ahead betokened snow. Then it came.

" It started with great whirling flakes like feathers about a gull's nesting-place," " Bartimeus " wrote, " a soundless ethereal

[1] Published by Messrs. Hodder & Stoughton.

vanguard of the storm, growing momentarily denser. The wind, from a temporary lull, reawakened with a roar. The air became a vast witch's cauldron of white and brown specks, seething before the vision in a veritable Bacchanal of Atoms. Sight became a lost sense : time, space, and feeling were overwhelmed by that shrieking fury of snow and frozen spray thrashing pitilessly about the homing grey hulls and the bowed heads of the men who clung to the reeling bridges. The grey, white-crested seas raced hissing alongside, and, as the engine-room telegraphs rang again and again for reduced speed, overtook and passed them."

" Sight became a lost sense." In the welter of snow and spray, with an utter lack of knowledge as to what speed the ships might be making good through the pounding, crashing seas, the exact position was more or less a matter of conjecture when once the visibility closed down to practically nothing. Moreover, the tides in the Pentland Firth are strong and erratic.

The *Narbrough* and *Opal* wallowed on.

An able seaman, No. 3 at the midship gun of the leading destroyer, flapped his arms to induce some semblance of warmth into his numbed fingers. He gazed forward towards the bridge, all but blotted out from view in the whirling snowflakes. With a supreme faith in those responsible for the safety of the ship, he felt no particular anxiety, for bad weather was no new thing. He was accustomed to heavy seas, to biting cold, to snow, and to fog. All he longed for was for the ship to be on an even keel again ; for that, and for hot food and a chance to warm his chilled limbs.

Nobody can say quite how it happened ; but through a rift in the veil of driving snowflakes those on the bridge must suddenly have caught sight of a parapet of rock close ahead, with the snow lying thickly in its gullies and crevices, and the sea surging tumultuously round its base.

The engine-room gongs clanged madly ; but it was too late.

The ship struck with a shuddering crash – lifted, was hurled forward on the back of a huge billow, struck again, and lurched over. A mighty wave towered up over her stern, broke thundering on board, and drove forward along the upper-deck to fill the engine-room.

The destroyer astern drove past with her siren yelping, her engines racing astern, but helpless to check her way in the seething backwash off the reef. She also struck, recoiled, struck again, and was thrown bodily on to the rocks with the seas erupting over her.

The able seaman on the gun platform of the leading destroyer was swept off his feet by a billow. Knocked against a funnel stay, he clung to it with grim desperation. The water receded. He managed to climb higher, until he was six feet above the crests of the highest waves.

The other destroyer had disappeared in the welter. He saw the forecastle of his own ship broken off and swept aside like a plaything, while on the deck beneath him some of his shipmates tried to launch a Carley float. He saw them swept away, to vanish in the smother of whitened foam.

The ship was rapidly being beaten out of existence. The wire to which he clung alternately sagged and tautened, threatened to hurl him overboard as if from a catapult.

Then the funnel itself, hammered by wave after wave, began to lean drunkenly over the side of the ship. The seaman, swaying to and fro, found himself suspended over the maelstrom. In a moment or two a racing sea tore him from his precarious hand-hold and hurled him into the water.

Plunged deep beneath the surface, his next feelings were those of bitter cold and suffocation. He came gasping to the surface, instantly to be hurled forward in the grasp of a mighty comber. By the mercy of Providence he missed the jagged fangs of rock, to find himself afloat inside a tiny cove edged with dark, threatening-looking cliffs all streaked with lying snow.

A wave rose behind, lifted him, and shot him forward at dizzying speed, straight towards the rocky base of the cliffs where the breakers surged and tumbled riotously. Then, caught in the backwash, sucked under water, flung head over heels, another sea flung him bodily on to a beach of pebbles. Battered and breathless, he managed to stagger forward a few paces before falling to his hands and knees on the edge of a snow-drift. For the time being, he was out of reach of those murderous waves.

Regaining his breath, he sat up and stared seaward. The dusk was falling. Nothing could be seen of the remains of those two destroyers – nothing but a succession of steep, smoking rollers moving relentlessly shoreward.

He was quite alone. Not a sign of another human being could be seen, not a soul drifting shoreward on some pitiful piece of flotsam.

Scrambling to his feet, he wondered what he should do. The

tiny beach upon which he stood would soon be covered by the incoming tide. Behind him, on all sides save to seaward, he was penned in by a buttress of sheer cliff. It seemed unclimbable.

But there was nothing for it but to climb if he wished to avoid being drowned or battered to pieces. Numbed with cold, his strength nearly exhausted, he started to claw his way up the steep rock.

The jagged edges and barnacles tore the skin from his hands as he fought his way up inch by inch, foot by foot. Three times, trusting his weight to an insecure hand-hold, he slipped and fell back to the bottom. At last, reaching a ledge half-way up, he rested awhile before continuing the dizzy ascent.

Within six feet of the summit he again had the misfortune to slip, to tumble heavily down to the ledge. Bruised, bleeding, his strength gone, he lay for a while. Then a sea broke over the ledge, drove him to his feet.

Utterly exhausted, he could do no more. The next heavy wave would filch him from his resting-place.

But the tide had reached its highest, though it was two hours or more, two hours of agony, during which he listened to the seas breaking and crashing in fury all round him, before he realised it.

Towards midnight, when the tide had fallen, he crept down from his ledge and followed the retreating water, filled with the idea that he could hear voices out at sea. The coming of the flood-tide drove him back to his eyrie, and the chill, grey dawn found him once more on his ledge, picking limpets from the rocks for a meal.

The sea was a riot of leaping breakers. It was nearly high-water. Of the remains of the *Narbrough* and *Opal* not a glimpse could be seen. No other man was anywhere in sight. Alone on that tiny, rocky islet, the able seaman must be the only survivor. The full realisation of the horror of it suddenly broke in upon him. One hundred and eighty odd of his shipmates and flotilla-mates had gone to their deaths within a hundred yards or so of where he lay. Unless some miracle had happened, he, only, remained alive. Alive, yes ; but would anyone find him before he perished from exposure and exhaustion ?

During the morning the weather brightened a little, and he saw some destroyers well out to seaward. They were searching for traces of their lost consorts. The A.B., tying his jumper to a piece of driftwood for a flag, waved it to and fro to attract their attention. But he was too far away for his signal to be sighted against the dark background, and those friendly ships, rolling and pitching in the seas, sometimes blotted out in driving spray, passed on, to vanish behind a headland.

It was not until the succeeding low tide, when the mangled steel-work of the wrecks was showing above the breaking water on the reefs, that another destroyer came into sight. The sharp eyes on her bridge, with their glasses on the little island, must have seen that tangled débris, for she slewed round, came slowly in towards the cove, stopped, and went astern.

His heart buoyed up with hope, the able seaman madly waved his flag. His signal was seen. The destroyer's siren wailed mournfully. He watched her lower a boat, watched it pull cautiously shoreward, at times all but disappearing in the troughs of the seas.

It was bitterly cold ; but the wildly plunging boat came closer, the bowman, his oar boated, crouching in the bows with a heaving line ready. The officer in the stern anxiously regarded the cliffs. It was ticklish work. The sea was still heavy. If once the frail boat touched the rock, every mother's son of her crew would find himself in the icy water.

The whaler approached as close as she dared, and her crew held water. The man with the heaving line flung it shoreward, the end landing almost at the castaway's feet. The lieutenant shouted to him to tie it round his waist. The boat could come no nearer without disaster. They would pull him on board.

The able seaman obeyed, slipped off his ledge into the water, and felt himself pulled through it. A moment later he bumped the whaler's planking and felt himself lifted over the gunwale.

The mouth of a flask was rammed between his chattering teeth. He swallowed gratefully. Someone wrapped him round in a blanket. A few minutes more and he was being helped up the grey steel side of his saviour. He found himself seated in front of a blazing stove, while kind, rough hands removed his sodden clothing, chafed his numbed limbs and body. When the warmth came back, he felt bruised and aching all over. The palms of his hands and fingers were raw and bleeding from that ghastly tussle with the rocks.

He was the only survivor.

CHAPTER XXIV

THE TWENTIETH FLOTILLA

I

I DO not think that in 1914 anyone seriously contemplated minelaying from destroyers. Indeed, when the war started, the only minelayers we possessed were seven old second-class cruisers of the *Apollo* type, which had a speed of little more than 14 knots. These were used for laying the first minefields in the Dover Straits, which had the effect of compelling all neutral merchant-vessels to pass through the Downs, where they were examined for contraband by the Downs Boarding Flotilla.

The standard British mine of 1914, the " B.E.," or British Elia, was popularly and rightly considered a " dud." It had a cumbrous cross-bar firing arrangement on top, and, judging from the numbers we habitually met at sea in the early months of the war and sank by gun or rifle fire, hundreds must have broken adrift from their moorings to drift aimlessly about the ocean.

The German horned mines, on the other hand, were unpleasantly potent, and early in the war large numbers were laid by surface ships off the east coast in positions where they were likely to damage naval vessels. The *Königin Luise*, for instance, a small converted German mail steamer, laid 150 on August 5th, 1914, the very day after war was declared. This ship was caught and sunk in daylight near the Galloper Lightship, by the light-cruiser *Amphion* and her destroyers from Harwich. On her way home, however, the *Amphion* herself ran into a minefield, and was blown up and sunk with a loss of 131 killed and drowned.

Another large German minefield laid early in the war was that placed thirty miles eastward of the Tyne, right in the usual track of shipping. We discovered it early on the morning of August 27th, 1914. I have reason to remember the occasion, as I happened at the time to be serving as the executive officer of the *Patrol*, the Captain (D)s ship of the local patrol flotilla.

We were lying at our moorings in the Tyne, and, as usual, I had turned out at 4 a.m. to keep the morning watch in the decoding office. At about 4.30 we received a wireless signal from one of our torpedo-boats patrolling outside to say that an Icelandic trawler had been blown up and sunk at 10 p.m. the night before. The survivors had been rescued by a South Shields drifter, which had communicated with the T.B. on her way in.

Our four minesweeping trawlers were sent off within an hour, but during the morning a small Norwegian steamer and a Danish sailing-vessel were both blown up and sunk. In the afternoon, too, two of the minesweeping trawlers shared the same fate, so that this one minefield accounted for 5 vessels, 3 of which were neutrals, and a loss of 20 men drowned, 15 of whom were neutrals. We thought at the time that it had been laid either to catch the battleship *Agincourt*, which had been built for the Turks and which had just been taken over by the Admiralty from her builders on the Tyne, Sir W. G. Armstrong, Whitworth & Co., or else to catch neutrals coming from Scandinavia.

I remember talking to the skipper of one of the blown-up mine-sweepers, an old North Country fisherman. He was in the wheel-house when the mine exploded under the ship's bottom. He didn't remember how he got out, but imagined he was blown through the roof, for the next thing he knew was when he found himself, drenched with water, running aft to hoist out the boat in the stern. The ship sank in five minutes, her boiler exploding as she went under.

He was a bit shaken, but full of pluck. We asked him what he intended to do. " Oh ! " said he, in broad North Country lingo, " I suppose they'll give me another trawler, so that I can have a bit of me' own back on them —— ! "

We had German mines on the brain after this, for undoubtedly they were efficacious. There was even a Naval and Military Conference to decide what should be done if suspicious vessels were sighted after dark off the Tyne or in the river itself. It resulted in an order being given by the responsible military authority that " No ships are to be afloat after sunset " ! A little drastic, we thought it. We realised, however, that the military gentleman's nautical terminology was at fault, and hastened to suggest a slight correction. An amendment came in due course : " In my Confidential Memorandum 54/B/2381, for ' afloat ' read ' under way.' "

Such slips of the pen occur in even the best-conducted circles. There was the occasion at the Royal Naval Staff College, when we were working out a scheme which involved the landing of troops on a hostile coast, when a very distinguished officer wrote in his orders : " The landing-places will be marked by black shapes by day and the same coloured lights by night " !

German minefields very soon appeared in increasing numbers, not merely off the east coast, but in the English Channel and still farther afield. Practically all of them were laid by submarines, and the positions chosen were most frequently near some focal point, headland, buoy, or lightship, or in the approaches to a naval or commercial port. The toll of our losses, principally merchant-men, increased rapidly.

It was not until 1917 that we had a really reliable mine of our own, and this was the " H.2 " mine with horns, of practically identical type to the German. And not until the end of this year were they being manufactured in sufficient quantities to make offensive minelaying on any considerable scale a practical pos-sibility.

As regards additional minelayers, four fast mail steamers were taken over soon after the outbreak of war and converted, being so successful that others were soon pressed into service. As time went on, however, and the laying of regular mine barrages in the Dover Straits, off the Belgian coast, and in the Heligoland Bight became the accepted policy, an old battleship and some old cruisers, together with specially built minelaying submarines, and converted flotilla-leaders and destroyers, were all used for the same purpose.

It was a simple matter to convert the destroyers for their new function. Mines rest on sinkers, which have small rollers at the bottom, each mine on its sinker weighing about half a ton. All that was needed was two pairs of rails like narrow tram-lines, to be bolted in a fore and aft direction along the deck, and a couple of chutes to be built over the stern. The mines were hauled aft by a winch, and were released at regular time intervals by the simple operation of a lever. To compensate for their weight, which in the case of the smaller destroyers with forty mines was twenty tons, and in the larger ones about double, the after 4-inch gun and after pair of torpedo-tubes were temporarily removed. It took less than twelve hours to replace them, when the mine-layer again became an ordinary destroyer.

The *Abdiel*, a flotilla-leader, was the first vessel so converted. Commanded by Commander Berwick Curtis, she joined the Grand Fleet early in 1916, and was soon being used for laying her " eggs " in the German-swept channels round about the Horns Reef. She had the great advantage of speed—32 knots—and light draught, and, going out entirely unescorted, laid her mines by night.

Her efforts were most successful, and it was this little ship, it may be remembered, which was sent off by Sir John Jellicoe at 9.30 p.m. after the Battle of Jutland to lay mines off the Vyl Lightship, just south of the Horns Reef. She " carried out this operation unobserved in the same successful manner as numerous other similar operations have been undertaken by this useful little vessel," as Sir John wrote in his despatch.

Berwick Curtis,[1] who was promoted to captain in June, 1916, was afterwards our Captain (D) in the 20th (Minelaying) Destroyer Flotilla based on Immingham, in the Humber. I came to know him very well. Our work, which I shall describe later, was rather hair-raising at times. It involved steaming in over the enemy minefields during high-water at night and depositing our " eggs " in the German swept channels well inside the Heligoland Bight.

Things went wrong sometimes, as things must when one is lay-ing mines in a sort of complicated herring-bone pattern without lights, and often in vile weather and low visibility. " Budge " Curtis was not merely responsible for his own ship, but for seven or eight working in company. But never once did we see him the least perturbed or flustered. His language was sometimes a little florid about things that did not matter, though no worse than our own ; but the only time I saw him really annoyed was when the Admiralty issued an order making the wearing of the war service chevrons compulsory.

After a little preliminary damning and blasting, he stroked his reddish beard and looked at us with a twinkle in his blue eyes. " When they present me with a set I'll be delighted to wear 'em," he said. " But you blokes must put 'em up, otherwise I shall have to issue a written order."

So we ordered the newly authorised gee-gaws from our outfitters at considerable expense to ourselves – a silver chevron for 1914, and golden ones for 1915, 1916, and 1917. Captain Curtis, on the other hand, caused his to be applied to the right sleeve of his sea-going monkey-jacket with Service aluminium and yellow paint !

He was a charming man to serve with, unassuming, unselfish, and a firm believer in letting people do their job without fuss and bother. He detested petty supervision as he hated paper-work, inefficiency, and B.F.s, and backed up his subordinates through

[1] Now (February, 1931) Rear-Admiral Berwick Curtis, C.B., C.M.S., D.S.O. and Bar.

thick and thin. To him, shocking weather or alarming incidents were merely " pretty fruity."

The " mothers' meetings " which sometimes took place in the captain's cabin of the *Abdiel* before some operation or other were generally unconventional and amusing. " You fellows know what to do," Captain (D) used to say, " so for heaven's sake do it. I'll issue operation orders by semaphore on the way out, as usual." Moreover, he had rather an exhilarating brand of cocktail and a pretty taste in light sherry. I hope he has still.

Yes. Officers and men loved " Budge " Curtis. Without being a stickler for etiquette and ceremony, he had our supreme trust and confidence. We would cheerfully have followed him to hell.

2

My first introduction to the minelaying business in destroyers was when, six months after promotion to commander in December 1916, I was appointed to the *Telemachus* after 2½ years' service in the *Murray* at Harwich. I took over this ship from her builders on the Clyde, and we presently found ourselves at Rosyth as one of the ordinary destroyers of the 13th Flotilla attached to the Battle-Cruiser Fleet.

I have written elsewhere in this book of our work in the *Telemachus* as a destroyer ; but for the first seven months of the commission we never quite knew whether we were a destroyer or a minelayer. On more than one occasion, when at sea off the Firth of Forth, we received orders to return into harbour forthwith, to complete with oil-fuel, proceed into the basin at Rosyth dockyard, remove our after gun and torpedo-tubes, and to convert ourselves into a minelayer. It generally took five or six hours, after which we proceeded up the river to Grangemouth to embark our forty mines.

When we got really into the swing of it we could take these on board with cranes in something under an hour. What took the time was their testing, and waiting for the tide at Grangemouth, the entrance to which could only be negotiated for two hours on either side of high-water. We were generally ready for service, however, within twenty hours of receiving the signal to convert. Then came another trip down the river and the receipt of a secret envelope containing operation and sailing orders. Finally, after a signal " Prime mines," away we went on our mission.

The first operation in which we took part was one carried out from Dover on the night of July 13th–14th, 1917, when four destroyers, the *Telemachus* and *Tarpon* from Rosyth, and the *Meteor* and one other from Dover, laid a line of mines in enemy waters within ten miles of Ostend.

We sallied forth from Dunkerque after dark, attended by a considerable escort of ordinary destroyers. These were to do the fighting if we met the enemy, which was likely enough, as the Germans had powerful flotillas based on the Belgian coast. We, the minelayers, were to concentrate on laying the mines in their correct position, and were not to fight unless actually attacked. I don't think anyone relished the idea of a night engagement with mines on board. One had an idea that a single shell in amongst our explosive cargo would cause a pyrotechnic display thoroughly satisfying to onlookers, but highly disintegrating to ourselves.

Dunkerque was enduring one of its usual air-raids when we sailed, with bombs crashing in the town, anti-aircraft guns thudding, and the heavens ablaze with the fiery trails of tracer shell and the orange flashes of bursting projectiles. Nieuport, where the opposing lines met the sea, was also most spectacular. The undersides of the low, dark clouds flickered redly in and out with the reflection of gun-flashes. The sky was punctuated with the dazzling white glares of star-shell, and strings of brilliant green flares popularly known as " flaming onions." The dull rumble of guns from the land front echoed ceaselessly seaward throughout the night. It had continued for nearly four years. The soldiers ashore had our sincere sympathy.

What a devil of a neighbourhood were the approaches to Dunkerque in wartime, with the many shoals, thick weather, fierce tides, and few navigational marks or buoys to fix by. Leaving the glare of Nieuport behind us, however, we skirted the banks and steamed on towards our objective.

Zero time came, and the whole force eased down to 12 knots. The rear destroyer laid the first half of her mines, swung to port to lay the other half, and disappeared. No. 3 followed suit, turning to starboard to lay her last twenty mines. Then No. 2, which swung to port. The mines, by the time we had finished laying them, were intended to be placed something like this

twenty mines in each leg of each \/ so to speak, or 160 in all. The idea of the curious patterns was to make it more difficult for them to be located and swept up.

Our turn came. An order went aft through the voice-pipe, and with a splash the first " egg " fell into the sea and went bobbing astern in our wake before taking up its depth.

" One – two – three – four – five——" came up the voice-pipe at regular intervals, as we heard the splashes over the stern. " Fourteen – fifteen——" then a lengthy pause.

" What the blazes has happened ? " I asked hurriedly, for we were steaming at 12 knots, and had to lay the mines 150 feet apart, neither more nor less.

" A sinker's jammed on the rails, sir," came back the answer. " They're doing their best to clear it."

Profanity on my part.

" Sixteen ! " came from aft. Then another pause.

I asked the sub-lieutenant with his stop-watch how much longer we had to run before turning to lay the second leg of our line.

" Five seconds, sir," he replied.

I sent the first lieutenant flying aft to do what he could. Meanwhile, all I could do was to turn on time, and to lay twenty-four mines on the second leg instead of twenty.

" Time, sir," said the sub.

" Hard a port ! Steer south fifty-six east, coxswain ! "

The ship swung round, steadied in the new direction, and the laying recommenced ; but very irregularly.

We discovered afterwards that the hauling-aft motors had gone wrong at the critical moment. Moreover, we were using old pattern mines, and the rollers of several sinkers had jammed in a curve on the rails, necessitating each mine and sinker being lifted and dragged aft by brute force. On the face of it this does not sound difficult. But a mine on its sinker weighs nearly half a ton, and the men were working on a deck encumbered with obstructions and in pitch darkness. Lights were quite out of the question in enemy waters.

Nevertheless, pulling, hauling, straining, and blaspheming, they managed to get them over somehow.

" Thirty-one – thirty-two – thirty-three," came up the voice-pipe. " Thirty-four – thirty-five——"

" Ships on the port bow, sir ! " came the sudden hail of the man on the look-out.

He was right. I could see the white bow-waves and dark shapes of two vessels like destroyers steaming fast on a course opposite to our own. They would pass us at a distance of about 500 yards.

Our escort had altered course to the westward when we had turned out of the line. We were alone, and the newcomers, from their position and course, could only be Germans.

It was an anxious moment. We had been ordered not to fight with mines on board unless attacked, and here we were steaming at only 12 knots, with the mines still jammed aft and the enemy flashing past us at high speed. It was a dark night and very calm, with the sky heavily overcast with low cloud. A gentle drizzle had set in, and the visibility was gradually shutting down. Even so, I did not see how those Germans could avoid spotting us.

We trained our two remaining guns and solitary pair of torpedo-tubes upon them, ready to reply if they opened fire upon us. My heart was in my mouth as I waited for the flash and the report of the first gun ; but nothing happened. The interval between when those ships were sighted, flashed past our beam, and then vanished in the darkness on the port quarter cannot have been more than a few seconds. But it seemed more like five minutes to me, and, staring in the place where they had finally disappeared, I could hardly make up my mind that the whole incident was not a mere trick of the imagination.

" Good God ! What fools ! " the first lieutenant said, his voice full of relief.

" Thank heaven ! " murmured I.

I afterwards went on board the senior officer's ship of our escort to find out if, by any chance, they had got out of position and had steamed past us at the exact time we were able to give them. None of them had. The ships we had sighted were undoubtedly German, and they had missed a most glorious opportunity. I can only imagine that either they did not sight us, or, since we were steaming at slow speed straight for Ostend, that they took us for a friend.

As for ourselves, we bundled the rest of the mines overboard as fast as we could and steamed off at full speed in the direction in which they had disappeared. There was some hope of finding and bringing them to action. But we had no luck. The visibility had closed down. We never saw them again.

This was not the only incident of the night, for on her way back to Dunkerque the *Tarpon,* our sister ship from Rosyth, struck a mine aft and was badly damaged. She was towed into Dunkerque and patched up before being taken to an English dockyard for repairs. Practically the entire after part of the ship had to be rebuilt, and it was six months before she finally rejoined us.

The officers lost most of their kits, what clothes were not damaged by sea-water being ruined by oil fuel. Their chief complaint, however, was that their twenty-guinea gramophone in its rosewood case, recently bought in Edinburgh, had gone overboard through the huge gash in the hull. They had purchased it, I believe, on the instalment system. Hence their peevishness at having to continue the instalments for an instrument whose battered remains probably drifted ashore somewhere near Zeebrugge.

Thus ended our first minelaying experience in enemy waters.

From time to time during the ensuing year we were again sent to Dover to lay minefields off the Belgian coast. On one of these occasions, in August 1918, a whole flotilla of us laid " M. sinkers " off Zeebrugge. These were nasty-looking yellow things each weighing a ton, dome-shaped contrivances of solid concrete which went straight to the bottom and remained there. Inside, besides the heavy explosive charge of amatol, they were fitted with a magnetic device which caused them to explode if a steel or iron ship passed within about 150 feet. Though most of the first lot we laid blew up through some defect in their interiors within forty minutes of laying – that is, as soon as the soluble safety-plugs of sal-ammoniac had melted – they were fearsome contrivances when finally perfected, for the reason that, unlike moored mines, they could not be swept up by ordinary minesweepers. Indeed, when it came to their having to be removed after the war, they had to be searched for and exploded by wooden drifters towing magnetic sweeps.

I remember one rather amusing incident when five of we minelaying destroyers were lying off Dunkerque ready for an operation the same night, with our mines all ready and primed. It was pitch dark, and because of an expected enemy destroyer raid, we received sudden orders to weigh and shift billet to an anchorage farther up the coast. Dunkerque Roads were rather crowded, and, while steaming ahead, the *Ferret* grazed a French trawler lying at anchor. The *Ferret's* mine-traps happened to be open, and before anybody could stop them, the slight shock sent two mines on their sinkers trundling gaily aft and overboard.

The Frenchman, already sufficiently peevish at being rammed, flung up his hands in horror, and burst into a flood of Gallic profanity when informed in execrable French by the *Ferret's* captain that there were two mines under his stern which would become dangerous as soon as their soluble plugs melted – otherwise, within about half an hour !

3

It was in February 1918, with the formation of the 20th Destroyer Flotilla at Immingham, that our strenuous work in the Heligoland Bight really started. We were rather a hybrid collection, with the *Abdiel* – Captain Berwick Curtis – as our flotilla-leader. The *Vanoc*, Commander E. O. Tudor ; *Vanquisher*, Lieutenant-Commander K. A. Beattie ; *Venturous*, Lieutenant-Commander G. P. Bowles ; and *Vehement*, Lieutenant-Commander Hammersley-Heenan, were all destroyers of the then new " V " class, craft of 1,300 tons. The sister ships *Telemachus*, Commander Taprell Dorling, and *Tarpon*, Lieutenant-Commander F. E. Wright, were slightly older destroyers of the " Admiralty R " class of about 1,065 tons, while the *Legion*, Commander F. A. Clutterbuck, was one of the 965-ton "L" class, built before the war. The *Sandfly*, Lieutenant-Commander E. H. Dauglish, Royal Indian Marine ; the *Ariel*, Lieutenant Rothera ; and the *Ferret*, Lieutenant A. H. L. Terry, were all 765-ton destroyers completed three years before the war.

Our task, which was to lay mines in the enemy swept channels in the Heligoland Bight, took us across the North Sea sometimes twice a week, sometimes more often. We had to pick our way in at night through the tortuous passages left between many lines drawn in red upon the chart – here, there, and everywhere – in the wet triangle bounded to the west by the line joining the Horns Reef to the Dutch island of Terschelling. The red lines represented previously laid British minefields, and, though their positions were supposedly exact, we could never really trust them to a mile or so. Mines, however, remain at a constant height above the sea floor, so we generally selected high water for our nocturnal activities over the other side.

The German minefields were an unknown quantity. We knew that many had been laid, some for the express purpose of putting a stop to our excursions. Many times we saw enemy " floaters." On several occasions yellow painted monstrosities, bristling with horns, came to the surface in the wake of one of us after its mooring wire had been cut by a fast-moving propeller. We simply had to take our chance, trusting to luck and the Almighty. I must confess, however, that when I saw the chart of the German minefields which was delivered up after the Armistice, I had an attack of cold shivering. Much of the water that we had considered innocuous, and had gaily careered over at 25 knots, teemed with explosive abominations.

There were other things to be considered, besides mines, and these were the patrols of German destroyers at sea in the Bight. As at Dover, we were not allowed to fight with mines on board unless first attacked, for the simple reason that one shell striking in among primed mines would bring about an explosion more spectacular than any firework display. We frequently sighted enemy patrols, but our main task was to lay the mines, and hence to evade anything we saw. If chased, we had to trust to our superior speed to escape.

The work at the time was considered very " hush-hush " and secret, and, in order that it should not be known what we were doing, the large white numbers painted on our bows were frequently altered to mystify anyone who might sight us at sea. For the same reason it was desirable to conceal the rows of mines on deck, which was done with canvas camouflage screens spread over the after part of the ship and painted with a gun, torpedo-tubes, and deck-fittings against a background of sky. One artist even ran riot and painted in a few seagulls and some men on deck. But the camouflage screens certainly served their purpose. At a few hundred yards, unless one suspected, it was impossible to tell that we were not ordinary destroyers.

The North and South Dogger Bank Lightships were the points from where we laid off our positions for the runs of anything between eighty and one hundred miles in to the laying positions in the Bight. After losing sight of them, we had to work on " dead reckoning," for there were no other lights to guide us. And steering a serpentine course between old minefields, often in wild weather, or in North Sea fogs so thick that the next ahead was invisible, must have been a nerve-racking business for the *Abdiel's* navigator. But I never knew him to fail, even if the spray was breaking heavily over the bridge and the chart in its open chart-table must have been reduced to the consistency of blotting-paper.

We worked in close order, and, of course, without navigation lights. Moreover, as flashing signals in enemy waters were impossible, all our operations had to be done by time. Some hours before arriving at the laying-ground, therefore, a zero time, indicated by a long flash on a shaded lamp, was made by the *Abdiel*, and stop-watches were started in every ship. The speed was reduced to the laying speed of 10, 12, or 15 knots later,

just before we arrived at the spot, and five minutes afterwards
the leader would swing round to the laying course. The rear
ship started to lay the first half of her mines immediately she
steadied on the new course, and then swung out of the line to lay
the rest. The last ship but one started her lay the moment her
next astern was seen to alter out, and so on to the head of the
line, with the result that the field was laid in a series of obtuse-
angled V's.

At the end of the operation all the laying destroyers were
supposed, theoretically, to arrive in a single line some distance
to the flank of the minefield. On the clearer nights this was
possible without much difficulty. On the really dark nights,
however, when hulls could not be seen at more than 200 yards,
or in fog or hazy weather, the manœuvre became positively
exciting. Moreover, as the evolution was worked out to fractions
of a minute, any delay caused by a ship putting her helm over a
few seconds late, or by a mine on its sinkers refusing to travel
along the rails, became cumulative, and affected every other
ship in the flotilla.

It was ticklish, anxious work, quite apart from the unknown
dangers.

The use of wireless, like flashing, was strictly forbidden while
anywhere near Germany. The reason was obvious. The enemy
had excellent directional stations, and, once a transmitting key
was touched, our position, and the position of the minefield,
would be known.

One remembers many incidents.

Once, during a thick fog well over the other side of the North
Sea, a sudden large alteration of course became necessary, and the
seventh destroyer, the *Sandfly*, lost her next ahead in the murk.
The *Abdiel*, as usual, was leading, and my own ship, the
Telemachus, came next. In addition to the fog, the night was
very dark, with a visibility of perhaps fifty yards.

We had altered course through 180°, and were jogging along at
10 knots, astern of the *Abdiel*, when, to my horror, I suddenly
saw a destroyer on the starboard bow steaming at right angles for
the narrow gap ahead of us. We must have sighted each other
simultaneously, and to rattle the engine-room telegraphs over to
full speed astern and yelp thrice with the siren was the work of a
moment. The helm also went over in a frantic effort to swing
clear.

But fifty yards is fifty yards. One cannot pull up 1,000 tons like a taxi-cab. Collision was inevitable from the moment we saw each other.

Looking anxiously over the bridge rails, I found myself gazing into the eyes of a white-faced little group of men on the *Sandfly's* forecastle as her bows slid past ours.

" Gaw' blimey ! " howled a voice. " Where the blinkin' 'ell are you coming to ? "

In point of fact, the boot was rather on the other foot, for we were in station and the *Sandfly* was not. But there was no time for further badinage. With a sickening bump and the grinding crash of twisting steel, our sharp bows struck the *Sandfly* fair in her foremost boiler-room. It carved a V-shaped gash through which the water poured like a mill-race.

It was a sickening moment, for the collision, through no fault of ours, had occurred within thirty miles of the enemy coast and a full 250 from home. The *Sandfly* was badly damaged, and would have to be towed, while we were in the very thick of probable enemy patrols. Daylight was due in an hour and a half, and our wireless operators could hear a Zeppelin chatting to a friend in Germany, and a ship within five miles chiming in. We prayed all we knew that the fog would continue.

The weather, luckily, was calm, but the *Sandfly* lay helpless and unable to steam. While she got out her collision-mats and started the pumps, we prepared to take her in tow. The 3½-inch wire was duly passed across from our stern to her forecastle, but the lame duck lay deep in the water and could not steer. Yawing wildly from side to side, the wire parted like a piece of string the moment we gathered speed.

She was taken in tow by another ship, and this time, as she had got her steering-gear in working order, it was successful.

Came daylight, with a continuance of the fog.

We started to crawl home at 8 knots, no other British ship being anywhere within supporting distance if the fog lifted and enemy patrols were sighted. Even if we had had a cruiser squadron at sea, it would have been asking for trouble to use our wireless. The old Zeppelin's *Telefunken* could be heard quite close, and if he once caught a glimpse of us we might expect a German light-cruiser or two or a destroyer flotilla to cut us off. So the spare destroyers were stationed on either bow and beam of the tow to ward off possible submarines, while two more steamed astern – one ready to dash alongside to rescue officers and men if the weather cleared and the enemy were sighted in force, the other, with her torpedoes ready, to sink the damaged *Sandfly*. Nobody felt really cheerful.

Usually we hated thick weather, but on this occasion we blessed it, and we had fog or mist throughout the day. The night, when it came, was as dark as " the inside of a cow," and by the next morning we were well over towards the English coast.

But it took us thirty-six interminable hours to get the damaged *Sandfly* home, take her up the Humber, and tuck her into a dry-dock at Immingham, safe but not quite sound.

As for the *Telemachus*, she was entirely undamaged, with hardly a scratch in the grey paint round her bows. But our steel submarine ram below the waterline had made a nasty mess of the *Sandfly*.

4

Sometimes, after one or other of our operations, we received a congratulatory telegram from the Admiralty on our return into harbour. This acted like a tonic upon officers and men, and it was pleasant to know that our efforts were appreciated. Nevertheless, we never quite knew why we were patted on the back for some excursions, and not for others.

I discovered the reason long afterwards. We were congratulated on our safe return when the British directional wireless stations had located enemy cruisers or destroyers at sea within a few miles of our minefield. Then I remembered that on one occasion, as we were laying our " eggs " in a thick fog, we had heard strange sirens very close, and had even felt the heavy wash in the otherwise flat calm sea caused by a large ship's passage through the water at high speed.

Occasionally we sighted the enemy, as witness the night when we passed a large bunch of German minesweepers escorted by destroyers steaming back to their base. Oblivious to all danger, they were talking to each other with their signalling-lamps, while we passed so close to leeward that we could smell the reek of coal from their funnels.

We could have made cat's meat of that little party had we been allowed to fight. But orders were peremptory. We must not fight with mines on board unless attacked. Had the night been clear and calm, instead of very dark, wet, and gusty ; had the Germans been keeping a better look-out ; someone might have fired a gun at that line of dark shapes which slid past them at no more than 500 yards, and we should have replied. But no such thing happened, and we sped on into the darkness ahead to do our dirty work thirty miles beyond.

Once again, having been delayed in making the North Dogger Bank Lightship through thick weather, we arrived at our mine-laying ground in the chilly light of the dawn instead of at midnight. It was a hazy morning – March 28th, 1918 – and just before we laid our mines we sighted three enemy outpost boats at anchor. We passed them at a distance of little more than 300 yards, and, beyond making a signal with a flashing lamp, they showed no signs of having seen us. Not a man could be seen on their decks. All their guns were still shrouded in their canvas covers.

The British and German naval ensigns were very similar, and they may have taken us for friends. But, whatever the reason, they maintained a masterly inactivity, and we went on and laid our mines a couple of miles beyond.

By the time it was finished it was broad daylight, and, though the Germans must have seen our White Ensigns, they did nothing. So two destroyers were told off to deal with each outpost boat.

We were just about to go alongside ours, when I saw a man rush aft along her deck and release something which fell into the water with a heavy splash. I realised what it was – a depth-charge – and promptly went full speed astern. It was as well. The depth-charge went off with a shattering explosion, and practically blew the stern off the outpost boat. Another few seconds, and it would have pulverised our bows as well. We rescued the crew from their boat, and made them prisoners.

We hoped at first to take the other two to England as prizes, for, hailed through megaphones and with guns trained upon them, they were made to slip their cables and steam off to the westward. But they were slow, ungainly craft, and we were within sixty miles of Heligoland. The enemy wireless was busy, as usual, while the wind had chopped round to the south-west and the sea was rapidly rising, sure signs of a " dusting " on our way home. Moreover, one of my English-speaking prisoners, who was in no way inclined to be killed by his own side, vouchsafed the information that a couple of light-cruisers and two flotillas of destroyers were at sea looking for us.

So the crews of the two prizes were ferried across with their impedimenta, and the ships themselves were scuttled with explosive charges.

We duly had our " dusting " on the way home and all hands,

particularly the prisoners, were supremely uncomfortable as we steamed through it at 22 knots, pitching, wallowing, rolling, and crashing as only destroyers can. We landed our guests under an armed guard on the jetty at Immingham, and, whatever other people may have thought, I certainly felt sorry for them. They were quite pleasant fellows, seamen like ourselves, and I noticed when they were put ashore that all their uniform buttons and cap-ribbons had disappeared. They had exchanged them for cigarettes and chocolates. Your British bluejacket is insatiable as a curio-hunter.

That morning's work brought the six destroyers taking part the sum of £360 in prize bounty, or £5 for each man captured.

But the little cherub who sits up aloft and watches over the poor sailors sometimes has a nap, and it was on the night of August 2nd-3rd, 1918 that we had our first real disaster.

It happened on a clear, dark night well to the eastward of the meridian of 5° east. We were steaming in single line at high speed, preparing to lay our mines within half an hour, when, at 11.45 p.m., there came the thudding crash of a heavy explosion from somewhere down the line.

We, in the *Telemachus*, were following the *Abdiel*, and, looking aft, we saw a brilliant gout of ruby and orange flame mingled with smoke and water standing out of the sea to a height of quite 200 feet. It was an unnerving sight. No British mines were in the vicinity. We were on top of a German minefield. The fifth ship in the line, the *Vehement*, had struck a mine. On exploding, it had detonated her foremost magazine.

For a moment there was dead silence, followed by splashing in the water as débris came raining down from the sky. Then the roaring below of escaping steam, and the sound of men's voices, some shouting, others, injured and in the water, calling piteously for help.

The *Abdiel* and *Telemachus*, signalling to the others to stop engines, circled round to help the *Vehement*. She was still afloat, her bows deep in the water and her stern well in the air. But the bows, from abaft the bridge to the stem, had almost completely disappeared. All that remained was a tangle of twisted steel plating, in which the oil fuel and cordite blazed in a sickly yellow glare, and clouds of black smoke went drifting slowly to leeward. It was a clear night. That flaming beacon must have been visible for many miles.

The *Abdiel*, going ahead, took what remained of the *Vehement* in tow, stern first. The rest of us, lowering boats, searched for survivors in the water. Several, blown through the air, owed their lives to a series of miracles. One, with a broken thigh, managed to swim a hundred yards before he collapsed in the rescuing boat. But Hammersley-Heenan, the commanding officer, had the most wonderful escape of all. Standing on his bridge when the explosion came, he was stunned and hurled through space, recovering his senses to find himself in the water a full 400 yards from the wreck of his burning ship. Though severely injured, he set about blowing up his life-saving waist-coat, and then succeeded in saving a drowning shipmate, an act of gallantry for which he subsequently received the life-saving medal of the Royal Humane Society.

But fate had not played its last trick, for at seven minutes past midnight, while the *Abdiel* was still busy with her preparations for towing, there came another roar and the flash of an explosion as the *Ariel* fouled a mine a quarter of a mile from the first. A ship at once hurried to help her and rescued some survivors, but again a magazine had exploded, and a quarter of an hour later the *Ariel* flung her bows skywards and disappeared.

The grey dawn was breaking in the east when the remains of the *Vehement*, still blazing furiously, and with an occasional shell or cartridge exploding in the heat of the fire, were finally in tow. Even so, the position was still one of horrible uncertainty, for we could not know which way to steer. The minefield might be laid in any direction. North, south, east, or west – all might be equally dangerous. We steered north, trusting to Providence. And Providence was kind. It was not until afterwards that I discovered the German minefield stretched twenty miles north and south.

But we were not out of the wood. An hour later a bulkhead collapsed in the *Vehement*, her bow portion dipped deeper in the water, and her stern lifted in the air, until rudder and propellers were out of the water. The wind was freshening, and the sea had started to rise. Further towing was impossible.

The survivors, many of them badly wounded, were rescued from the wreck, and the guns of my ship and a couple of depth-charges sent the remains of the *Vehement* to her doom. She sank quietly, to leave a pitiful little collection of flotsam in the midst of an ever-widening patch of oil floating on the surface of the sea.

We turned our bows to the westward and steamed away. We

had left our base 9 strong and returned 7. In the brief space of twenty-two minutes over 100 of our flotilla-mates had gone to their death.

But we carried on, because we had to. Less than a week afterwards we were laying mines within seven miles of Zeebrugge.

5

Between February 19th and August 31st, 1918, the *Telemachus*, in which I served, carried out 36 minelaying operations in enemy waters and laid 1,440 mines. During the same period, at the most modest estimate, the 20th Flotilla must have laid 15,000.

We never knew the results officially, but it was Sir Eric Geddes, in a speech quoted by *The Times* of January 6th, 1919, who said that over 100 enemy vessels – destroyers, minesweepers, and outpost craft, with, I believe, a couple of submarines – had been caught and sunk by our mines during the first six months of 1918. And Sir Eric Geddes should have known what he was talking about, for at that time he was First Lord of the Admiralty.

CHAPTER XXV

ZEEBRUGGE[1]

I

DURING the afternoon of April 22nd, 1918, the eve of St. George's Day, an observer standing on the wind-swept summit of the cliffs by the North Foreland Lighthouse might have noticed an unusual concourse of vessels some distance out at sea. The area, even in war, was ever a busy one, with the passage of mercantile traffic in and out of the Downs and the Thames estuary; but on this particular afternoon something out of the ordinary was evidently afoot. He would have seen the obsolete cruiser *Vindictive* conspicuous by reason of her three lean funnels and the absence of masts, save for a stump of fore-mast crowned with its circular fighting-top; the *Thetis*, the *Intrepid*, and the *Iphigenia*; the *Brilliant* and the *Sirius*, all small cruisers completed for sea in the 'nineties, vessels which had shown the White Ensign of Britain all over the world, but were now destined to end their days gloriously under the very muzzles of the enemy's guns. Old ships every one of them – ships that were long past their best days and could serve no useful purpose with a modern fleet. Nothing as a rule is more pathetic than a superannuated man-of-war, but the names of these vessels, together with those of the gallant souls who manned them, will pass down to posterity in the annals of the Royal Navy.

There were many more craft present – the *Iris* and the *Daffodil*, single-funnelled, stubby-looking little ferry-boats from the Mersey; a couple of old submarines; the ubiquitous destroyers; and a swarm of coastal motor-boats and motor-launches. And farther afield, at Dover and at Dunkirk, other forces were under steam in readiness – monitors and more destroyers, motor-launches and coastal motor-boats – all to take part in the great adventure, an enterprise compared with which the risks of ordinary naval warfare seem to fade into insignificance.

It was no haphazard operation, designed on the spur of the moment. Zeebrugge and Ostend, both used as submarine and

---

[1] This account originally appeared in *A Little Ship*, written by myself, and published by Messrs. W. & R. Chambers in 1918. I am indebted to the publishers for permission to reprint it here.

destroyer bases by the enemy, had long proved thorns in our side, and in November 1917, in the absence of any more certain method, plans were first set on foot for the blocking of the two Flanders ports.

The mole at Zeebrugge consists of a long, curved breakwater of solid concrete jutting out into the sea, and affording the necessary protection to the twin-piers guarding the entrance to the inner basins and the Bruges Canal. At the shore end of the mole is a lattice-work viaduct which allows for the free flow of the tide, and without which the harbour could not have been prevented from silting up. The mole itself is about a mile long and eighty yards wide, and, like the foreshore bordering the entrance to the canal, was known to be studded with guns of all sizes, and with searchlights.

It was a foregone conclusion that the actual blocking-ships could never hope to get into the harbour unless the attention of the enemy was to be diverted by other means ; and, some time before they were due to arrive at their destinations, both Zeebrugge and Ostend were to be heavily bombarded by monitors at sea, by our shore batteries in the neighbourhood of Nieuport, and bombed by aircraft. Then, at the right moment, the *Vindictive*, *Daffodil*, and *Iris*, advancing in a smoke-screen to shield them from the enemy's view, were to dash alongside the Zeebrugge mole, land their storming-parties, capture the mole batteries, prevent the guns from firing on the blockships when they came in, and generally to distract attention. At much the same time, two old submarines filled with explosives were to make for the viaduct connecting the mole with the land, and, having wedged themselves in under the lattice-work, were to blow themselves up, destroy the viaduct, and make it impossible for any reinforcements to pass on to the mole proper. When this and the *Vindictive's* task had been effected, the *Thetis*, the *Intrepid*, and the *Iphigenia*, under the cover of another artificial fog, were to steam in and sink themselves in the canal entrance, their crews, together with those of the submarines, being taken off by motor-craft specially detailed for the purpose.

A very similar scheme was to be carried out at Ostend, except that, as there was no protecting mole at this place, the storming-parties and the submarines were not required.

Critics, had they known of the project, might well have held up their hands in horror. They could have drawn attention to Hobson's gallant but futile effort in the *Merrimac* to block the entrance to Santiago Harbour, and the desperate and repeated efforts of the Japanese to bottle the Russian fleet in Port Arthur. All these exploits ended in failure. And how could we, in the face of far greater difficulties, ever hope to seal Zeebrugge and Ostend ?

The blockships, remember, had to be taken through mined waters before reaching their objectives, through areas in which hostile destroyers would almost certainly be patrolling. This having been achieved unseen, they, with over fifty attendant craft in the shape of destroyers, motor-launches, and fast motor-boats, were then to be run into the very jaws of harbours situated in a flat, unlighted coast well provided with searchlights, and studded with guns of every calibre, from 15-inch downwards – weapons which could make accurate shooting at something over twenty miles.

Wind, weather, visibility, and the state of the tide had all to be taken into account. The operation could never be successful with an off-shore breeze, which would roll the smoke-screen seaward, and so expose the attackers to view. Moreover, bad weather, with a resultant sea, would effectually stultify the operations of the smaller craft, and prevent the *Vindictive*, the *Daffodil*, and the *Iris* from getting their storming-parties ashore. The tide, also, was an important factor, for the water had to be a certain height to permit the *Vindictive's* hinged brows, or gang-ways, to reach the mole ; while there must be no thick fog, but, for preference, a slight haze. The conditions, indeed, had to be ideal. And how often do four important factors work in con-junction ? Very rarely.

Did people in responsible positions ever really imagine that the armada would get within a mile of its destination without being sunk, let alone through the outer harbours and into the narrow bottle-necks of the inner basins themselves ?

But in war, given the right men, nothing is impossible.

A full five months before the attempt was actually made the preparations began. Not only had voluminous orders and instructions to be drafted out for every unit taking part, but the ships themselves had to be specially prepared, and, what was far more important, suitable officers and men obtained. Precisely how the volunteers were selected one cannot say ; but it is said that not even they themselves were aware, until well on into the proceedings, exactly what was the " hazardous service " they were being called upon to undertake. Not that there would have been any hanging back if they had. If the news of the intended operation had been published broadcast, and volunteers publicly called for from the entire British Navy, the situation would have been impossible – but much the same as in Togo's small fleet before Port Arthur, where, when less than a hundred men were required to man the blockships, several thousands applied, many of them signing their applications in their own blood.

The task of selection had to be done privily, and men were chosen from the Grand Fleet, from the naval depots at Portsmouth, Chatham, and Devonport, and from ubiquitous and gallant corps, the Royal Marines, both artillery and light infantry. Australia, New Zealand, Canada, South Africa, and every other oversea dominion, were represented.

Once chosen, every officer and man had to be specially trained for the part he was to play. The storming-parties had to be drilled in every detail of the operation. Men using hand-grenades, bombs, explosives for demolition purposes, *flammenwerfers*, and other unfamiliar and diabolical contrivances, had to be accustomed to their use. And not only this, they had to rehearse and rehearse again the whole operation on a full-scale model of Zeebrugge mole marked out on the ground. Every detail had to be considered. Each article of equipment had to be thought of. It had to be borne in mind that certain members of the storming-parties were to be provided with goggles, others with wire-nippers with insulated handles for cutting barbed wire. Some were to wear rubber-soled gymnastic shoes for a surer foothold ; and each man a large white patch on his back and his chest, so that friend could recognise friend in the dark.

The actual blockships had to be filled up with rubble and cement, provided with protection for their bridges, and gutted of all valuable fittings. The *Vindictive* had to be supplied with special fenders for going alongside, fitted with ramps and hinged brows for disembarking her storming-parties in the shortest possible time, and a variety of guns, howitzers, mortars, and *flammenwerfers*. Even the little *Daffodil* and the *Iris* had to be adapted for their special *rôle*, while no inconsiderable number of motor-craft had to be supplied with special smoke-producing plant for the creation of the necessary fog.

It was no small undertaking, and everything had to be kept a dead secret. If once the enemy got wind of the intention, the operation was foredoomed. But in spite of the multitude of men engaged in the work of preparation, and those who were to be participators in the great event, the secret was kept. Those who knew of it kept their mouths tight shut. The officers and men in the Grand Fleet were completely in the dark. As for the general public, the news of the exploit came as a complete surprise. By the Germans the attack was not unexpected.[1]

Before the actual operation there were two abortive attempts, when, at the eleventh hour, the weather rendered the undertaking impossible. The delay was a bitter disappointment to all concerned, but the experience was invaluable. But at last, on the eve of St. George's Day, they set out on their desperate enterprise. Some of them were going to almost certain death. Many did die gloriously in the face of the enemy ; but one and all proved to the world that the hardy spirit of their seaman ancestors still surged uppermost in their hearts.

2

The *Vindictive* was timed to reach her destination exactly at midnight, but some time before this the aerial attacks and bombardments of Zeebrugge and Ostend were already in progress. Before long the flotilla of motor launches and coastal motor-boats went ahead in the darkness to lay the necessary floats for making the smoke-screen across the harbour entrance. Presently, the deep throbbing of heavy gunfire, with the unearthly brilliance of star-shell bursting in the sky to the south-westward, showed that they had been seen and were being fired upon by the shore batteries.

The breeze, which up to this time had been blowing in a direction favourable to the attack – that is, towards the land – now died away, and, before many minutes had passed, light airs, steadily increasing in force, were stealing seaward. This meant that the smoke, drifting out to sea, would leave the attackers clear in view of the enemy when they emerged from the pall.

It was a misfortune – a serious misfortune ; but they did not hesitate. They were already committed to the venture, wind or

[1] According to an account of the operations prepared by the German Captain Karl Schultz in 1929 from materials in the German official archives, a British coastal motor-boat was found aground on April 12th after a night bombardment of Ostend by monitors, and aircraft attacks on Zeebrugge. Operation orders found in this boat caused the Commander of the Marine Corps to order the whole Flanders coast in a constant state of readiness. Newly laid buoys subsequently found in the outer approaches to Ostend pointed to further attacks, and from conditions of weather and tide the night of April 22nd-23rd was considered a likely period. Except as to the precise method of procedure, therefore, the assault and blocking attempts did not come as a surprise, which makes them all the more remarkable.

no wind, and at seven minutes to midnight the *Vindictive* ran into a bank of artificial fog so thick that it was impossible to see more than half the length of her forecastle. Three minutes later she had passed through it, and, emerging into the clearer darkness beyond, immediately sighted the lighthouse at the head of the mole a few hundred yards distant on her port bow. Captain Carpenter promptly increased to full speed and altered course to go alongside.

Owing to the shift in the wind, and the fact that the enemy had succeeded in sinking several of the smoke-floats by gunfire, the ship was now in full view of the batteries ashore, and almost at once every enemy weapon which would bear opened fire. The *Vindictive* replied, and in an instant the night became hideous with the deep, thudding roll of the discharges, the whinnying screech of projectiles, and the nerve-shattering crash, roar, and jangle as they drove home and burst.

Ahead, the orange flashes of the guns danced in and out of the dark shadows of the buildings ashore in a constant sparkle of flame. Star-shell and " flaming onions " soared ceaselessly skywards, to bathe the scene in their dazzling greenish-white glare until it was almost as bright as daylight ; while the white, finger-like beams of many searchlights, with wreathing eddies of smoke from the guns filtering fantastically through their rays, added to the illumination. Nearer at hand the water spouted and boiled as projectiles fell.

The *Vindictive* was advancing into the mouth of hell. The hostile guns were firing at point-blank range, so that they could hardly miss. But she never wavered. She drove steadily on, as steadily as the Light Brigade on the blood-stained field of Balaclava.

In the brief five minutes during which the ship ran the gaunt-let – between the times she emerged from the friendly smoke-screen and arrived alongside the mole – she was hit repeatedly. Captain Halahan, in charge of the bluejacket storming-party, was killed as he stood in readiness to lead his men on to the mole. Lieutenant-Colonel Elliot, in command of the marines, together with his second in command, Major Cordner, shared the same fate. Many other men, clustered on deck with their weapons in readiness to leap ashore the moment the ship got alongside, were also struck down, killed or wounded. Several of the hinged brows were demolished. But the *Vindictive* moved on, her guns booming defiance.

It must have been an uncanny moment for any Germans on the mole when first they saw the ship appearing out of the smoke-curtain. Her ghostly grey shape, magnified out of all proportion by her proximity, wreathed in a reek of smoke from her guns and exploding shell, sparkling with the wicked-looking flashes of her weapons and the redder gouts of flame from shell bursting, must have seemed something from another world, something ghastly and supernatural, as she drove remorselessly towards them. But they were not afforded much time to analyse their feelings. At one minute past midnight, with her pom-poms and machine-guns sweeping the mole, her mortars lobbing bombs over the parapet, and her heavy guns and howitzers firing shell at the hostile bat-teries, the ship was alongside.

She rubbed the wall with scarcely a tremor, and orders were given to let go an anchor. The *Daffodil*, however, which was to push her larger sister bodily into the mole, had been left behind when the *Vindictive* increased speed, and for some minutes the position was very precarious. Orders were inaudible in the up-roar of the guns. Owing to a strong tide alongside the mole, and a heavy swell causing the ship to roll, the *Vindictive* could not get close enough to land her storming-parties. Whichever way she put her helm, to starboard, to port, or amidships, the brows in the centre portion of the ship could not be made to reach the wall. Nor could the special anchors for making her fast be properly secured. It was a terrible time, and the awful three or four minutes which elapsed until the *Daffodil* arrived must have seemed a veritable purgatory.

But at last the little passenger-tender from the Mersey put her bows into the side of the cruiser and pushed her in. Two brows were dropped. All the others had been destroyed or temporarily disabled by shell fire. The storming-parties, led by their officers, instantly started to scramble ashore as best they could.

How the men ever landed seems little short of a miracle. The ship was rolling heavily in the backwash, and at one moment the ends of the brows were crashing against the mole, while the next they were eight or more feet in the air. Bluejackets and marines, fully accoutred and wearing gas-masks and steel helmets, some with rifles and fixed bayonets, some with Lewis guns, some with bombs and explosives, others with portable flame-throwers and all manner of other contrivances, had to make their way up these steep, wildly swaying bridges at peril of their lives. They were under the close-range fire of many machine-guns ; shells were still dropping all round them and bursting overhead, while a stumble or a false foothold might have sent any of them tumbling to a certain and horrible death in the thirty-foot chasm between the ship and the mole.

It was enough to appal the bravest man ; but again there was no wavering. The survivors of the storming-parties, leaving many dead and wounded behind them, swept ashore with a rush.

The *Daffodil*, on board of which were the officers and men of the demolition-parties, was ordered by Captain Carpenter to continue pushing the *Vindictive* into the wall, and remained doing this the whole time the larger vessel was alongside. At first it was thought that the little ship's boilers would not develop a sufficient head of steam for this difficult task, but, thanks to the wonderful work of Mr. Sutton, her artificer-engineer, who succeeded in maintaining 160 lbs. pressure to the square inch in boilers only intended for eighty, the task was successfully accomplished.

The *Iris*, which had on board some further storming-parties, went alongside the mole ahead of the *Vindictive* to land her contingent. She had the greatest difficulty in securing, as there was a heavy swell and her grapnels would not span the parapet. Lieutenant-Commander Bradford gallantly swarmed up a violently swaying derrick in an effort to secure the ship ; but was shot almost as soon as he appeared over the parapet, to fall between the wall and the ship's side. Lieutenant Hawkins also climbed up a ladder and sat astride the wall trying to make the ship fast. He also was killed. Landing the men in these conditions was impossible, and, to save further useless sacrifice of valuable lives, she left her position, went alongside the *Vindictive*, and landed a few of her men across that ship.

Whilst alongside the mole the *Vindictive's* hull was comparatively immune from shell fire, but funnels, upper works, and ventilators showed above the wall, and were struck every few seconds. The fighting-top above the bridge, in which were stationed marines manning pom-poms and Lewis guns, sustained direct hits from shell which, on bursting, killed every man except two. But Sergeant Finch, of the Royal Marine Artillery, himself badly wounded and streaming with blood, continued to use his gun until the top was finally wrecked. He now wears the coveted Victoria Cross.

The crew of the 7.5-inch howitzer on the forecastle were killed or wounded to a man. The weapon was instantly manned by a fresh crew; but they, too, were exterminated. Nothing daunted at the fate of their predecessors, a third party manned the gun and continued to fire. Many of the deeds performed on that awful night passed unnoticed in the turmoil of battle. The men, to quote the opinion of their officers, behaved magnificently.

The main deck of the *Vindictive* was a ghastly shambles crowded with stricken men. Ever since about 11.50, when the ship first came under fire, a ceaseless flow of casualties had been going below, until the temporary dressing-stations on the mess-deck and in the sick-bay overflowed. Room had to be found for the wounded in the wardroom, the cabins, and any spare space available. Most of the wounds were severe. Some of the men were on the threshold of death, but one and all were possessed by the same indomitable spirit.

" Have we won, sir ? " they anxiously asked Captain Carpenter as he went round. " Have we won ? "

There is something sublime in the spirit of self-abnegation which animated the men on that memorable night. All ideas of self seemed to vanish utterly. Many of the brave fellows who lay there gritting their teeth in agony knew that their hours were numbered, but the thoughts of every one of them centred on that all-important question – " Have we won ? "

No written description can ever convey an adequate idea of the awful nature of the fighting on the mole itself. Shelled by heavy guns, fired upon at close range by snipers and machine guns, the storming and demolition parties did what they set out to do. The arrangement of the mole itself, with its batteries, its concrete shelters, its sheds, and its seaplane station, was more or less known beforehand. But studying its geography from plans and aeroplane photographs in peace and quietness, and storming the place at midnight under heavy fire and in the dazzling glare of searchlights and star-shell, are two very different things. There were pitfalls everywhere – railway lines for heavily laden men to trip over, barbed-wire entanglements to catch them if they were unwary, sheer drops of a dozen feet on to the solid concrete below. And through it all the unremitting swish and crackle of the machine-gun bullets, the roar, crash, and thunder of exploding shell.

On the other side of the mole, abreast of where the *Vindictive* lay, was a German destroyer. She was heavily fired upon, and a few of her men scrambled on to the mole, instantly to be bayoneted or shot by the storming-parties. Other men pelted the destroyer with bombs and explosives, and there seemed little doubt that she was sunk.

Buildings, gun-emplacements, and bomb-proof shelters were attacked in turn, while several isolated parties of the enemy were cut off and disposed of. Side by side with the bluejackets and the marines went a little party of air mechanics with portable *flammenwerfers* and phosphorus bombs. Their work was invaluable. But the casualties among the storming-parties were very severe, for, in addition to the heavy and accurate fire from the shore-batteries and the machine-guns on the mole itself, the German destroyers alongside also joined in the battle.

And so the struggle on the mole continued, the men fighting shoulder to shoulder to storm the gun-positions – shooting, bayoneting, bombing in the glare and sulphurous smoke of the shell explosions ; men dropping right and left, and the wounded crawling painfully back to the doubtful shelter of the *Vindictive*.

Meanwhile, from another direction, a gallant little band of six men were slowly approaching the viaduct at the shore end of the mole in an antiquated C.3, filled with explosives. Their names – Lieutenants Sandford, of the Royal Navy, and Howell Price, of the Royal Naval Reserve ; Petty Officer W. Harner ; Engine-Room Artificer G. Roxburgh ; Leading Seaman Maver ; and Stoker H. C. Bindall – deserve to be remembered, for theirs was probably the most hazardous and nerve-testing task of that eventful night.

It had originally been intended to attack the viaduct with two submarines, but the second, due to a mishap which nobody could have avoided, was not able to reach her destination in time to take her share. Bitterly disappointed, her officers and men proffered their services for another attempt immediately on their return.

C.3 was provided with an automatic steering-device to enable her to maintain a steady course if the men abandoned her a few hundred yards from the viaduct, while a small skiff fitted with a motor provided the means for the crew to escape. But there was always the chance that something might go wrong with the steering-gear at the last moment, and, sooner than leave anything to chance, Lieutenant Sandford and his brave fellows determined not to abandon their craft until they had wedged her firmly in underneath the viaduct.

It was a heroic resolve. The viaduct, they well knew, would be crowded with the enemy, and there was every prospect that the motor-skiff would be shot to pieces by gun and rifle fire before ever they reached their destination. As an alternative method of escape they might possibly scramble ashore and make their way to the *Vindictive* along the mole. If they were unable to effect this, they had every intention of lighting the fuse, and of perishing in the resulting explosion.

It was no desperate plan made on the spur of the moment, in the heat of battle. It was premeditated, and these six volunteers were unanimous. Life was as dear to them as it is to other men, but they realised that their task was merely part and parcel of an operation, the success of which must not be jeopardised through their unwillingness to make the supreme sacrifice. Whatever happened, the viaduct must be blown up. They, if necessary, would go with it.

While the submarine was still at a distance of over a mile from her objective she was lit up in the glare of a star-shell. At about the same time a few rounds were fired at her. The enemy, however, soon ceased his attentions, and by about midnight the mole and the viaduct, clearly silhouetted against the glare of flares burned by the enemy, was within half a mile. The crew were mustered on deck in readiness for the final effort, and almost at once the boat was temporarily illuminated in the beams of two searchlights.

The hostile guns, however, refrained from firing. Possibly they were too busy with other targets, or else the Germans imagined that the submarine was trying to get into the harbour, had missed her way, and was blindly blundering into collision with the mole, in which condition they could make short work of her, even capture her. They little guessed her real errand. If they had, they would have opened fire with every gun that would bear.

A few minutes later she altered course straight for the viaduct at full speed, a little more than 9 knots. The lattice-work itself, true to their expectation, was crowded with riflemen, though, imagining the submarine to be running crazily to certain destruction, they did not open fire.

Nearer and nearer came the viaduct. The crash came, and C.3 struck under their very noses. She took the structure exactly between two uprights, and, lifting bodily into the air as she rode over the horizontal girders, drove on until the foreside of her conning-tower crashed into the lattice-work. There she brought up.

The motor-skiff was lowered at once, but, as the boat was dropped into the water, the propeller became hopelessly damaged against a projection. The crew took their places in her and manned the two oars, leaving Lieutenant Sandford on board the submarine to light the fuses. Having done this, he joined his men in the boat. Shoving off, they started to pull away for their lives against the strong current. They could hear orders shouted overhead, could see Germans dropping down from the viaduct on to the deck of the submarine. A moment later two searchlights blazed out, and the frail cockle-shell instantly became a target for every pom-pom, machine-gun, and rifle in the vicinity. They were shooting at point-blank range, and so great was the volume of fire that one man of the party states that the swish and plop of the bullets striking the boat and dropping into the water all round completely drowned the sounds of the firing.

The skiff was soon holed in many places. It was only by dint of using a pump, which had luckily been provided as an afterthought, that they succeeded in keeping her afloat. Then Lieutenant Sandford was hit twice in rapid succession, followed almost immediately afterwards by the petty officer and the stoker. But the others still tugged at the oars, nerving every effort to get to a place of safety before the inevitable explosion. With only two oars in the teeth of the current, their progress was appallingly slow.

At last, at twenty minutes past midnight, when the boat was still within three hundred yards of the viaduct, the charge detonated. There came the shattering roar of a huge explosion. A blinding sheet of orange flame, mingled with pieces of wreckage from the submarine and the viaduct itself shot skywards. An arch of liquid fire, caused by blazing petrol from the submarine's fuel-tanks, curved across the heavens over the heads of the men in their boat and fell sizzling and steaming into the water beyond. A shower of débris, mingled with fragments of solid masonry and perhaps the mutilated bodies of Germans, came raining down into the sea all round them. . . .

The searchlights ashore suddenly vanished. The firing ceased, and in that brief instant the viaduct was utterly demolished and many of the enemy went to their death. There came a few minutes' silence, followed by a roar of frenzied cheering from the *Vindictive's* storming parties on the mole. Then the crackle of musketry and the roar and thunder of the heavier guns broke out afresh as the fight recommenced.

The men of C.3 had successfully accomplished their mission. A few minutes later the gallant little party was picked up by a picket-boat specially detailed for the purpose, and commanded by Lieutenant-Commander Sandford, Lieutenant Sandford's brother, who took his boat in under the fire of the guns to effect the rescue. The picket-boat was holed in the process, but got away in safety. Having transferred the wounded, she eventually managed to return to Dover under her own steam.

3

At twenty minutes past midnight the *Thetis*, the leading block-ship, commanded by Commander Ralph S. Sneyd, D.S.O., steamed past the end of the mole. After her came the *Intrepid*, Lieutenant Stuart Bonham-Carter, and the *Iphigenia*, Lieutenant Edward W. Billyard-Leake.

Theirs was the most important phase of the operation, for the storming of the mole by the *Vindictive's* men, and the blowing up and destruction of the viaduct by the submarine, were both subsidiary and contributory to the actual blocking of the harbour entrance.

Rockets fired from the *Vindictive* gave the *Intrepid* a chance of seeing her whereabouts, and, rounding the lighthouse at the end of the mole, she steered straight for the entrance in the boom, a contrivance of nets and heavy wires strung out between barges. As she came in, her guns opened fire on the hostile batteries, she in turn being subjected to a tornado of fire from the guns ashore. She was hit repeatedly. Those who witnessed her entry say that her grey hull, wreathed in smoke, dim and ghostly against the brilliance of the searchlights beyond, sparkled with the flame of her own guns, and glowed with the bursts of exploding shell. It was a sight never to be forgotten.

The *Thetis* steamed on towards the opening between the barges. But she was swinging fast and could not be checked in time, and had the misfortune to run into the net obstruction, which, being gathered into her propellers, soon brought them to a standstill. Carrying her way, she still forged ahead, taking the nets with her, until, practically unmanageable, she bumped on the bottom. She eventually slid off again into the deeper water of the dredged channel, but, having been frequently hit, was heeling over and settling down fast.

The piers at the canal entrance were actually in sight, but nothing further could be done. Signalling to the *Intrepid* and the *Iphigenia* to point out the clear passage, Commander Sneyd gave orders for his vessel to be abandoned. Waiting until the engine- and boiler-rooms were clear of men, he then pressed the firing-keys and blew her up. The ship began to sink fast, and her ship's company, many of them wounded or suffering from the effects of gas, manned the single cutter which was left to them and rowed to their attendant motor-launch.

The *Thetis*, thanks to a series of circumstances which no power on earth could have guarded against, was therefore denied the supreme satisfaction of sinking herself exactly in the position laid down for her between the jetties leading to the inner harbour. But she was in the fairway outside, where she was scarcely less useful in blocking the exit. Moreover, her signals to her consorts played no small part in helping them to achieve complete success.

The second blockship, the *Intrepid*, commanded by Lieutenant Stuart Bonham-Carter, was following close on the heels of the *Thetis*. Passing that ship as she lay sinking, she steered straight for the mouth of the canal. Owing to delay some time before in a motor-launch getting alongside to take off her spare crew, and due also, it is said, to the extreme reluctance on the part of the men themselves to miss the fight, she went in with her spare watch of stokers still on board, so that her ship's company, instead of fifty-four, numbered eighty-seven souls.

Most of the hostile guns were concentrating their fire on the *Vindictive*, the mole, and the *Thetis*, and passing between the piers, the *Intrepid* steamed on up the canal without much inter-ference beyond shrapnel-fire. Having reached a position several hundred yards inside the line of the shore, Lieutenant Bonham-Carter put the bows of his ship in towards the western bank, and worked the propellers to swing the stern well across the canal. There, having given orders to abandon the ship, he exploded the charges to sink her.

The greater number of the officers and men got away in boats, and were duly picked up; but the commanding officer himself, two other officers, and four petty officers were reduced to nothing better than a Carley float. Launching this un-wieldy contrivance, a calcium light attached to which burst into brilliant flame the moment it touched the water, they paddled slowly down the canal, with bullets from the machine-guns on the bank pattering into the water all round them. How this party ever succeeded in making their escape is nothing short of a miracle. They had nothing with which to propel their lumbering float except a few short paddles, and had it not been for Lieutenant Percy T. Dean, R.N.V.R., of Motor-Launch 282, who brought his little ship into the canal on the heels of the *Intrepid* and rescued them under the withering fire of the machine guns, they could hardly have survived to tell the tale.

The *Iphigenia*, the third blockship, in command of Lieutenant E. W. Billyard-Leake, arrived soon after the *Intrepid*. She also came under fire as she passed through the outer harbour, while a bursting shell severed a steam-pipe and shrouded the forepart of the vessel in clouds of steam. The smoke from the *Intrepid*, moreover, was floating about the canal entrance, and made it very difficult to see. But driving in between a dredger and a barge, and carrying the latter with her, Lieutenant Billyard-Leake steamed his ship on up the canal. He then manœuvred to place the *Iphigenia* in the gap between the *Intrepid* and the eastern bank, and, after ringing the alarm-gong for the ship to be abandoned, exploded the charges.

The crew left the ship in one cutter, the other being too badly damaged by shell fire to be of any use. Peppered by bursting shrapnel and pelted by machine-guns, they pulled clear of the sinking ship. Motor-launch 282 was still in the vicinity, rescuing men of the *Intrepid*, and, seeing her near the bows of his own ship, Lieutenant Billyard-Leake went alongside and transferred most of his men. The others stayed in the cutter, which was made fast to the bow of the motor-launch, which went full speed, stern first, down the canal.

It was realised from the very beginning that the crews of the blockships had a very slender chance of getting away with their lives. They had to sink their ships well inside the jaws of a narrow harbour fringed with machine-guns, the approaches to which were commanded by guns of all sizes and illuminated by searchlights. Having abandoned their vessels, they then had to run the gauntlet in their boats. Had it not been for the magnificent work of Lieutenant Dean and his volunteer crew in their motor-launch, hardly one of them could have escaped.

A motor-launch is unarmoured. She has a wooden hull, which can be pierced by any bullet, and in the most ordinary circumstances is none too easy to handle. Yet, without the least regard for their own personal safety, the lieutenant and his men took their craft up the canal in face of the fire from the banks, hovered about picking men out of the water and from boats of the blockships, and then retired with their little ship so crammed with the one hundred and fifty men aboard that she was in imminent danger of capsizing. To make matters worse, she suffered many casualties from the incessant fire of the machine-guns ; while her steering-gear jammed on leaving the canal, necessitating the undesirable expedient of steering with the screws. Lieutenant Dean received the Victoria Cross for his gallantry. Never has the decoration been more richly deserved.

4

Included in the swarm of other vessels detailed to take part in the operation were numbers of coastal motor-boats, small, powerfully engined craft built on the hydroplane principle, and capable of a speed of something over 30 knots in calm water. For many months they had been used with conspicuous success off the Belgian coast, darting in at night close under the enemy's guns and searchlights to attack destroyers with their torpedoes, and for reconnaissance work generally. They were particularly suitable for this function on account of their light draught, great speed, and small size, which, besides permitting them to work in shoal water at all stages of the tide, made it extremely difficult for the German gunners to knock them out. It is one thing to put a shell into a large and slowly moving ship, but quite another proposition to hit a small object with nothing visible to aim at except two enormous feathers of water careering along in the darkness at the speed of an ordinary passenger-train.

These craft, as may well be imagined, were officered and manned by young men who gave no thought for the morrow. They were used to hurtling about within point-blank range of the guns, and on the night of April 22nd–23rd they again proved their value. Some were detailed for making the necessary smoke-screens off the harbour entrance – work which brought them their fair share of attention from the batteries. Others had the more exciting tasks of attacking the mole with Stokes guns before the *Vindictive* got alongside, with the object of making the German gunners take shelter in their bomb-proofs, or of firing their torpedoes at vessels alongside the inner face of the mole when once the blockships had passed.

As an example of the spirit which animated the personnel of these C.M.B.s, and to show their firm determination not to miss the fight, there is the case of No. 35a, commanded by Lieutenant Edward Hill. This boat sailed from Dover with the others at about 3.30 on the afternoon of April 22nd, but a few hours later,

when eighteen miles from her starting-place, had the misfortune
to foul her propellers.   Nothing could be done on the spot to
clear them, but at 6.30 a drifter arrived on the scene, took the
damaged craft in tow, and arrived with her at Dover at 8 o'clock.
She was immediately hoisted out of the water, when, besides
fouled propellers, it was found she had sustained other damage.
This was rectified, and at 9.40 she was once more in the water,
and set off at full speed for her rendezvous off the Belgian coast.
She eventually arrived at Zeebrugge, a matter of some seventy
miles, ten minutes before midnight, and proceeded to carry out
her share in the smoke-screening operations as if nothing at all
out of the ordinary had happened.

Most of the destroyers present were employed in covering
the flotillas of motor-launches and motor-boats responsible for
making the smoke-screens.   Though the greater number of them
came under fire at one time or another, it is not possible here to
give details of their movements.

The *Warwick*, Commander Victor Campbell, D.S.O., on board
of which was Sir Roger Keyes himself, together with the *Phœbe*
and the *North Star*, was stationed close inshore to attack any
hostile destroyers leaving the harbour.   Throughout the operation, sometimes under heavy fire, the *Warwick* remained within
a few hundred yards of the *Vindictive* as she lay alongside the
mole.   But of all the destroyers present, the *North Star* and the
Phœbe had the most thrilling experience.

The first-named, commanded by Lieutenant-Commander K. C.
Helyar, lost touch in the thick smoke, and, after casting round
to find the *Vindictive* or her consorts, sighted land ahead shortly
before one o'clock.   Altering course again, she presently found
herself actually inside the area enclosed by the curved mole, with
the blockships in sight ahead, and the mole itself, with several
German destroyers alongside it, to starboard.   She was instantly
lit up by a searchlight, and firing a torpedo at one of the hostile
vessels, put her helm hard over to escape from her unenviable
position.   The ship swung rapidly, but while she slewed towards
the mole the batteries opened a furious fire.   Shell fell all round
her, many driving home.   Firing more torpedoes, she still continued to turn.   The lighthouse at the extremity of the mole was
sighted, and at first it was touch-and-go whether or not she could
clear it.   This she succeeded in doing, but, on passing at little
more than a hundred yards, was struck by two successive salvos
of shell in the engine- and boiler-rooms.   Engines and boilers

were rendered useless, and, with her motive-power gone, the *North Star* finally came to rest within 400 yards of the end of the mole, a searchlight still blazing full upon her and shell crashing home every few seconds.

But help was forthcoming. The *Phœbe*, commanded by Lieutenant-Commander H. E. Gore-Langton, which was outside, had observed through a rift in the smoke the *North Star* passing the mole-head on her way out, and had seen her struck and brought to a standstill. He at once proceeded to her assistance, and steaming between the injured vessel and the mole, made a smoke-screen to shield her from view. Having done this, he placed his ship ahead of the *North Star* and passed a wire across to tow her out of action. By the time this was completed both ships had drifted some distance to the north-eastward, with the *North Star* lying approximately at right angles to the *Phœbe*. A shift in the wind, however, had dissipated the smoke-screen, and once more both vessels were lit up in the rays of searchlights and the glare of star-shell, and were being heavily fired upon at short range. Going slowly ahead, the *Phœbe* then tried to drag her damaged consort round to the desired course, but the *North Star*, badly battered, and with her engine- and boiler-rooms flooded, lay waterlogged, so that the towing-wire snapped like pack-thread as soon as the strain came upon it.

Lieutenant-Commander Gore-Langton then turned his ship and secured alongside the wreck, with the intention of drawing her farther out before again attempting to tow from ahead. During this period both ships were once more fairly illuminated. Several salvos of shell struck, cutting the securing wires, blowing the *North Star's* capstan overboard, and killing and wounding many men. Unable to carry out her intention, the *Phœbe* thereupon cast off, made another smoke-screen between the *North Star* and the shore, and, lying off, sent a boat to rescue some of the survivors. The *North Star* also lowered her boats and ferried a few of her men across.

Both ships were still under accurate and heavy fire. Circling round again, however, Lieutenant-Commander Gore-Langton made a further smoke-screen to cover his movements, and then, for the third time, closed the wreck and went alongside. Once more he attempted to tow her clear, but again the *North Star* was hit repeatedly; and seeing that she was sinking fast, and that further efforts would only result in the loss of both ships, he reluctantly gave orders for her to be abandoned. The men scrambled across, and the *Phœbe* backed astern. Then it was noticed that one seaman had been left behind. The wreck was reapproached to effect his rescue, but as the *Phœbe* came alongside the poor fellow was killed by a bursting shell.

The port side of the *North Star* was riddled like a sieve, the water was gaining fast, and more shell were bursting on board every moment. Finally, seeing she was doomed, the *Phœbe* left her to her fate and retired under heavy fire.

From first to last she had stood by her stricken friend for nearly an hour under the unremitting and accurate close-range fire of the batteries. The rescue of the *North Star's* crew, which was effected in circumstances which might also have involved the loss of the *Phœbe*, was entirely due to the coolness and gallant conduct of Lieutenant-Commander Gore-Langton and his ship's company, behaviour in which the officers and men of the *North Star* were not one whit behindhand. It has never been the custom in the British Navy to desert a comrade in distress, and on this occasion the old tradition was more than upheld.

5

At about ten minutes to one, as the blockships were in and the submarine had accomplished her purpose, Captain Carpenter, in the *Vindictive*, gave the necessary signal for the retirement of the storming-parties on the mole. A quarter of an hour later it was reported that no further officers or men were coming on board, and, after another five minutes' grace, the *Daffodil* started to tow the *Vindictive's* bows away from the wall.

The *Iris*, which had shoved off some minutes previously, had come under very heavy fire on getting clear. Crowded with men, she suffered very heavy casualties, including Commander Valentine Gibbs, who was mortally wounded by a shell which severed both legs, and Lieutenant Spencer, R.N.R., the navigating officer. Serious fires also broke out on board, due to shell igniting some ammunition. Taking charge of the ship, the next officer, Lieutenant Oscar Henderson, took her seaward. Luckily the engines and boilers were intact ; but her casualties were enormous – 8 officers and 69 men being killed, and 3 officers and 102 men wounded.

Presently, blazing like a furnace, her flaming funnels torn and battered out of all recognition, and her upper deck a shambles of twisted steel, the *Vindictive* left the mole, circled round and made for home. Captain Carpenter had just been wounded, but took the wheel himself. Followed by salvos of German shell which fell into the water all round her, the gallant old ship disappeared in the billowing clouds of smoke to seaward.

The *Sirius* and the *Brilliant*, the two blockships detailed to seal the harbour entrance at Ostend, owing to the removal of a buoy and the off-shore wind blowing the smoke-screens seaward, did not succeed in reaching their objective. They came into full view of the enemy's guns, were heavily pounded, and, having failed to find the entrance, grounded some distance to the eastward. It was nobody's fault. It was a mere vicissitude of war. Commander Godsal, who commanded the *Sirius* in the first endeavour, had charge of the *Vindictive* on the second and final attempt to seal the harbour. It was successful, but the gallant commander met his death after having placed his ship in the entrance.

When the sun rose on St. George's Day, an antiquated cruiser, many destroyers, and numbers of motor-launches and coastal motor-boats might have been seen wending their way homeward towards their respective bases. They had left something tangible behind them, in the shape of two charred, shell-riven wrecks in the canal at Zeebrugge, and two more on the beach near Ostend. But something even more imperishable had risen out of those battered hulls. Ships may come and ships may go ; men may rise to fame and pass away ; but the memory of the gallant dead, those of that band of brothers who strove and fought for Britain on St. George's Day, will surely never fade.

CHAPTER XXVI

BRITISH DESTROYER STRENGTH AND WAR CONSTRUCTION

(*Flotilla-Leaders, Destroyers, Patrol-Boats, Torpedo-Boats*)

I. FLOTILLA-LEADERS

THE flotilla-leader type really originated with the *Swift*, an experimental ocean-going vessel of the destroyer class launched in 1907. She had a displacement of 2,170 tons, was fitted with turbines and oil-fired boilers, and attained a speed of 35.1 knots on her trials. Her armament consisted of four 4-inch guns and a couple of torpedo-tubes.

For a time this type was allowed to lapse. Before the war, the Captains (D) commanding destroyer flotillas, which at that time consisted of from 16 to 20 destroyers, were invariably accommodated in light-cruisers. Even during the war, when more flotilla-leaders became available, some Captains (D) were still in small cruisers, and others in flotilla-leaders. At Jutland, for instance, Captain J. W. Farie, Captain (D) of the 13th Flotilla, attached to the Battle-Cruiser Fleet, was in the light-cruiser *Champion*, and had no flotilla-leaders under his command. Captain Wintour, however, of the 4th Flotilla, was in the flotilla-leader *Tipperary*, while his second-in-command, Commander Allen, was in her sister vessel *Broke*. Captain Stirling, too, of the 12th Flotilla, was in the flotilla-leader *Faulknor*, and his second-in-command in the *Marksman*.

The general policy arrived at when flotilla-leaders became available, was to provide two of these vessels to each flotilla of 16 destroyers, the usual destroyer tactical unit consisting of 4 ships, which always worked together as a division when serving with the fleet. When destroyers were used for patrol and convoy purposes, however, the divisional system went by the board, and even flotillas became intermingled.

Nowadays, a flotilla consists of 8 destroyers commanded by a Captain (D) accommodated in a flotilla-leader. This means a total of 9 vessels, so that, for attacking purposes, the modern

NOTE. – A list of all flotilla-leaders in service during the war will be found in Appendix I. War losses appear in Appendices III.–VI.

408

flotilla may be divided into three units each of three vessels. One unit of three destroyers is headed by the leader, and the other two by half or divisional leaders.

It was in 1913 that it was considered desirable that Captains (D) of flotillas should be accommodated in vessels of destroyer type and characteristics, and this led to the design of ships with increased living accommodation for the staff officers and additional ratings, adequate bridge space with increased facilities for visual and other signalling, and larger endurance and the same speed as the destroyers commanded. These features called for larger vessels than destroyers, and the consequent increase in size permitted a heavier gun armament to be carried.

The *Lightfoot* and *Marksman*, of the 1913–14 programme, and the *Kempenfelt* and *Nimrod*, of the 1914–15 programme, were all in various stages of building when the war started. They were really large destroyers – craft of 1,605 tons, driven at 34 knots by turbines and oil fuel, and mounting four 4-inch and two 2-pounder pom-poms, together with two pairs of 21-inch torpedo-tubes. These four ships were all completed before the end of 1915.

At the outbreak of war four large Chilean destroyers were being built by Messrs. J. S. White, of Cowes. These, renamed *Botha*, *Tipperary*, *Faulknor*, and *Broke*, were all taken over by the Admiralty. Their displacement was something over 1,700 tons, and they mounted six 4-inch guns, one 1½-pounder pom-pom, and either two double or four single 21-inch torpedo-tubes. Their designed speed was between 31 and 32 knots, they were driven by turbines, and carried 403 tons of coal and 83 tons of oil fuel.

The *Tipperary* was sunk at Jutland, but the *Botha*, *Faulknor*, and *Broke* were reconditioned and returned to Chile at the end of the war. They are now known as the *Almirante Williams*, *Almirante Riveros*, and *Almirante Uribe* respectively.

Thirty-one more flotilla-leaders of varying types were ordered between November 1914 and April 1918. Their names and main characteristics will be found in Appendix I. Four of the last batch of six were countermanded on the cessation of hostilities, while five, the " V " class leaders ordered in April 1916, were practically the same as the " V " class destroyers ordered four months later. Of the 34 vessels of this type building at the outbreak of war, or ordered during hostilities and subsequently completed, Messrs. Cammell Laird built 17 ; Messrs. Samuel White. 6 ; Messrs. Denny and Thornycroft, 4 each ; and Messrs. Hawthorn Leslie, 3.

2. DESTROYERS

At the outbreak of war the names of 243 destroyers figured in the Navy List. Ten of these were craft of the old 27-knot type, completed for sea between 1894 and 1900, and 63 more 30-knotters, dating from between 1895 and 1901. Two, the *Bonetta* and *Albacore*, of slightly different type, were bought in 1909 for replacement purposes.

All these 73 vessels were of the same general type and characteristics – little ships of between 300 and 450 tons, with low sloping turtle-backs forward instead of high forecastles, and armed as a rule with one 12-pounder and five 6-pounder guns, together with a couple of 18-inch torpedo-tubes. They were the lineal descendants of the first destroyer ever built – the *Havock*, ordered in 1892.

Destroyers, when they originally came into being, were intended more for use in coastal waters than to accompany a fleet to sea in all weathers. But numbers of these older craft served on foreign stations and cruised extensively. I can only trace one of these vessels actually abroad when the war started, the 340-ton, 30-knotter *Fame*, at Hong-Kong.[1] It was this little ship, commanded by Lieutenant Roger Keyes (now Admiral of the Fleet Sir Roger Keyes, Bart., G.C.B., K.C.V.O., C.M.G., D.S.O., LL.D., D.C.L.), which, with the destroyer *Whiting*, Lieutenant Colin Mackenzie (now Rear-Admiral Colin Mackenzie, C.I.E., D.S.O.), captured four German-built Chinese destroyers in the Peiho River during the bombardment of the Taku Forts on June 17th, 1900. Three days later I remember both the *Fame* and *Whiting* coming alongside the ship in which I was then serving as a midshipman, the cruiser *Terrible* (Captain Percy Scott), to disembark troops and seamen for active service ashore.

In spite of their age, their small size, and their indifferent sea-keeping qualities, these veteran craft did yeoman service in coastal patrol, escort, and convoy work during the war. Several had the good fortune to distinguish themselves by sinking enemy submarines, while twelve were lost.

[1] In the Navy List for November, 1914, the 30-knotters *Otter*, *Whiting* and *Virago*, together with the ex-Chinese *Taku*, captured at the Taku Forts in 1900, are shown as being for sale at Hong-Kong. All these vessels had served for a good many years on the China Station. The name of the 27-knot *Handy* is omitted, probably in error, as this ship, with the *Otter*, *Whiting*, and *Taku*, was sold at Hong-Kong during the war.

Note. – The names and characteristics of all destroyers which served, or were built, during the war will be found in Appendix II. Losses will be found in Appendices III.-VI.

As time went on these early destroyers were found to be unsuitable for work with the fleet at sea in all weathers. So in 1902–3 were built the first of what were popularly known as the " River " class, so called because they were all named after rivers of the United Kingdom. They were much more seaworthy than the earlier types, being craft of between 550 and 600 tons, with high forecastles instead of the old-fashioned turtle-backs.

They were the first British T.B.D.s to have cabins for all their officers, and rare luxuries they were considered. But what one gained in comfort one lost in emoluments, for the Admiralty eventually did away with the " hard-lying money " – 1s. 6d. a day for officers and 6d. a day for men – which all those serving in torpedo-craft used to receive.

In some of the oldest of the 27-knotters' the captain had no cabin of his own, and lived in the wardroom. This was the case in the *Lynx*, dating from 1894, which was my first command fourteen years later. We all slept on cushioned lockers in the wardroom, which were as hard as the nether millstone. And the gunner snored, in two keys. However, as I talked in my sleep, and the artificer-engineer smoked strong Navy tobacco after turning in, we were more or less quits.

The " River " class had a speed of 25½ knots, were armed with two torpedo-tubes, and, originally, one 12-pounder and five 6-pounder guns. As a result of the destroyer fighting of the Russo-Japanese War, however, the five 6-pounders were replaced by three light 12-pounders. The " River " class were always satisfactory as seaboats. Two of them, the *Exe* and the *Dee*, actually went through the middle of a typhoon in the China Sea. During the war they also did excellent service in escort and patrol work, while one was present at the capture of Tsingtau and others in the Dardanelles, where they did particularly fine work. Thirty-three of them figured in the Navy List for November 1914, and 6 were lost during the war.

Up till 1899, reciprocating engines and water-tube boilers had been used entirely, and, in spite of attempts to produce higher speeds, it was found impossible to attain more than 31 knots with this type of machinery. In 1897 the official trials of the *Turbinia*,[1] a small experimental vessel of 45 tons driven by turbines invented by the Hon. Sir Charles Parsons, produced a speed of 32.75 knots. This result, and the *Turbinia's* subsequent appearance at the

[1] Now in the Science Museum in South Kensington.

Diamond Jubilee Review of 1897, created something of a sensation.

The Admiralty took up the new idea, and in 1899 ordered the *Viper* and purchased the *Cobra*, the first vessels of war ever to be driven by turbines. They were of the old 30-knotter type, but the *Viper* attained the then phenomenal speed of 34 knots on a very economical coal consumption. Both these ships came to an untimely end, the first through breaking her back and foundering in heavy weather near the Outer Dowsing, off Cromer, and the second through running ashore near the Casquets, in the Channel Islands, in a fog during manœuvres.

But the turbine had come to stay, and in 1904, when the Committee on Designs recommended the use of oil fuel instead of coal for destroyers, a great advance was made.

Oil had many advantages. It lessened the strain on the personnel when steaming at high speeds, when every ounce of coal had to be shovelled into the furnaces ; reduced the numbers of men necessary in the boiler-rooms ; and made the task of refuelling much easier. In the older method of "coaling ship" every pound of coal had to be dug out of the hold of a collier, shovelled into bags, and then hoisted on board the ship and tipped down into her bunkers. It was a laborious, exhausting business, which took much time. In a ship burning oil fuel, however, she merely goes alongside an oiler, connects up a few hoses, and the pumps do the rest.

Whatever people may say, oil fuel is a blessing that makes for efficiency. During the war we could never have done the sea-time we sometimes had to do if we had been coal-burners. I can imagine no more dismal prospect than returning into harbour after four or five days' buffeting at sea, immediately to start in on the wearisome, dirty task of digging coal out of a collier and hoisting it on board in bags, a ton at a time.

It was different for battleships and cruisers. They had large ships' companies, in addition to which few of them spent the time at sea that we did. Moreover, they were more or less comfortable even in the vilest weather. We, who sometimes lived in a cross between an oscillating switchback and a waterfall, usually returned into harbour weary, jaded, and anxious only for a few hours' sleep and some really edible food. So I hope that nobody will ever be misguided enough to revert to coal for the use of destroyers. The only coal we carried in the war was the few tons for use in the warming stoves and galley.

The first turbine-driven, oil-fired destroyers in the British Navy built as a class were the twelve *Tribals*, produced between 1906 and 1908.   They varied in size between 865 and 1090 tons, and while the earlier ships of the type carried from three to five 12-pounder guns, the later ones mounted a 4-inch gun, the first destroyers to be so armed.   Their speed was 33 knots, though on her official trials the *Tartar* is said to have done over 37.   These twelve ships figured largely in the work of the Dover Patrol during the war, four of them being lost.

The sixteen vessels of the *Beagle* class, which followed in 1908–9, were much the same as the *Tribals*, but had a speed of only 27 knots, and burnt coal.   These craft, which were the first destroyers to carry 21-inch torpedo-tubes, were in the Mediterranean when the war broke out, and did particularly fine work in the Dardanelles.

The class which followed them, the twenty ships of the *Acorn* type, were slightly smaller, though they burnt oil fuel and carried one more 4-inch gun.   The " Improved *Acorn* " class of 20 vessels completed in 1912–13, were practically similar, but carried 30 tons more oil fuel and had a speed of 28 instead of 27 knots.   The *Acorn* class were with the Grand Fleet during the earlier part of the war, but reverted to other duties when relieved by newer craft. The " Improved *Acorns* " served with the Harwich Force under Commodore Reginald Tyrwhitt in 1914–15, but were relegated to other duties in the latter year.

The *Firedrake, Lurcher,* and *Oak* were of much the same design, but considerably faster, having speeds of 32–33 knots.   The two first-named served with submarines during the war, and the *Oak* as the special despatch vessel of the commander-in-chief of the Grand Fleet.

The *Acasta* class of eighteen destroyers, completed in 1913–14, were with the Grand Fleet during the war, many of them being present at the Battle of Jutland.   They were somewhat larger than their immediate predecessors, being of 935 tons, with a speed of about 29 knots, and armed with three 4-inch guns.

The newest destroyers actually at sea on the outbreak of hostilities were the destroyers of the " L " class of the 1912–13 programme, craft of 965 tons and 29 knots speed, armed with three 4-inch guns and four 21-inch torpedo-tubes.   They, like the " Improved *Acorns*," served at Harwich during the early part of the war.   Many were in action at Heligoland in August 1914, in the battle-cruiser action off the Dogger Bank in the following

January, besides the many little-known destroyer actions in the Narrow Seas. Four also were present at Jutland.

The first 13 vessels of the "M" class, of the 1913–14 programme, were beginning to be delivered from their builders soon after the commencement of the war. They were slightly larger than the "Ls" with a nominal speed of 34 knots, but carried the same armament.

The experience of the war fully justified the main features of the pre-war design of British destroyers, and no other type of warship required less alteration. The conditions under which they had to work were much more severe than in the German Navy, and to meet these conditions they had to possess considerable freeboard and high forecastles to ensure good sea-keeping qualities, large fuel capacity, and good living-spaces to ensure habitability in all seasons and weather conditions likely to be experienced.

The German pre-war destroyers, with their low freeboard and turtle-back forecastles, were less well adapted than the British for keeping their speeds in bad weather, while their crew-spaces were much inferior. They had the advantage, however, in that they could choose their own time of attack, and carried only the necessary quantities of fuel and stores for the actual operation intended. This gave them a high smooth-water speed which was very noticeable in the actions which took place from time to time in the Dover Straits and off the Dutch coast.

The strength of our destroyers was amply shown in bad weather, and few, if any, of the British vessels had to be dealt with for structural weakness. The efficiency of their watertight sub-division was most noticeable. Remarkable also was the length of time that some of them remained afloat after being severely damaged by enemy shell, mines, or torpedoes, or in collision. Numbers of them were safely brought into harbour with, in some cases, their bows and stems completely missing. Scuttling a destroyer, on the rare occasions it became necessary to do so, was always a matter of difficulty. When I had to sink the stern portion of the *Vehement* on August 3rd, 1918, her bows as far as the foremost funnel having already been blown off by a German mine and the explosion of her magazine, no amount of 4-inch shell along her waterline seemed to have any effect. It was only by backing astern, steaming past the wreck at 20 knots at the distance of a few feet, and letting go two depth-charges, that her remains were finally sent to the bottom.

With the outbreak of war there was a huge increase in our destroyer building, 20 more of the " M " class being ordered in September 1914 ; 32 more in November ; 18 in February 1915 ; and 20 in May.

Slight improvements were brought in from time to time, the chief of which was a sharp, square ram stem to stiffen up the structure in the bows of the ship when ramming submarines. It was most efficacious if a submarine were hit. The *Milne*, for instance, incurred no damage whatsoever, and came away with portions of the U-boat's plating still sticking to her under-water ram. Of these 70 vessels of the " M " class ordered after the outbreak of war, many perforce had names beginning with N, O, or P.

The " R " class, the first of which were ordered in May 1915, had a designed speed of 36 knots. Their general arrangement was similar to the " Ms " ; but, to give better conditions on the bridge at high speed in bad weather, their forecastles were raised one foot, the flare, or curve, of their bows was increased, and they had raked instead of straight stems. Their third 4-inch gun on the quarterdeck was also raised on a circular platform above the upper deck to keep it clear of spray and to prevent it washing down in bad weather, while the structure was slightly heavier to meet the increase in weights. Two of the " R " class were ordered in May 1915 ; 24 in July ; 10 in December ; and 15 in March 1916.

The " Modified Rs " were originally ordered as " R " class repeats ; but their forecastles were extended, as it was desired to have the bridges farther aft to give still better protection to the bridge personnel in bad weather. They also had newer pattern 4-inch guns, with 30° elevation and a range of 12,000 instead of 10,000 yards. Eleven " Modified Rs " were ordered in March 1916.

In order to meet the heavier gun armaments reported to be carried by the German destroyers in the middle of 1916, it was necessary to have destroyers with heavier gun armaments than the " R " class. The " V " class flotilla-leaders had already been ordered, and to obtain the new vessels within the minimum time for construction the " V " class destroyers were of the same dimensions, form, and arrangement as the leaders, with simplified accommodation and bridge to render them more suitable for destroyer work. They carried four 4-inch guns – two superimposed forward, and two aft ; one 3-inch anti-aircraft gun ; and

two sets of double 21-inch torpedo tubes. They had a displacement of about 1,330 tons, and a designed speed of 34 knots.
Twenty-five " V " class were ordered in July 1916.

The 21 " W " class, ordered in December 1916, which included
the *Voyager*, were precisely the same as their predecessors, except
that they mounted two sets of triple instead of double torpedo-
tubes.

Further information of the new German torpedo-craft showed
that there were only a small number of vessels of superior gun-
power corresponding to our flotilla-leaders. This enabled the

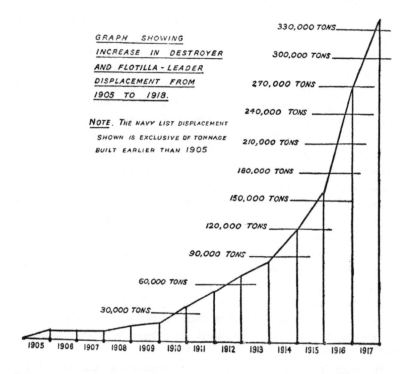

GRAPH SHOWING
INCREASE IN DESTROYER
AND FLOTILLA - LEADER
DISPLACEMENT FROM
1905 TO 1918.

NOTE. THE NAVY LIST DISPLACEMENT
SHOWN IS EXCLUSIVE OF TONNAGE
BUILT EARLIER THAN 1905

British constructors to revert to a smaller and less expensive
type of destroyer, which would be faster than the " Vs " and
" Ws " and would take less time to build. These ships were
those of the " S " class, which were slightly larger than the
" Modified Rs." To make them even better as sea-boats, the
sheer forward of the forecastle was increased by two feet to
give an upstanding bow, and the after end was lowered one
foot. The sides of the forecastle deck were rounded off, while
the bridge and chart house were altered in shape to withstand

heavy seas. An increase in the size of the bridge also became necessary to accommodate control officers on the introduction of director firing for guns and torpedoes, which incidentally, was made retrospective to all destroyers as far back as the " L " class.

The gun and torpedo armament of the " S " class were the same as that of the " Modified Rs," except that they were provided with one single 18-inch revolving torpedo-tube on each side of the upper deck under the break of the forecastle for use against enemy destroyers at night. Two 14-inch torpedo-tubes, one fixed on each beam, had previously been fitted on the upper deck at the break of the forecastle in some of the " M " and " R " class destroyers on the Dover Patrol and at Harwich.

Thirty-three " S " class destroyers were ordered in April 1917, and 36 in June. Two were cancelled on the cessation of hostilities, and, of the total of 69 ordered, about 25 were completed between March 1918 and the end of the war.

The proved superiority of the " V " and " W " classes of destroyers over the " R " class, together with the increasing need for a long range gun armament, led to a placing of orders in January and April 1918 for a further 54 vessels of the " V " class design. It was decided, however, to provide these new ships with heavier guns, and the armament eventually consisted of four 4.7-inch guns, superimposed in pairs forward and aft, one 3-inch anti-aircraft gun, and two sets of triple 21-inch torpedo-tubes.

None of these vessels was completed for sea before the end of the war, and the orders for 38 were cancelled. The remaining 16, completed in 1919–20, are now in service.

An examination of the list of the 303 destroyers in process of completion at the beginning of the war, or actually ordered during hostilities and subsequently completed, shows that the work of building these fast craft is highly specialised, and that the bulk of the orders were placed with a few firms of world-wide renown. So far as can be discovered, Messrs. John Brown completed 37 ; Messrs. Swan Hunter, 29 ; Messrs. Thornycrofts, Messrs. Yarrow, and the Fairfield Shipbuilding Company, 26 each ; Messrs. Hawthorn Leslie, 22 ; Messrs. Denny, Doxford, and Samuel White, 21 each ; Messrs. Palmer, 18 ; Messrs. Stephen, 17 ; Messrs. Scotts, 15 ; Messrs. Beardmore, 13 ; and Messrs. Harland & Wolff, 6.

When we realise the treatment that these little vessels received during the war, the work they did, and the damage they sometimes sustained without foundering, it will be realised how immeasurably the Royal Navy in general, and those who went down to the sea in destroyers in particular, stand in the debt of those who built, engined, and designed the stout, speedy little vessels that withstood so much. British destroyers, if carefully handled, could face practically any sea without damage to the main structure, and I have heard of no case of any vessel having to be specially strengthened during the war. On the other hand, and without in the least wishing to disparage their wonderful work, I understand that some of the American destroyers serving at Queenstown had to be strengthened during the winter of 1917–18 to enable them to compete with the heavy seas of the open Atlantic and the western approaches to the Channel.

The building of destroyers, as already pointed out, is a highly specialised art. Though foreign craft may sometimes attain phenomenal speeds in artificial conditions, speeds which are no real use on service and for which, as a rule, there must be a corresponding decrease in strength, the war proved over and over again that for general, all-round purposes the British destroyers were the best in the world.

Even during the last few months certain Italian firms have been reporting phenomenal trial speeds for destroyers they have built. I have reason to know that these speeds, instead of being the means of six runs, with and against the tide and wind, or both, are the maximum speeds obtained in the most favourable circumstances – that is, with the wind and tide, and generally on the last trial run, when, with fuel and boiler water largely exhausted, the vessels are at their lightest displacement. On such occasions, moreover, the ships have often been lighter than they should be, the guns being left out, and the power being " boosted " for the test minutes or quarter of an hour required for the run. Abnormal speeds may thus be obtained which can never be repeated during the vessels' service at sea, and not infrequently have the effect of straining and permanently damaging the propelling installations.

The published trial speeds of British destroyers, on the other hand, are mean speeds with the vessels complete and in a service condition and without any overload on the machinery. These speeds can be reproduced on actual service and over extended periods, and represent more truly the service performances of the vessels.

No records are available as to the number of British destroyers which were severely damaged during the war by gunfire, torpedo, mine, or collision. But the number was prodigious, and it was little short of miraculous how some of the ships ever remained afloat, to be towed home, or to steam home, as battered wrecks, and to be refitted, some in the royal dockyards, but the majority by private firms. There seems to have been more anxiety to get the damaged ships to sea again than to make notes of precisely what was done. The shipbuilding firms of Great Britain rose nobly to the occasion, which makes the present state of depression in this national industry all the more distressing.

But the truly amazing thing about destroyers in the war – and here I speak from personal experience – was their vitality. This, let me reiterate, quite apart from their armament and seagoing speed in service conditions, proved time and time again that the British destroyers need fear no foreign competitors.

During the eventful four years of hostilities there was hardly a purpose for which they were not utilised at one time or another. With the battleships of the Grand Fleet – indeed, with all detachments of heavy ships – they were used as permanent anti-submarine screens at sea in all weathers, as well as in action for beating off hostile destroyer attacks with their guns, attacking the enemy heavy ships with torpedoes, and making smoke-screens. They escorted minelayers and aircraft-carriers, and towed kite balloons. Provided with rams, explosive sweeps, depth-charges, and, in the later stages of the war, with listening devices, they hunted submarines.

They were used for coastal patrols, escorted vessels of the cross-Channel services between England and Havre, Dieppe, Boulogne, Calais, and Dunkerque. Large numbers were pressed into the convoy service during the later stages of the war during the unrestricted submarine campaign, when they not only convoyed transports and merchantmen through the particularly dangerous waters contiguous to the British Isles, but to and fro throughout the Mediterranean and half way across the Atlantic. In the Dardanelles they were used for landing troops, while in the same campaign, in the Suez Canal, and on the Flanders coast, they bombarded enemy troops and positions ashore. They were even utilised as minelayers and minesweepers.

Their casualties, as I have pointed out elsewhere in this book, including flotilla-leaders, amounted to 67 vessels lost during the 4 years 3 months and 7 days that the war lasted – 17 in action,

8 sunk by submarines, 20 by mines, 12 in collision, 8 wrecked, and 1 through a cause unknown. I do not think I exaggerate if I say that the destroyers, together with the light-cruisers, trawlers, and drifters, were the hardest worked vessels of the war. Their number was legion. Like the Royal Artillery, their motto might well be

UBIQUE

3. PATROL-BOATS

Experience gained in the first months of the war showed the necessity for many more vessels of the destroyer type for the strenuous and continuous duties of general patrol, submarine hunting, and escort work. The huge destroyer programme already referred to was largely the result of the increasing effectiveness of the German submarine warfare, and all the firms accustomed to constructing destroyers were fully occupied in building them. Any further output of patrol craft had therefore to be undertaken by contractors unaccustomed to Admiralty requirements in the construction of torpedo-craft.

In April 1915 proposals were put forward for a number of easily manœuvred vessels of moderate speed, a powerful defensive armament, and low visibility. The Admiralty further suggested that they should have the general appearance of steam submarines on the surface, and that their light, mild-steel hulls should be capable of being built by contractors unused to the more stringent conditions of destroyer hulls. Low-powered machinery would provide the " moderate " speed required, and all the vessels would be provided with hardened steel rams for dealing with submarines.

In May 1915, 24 of these vessels, numbered P11 to P34 inclusive, P13 being numbered P75, were ordered from 18 different firms, most of which were accustomed to the building of merchant-ships. They were all completed between January and December 1916, and were ships of about 570 tons, with geared turbines and oil-fired boilers. Their designed speed was 20 knots, though most of them could steam 22. Their armament consisted of one 4-inch gun, a 2-pounder pom-pom, and a couple of fixed 14-inch torpedo-tubes, one on each quarter. Depth-charges and

NOTE. – War losses of patrol-boats will be found in Appendices III–VI.

depth-charge throwers were also provided, though all torpedo-tubes were eventually surrendered for increased depth-charge outfits.

The time of building varied from 9 to 18 months, and the approximate cost of each vessel was about £104,000. Owing to their low forecastles and peculiar cut-away sterns, the P-boats were rather wet in anything approaching bad weather. Generally speaking, however, their seaworthiness in almost any weather left little to be desired.

Another 6 P-boats were ordered in February 1916 – P35 to P40 inclusive – making a total of 30 of these first two batches actually completed by May 1917.

The general features of their first design were continued until December 1916, when it became definitely known that the Germans intended to make unrestricted use of their submarines against merchant-shipping. The P-boats were considered to be about the right size for disguising as small merchant-ships, and, of the 34 further vessels ordered between March 1916 and June 1917, 21 were converted to, or built as, P.C. boats.

These vessels, P.C.s 42 to 45, 51, 55, 56, 60 to 63, 65 to 74, were really decoy ships of mercantile appearance. Their hulls were built up to increase the freeboard, and they were provided with a short forecastle, poop, and midship structure, the usual perpendicular funnel amidships, and two perpendicular masts complete with dummy derricks. The armament, which consisted of one 4-inch gun, two 12-pounders, and four depth-charges, was concealed ; the depth-charges under the poop, the 4-inch gun under a screen just before the mainmast, and the 12-pounders one either side underneath the bridge.

Due to the additional structure, their displacement was brought up to 692 tons, and their average price to £116,000 per ship. Their maximum draught was under 9 feet, which meant that they were far less likely to be torpedoed or mined than ordinary merchant-ships. Their speed of 20½ knots also gave them every chance of successfully dealing with a submarine which might be beguiled into thinking she was dealing with an ordinary merchantman.

So far as can be ascertained from the records, P. and P.C. boats actually destroyed 5 submarines during the war, while one was lost through the explosion of a mine and another by collision. The measure of their success, however, can by no means be estimated by the number of submarines actually disposed of. They were invaluable for patrol and convoy work, and, like the destroyers, were always busily employed.

NOMINAL LIST OF FLOTILLA-LEADERS IN SERVICE DURING THE WAR.

Swift – Completed 1908. 1,825 tons. 38.3 knots. Four 4-inch guns. 2 torpedo-tubes. Oil fuel. Turbines. A 6-inch gun was fitted on the forecastle of the *Swift* during the war to meet the German Channel raiders while she was serving on the Dover Patrol. It was not very successful, and was afterwards removed.

Lightfoot	(White)	Completed Aug. – Sept. 1915. 1,605 tons. 34 knots. Four 4-inch guns. Two 2-pdrs. 2 pairs 21-inch torpedo-tubes. Oil fuel. Turbines.
Marksman	(Hawthorn Leslie)	
Kempenfelt	(Cammell Laird)	
Nimrod	(Denny)	

Botha	(White)	Completed Aug. 1914 – June 1915. Building for Chile. 1,700 tons approx. 31–32 knots. Six 4-inch guns. 2 pairs, or 4 single, 21-inch torpedo-tubes. Coal. Oil fuel. Turbines.
Tipperary[1]	,,	
Faulknor	,,	
Broke	,,	

Abdiel	(Cammell Laird)	Completed March – Aug. 1916. Similar to *Lightfoot*. *Abdiel* fitted as minelayer.
Gabriel	,, ,,	
Ithuriel	,, ,,	

Parker	(Cammell Laird)	
Grenville	,, ,,	
Hoste[1]	,, ,,	Completed Aug. 1916 – April 1917. Similar to *Lightfoot*.
Seymour	,, ,,	
Saumarez	,, ,,	
Anzac	(Denny)	

Valkyrie	(Denny)	Completed June – Sept. 1917. 1,330 tons. 34 knots. Four 4-inch guns. One 3-inch H.A. 2 pairs 21-inch torpedo-tubes except *Vampire*, which had 2 sets of triple tubes.
Valorous	,,	
Valentine	(Cammell Laird)	
Valhalla	,, ,,	
Vampire	(White)	

Shakespeare	(Thornycroft)	
Spenser	,,	
Scott[1]	(Cammell Laird)	All except *Campbell*, *Mackay*, *Malcolm*, and *Stuart*, completed before the end of the war. 1,800 tons. 36½ knots. Five 4.7-inch guns. One 3-inch H.A. 2 sets of triple 21-inch torpedo-tubes.
Bruce	,, ,,	
Douglas	,, ,,	
Campbell	,, ,,	
Mackay	,, ,,	
Malcolm	,, ,,	
Montrose	(Hawthorn Leslie)	
Stuart	,, ,,	

[1] Lost during the war.

Keppel   (Thornycroft)

Rooke (now *Broke*)   (Thornycroft)

Six of this class were ordered ; but four were cancelled owing to termination of hostilities. *Keppel* and *Broke* were completed in 1925. Details as for preceding class.

Of the 34 flotilla-leaders building at the outbreak of war, or ordered during hostilities and subsequently completed, Cammell Laird built 17 ; White's 6 ; Denny and Thornycroft, 4 each ; and Hawthorn Leslie, 3.

NOMINAL LISTS OF BRITISH DESTROYERS IN SERVICE DURING THE WAR

27 AND 30 KNOT TYPES.

300–450 tons. Mostly completed for sea between 1895 and 1901, except *Albacore* and *Bonetta*, which were built as stock-boats by Messrs. Palmers and taken over by the Admiralty in about 1909. Nominal speeds of 27 and 30 knots. Armament usually one 12-pounder and five 6-pounder guns, and two 18-inch torpedo-tubes.

Albacore, Albatross, Angler, Arab, Avon, Bat, Bittern,[1] *Bonetta,* BOXER,[1] *Brazen, Bullfinch, Cheerful*[1] CONFLICT, *Coquette,*[1] *Crane, Cygnet, Cynthia, Desperate, Dove, Earnest, Electra, Express, Fairy,*[1] *Falcon,*[1] *Fame, Fawn,* FERVENT, *Flirt,*[1] *Flying Fish, Gipsy, Greyhound, Griffon, Kangaroo, Kestrel, Leopard, Leven,* LIGHTNING,[1] *Lively, Locust, Mallard, Mermaid, Myrmidon,*[1] OPOSSUM, *Orwell, Osprey, Ostrich, Panther, Peterel,* POR-CUPINE, *Quail, Racehorse, Recruit,*[1] *Roebuck, Seal, Spiteful, Sprightly, Stag, Star, Success,*[1] SUNFISH, SURLY, *Sylvia, Syren, Thorn, Thrasher, Velox,*[1] *Vigilant, Violet, Vixen, Vulture,* WIZARD, *Wolf,* ZEPHYR.

NOTE. – *The ten names in capitals are those of the old 27-knotters completed for sea between* 1894 *and* 1896.

"RIVER" CLASS

550–600 tons. Mostly completed for sea between 1904 and 1907. The first destroyers to have high forecastles. $25\frac{1}{2}$ knots. Armament, four 12-pounders and two 18-inch torpedo-tubes.

Arun, Boyne, Chelmer, Cherwell, Colne, Dee, Derwent,[1] *Doon, Eden, Erne,*[1] *Ettrick, Exe, Foyle,*[1] *Garry, Itchen,*[1] *Jed, Kale,*[1] *Kennet, Liffey, Moy, Ness, Nith, Ouse, Ribble, Rother, Stour, Test, Teviot, Ure, Usk, Waveney, Wear, Welland.*

"TRIBAL" CLASS

865–1,090 tons. Completed for sea 1908–10. The first ocean-going destroyers, and the first to have entirely oil fuel and turbines. Designed speed 33 knots; but most of them exceeded it. *Tartar* did 37.4 on trials. Armament either five 12-pounder guns or two 4-inch, with the usual couple of 18-inch torpedo-tubes.

Afridi, Amazon, Cossack, Crusader, Ghurka,[1] *Maori,*[1] *Mohawk, Nubian,*[1],[2] *Saracen, Tartar, Viking, Zulu.*[1],[2]

"BEAGLE" CLASS

860–940 tons. Completed 1910–11. Coal burning. Turbines. One 4-inch and three 12-pounder guns. Two 21-inch torpedo-tubes, the first destroyers to have torpedoes of this size.

Basilisk, Beagle, Bulldog, Foxhound, Grampus, Grasshopper, Harpy, Mosquito, Pincher,[1] *Racoon,*[1] *Rattlesnake, Renard, Savage, Scorpion, Scourge, Wolverine.*[1]

[1] Lost during the war.
[2] Bow of *Zulu* and stern of *Nubian* joined together to make one ship called *Zubian.*

" Acorn " Class

780 tons. Completed 1911–12. Oil fuel. Turbines. 27 knots. Two 4-inch and two 12-pounder guns. Two 21-inch torpedo-tubes.

Acorn, Alarm, Brisk, Cameleon, Comet,[1] *Fury, Goldfinch,*[1] *Hope, Larne, Lyra, Martin, Minstrel, Nemesis, Nereide, Nymphe, Redpole, Rifleman, Ruby, Sheldrake, Staunch.*[1]

Improved " Acorn " Class

780 tons. Completed 1912–13. Oil fuel. Turbines. 28 knots. Two 4-inch and two 12-pounder guns. Two 21-inch torpedo-tubes.

Acheron, Archer, Ariel,[1] *Attack,*[1] *Badger, Beaver, Defender, Druid, Ferret, Forester, Goshawk, Hind, Hornet, Hydra, Jackal, Lapwing, Lizard, Phœnix,*[1] *Sandfly, Tigress.*

Special Type, much the same as *Acorn* class, but with speeds of about 32–33 knots. Completed 1912.

Firedrake, Lurcher, Oak.

" Acasta " Class

935 tons. Completed 1913–14. 29 knots. Three 4-inch guns. Two 21-inch torpedo-tubes.

Acasta, Achates, Ambuscade, Ardent,[1] *Christopher, Cockatrice, Contest,*[1] *Fortune,*[1] *Garland, Hardy, Lynx,*[1] *Midge, Owl, Paragon,*[1] *Porpoise, Shark,*[1] *Sparrowhawk,*[1] *Spitfire, Unity, Victor.*

" L " Class

965 tons. Completed 1914–15. 29 knots. Three 4-inch guns. Two pairs of 21-inch torpedo-tubes. Seven of this class were still completing when war broke out.

Laertes, Laforey,[1] *Lance, Landrail, Lark, Lassoo,*[1] *Laurel, Laverock, Lawford, Legion, Lennox, Leonidas, Liberty, Linnet, Llewellyn, Lookout, Louis,*[1] *Loyal, Lucifer, Lydiard, Lysander.*

" M " Class

880–1,055 tons. Completed 1914–15. 34–35 knots. Three 4-inch guns. Two pairs of 21-inch torpedo-tubes. 1913–14 programme. All building when war broke out.

13 on order in August 1914.

Manly	(Yarrow)	*Minos*	(Yarrow)
Matchless	(Swan, Hunter)	*Morris*	(John Brown)
Milne	(John Brown)	*Mastiff*	(Thornycroft)
Moorsom	,, ,,	*Meteor*	,,
Myngs	(Palmers)	*Miranda*	(Yarrow)
Mansfield	(Hawthorn Leslie)	*Murray*	(Palmers)
Mentor	,, ,,		

[1] Lost during the war.

20 ordered September 1914

Mons	(John Brown)	*Mary Rose*[1]	(Swan, Hunter)
Marne	,, ,,	*Menace*	,, ,,
Mystic	(Denny)	*Michael*	(Thornycroft)
Mænad	,,	*Milbrook*	,,
Manners	(Fairfield)	*Minion*	,,
Mandate	,,	*Munster*	,,
Magic	(White)	*Moon*	(Yarrow)
Moresby	,,	*Morning Star*	,,
Marmion[1]	(Swan, Hunter)	*Mounsey*	,,
Martial	,, ,,	*Musketeer*	,,

10 ordered November 1914 (first order)

Mameluke	(John Brown)	*Negro*[1]	(Palmers)
Marvel	(Denny)	*Nepean*	(Thornycroft)
Mindful	(Fairfield)	*Nereus*	,,
Mischief	,,	*Nessus*	Swan, Hunter)
Nonsuch	(Palmers)	*Nerissa*	(Yarrow)

22 ordered November 1914 (second order)

Nestor[1]	(A. Stephen)	*Onslaught*	(Fairfield)
Noble	,,	*Onslow*	,,
Nizam	,,	*Opal*[1]	(Doxford)
Nomad[1]	,,	*Ophelia*	,,
Nonpariel	,,	*Opportune*	,,
Norman	(Palmers)	*Oracle*	,,
Northesk	,,	*Orestes*	,,
North Star[1]	,,	*Orford*	,,
Nugent	,,	*Orpheus*	,,
Obedient	(Scotts)	*Octavia*	,,
Obdurate	,,	*Ossory*	(John Brown)

18 ordered February 1915

Napier	(John Brown)	*Oriana*	(Fairfield)
Narbrough[1]	,,	*Oriole*	(Palmers)
Narwhal	(Denny)	*Osiris*	,,
Nicator	,,	*Paladin*	(Scotts)
Norseman	(Doxford)	*Parthian*	,,
Oberon	,,	*Partridge*[1]	(Swan, Hunter)
Observer	(Fairfield)	*Pasley*	,, ,,
Offa	,,	*Patrician*	(Thornycroft)
Orcadia	,,	*Patriot*	,,

[1] Lost during the war.

20 ordered May 1915

Plucky	(Scotts)	*Petard*	(Denny)
Portia	,,	*Peyton*	,,
Pheasant[1]	(Fairfield)	*Prince*	(A. Stephens)
Phœbe	,,	*Pylades*	,,
Pigeon	(Hawthorn Leslie)	*Medina*	(White)
Plover	,, ,,	*Medway*	,,
Penn	(John Brown)	*Rapid*	(Thornycroft)
Peregrine	,, ,,	*Ready*	,,
Pelican	(Beardmore)	*Relentless*	(Yarrow)
Pellew	,,	*Rival*	,,

DESTROYERS BUILDING FOR GREEK GOVERNMENT TAKEN OVER BY THE ADMIRALTY

These four vessels were practically the same as the " M " class.

Medea	(John Brown)	*Melampus*	(Fairfield)
Medusa[1]	,, ,,	*Melpomene*	,,

DESTROYERS BUILDING FOR TURKISH GOVERNMENT TAKEN OVER BY THE ADMIRALTY

1,098 tons. Completed Jan.–March 1916. 32 knots. Five 4-inch guns. 2 pairs of 21-inch torpedo-tubes.

Talisman, Turbulent,[1] *Trident, Termagant* (all Hawthorn Leslie).

DESTROYERS BUILDING FOR PORTUGUESE GOVERNMENT TAKEN OVER BY THE ADMIRALTY

About 600 tons. Four 12-pounder guns. Three 18-inch torpedo-tubes.

Arno.[1] Building by Messrs. Ansaldo of Genoa.

" R " CLASS.

Slightly larger and faster than the " M " class, but same armament. Forecastle raised one foot for better seaworthiness. Designed speed, 36 knots.

2 ordered May 1915
Radstock, Raider (both Swan, Hunter)

24 ordered July 1915

Romola	(John Brown)	*Sylph*	(Harland & Wolff)
Rowena	,, ,,	*Sarpedon*	(Hawthorn Leslie)
Restless	,, ,,	*Sable*	(White)
Rigorous	,, ,,	*Setter*[1]	,,
Rocket	(Denny)	*Sorceress*	(Swan, Hunter)
Rob Roy	,,	*Rosalind*	(Thornycroft)
Red Gauntlet	,,	*Radiant*	,,
Redoubt	(Doxford)	*Retriever*	,,

[1] Lost during the war.

Recruit[1]	(Doxford)	*Sabrina*	(Yarrow)
Sturgeon	(A. Stephen)	*Strongbow*[1]	,,
Sceptre	,,	*Surprise*[1]	,,
Salmon	(Harland & Wolff)	*Sybille*	,,

10 ordered December 1915

Satyr	(Beardmore)	*Stork*	(Hawthorn)
Sharpshooter	,,	*Skilful*	(Harland & Wolff)
Simoom[1]	(John Brown)	*Springbok*	,, ,,
Skate	,, ,,	*Taurus*	(Thornycroft)
Starfish	(Hawthorn)	*Teazer*	,,

15 ordered March 1916

Tancred	(Beardmore)	*Tormentor*	(A. Stephen)
Tarpon	(John Brown)	*Tornado*[1]	,,
Telemachus	,, ,,	*Torrent*[1]	(Swan, Hunter)
Tempest	(Fairfield)	*Torrid*	,, ,,
Tenacious	(Harland & Wolff)	*Truculent*	(Yarrow)
Tetrarch	,, ,,	*Tyrant*	,,
Thisbe	(Hawthorn Leslie)	*Ulleswater*[1]	,,
Thruster	,, ,,		

MODIFIED " R " CLASS
Bridge moved slightly aft and forecastle lengthened for better sea-worthiness. Otherwise same as " R " class.

11 ordered March 1916

Trenchant	(White)	*Ulysses*[1]	(Doxford)
Tristram	,,	*Umpire*	,,
Tower	(Swan, Hunter)	*Undine*	(Fairfield)
Tirade	(Scotts)	*Urchin*	(Palmers)
Ursula	,,	*Ursa*	,,
Ulster	(Beardmore)		

" V " CLASS
Same design as " V " class leaders to accelerate construction. These destroyers were designed to meet the heavier gun armaments of German destroyers. About 1,330 tons, and 34 knots designed speed. Four 4-inch guns, one 3-inch H.A., and 2 pairs of double 21-inch torpedo-tubes.

25 ordered July 1916

Vancouver (now *Vimy*)	(Beardmore)	*Verulam*[2]	(Hawthorn Leslie)
Vanessa	(Beardmore)	*Vesper*	(A. Stephen)
Vanity	,,	*Vidette*	,,

[1] Lost during the war.   [2] Lost in Baltic after Armistice.

Vanoc	(John Brown)	*Violent*	(Swan, Hunter)
Vanquisher	,, ,,	*Vimiera*	,, ,,
Vega	(Doxford)	*Vittoria*²	,, ,,
Velox	,,	*Vivacious*	(Yarrow)
Vehement ¹	(Denny)	*Vivien*	,,
Venturous	,,	*Vectis*	(White)
Vendetta	(Fairfield)	*Vortigern*	,,
Venetia	,,	*Viceroy*	(Thornycroft)
Verdun	(Hawthorn Leslie)	*Viscount*	,,
Versatile	,, ,,		

" W " CLASS

The vessels of this order were repeats of the " V " class, except that they had two sets of triple torpedo-tubes instead of double.

21 ordered December 1916

Voyager	(A. Stephens)	*Warwick*	(Hawthorn Leslie)
Walrus	(Fairfield)	*Wessex*	,, ,,
Wolfhound	,,	*Whirlwind*	(Swan, Hunter)
Wakeful	(John Brown)	*Wrestler*	,, ,,
Watchman	,, ,,	*Wryneck*	(Palmers)
Westminster	(Scotts)	*Waterhen*	,,
Windsor	,,	*Walpole*	(Doxford)
Walker	(Denny)	*Whitley*	,,
Westcott	,,	*Wolsey*	(Thornycroft)
Winchelsea	(White)	*Woolston*	,,
Winchester	,,		

" S " CLASS

33 ordered April 1917

Improvements on Modified " R " class

Simoom	(John Brown)	*Sepoy*	(Denny)
Scimitar	,, ,,	*Seraph*	,,
Scotsman	,, ,,	*Swallow*	(Scotts)
Scout	,, ,,	*Swordsman*	,,
Shark	(Swan, Hunter)	*Steadfast*	(Palmers)
Sparrowhawk	,, ,,	*Sterling*	,,
Splendid	,, ,,	*Tribune*	(White)
*Sabre*³	(A. Stephen)	*Trinidad*	,,
Saladin	,,	*Torch*	(Yarrow)
Sikh	(Fairfield)	*Tomahawk*	,,
Sirdar	,,	*Tryphon*⁴	,,
Somme	,,	*Tumult*	,,

¹ Lost during the war.
² Lost in Baltic after Armistice.
³ Completed by Fairfield.
⁴ Wrecked at Mudros, 1919.   Towed to Malta and there sold.

Success	(Doxford)	*Turquoise*	(Yarrow)
Shamrock	,,	*Tuscan*	,,
Shikari	,,	*Tyrian*	,,
Senator	(Denny)	*Speedy*[1]	(Thornycroft)
Tobago	,,		

36 ordered June 1917.   2 cancelled due to cessation of hostilities

Turbulent	(Hawthorn Leslie)	*Searcher*	(John Brown)
Tenedos	,, ,,	*Seawolf*	,, ,,
Thanet	,, ,,	*Sardonyx*	(A. Stephen)
Thracian	,, ,,	*Stonehenge*[2]	(Palmers)
Serapis	(Denny)	*Stormcloud*	,,
Serene	,,	*Sportive*	(Swan, Hunter)
Sesame	,,	*Stalwart*	,, ,,
Trojan	(White)	*Tilbury*	,, ,,
Truant	,,	*Tintagel*	,, ,,
Trusty	,,	*Spear*	(Fairfield)
Tactician	(Beardmore)	*Spindrift*	,,
Tara	,,	*Strenuous*	(Scotts)
Tasmania	,,	*Stronghold*	,,
Tattoo	,,	*Sturdy*	,,
Scythe	(John Brown)	*Torbay*	(Thornycroft)
Seabear	,, ,,	*Toreador*	,,
Seafire	,, ,,	*Tourmaline*	,,

REPEAT " W " CLASS

The proved superiority of the " V " and " W " class destroyers over the earlier types led to the placing of further orders. The repeat " W " class had four 4.7-inch guns instead of the 4-inch of the " Vs " and " Ws."

16 ordered January 1918, but 7 cancelled due to cessation of hostilities

Vansittart	(Beardmore)	*Whitehall*	(Swan, Hunter)
Volunteer	(Denny)	*Wren*	(Yarrow)
Venomous	(John Brown)	*Wishart*	(Thornycroft)
Verity	,,	*Witch*	,,
Wanderer	(Fairfield)		

REPEAT " W " CLASS

38 ordered April 1918, but 31 cancelled due to cessation of hostilities

Veteran	(John Brown)	*Wivern*	(White)
Whitshed	(Swan, Hunter)	*Wolverine*	,,
Wild Swan	,, ,,	*Worcester*	,,
Witherington	(White)		

[1] Sunk in collision, Sea of Marmora, 1922.
[2] Wrecked near Smyrna, 1920.

Of the 303 destroyers in process of completion at the beginning of the war, and actually ordered during hostilities and completed, John Brown built 37 ; Swan, Hunter, 29 ; Thornycroft, Fairfield, and Yarrow, 26 each ; Hawthorn Leslie, 22 ; Denny, Doxford, and White, 21 each ; Palmers, 18 ; Stephen, 17 ; Scotts, 15 ; Beardmore, 13 ; and Harland & Wolff, 6.

LIST OF LOSSES

OF FLOTILLA-LEADERS, DESTROYERS,
TORPEDO-BOATS, AND PATROL-BOATS, ARRANGED ACCORDING TO YEARS

(Compiled from a White Paper, "Navy Losses," of August 1919)

Class	Name	Displacement	Date of Launch	Date of Completion	Date of Loss	How Lost and Where
Destroyers	*Success*	385	21/3/01	May 1902	**1914** Dec. 27th	Wrecked off Fifeness
	Erne	550	14/1/03	Feb. 1904	**1915** Feb. 6th	Wrecked off Rattray Head
	Goldfinch	747	12/7/10	Feb. 1911	Feb. 18–19th	Wrecked off Orkney Islands
	Recruit (old)	385	22/8/96	Oct. 1900	May 1st	Sunk by submarine off Galloper
	Maori	1,035	24/5/09	Nov. 1909	May 7th	Sunk by mine off Belgian Coast
	Lightning	320	10/4/95	Jan. 1896	June 30th	Sunk by mine in North Sea
	Lynx	935	20/3/13	Jan. 1914	Aug. 9th	Mined off Moray Firth
	Velox	420	11/2/02	Feb. 1904	Oct. 25th	Mined off Nab Light-Vessel
	Louis	965	30/12/13	May 1914	Oct. 31st	Wrecked in Suvla Bay
Torpedo-boats	064	87	—	Sept. 1886	March 21st	Wrecked in Ægean Sea
	10	245	13/2/07	May 1907	June 10th	Mined in North Sea
	12	263	15/3/07	May 1907	June 10th	
	96	130	—	April 1896	Nov. 1st	Sunk in collision off Gibraltar
	046	79	—	July 1886	Dec. 27th	Wrecked by heavy weather while in tow in Eastern Mediterranean

Class	Name	Displacement	Date of Launch	Date of Completion	Date of Loss	How Lost and Where
					1916	
Flotilla-leaders	Tipperary	1,737	5/3/15	May 1915	May 31st	Sunk in action in North Sea
	Hoste	1,666	16/8/16	Nov. 1916	Dec. 21st	Sunk in action in collision
Destroyers	Coquette	355	25/11/97	Nov. 1899	Mar. 7th	Sunk by mine in North Sea
	Medusa	1,007	27/3/15	June 1915	Mar. 25th	Sunk after collision in North Sea
	Ardent	981	8/9/13	Feb. 1914	May 31st	
	Fortune	1,000	17/3/13	Dec. 1913	May 31st	
	Nestor	1,025	22/12/15	April 1916	May 31st	
	Nomad	1,025	7/2/16	April 1916	May 31st	Sunk in action in North Sea, Battle of Jutland
	Shark	935	30/7/12	April 1913	May 31st	
	Sparrowhawk	935	12/10/12	May 1913	May 31st	
	Turbulent	1,080	5/1/16	May 1916	May 31st	
	Eden	540	14/3/03	June 1904	June 18th	Sunk in collision in English Channel
	Lassoo	1,010	24/8/15	Oct. 1915	Aug. 13th	Sunk by mine in North Sea
	Flirt	380	15/5/97	April 1899	Oct. 27th	Sunk in action in Straits of Dover
	Zulu	1,027	16/9/09	Mar. 1910	Oct. 27th	Damaged in action afterwards made into one ship named Zubian
	Nubian	1,062	20/4/09	Sept. 1909	Oct. 27th	
	Negro	1,025	8/3/16	May 1916	Dec. 21st	Sunk in North Sea by collision
Torpedo-boats	13	270	10/7/07	May 1908	Jan. 26th	Sunk by mine in North Sea
	11	263	9/1/07	May 1907	Mar. 7th	Sunk by collision in North Sea
	9	247	18/3/07	June 1907	July 26th	
					1917	
Destroyers	Simoom	1,072	30/10/16	Dec. 1916	Jan. 23rd	Sunk in action in North Sea
	Ghurka	880	29/4/07	Dec. 1908	Feb. 8th	Sunk by mine in English Channel
	Pheasant	1,025	23/10/16	Nov. 1916	Mar. 1st	Sunk off Orkneys, apparently by floating mine
	Foyle	550	25/2/03	Mar. 1904	Oct. 27th	Sunk by mine in Dover Straits
	Paragon	917	21/2/13	Dec. 1913	Mar. 15th	Sunk in action in Dover Straits
	Laforey	995	22/8/13	Feb. 1914	Mar. 18th	
	Myrmidon	370	26/5/00	May. 1901	Mar. 23rd	
	Derwent	555	14/2/03	July 1904	Mar. 26th	Sunk by mine in English Channel
					May 2nd	

Class	Name	Displacement	Date of Launch	Date of Completion	Date of Loss	How Lost and Where
					1917	
Destroyers	*Setter*	1,040	18/8/16	Feb. 1917	May 17th	Sunk by collision in North Sea
	Cheerful	370	14/7/97	Feb. 1900	June 30th	Sunk by mine off Shetland Islands
	Itchen	550	17/3/03	Jan. 1904	July 6th	Sunk by submarine in North Sea
	Recruit (new)	1,075	9/12/16	April 1917	Aug. 9th	Sunk by mine in North Sea
	Contest	957	7/1/13	June 1913	Sept. 18th	Sunk by submarine in English Channel
	Mary Rose	1,017	8/10/15	Mar. 1916	Oct. 17th	Sunk in action in North Sea
	Strongbow	898	30/9/16	Nov. 1916	Oct. 17th	
	Marmion	1,029	28/5/15	Sept. 1915	Oct. 21st	Sunk by collision in North Sea
	Staunch	748	29/10/10	Mar. 1916	Nov. 11th	Sunk by submarine off coast of Palestine
	Partridge	1,016	4/3/16	June 1916	Dec. 12th	Sunk in action in North Sea
	Wolverine	986	15/1/10	Sept. 1910	Dec. 12th	Sunk by collision off Irish coast
	Surprise	910	25/11/16	Jan. 1917	Dec. 23rd	
	Tornado	1,091	4/8/17	Nov. 1917	Dec. 23rd	Sunk by mine in North Sea
	Torrent	1,069	26/11/16	Feb. 1917	Dec. 23rd	
	Attack	785	21/12/11	May 1912	Dec. 30th	Sunk by mine off Alexandria
Torpedo-boats	24	319	19/3/08	June 1909	Jan. 28th	Wrecked off Dover breakwater
	117	197	18/2/04	Sept. 1904	June 10th	Sunk by collision in English Channel
Patrol-boat	P.26	613	22/12/15	May 1916	April 10th	Sunk by mine in English Channel
					1918	
Flotilla-leader	*Scott*	1,801	18/10/17	Jan. 1918	Aug. 15th	Sunk by submarine in North Sea
Destroyers	*Racoon*	913	15/2/10	Oct. 1910	Jan. 9th	Wrecked off North Irish coast
	Narbrough	1,010	2/3/16	April 1916	Jan. 12th	Wrecked in Pentland Firth
	Opal	1,000	11/9/15	April 1916	Jan. 12th	
	Boxer	280	28/11/94	June 1895	Feb. 8th	Sunk by collision in English Channel
	Arno	550		June 1915	Mar. 23rd	Sunk by collision off Dardanelles
	Kale	545	8/11/04	Aug. 1905	Mar. 27th	Sunk by mine in North Sea
	Falcon	408	28/12/99	Dec. 1901	April 1st	Sunk by collision in North Sea
	Bittern	360	1/2/97	April 1899	April 4th	Sunk by collision in English Channel

Class	Name	Displacement	Date of Launch	Date of Completion	Date of Loss	How Lost and Where
Destroyers	North Star	1,042	9/11/16	Feb. 1917	**1918** April 23rd	Sunk in action at Zeebrugge
	Phoenix	765	9/10/11	May 1912	May 14th	Sunk by submarine in Adriatic
	Fairy	380	29/5/97	Aug. 1898	May 31st	Sunk after ramming and destroying enemy submarine in North Sea
	Pincher	975	15/3/10	Sept. 1910	July 24th	Wrecked on Seven Stones
	Vehement	1,300	6/7/17	Oct. 1917	Aug. 2nd	Sunk by mine in North Sea
	Ariel	763	26/9/11	March 1912	Aug. 2nd	Sunk by mine in North Sea
	Comet	747	23/6/10	Jan. 1911	Aug. 6th	Sunk by submarine in Mediterranean
	Ulleswater	923	4/8/17	Sept. 1917	Aug. 15th	Sunk by submarine in North Sea
	Nessus	1,022	24/8/15	Nov. 1915	Sept. 8th	Sunk by collision in North Sea
	Ulysses	1,090	24/3/17	June 1917	Oct. 29th	Sunk by collision in Firth of Clyde
Torpedo-boat	90	130	—	Nov. 1895	April 25th	Capsized and sank in Straits of Gibraltar
Patrol-boat	P 12	613	4/12/15	Feb. 1916	Nov. 4th	Sunk by collision in English Channel

SUMMARY OF LOSSES OF FLOTILLA-LEADERS, TORPEDO-BOAT DESTROYERS, TORPEDO-BOATS, AND PATROL-BOATS

Class	Aug. 4th, 1914 to Dec. 31st, 1914	1915	1916	1917	Jan. 1st, 1918 to Nov. 11th, 1918	Total number lost
Flotilla-leaders	—	—	2	—	1	3
Torpedo-boat destroyers	1	8	14[1]	23	18	64[1]
Torpedo-boats	—	5	2	2	1	11
Patrol-boats	—	—	—	1	1	2
	1	13	18	26	21	80

[1] Including *Zulu* and *Nubian*, damaged in action and afterwards made into one ship named *Zubian* (counted as one lost).

APPENDIX V

ANALYSIS OF CAUSE OF LOSS

Class	Action	Submarine	Mine	Collision	Wrecked	Unknown	Total
Flotilla-leaders	I	I	—	I	—	—	3
Torpedo-boat destroyers	16	7	20	12	8	I	64[1]
Torpedo-boats	—	—	3	4	4	—	II
Patrol-boats	—	—	I	I	—	—	2
	17	8	24	18	12	I	80

[1] *Nubian* and *Zulu* counted as one.

CLASSIFIED NOMINAL LIST OF LOSSES

Flotilla-leaders	Torpedo-boat destroyers	Torpedo-boats	Patrol-boats
Hoste	Ardent	046	P 12
Scott	Ariel	064	P 26
Tipperary	Arno	9	
	Attack	10	
	Bittern	11	
	Boxer	12	
	Cheerful	13	
	Comet	24	
	Contest	90	
	Coquette	96	
	Derwent	117	
	Eden		
	Erne		
	Fairy		
	Falcon		
	Flirt		
	Fortune		
	Foyle		
	Ghurka		
	Goldfinch		
	Itchen		
	Kale		
	Laforey		
	Lassoo		
	Lightning		
	Louis		
	Lynx		
	Maori		
	Marmion		
	Mary Rose		
	Medusa		
	Myrmidon		
	Narbrough		
	Negro		
	Nessus		
	Nestor		
	Nomad		
	North Star		
	Nubian¹		
	Opal		
	Paragon		
	Partridge		
	Pheasant		
	Phœnix		
	Pincher		
	Racoon		
	Recruit (old) and (new)		
	Setter		
	Shark		
	Simoom		
	Sparrowhawk		
	Staunch		
	Strongbow		
	Success		
	Surprise		
	Tornado		
	Torrent		
	Turbulent		
	Ulleswater		
	Ulysses		
	Vehement		
	Velox		
	Wolverine		
	Zulu¹		
=3	=64	=11	=2

¹ *Nubian* and *Zulu* counted as 1.

INDEX

(i) Names of flotilla-leaders and destroyers are printed in capitals—all other ships in italics.
(ii) In most cases the ranks of officers and men mentioned are those held during the war.

A

A.7. (German T.B.), 262
A.19 (German T.B.), 262
Abbett, Lt.-Cdr. H. J., 338
ABDIEL, 149, 184, 372 et seq., 423
ACASTA, 174, 175, 178–182, 204
ACHATES, 184, 189, 195, 196, 198, 426
ACHERON, 152n, 269, 426
ACORN, 426
Adelaide, 289
A.E.1 (Aust. Sm.), 289, 290, 294
A.E.2 (Aust. Sm.), 289, 290, 296
AFRIDI, 266, 425
Agamemnon, 51, 52
Agincourt, 206, 371
ALARM, 426
ALBACORE, 410, 425
ALBATROSS, 425
Albion, 51
Alexander-Sinclair, Commodore E. S., 151
Alison, Lt.-Cdr. R. V., 163, 164, 216, 217
Allen, Comdr. W. L., 194
Allsup, Comdr. C. F., 20
AMAZON, 248, 253, 425
AMBUSCADE, 189, 195–198, 426
Amedroz, Lt.-Cdr. R. T., 66, 90
American destroyers, 327, 343
Amethyst, 22, 27n, 43, 50
Amphion, 22–24
ANGLER, 425
Anglia (S.S.), 245
ANZAC, 423
Anzac Cove, 60, 61, 63, 65, 69, 70, 77, 83
Anzac, evacuation of, 86 et seq.
Aquitania, 340–342
ARAB, 425
ARCHER, 426
ARDENT, 189, 195–199, 204, 426, 439
Arethusa, 24, 26–29, 31–43, 102 et seq., 127
Argyll, 227–229
Ariadne (German cruiser), 33, 40, 41
ARIEL, 36, 124, 152n, 267, 269, 379, 386, 426, 439
ARNO, 80, 428, 439
Arnold, Alfred (German Sm. officer), 274
ARUN, 425
Ashton, Eng.-Lt.-Cdr. James, 140
Aster, 80
ATTACK, 152n, 269, 426, 439
Australia, 289–296

Australian Navy, Royal, 288 et seq.
Australian troops, 61–69, 75, 82, 87, 295, 296
AVON, 425

B

Bacchante, 71
Bacchus, Lt.-Cdr. R., 66
Bacon, Adm. Sir R., 136n, 241, 250, 330
BADGER, 152n, 176, 264, 426
Bagley, Lt.-Cdr. D. W. (U.S.N.), 335–337
Barnish, Lt. G. H., 276
Barham, 152, 168, 206
Barron, Lt.-Cdr. J. O., 178, 182
Barrow, Comdr. B. W., 251, 266
Bartlett, Ellis Ashmead-, 45
Barttelot, Lt.-Cdr. N. K. W., 38
BASILISK, 53, 70, 80, 425
Bayly, Adm. Sir Lewis, 328 et seq.
BEAGLE, 14, 60, 70, 80, 82, 413, 425
Beattie, Lt.-Cdr. K. A., 210, 379
Beatty, Admiral of the Fleet Earl, 25, 34–36, 41–43, 149 et seq.
Beardmore, Messrs., 417, App. II
BEAVER, 426
Belgian Prince (S.S.), 272
Bennett, Gunner A. J., 276
Bernard, Comdr. M. R., 253
Besant, Lt.-Cdr., H. F., 294
Bethell, Lt. M. J., 161
Biarritz, 135, 136
Billyard-Leake, Lt. E. W., 400, et seq.
Bindall, Stoker H. C., 397
Bingham, Comdr. Hon. Barry, 155, 156, 158, 159, 161, 162, 228, 352, 353
Birdwood, General, 65
Birmingham, 25, 168, 186–188, 264
Birnie, Lt.-Cdr. H. C., 275
BITTERN, 425, 439
Black Sea, Aust. T.B.D.'s in, 307
Blackwood, Lt.-Cdr. M. B. R., 247
Blake, Lt.-Cdr. C. P., 156, 163
Blenheim, 56, 73, 91, 92, 97
Blunt, Capt. W. F., 24, 28, 34
Bombs, lance, 266
Bond, Comdr. A. G. H., 306, 307
BONETTA, 410, 425
Bonham-Carter, Lt. S., 400 et seq.
BOTHA, 223, 260–263, 409, 423
Bouvet, 51, 53, 54
Bowen, Lt. (R.A.N.), 293
Bowles, Lt.-Cdr. G. P., 379
Bowyer, Lt. R. T., 253
BOXER, 425, 439
BOYNE, 425